Mohutangi

NORTHLAND

Opononi • Whangarei

Orewa

• Auckland

AUCKLAND

Thames

Hamilton

Cambridge

Te Araroa

THE CENTRAL
NORTH ISLAND

Taupo

New Plymouth

Gisborne

Napier

Hastings

WELLINGTON
AND
THE SOUTH

Wellington

H

Blenheim

0 kilometres   100

0 miles   100

DK EYEWITNESS TRAVEL

New Zealand

EYEWITNESS TRAVEL

New Zealand

Penguin
Random
House

Produced by Editions Didier Millet,
Kuala Lumpur
Editorial Director Timothy Auger
Project Manager Noor Azlina Yunus
Editors Dianne Buerger, Zuraidah Omar
Designers Theivanai Nadaraju,
Yong Yoke Lian

Contributors
Helen Corrigan, Roef Hopman, Gerard
Hutching, Rebecca Macfie, Geoff Mercer,
Simon Noble, Peter Smith, Michael Ward,
Mark Wright

Photographers
Peter Bush, Gerald Lopez, Lloyd Park,
Ron Redfern

Illustrators
Yeap Kok Chien, Tan Hong Yew,
Denis Chai Kah Yune

Maps
ERA-Maptec Ltd, Dublin, Ireland

Printed and bound in China

First American Edition, 2001

18 19 20 21 10 9 8 7 6 5 4 3 2 1

Published in the United States by
DK Publishing, 345 Hudson Street, New York,
New York 10014

**Reprinted with revisions 2002, 2003,
2005, 2006, 2008, 2010, 2012,
2014, 2016, 2018**

Copyright 2001, 2018 © Dorling Kindersley
Limited, London

A Penguin Random House Company

Published in Great Britain by
Dorling Kindersley Limited.

A catalog record for this book is available
from the Library of Congress.

ISSN 1542-1554

ISBN 978-1-4654-6873-4

Throughout this guide, floors are
numbered according to local usage,
ie the "first floor" is the floor above
ground level.

MIX
Paper from
responsible sources
FSC™ C018179
www.fsc.org

Introducing
New Zealand

Inner-city tram on Cashel Street in the
city of Christchurch

New Zealand
Area by Area

Flowers in bloom at the Clay Cliffs Scenic Reserve, New Zealand

---

**The information in this
DK Eyewitness Travel Guide is checked regularly.**
Every effort has been made to ensure that this book is as up-to-date as possible
at the time of going to press. Some details, however, such as telephone numbers,
opening hours, prices, gallery hanging arrangements and travel information are
liable to change. The publishers cannot accept responsibility for any consequences
arising from the use of this book, nor for any material on third-party websites, and
cannot guarantee that any website address in this book will be a suitable source of
travel information. We value the views and suggestions of our readers very highly.
Please write to: Publisher, DK Eyewitness Travel Guides, Dorling Kindersley,
80 Strand, London, WC2R 0RL, UK, or email: travelguides@dk.com.

◀ **Title page** Stunning Tupou Bay, Northland   **Front cover image** Lake Mangamahoe and Mount Taranaki/Egmont, Egmont National
Park, North Island   **Back cover image** Moeraki boulders on Koekohe Beach at sunrise, Otago coast, South Island

Contents

Ethereal Māori carvings of the faces of a man and a woman

Red glass vase, an example of New Zealand glassware

Olveston Historic Home, Dunedin

HOW TO USE THIS GUIDE

This guide helps you to get the most from your visit to New Zealand. *Introducing New Zealand* maps the country and sets it in its historical and cultural context. The seven area chapters in *New Zealand Area by Area* describe the main sights, with photographs, illustrations and maps. Features cover topics relating specifically to the North and South Islands as well as subjects of regional interest. Restaurant and hotel recommendations can be found in *Travellers' Needs*, while the *Survival Guide* has practical tips on everything from making a telephone call to transport.

New Zealand Area By Area

New Zealand has been divided into seven main sightseeing areas, coded with a coloured thumb tab for quick reference. A map illustrating how the two main islands have been divided can be found on the inside front cover of this guide. The sights listed within the individual areas are plotted and numbered on a Regional Map.

Each area of New Zealand can be identified quickly by its colour coding.

1 Introduction
The landscape, history and character of each region is described here, showing how the area has developed over the years and what it has to offer the visitor today.

A locator map shows the region in relation to the other areas of New Zealand.

2 Regional Map
This gives an illustrated overview of the whole area. All the sights covered in the chapter are numbered and there are useful tips on getting around by car and public transport.

3 Detailed Information
All the important towns and other places of interest are described individually. They are listed in order, following the numbering on the Regional Map. Within each entry there is detailed information on the important buildings and other major sights.

Features and story boxes highlight special or unique features of an area or sight.

4 Major Towns
All the important towns are described individually. Within each entry there is further detailed information on interesting buildings and other sites. The Town Map shows the location of the main sights.

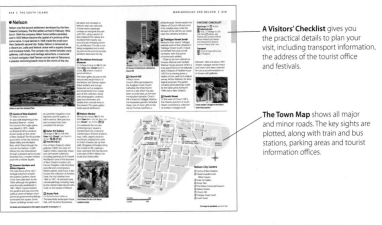

A Visitors' Checklist gives you the practical details to plan your visit, including transport information, the address of the tourist office and festivals.

The Town Map shows all major and minor roads. The key sights are plotted, along with train and bus stations, parking areas and tourist information offices.

5 Street-by-Street Map
Towns or districts of special interest to the visitor are given a bird's-eye view in detailed 3-D with photographs and descriptions of the most important sights.

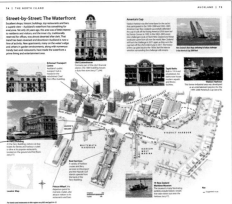

A suggested route for a walk covers the most interesting streets in the area.

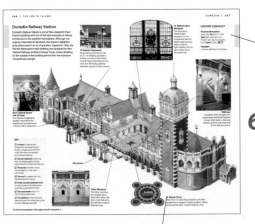

Opening hours, the telephone number and transport details for the sight are given in the Visitors' Checklist.

6 The Top Sights
These are given two or more pages. Historic buildings are dissected to reveal their interiors; national parks have maps showing facilities and trails; museums have colour-coded floorplans. Photographs highlight the most interesting features.

Stars indicate sights that visitors should not miss.

INTRODUCING NEW ZEALAND

DISCOVERING NEW ZEALAND

The following itineraries have been designed to take in as many of New Zealand's highlights as possible, while keeping long-distance travel manageable. Ideally you'll want to divide your time evenly between the North Island and the South Island. First comes a one-week tour of the North Island, supplemented by a three-day jaunt around Northland and a couple of days in the capital, Wellington. For those with more time, there are some suggestions for extending these trips, including a few days around the East Cape. The two-week grand tour of the South Island takes in the best on offer, but again, this can be extended with trips to Golden Bay and the country's third major landmass, Stewart Island. Pick, combine and follow your favourite tours, or simply dip in and out and be inspired.

White-water rafting on Shotover River, Queenstown
New Zealand's fast-flowing rivers are perfect for white-water rafting. The Oxenbridge Tunnel Rapid on the Shotover River leads through the exhilarating rapids of the Skippers Canyon.

Key

— One Week in the North Island

— Three Days in Northland

— Two Weeks in the South Island

Two Weeks in the South Island

- Watch whales, swim with dolphins and get close to fur seals at picturesque **Kaikoura**.

- Sip a Marlborough Sauvignon at **Wairau Valley**, then cruise the nearby **Queen Charlotte Sound**.

- Kayak the crystal-clear waters or hike the easy Coast Track in the **Abel Tasman National Park**.

- Go adventure-crazy in **Queenstown** or simply just appreciate the stunning scenery.

- Thread your way along the bush-cloaked, narrow waterways of remote **Fiordland**.

- Take the slower, winding road along the **Catlins Coast**, with its leaping dolphins, petrified forest and dramatic coastlines.

0 kilometres 100
0 miles 100

Paparoa
National Park

SOUTH
ISLAND

Westland/Tai Poutini
National Park
Fox Glacier
Haast
Haast Pass
Mount Aspiring
National Park
Milford Sound
Fiordland
National Park
Doubtful
Sound
Te Anau
Manapouri
Arrowtown
Queenstown
Lake
Wakatipu
Wanaka
Franz Josef Glacier
Aoraki/Mount Cook
National Park
Christchurch
Lake Tekapo
Lake Pukaki
Lyttelto
Aka
Oamaru
Moeraki
Otago Peninsula
Dunedin
Invercargill
Catlins
Nugget Point
Stewart
Island
Curio
Bay
Porpoise Bay

◀ Māori fortified village or *pah* in Taranaki, New Zealand (mid 1800s)

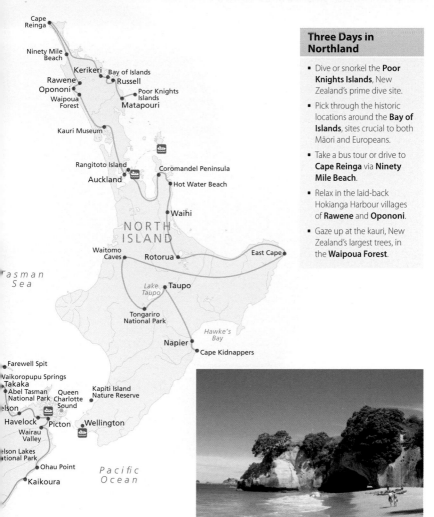

Cape Reinga
Ninety Mile Beach
Kerikeri — **Bay of Islands**
Rawene — **Russell**
Opononi
Poor Knights Islands
Waipoua Forest
Matapouri
Kauri Museum
Rangitoto Island — **Coromandel Peninsula**
Auckland
Hot Water Beach
Waihi

NORTH
ISLAND

Waitomo Caves — **Rotorua** — **East Cape**

Tasman Sea

Lake Taupo **Taupo**
Tongariro National Park
Hawke's Bay
Napier
Cape Kidnappers

Farewell Spit
Waikoropupu Springs
Takaka
Abel Tasman National Park — **Queen Charlotte Sound** — **Kapiti Island Nature Reserve**
Nelson
Havelock — **Picton** — **Wellington**
Wairau Valley
Nelson Lakes National Park
Ohau Point
Kaikoura

Pacific Ocean

Three Days in Northland

- Dive or snorkel the **Poor Knights Islands**, New Zealand's prime dive site.
- Pick through the historic locations around the **Bay of Islands**, sites crucial to both Māori and Europeans.
- Take a bus tour or drive to **Cape Reinga** via **Ninety Mile Beach**.
- Relax in the laid-back Hokianga Harbour villages of **Rawene** and **Opononi**.
- Gaze up at the kauri, New Zealand's largest trees, in the **Waipoua Forest**.

Cathedral Cove
A natural stone arch separates the two sandy beaches at Cathedral Cove on the Coromandel Peninsula.

One Week in the North Island

- See the best of Māori, Pacific and wider New Zealand art at the galleries of **Auckland**.
- Explore the beautiful **Coromandel Peninsula** and dig a hot spring hole in the sand at **Hot Water Beach**.
- Smell the sulphur and see geysers, silica terraces and boiling mud pools in and around **Rotorua**.
- Delve into the glowworm-illuminated underworld of **Waitomo**.
- Take a scenic stroll or a full-day hike through the volcanic wonders of **Tongariro National Park**.
- Admire **Napier's** Art Deco city centre, then sample some superb Syrah and Chardonnay wines in the **Hawke's Bay Vineyards**.

- **Arriving** Auckland airport is 20 km (12 miles) south of the city centre. Buses and taxis connect it to the city centre.
- **Transport** A car or campervan is the best option, but everywhere can be reached by fairly infrequent bus services.

Lake Rotorua seen from the North Crater on the Tongariro Alpine Crossing

Day 1: Auckland

Culturally minded visitors should pay visits to the **New Zealand Maritime Museum** (p77), the beautifully renovated **Auckland Art Gallery** (p80) and the **Auckland War Memorial Museum** (pp82–3). Alternatively, take a short cruise to **Rangitoto Island** (p93) with its unique pohutukawa forest, unusual lava tubes and great views of the city.

Day 2: Coromandel Peninsula

Loop around the beautiful Coromandel Peninsula, winding into the hills at **Driving Creek Railway** (p128), soak in the hot pools at **Hot Water Beach** (p129), swim at golden **Cathedral Cove** (p129) and check out the vibrant **arts and crafts scene** (p131).

Day 3: Rotorua

It is about a 4-hour drive south to Rotorua, a journey best broken at **Waihi** (p130) with its massive gold-mining hole right in the centre of town. Learn about the genesis of New Zealand's first tourist town by

Wood carving at the Māori Meeting House, Auckland War Memorial Museum

visiting the **Rotorua Museum** (p138) and surrounding **Government Gardens** (p138). Next, stroll around the lakeshore to **St Faith's Anglican Church** (p139) in the original Māori village of Ohinemutu. Set aside the evening for a visit to **Tamaki Māori Village** (p141) with its demonstration of Māori customs and a *hangi* dinner cooked in an earth oven.

Day 4: Rotorua

Drive out to **Wai-o-tapu Thermal Wonderland** (p144) in time for the clockwork 10:15am geyser eruption. While there, admire pools of boiling mud and wander past the vibrantly coloured Champagne Pool, Primrose Terraces and Artist's Palette. In the afternoon, choose from: historical explorations at **The Buried Village** (p141); madcap laughs on the Shweeb and bungy jumping at **Agroventures** (p140) or **ZORB® Rotorua** (p140); or simply soak the afternoon away at the **Polynesian Spa** (p138).

> **To extend your trip…**
> Spend a couple of days (or longer if you have the time) soaking up the relaxed pace of the **East Cape** (pp136–7), New Zealand's remotest populated corner. It feels like you're stepping back in time 30 or even 50 years.

Day 5: Waitomo Caves

New Zealand's most celebrated netherworld wonders can be experienced at **Waitomo Caves** (pp124–5) where the **Glowworm Caves** (p125) combine viewing stalactite formations with a boat ride under a constellation of glowworms. The wetsuit-clad adventure trip **Lost World** (p125) will get you abseiling, cave tubing and jumping into dark pools. Back above ground, take the short but lovely walk to the **Ruakuri Natural Tunnel** (p124).

Day 6: Tongariro National Park and Taupo

Take a couple of short walks on the slopes of the three occasionally active volcanoes in **Tongariro National Park** (pp146–7), then head north past the **National Trout Centre** (p145) to the fishing mecca of **Taupo** (p145). Its eponymous lake empties down the Waikato River, which plunges spectacularly over **Huka Falls** (p144).

> **To extend your trip…**
> Set aside an extra day to hike the strenuous **Tongariro Alpine Crossing** (p147), one of the finest day walks in the country.

Day 7: Hawke's Bay

Explore one of the world's finest small-scale Art Deco townscapes at **Napier** (pp150–51) before lunching at a winery and touring the **Hawke's Bay vineyards** (p154). Alternatively, take a tractor tour along a rugged beach to see the nesting gannets at **Cape Kidnappers** (p153): the tours are tide-dependent, so check times online and book ahead.

For practical information on travelling around New Zealand see pp352–61

Three Days In Northland

- **Arriving** Auckland airport.
- **Transport** Driving is easiest, but bus services do cover these routes.

Day 1: The Poor Knights and the Bay of Islands

Divers and snorkellers shouldn't miss the **Poor Knights Islands** *(p103)*, followed by short visits to the gorgeous coves at **Matapouri** *(p103)* and **Whale Bay** *(p103)*. Alternatively, head straight to the Bay of Islands and historic Russell, home to **Pompallier Mission** *(p106)*. Across the Bay, the **Waitangi Treaty Grounds** *(pp108–9)* are the birthplace of modern New Zealand, while **Kerikeri's Stone Store** *(p110)* and **Kemp House** *(p110)* formed one of its first European settlements.

Day 2: Cape Reinga and Ninety Mile Beach

Take a long day-trip to the island's northern tip at **Cape Reinga** *(p112)*, including a drive along the sands of **Ninety Mile Beach** *(p112)*. Driving the beach is hazardous for the inexperienced, so it's best to take a bus tour: book ahead.

Day 3: Hokianga Harbour and the Waipoua kauris

Explore the Hokianga Harbour's backwater villages of **Rawene** *(p114)* and **Opononi** *(p114)*, admire the sheer majesty of the kauri trees in

The Beehive, part of New Zealand's Parliament Buildings

Waipoua Forest *(p115)* and spend an hour at the engaging **Kauri Museum** *(p115)* at Matakohe before returning to Auckland.

Two Days in Wellington

The nation's compact capital has a great setting, a strong café culture, a vibrant arts scene and many interesting sights.

- **Arriving** Drive down from Auckland or fly to Wellington airport, 6 km (4 miles) from the city centre.
- **Moving on** Head across Cook Strait to Picton, on the South Island, using the Inter-Island Ferry Services *(p356)*, a gorgeous 3-hour journey through the Tory Channel and Queen Charlotte Sound *(p207)*.

Day 1

Kick-start your day with a coffee in one of Wellington's cutting-edge **cafés** *(pp319–21)*, then set aside the morning to explore **The Museum of New Zealand Te Papa Tongarewa** *(pp170–71)*. Take the **Wellington Cable Car** *(p164)* up to the suburb of Kelburn, then walk through the **Wellington Botanic Garden** *(p164)* towards the **Parliament Buildings** *(p162)*, the two **cathedrals** *(p162)* and **Katherine Mansfield House and Garden** *(p163)*.

Day 2

Bird-watchers should not miss a day-trip to **Kapiti Island Nature Reserve** *(p175)*, while *Lord of the Rings* and Peter Jackson fans will love to explore **Weta Workshop** *(p160)*. Alternatively, take a lovely **Marine Drive Tour** *(pp172–3)* around the city's wild and windy coast or see the great art at the **City Gallery Wellington** *(p168)*.

The stunning Whale Bay on the Tutukaka Coast, Northland

Two Weeks in the South Island

- **Arriving** Fly into Christchurch, or join the tour at Picton (Day 3), the South Island terminus of the Cook Strait ferries from Wellington.

- **Transport** A car will get you around in good time. It is possible to do the tour by infrequent buses but you'll probably want to allow a few extra days.

- **Booking ahead** Book the Kaikoura whale-watching trip a few days in advance: rough seas often cause trips to be cancelled, so build an extra day into your schedule if you can.

Day 1: Christchurch
See how Christchurch is rising from the rubble of the devastating earthquakes of 2011. There's a great deal of work still to do, but necessity has pushed the residents to find innovative ways to keep the city going – visit the transitional **Cardboard Cathedral** (p227). Christchurch's traditional charms haven't all been lost: punting from the **Antigua Boat Sheds** (p231) and strolling through the **Botanic Gardens** (pp232–3) is still a superbly relaxing way to experience the South Island's capital. In the late afternoon, head to Kaikoura (a 2-hour drive) for an early start the next day.

Day 2: Kaikoura
The crack of dawn is the best time to go cetacean-spotting

Hikers in Abel Tasman National Park

with Whale Watch **Kaikoura** (p213). Top up your marine mammal quota by joining one of the **dolphin swimming** cruises (p213) or by simply walking around the rugged coastline, which was uplifted several meters by the Kaikoura earthquake in November 2016. On the way to Marlborough, pause at **Ohau Point** (p213), where New Zealand fur seals cover the rocks beside the highway.

Day 3: Marlborough and Queen Charlotte Sound
Spend the morning supping New Zealand's wine gift to the world, Marlborough Sauvignon Blanc, sampled at one of the dozens of wineries around the **Wairau Valley** (pp210–11), some of which serve excellent lunches beside the vines. Continue to **Picton** (p204), where you can take a short water-taxi ride to one of the delightful **waterfront lodges** (p299) beside the **Queen Charlotte Track** (p207).

Day 4: Nelson
Take a water-taxi back to Picton, then drive the winding, delightful **Queen Charlotte Drive** (pp204–5) past **Havelock** (p205) and the pretty **Pelorus Bridge Scenic Reserve** (p205) to laid-back **Nelson** (pp214–15). Either visit the **Nelson Provincial Museum** (p214), with its fascinating collection of Māori artifacts, and the **Suter Art Gallery** (p214) or head west to **Höglund Art Glass** (p216) and **McGlashen Pottery** (p216).

Day 5: Abel Tasman National Park
If it's Saturday, browse in the excellent **Nelson Market** (p214) for an hour. Spend the rest of the day in **Abel Tasman National Park** (pp218–19), either hiking sections of the easy **Coast Track** or **kayaking** from **Marahau** (p219), with easy water-taxi access to avoid retracing your steps or paddle strokes.

> **To extend your trip...**
> Slow the pace in Golden Bay, visiting **Waikoropupu Springs Scenic Reserve** and **Farewell Spit** (p221) from bohemian **Takaka** (p220).

Day 6: The West Coast
There's a lot of driving involved on Day 6, so take a quick peek at **Nelson Lakes National Park** (p216) en route to the Pancake Rocks in **Paparoa National Park** (p240). Check out the **greenstone carving** (p241) at Hokitika, then push on to Franz Josef and Fox glaciers in **Westland/Tai Poutini National Park** (pp242–3).

Day 7: Wanaka
Admire the reflective waters of **Lake Matheson** (p242), then take a long drive through the temperate rainforest towards **Haast** (p277) and through the **Gates of Haast** (p277) to the open rolling countryside around **Wanaka** (p274). Set off early and you'll make it in time to visit **Stuart Landsborough's Puzzling World** (p274) or the dramatically sited **Rippon Vineyard** (p274).

Antigua Boat Sheds on the Avon River in Christchurch

For practical information on travelling around New Zealand see pp352–61

Day 8: Queenstown

If you fancy some hiking in magnificent scenery, head up the Matukituki Valley into **Mount Aspiring National Park** *(pp276–7)*. Otherwise, drive over the Crown Range to pretty **Arrowtown** *(p282)*, then continue to **Queenstown** *(pp280–81)* to catch a late-afternoon cruise aboard the TSS *Earnslaw* on **Lake Wakatipu** *(p280)*, or ride the **Skyline Gondola** *(p281)* up Bob's Peak, where you can dine overlooking the town.

Day 9: Queenstown

Experience the Adventure Capital of New Zealand *(p280)*. Go bungy jumping, white-water rafting, jet-boating, tandem parapenting or heli-biking, possibly all of them in one day with a combo deal. If this does not appeal, take a lakeside drive to scenic **Glenorchy** *(p282)*, or just relax in the **cafés and bars** *(pp324–5)*.

> **To extend your trip…**
> If a multi-day hike sounds appealing, set aside 3 or 4 days to hike in either **Mount Aspiring National Park** *(p276)* or **Fiordland National Park** *(pp284–5)* where the Milford, Routeburn and Kepler tracks are the star picks.

Day 10: Fiordland

The perennial tourist dilemma is whether to visit Milford Sound or Doubtful Sound. Both are dramatic and beautiful but **Milford Sound** *(p287)* is the most popular, with the widest range of cruises, kayak trips and the most people (though it is hardly crowded). By contrast, **Doubtful Sound** *(pp288–9)* is remoter and far less visited, and getting there is all part of the adventure.

Day 11: The Catlins Coast

Pay a short visit to the ancient, lizard-like tuataras at Invercargill's **Southland Museum and Art Gallery** *(p290)* en route to the sparsely populated **Catlins** *(pp294–5)* where the

Observers watching a parapenter (paraglider) passing overhead

winding roads force drivers to adopt a measured pace. Take your time, calling in at the petrified forest in **Curio Bay** *(p294)*, the cute Hector's dolphins at **Porpoise Bay** *(p295)* and the rugged promontory of **Nugget Point** *(p294)*.

> **To extend your trip…**
> There's a real island-life feel to **Stewart Island** *(pp292–3)*, where you can easily spend 2 or 3 days watching the endangered birds on **Ulva Island** *(p292)* and walking the **Rakiura Track** *(p293)*.

Day 12: Dunedin and the Otago Peninsula

The buildings of **Robert Lawson** *(p263)* provide the focus of a walking exploration of **central Dunedin** *(pp262–9)*, where you should also visit the **Dunedin Railway Station** *(pp266–7)* and **Olveston Historic Home** *(p269)*. Wildlife enthusiasts may prefer

to focus on the **Otago Peninsula** *(pp270–71)*, particularly the **Royal Albatross Centre** *(p270)* and the **Penguin Place** *(p271)*. A stroll along the **Tunnel Beach Walkway** *(p268)* is ideal on a long summer evening.

Day 13: Oamaru and Mt Cook

Make a leisurely start and then spend half an hour at **Moeraki Boulders Scenic Reserve** *(p271)* before lunching in Moeraki. Walk off your meal around wonderfully preserved mercantile buildings in the "whitestone" town of **Oamaru** *(pp272–3)* before turning inland to **Aoraki/Mount Cook National Park** *(pp256–7)*. The park's diminutive township centres on **The Hermitage** *(p256)*, a classy hotel with fine views of New Zealand's highest mountain. **Hike the tracks** *(p257)*, take a **flightseeing trip** *(p256)* or kayak the terminal lake of the **Tasman Glacier** *(p256)*.

Day 14: Christchurch and Akaroa

Spot black stilts (the world's rarest wading bird) at the Twizel's **Kaki Visitor Hide** *(p255)*, then head through the dry grasslands of the Mackenzie Country, where the opaque-blue waters of **Lake Tekapo** *(p254)* and **Lake Pukaki** *(p254)* form part of the monumental **Upper Waitaki Hydro-Electric Development Scheme** *(p255)*. Continue to **Christchurch** *(pp226–33)* and, if you have time, consider a trip to quirky **Lyttelton** *(p234)* or the French-style harbour village of **Akaroa** *(p235)*.

Nugget Point promontory on the Catlins Coast

Putting New Zealand on the Map: The North Island

New Zealand lies in the South Pacific Ocean, 1,600 km (990 miles) to the east of Australia, 10,000 km (6,210 miles) from San Francisco and a similar distance from Tokyo. Comprising two large islands and a number of smaller ones, its total land area is 270,530 sq km (104,420 sq miles), making it comparable in size to Japan or the British Isles. The main North and South islands are separated by Cook Strait, 22 km (14 miles) wide at its narrowest point. Two-thirds of the country's population of almost 4.8 million live in the North Island, and of these 1.5 million live in Auckland, the country's largest city and the world's most populous Polynesian centre. New Zealand's capital is Wellington, at the southern end of the North Island.

New Zealand and its Environs

Key to Colour Coding

North Island

- Northland
- Auckland
- Central North Island
- Wellington and the South

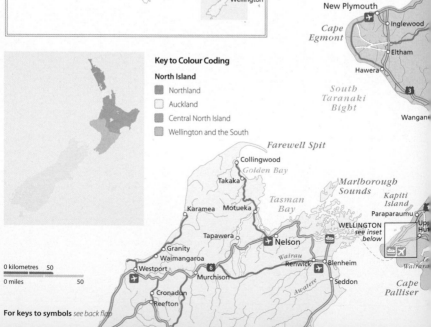

0 kilometres 50

0 miles 50

For keys to symbols *see back flap*

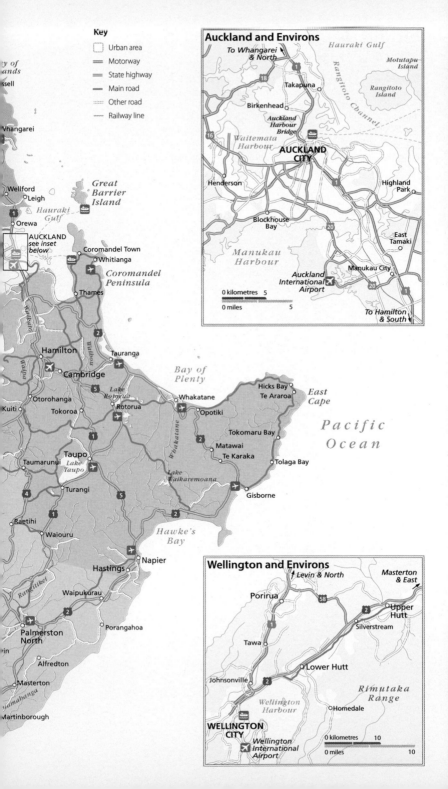

Putting New Zealand on the Map: The South Island

The South Island, 150,440 sq km (58,070 sq miles) in area, is slightly larger than the North Island. The Southern Alps mountain chain runs almost the length of the island, with 223 named peaks higher than 2,300 m (7,550 ft). The eastern side of the alps is dry and largely non-forested, while the West Coast has high rainfall and magnificent forests, mountains and glaciers. Christchurch, the largest city in the South Island, with almost 395,000 inhabitants, has good international travel links. To the south, Dunedin is an important university town. Stewart Island, south of Invercargill, is New Zealand's third largest island.

Key to Colour Coding

South Island

- Marlborough and Nelson
- Canterbury and the West Coast
- Otago and Southland

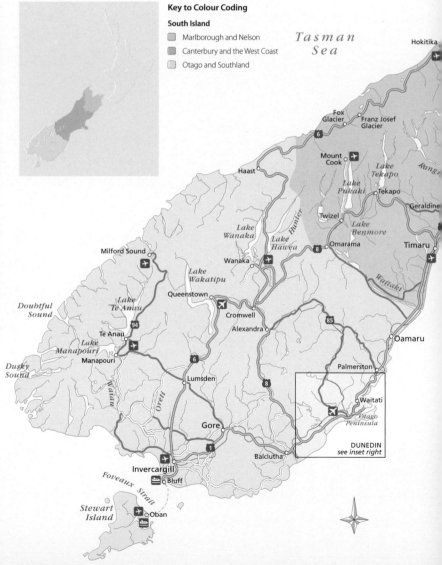

Tasman Sea

Hokitika

Fox Glacier

Franz Josef Glacier

Mount Cook

Haast

Lake Tekapo

Lake Pukaki

Tekapo

Geraldine

Twizel

Lake Benmore

Timaru

Lake Wanaka

Lake Hawea

Hunter

Omarama

Milford Sound

Wanaka

Lake Wakatipu

Waitaki

Doubtful Sound

Lake Te Anau

Queenstown

Cromwell

85

Alexandra

Oamaru

Te Anau

94

Lake Manapouri

Manapouri

6

Dusky Sound

Lumsden

8

Palmerston

Waitati

Otago Peninsula

Waiau

Oreti

Gore

DUNEDIN
see inset right

1

Balclutha

Invercargill

Bluff

Foveaux Strait

Stewart Island

Oban

For keys to symbols *see back flap*

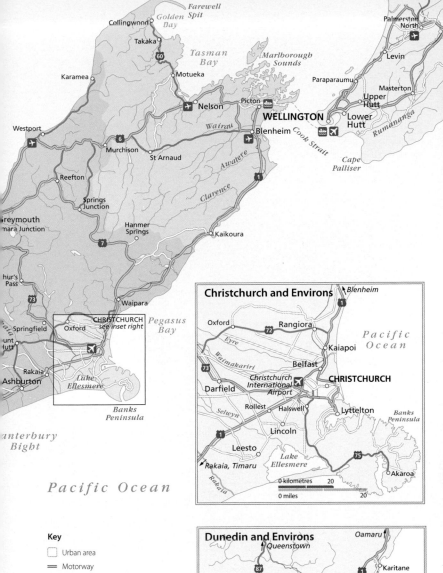

Key

- ☐ Urban area
- ▬ Motorway
- ▬ State highway
- ━ Main road
- ⋯ Other road
- — Railway line
- -- Ferry route

A PORTRAIT OF NEW ZEALAND

New Zealand is one of the most isolated countries in the world and was the last major land mass to be colonised by people. Māori, some of the early arrivals from the Pacific, called it Aotearoa, "the land of the long white cloud" – the first indication to these canoe voyagers of the islands' presence was the cloud covering their high ranges. New Zealand's island location and spectacular terrain affects its climate, its history and its contemporary character.

Spanning latitudes 34 degrees and 47 degrees South, the islands of New Zealand are in the path of "the roaring forties", the winds that circle this lower part of the globe, and are separated from the nearest landmass, Australia, by 1,600 km (990 miles) of the Tasman Sea. Adjacent to the International Date Line, New Zealand is opposite the Greenwich Meridian of zero degree, and claims to be the first country to see the sun rise.

The climate ranges from subantarctic to subtropical. The maritime setting creates regular rainfall and abundant vegetation. There is extensive bird and fish life but other than two bat species, the only land mammals are those introduced by early Māori and Europeans. It is a comparatively recent settlement and one of the least populated countries in the world, with a population of almost 4.8 million, New Zealand retains in many areas a clean, natural and untouched environment.

The snow-covered Southern Alps and glacial-formed lakes and fiords provide spectacular scenery, and there is extensive volcanic and thermal activity on the North Island central plateau. The country's coastline provides both sheltered bays and harbours and superb beaches. New Zealand's tourist industry focuses on the natural environment, the urban aspect is much less significant by comparison.

The silver fern, one of the symbols of New Zealand

◀ Lake Pukaki and Mount Cook

The coastline as seen from Tunnel Beach, south of Dunedin

Settlement

Captain James Cook's circumnavigation and charting of the main islands in 1769–70 paved the way for the sealing and whaling industry. The unruly conditions, the concerns of missionaries over friction with the Māori and pressure from Edward Gibbon's Colonising Society prompted the British to pursue a treaty with the Māori to establish sovereignty. At Waitangi in

Captain James Cook

the Bay of Islands, a treaty was signed between the British Crown, represented by Captain William Hobson, and a number of Māori chiefs. Although the Treaty of Waitangi provided for protection of Māori and their natural resources, alienation of Māori land occurred well into the 20th century. Māori leaders pressed for justice and organized land marches. In 1975, the treaty was reconsidered and the Treaty of Waitangi Act passed by parliament set up the Waitangi Tribunal, which still considers land claims today.

Planned settlement in the 1840s was mainly by English and Scottish enterprises. Today the character of cities such as Christchurch and Dunedin still reflects those origins. Auckland, the country's former capital and now its commercial centre, remains more cosmopolitan. Wellington's early establishment as the capital contributes to its political character.

The independent spirit of modern New Zealanders can be said to derive from the determination of the first settlers, who worked hard to clear extensive areas of forest for farmland and for timber. The people of New Zealand came from a cross section of English, Scottish and Irish society, and all were united in their desire to make their country prosper.

Māori leader Dame Whina Cooper setting out for a land march (*Hikoi*) in October 1975

Society

Though New Zealand is an independent state, New Zealand's parliament, based on the Statute of Westminster, pays allegiance to the British sovereign through its governor-general. However, proposals that New Zealand become a republic have some support in the country.

New Zealanders take pride in their history of social reform. The first country in the world to give all women the vote in 1893, New Zealand had established compulsory, free primary schooling by 1877, and by 1938 a state-supported health system, universal superannuation and a liberal social welfare structure. The country declared its non-nuclear stance in 1986. This has resulted in non-alignment of its armed forces, though New Zealand troops are used in peacekeeping and training roles.

Although the Waitangi Tribunal has enabled substantial compensation for Māori whose land was confiscated, there are still some grievances to settle. The governments of the 1960s, seeking to build a labour force, encouraged the immigration of Pacific Islanders. This has created a greater ethnic diversity, as has the influx of Asian immigrants since the 1990s.

The Beehive, which houses the Ministers' offices, is part of the Parliament Buildings in Wellington

Today, visitors frequently comment on the friendliness and welcoming attitude of New Zealanders. This probably stems from the fact that they are a small population living, by world standards, in good quality housing, in small cities that do not suffer from congestion or widespread crime. All have easy access to a superb natural environment. There is also a curiosity

The Nelson market, selling fresh local produce and regional artisan crafts

New Zealand's All Blacks rugby team playing against Italy

about the world and New Zealanders travel abroad a great deal. The great " OE" (overseas experience) is still popular with the young.

In spite of the fact that there is a widening gap between rich and poor, New Zealand remains an egalitarian society. There are some social differences based upon wealth and occupation, but there is no class system in New Zealand based on birth and inheritance. Enterprise and energy can secure good employment and quality of life. Almost 86 per cent of the population is urban, with 75 per cent resident in the North Island. In the last 100 years or so the Māori population has increased and now makes up 17.5 per cent of the country's total. However, the social and economic status of some Māori is still below average, a situation that will hopefully be corrected in time by affirmative government education, employment and health policies.

Work and the Economy

Today, tourism in New Zealand caters to all tastes and is important to the economy – in 2016 it was the country's highest earning industry. Although agriculture is still a major industry, with dairy, meat, fish and timber products predominating, a need to compete in the world markets has required diversification. A pioneer in agricultural research, New Zealand is a leader in animal and crop technology. Its wines, particularly whites, are internationally recognized and its quality foodstuffs are exported to many countries.

Sheep droving on a state highway

Being a small nation that has to transport its exports long distances to foreign markets, New Zealand is vulnerable to the international economy. It does not possess substantial mineral resources, but it has been able to utilize its own natural gas, oil and coal reserves. It is the world's leading exporter of dairy products, and signs of an export market in information technology, electronics and ship-building are encouraging.

The recession in the 1980s prompted a move from welfare state to "user pays" policies, with privatization of state-owned enterprises. The major political parties are Labour (centre left) and National (centre right), with minor parties influencing the balance of power.

Sport and Culture

New Zealand is a sport fan's paradise. The successful defence of the America's Cup in 2000 attracted one of the world's largest gatherings of mega-yachts. Rugby is the most popular game (the All Blacks won the Rugby World Cup in 2011 and again in 2015), followed by netball and cricket. A wide range of international entertainers, musicians, artists and dance companies make frequent visits to the country. Festivals of Pacific Island and Māori culture coincide with a resurgence of Māori and Pacific Island art and artists. New Zealanders can claim some notable firsts. Lord Ernest Rutherford from

Alfresco dining at Queenstown Marina

Brightwater was the first to split the atom and Sir Edmund Hillary, with Sherpa Tenzing, was the first to reach the summit of Mount Everest. Others of international reputation are author Katherine Mansfield, opera diva Dame Kiri Te Kanawa, soprano Hayley Westenra, film director Peter Jackson and space scientist Sir William Pickering.

New Zealand is today a vibrant, hospitable, multicultural nation that has forged a unique identity derived from a combination of Māori heritage and colonial culture.

Street buskers providing entertainment in Auckland

New Zealand's Landscape

New Zealand is an old land with a young landscape: some of the rocks that underlie the country are, at 540 million years old, relatively ancient. However, the landforms that have been created from them are very young. The Southern Alps, for example, began to emerge only five million years ago and volcanic explosions and earthquakes continue to create new forms. The overriding feature of the landscape is its diversity: mountains, lakes, rivers, beaches, hills, plains, volcanoes, rainforests and fiords are all contained in a relatively small area.

Mount Ruapehu, like other New Zealand cone volcanoes, erupts frequently. It sits astride one of the world's major volcanic centres (*see pp68–9*).

The foothills of the Southern Alps, the Great Divide between the west and east coasts, shelter the Canterbury Plains from prevailing westerly winds.

New Zealand's coastline is roughly 16,000 km (9,900 miles) long. About 80 per cent is exposed to open sea while 20 per cent borders sheltered waters. The coasts harbour marine life and are popular playgrounds for watersports, fishing and gathering of *kai moana* (seafood).

Tectonic Plate Formation

Alpine fault

Oceanic crust

Continental crust

Indo-Australian Plate

Pacific Continental Plate

For the last 20–25 million years, New Zealand has been lying astride two of the world's 15 moving "plates". In the North Island, the Pacific Continental Plate pushes under the Indo-Australian Plate, forming volcanoes in between. In the South Island, the Indo-Australian Plate pushes under the Pacific one, forming an Alpine fault line.

South Canterbury and Southern Alps

Large-scale farming has transformed tussock plains into a landscape of grasslands dissected by rivers and dotted with livestock. The distant Southern Alps bear testimony to the powerful geological forces which have been shaping the country for the last 600 million years.

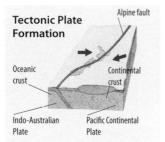

Tussock grasslands cover about 10 per cent of New Zealand's land area. Much of this area was covered in forest or scrubland before the early Māori burned it while hunting for moa.

The Bay of Islands comprises 144 offshore islands, all within 50 km (30 miles) of the coast. During glacial periods, when sea levels were lower, the islands were connected to the mainland.

Braided rivers *(see p195)* transport shingle and sediments from the Southern Alps to create fertile farmlands.

Sheep, farmed for both wool and meat, thrive on South Canterbury's hill country and rolling downs.

The fiords of southwest New Zealand, carved out over millions of years by successive Ice Ages – the last 10,000 years ago – are among the most spectacular in the world *(see pp284–5)*. The coastline of the fiords extends 1,000 km (620 miles). Doubtful Sound, at 420 m (1,380 ft) is the deepest of the fiords, while Dusky Sound, which stretches 40 km (25 miles) inland, is the longest.

The Gondwanaland Connection

Until about 80 million years ago, New Zealand formed part of the great super continent, Gondwanaland, which comprised present-day Antarctica, Australia, India, Africa and South America. Once New Zealand floated off into isolation, many of its plants and animals evolved into forms which were never seen on other landmasses.

180 million years ago, New Zealand occupied a corner of Gondwanaland, one of the world's two massive continents; the other is called Laurasia.

135 million years ago, Gondwanaland began to split apart into the present-day continents. At this time, New Zealand was still attached to Australia.

Today, the Tasman Sea separates New Zealand and Australia, and the continents continue to drift apart. New Zealand is moving northwards towards the equator at the rate of about 30 mm (1.2 inches) a year.

Flora and Fauna

New Zealand has been a land apart for 80 million years, with the result that it is home to a collection of plants and animals found nowhere else in the world. It has only two native land mammals (both bats), although seals, whales and dolphins are found around the coasts. Flightless birds, a diversity of lizards, giant snails, primitive frogs and plants that are as old as the dinosaurs combine to make New Zealand unique. Despite the impact of humans on flora and fauna over the last 1,000 years, much remains to fascinate the visitor.

The tuatara is the sole remaining species of an order of reptiles that evolved about 220 million years ago. One good place to see a tuatara is at the tuatarium in Invercargill *(see p290)*.

Kauri Forests

Northland's forests are dominated by massive, straight-trunked kauri trees interspersed with a mix of subtropical plants. So valuable was the timber for boat building, housing and carving that the forests have been depleted since the 1790s.

Kiwi are found in forests on North, South and Stewart islands, where they use their long beaks to dig for food.

Giant weta, flightless "crickets" as large as a person's hand, are harmless inhabitants of islands and kauri forests.

The silver fern or ponga, widely adopted as a national symbol, takes its name from the silvery underside of the fronds.

Shrublands

Shrublands consist of short, scrubby plants. They are home to many species of animals and are nurseries for mature forest. Widespread throughout the country, shrublands are often areas that were once logged and are now regenerating.

The green gecko lives on the outer branches of shrubs and is a daytime hunter. It bears live young in contrast to other species which lay eggs.

Kowhai, New Zealand's official national flower, has striking drooping yellow blooms in spring.

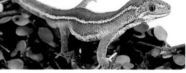

Manuka is a key pollen and nectar plant for bees.

Birds of New Zealand

New Zealand is famed for its unusual birds. Evolving without significant predators, such as rats, cats or dogs, to menace them, they lost any reason to fly. Some not only became flightless, but also developed into

some of the largest birds ever to have lived. When Māori arrived, they discovered the moa, the largest species of which stood 2 m (7 ft) tall to the top of its back. As a result of being hunted, the moa became extinct 300–500 years ago. Today, many of New Zealand's ancient bird species survive in limited numbers, among them the kiwi, kakapo, takahe, black robin and kea, and enormous efforts are being made to ensure their survival.

The kakapo is a large, flightless, nocturnal parrot.

Kokako are poor fliers but are noted for their singing abilities.

Alpine Landscape

New Zealand's alpine region begins at about 1,300 m (4,270 ft) above sea level in the North Island but drops to 900 m (2,950 ft) in the South Island. Intense cold, heat, dryness and wind combine to produce tussock and shrubs adapted to cope with the climate.

Kea are South Island mountain parrots. They have a reputation for playfulness and intelligence.

The vegetable sheep plant is a mass of thousands of small, separate plants which together resemble the wool of a sheep.

Alpine plants climb above the competition to be noticed by pollinating alpine insects.

Around the Coast

Rocky shores, sandy beaches and muddy estuaries provide a diversity of habitats for coastal flora and fauna. Many native plants thrive in the salty environment, thanks to adaptations such as tough leaves which retain moisture in dry conditons.

The royal albatross breeds at Taiaroa Head on the Otago Peninsula (see p270) upon returning from its winter feeding grounds.

The pohutu-kawa's crimson flowers along the coasts of the North Island herald the arrival of Christmas.

New Zealand fur seals are commonly seen lolling on rocks around the coastline.

New Zealand's National Parks and Reserves

From the snow-capped volcanoes of Tongariro National Park to the sheer cliffs of Fiordland, New Zealand's national parks contain an awe-inspiring range of scenery, beautiful walking tracks, and numerous plants and animals found nowhere else in the world. The 14 national parks cover over 30,000 sq km (19,000 sq miles) or about 8 per cent of the country's land surface. There are also over 30 conservation and forest parks, thousands of reserves and 44 marine reserves. Keep safe when tramping or hiking by being well prepared and equipped, and respect the natural environment by leaving the land undisturbed.

Abel Tasman National Park's golden sand beaches fringe bush-clad cliffs. Inland, deep caves and underground rivers are a feature of the limestone landscape *(see pp218–19).*

Paparoa National Park's limestone landscape gives this area its special flavour. Along the coast, constant pounding by the Tasman Sea has sculpted the limestone into the Pancake Rocks and blowholes *(see p240).*

Aoraki/Mount Cook National Park contains the highest mountain in Australasia, Mount Cook, known as Aoraki or "cloud piercer" by the Ngai Tahu tribe, as well as New Zealand's longest glacier *(see pp256–7).*

0 kilometres 100

0 miles 100

Fiordland National Park is a vast, remote wilderness, with snow-capped mountains, fiords, glacial valleys and lakes, waterfalls, islands and dense temperate forest *(see pp284–5).*

Abel Tasman National Park

Kahurangi National Park

NELSO

Nelson Lakes National Park

Paparoa National Park

Westland / Tai Poutini National Park

Arthur's Pass National Park

Aoraki / Mount Cook National Park

CHRISTCHURCH

Banks Peninsula

Mount Aspiring National Park

QUEENSTOWN

Fiordland National Park

Otago Peninsula

INVERCARGILL   DUNEDIN

Foveaux Strait

Rakiura National Park

Stewart Island

Key

National parks

Conservation parks

Reserves

Marine reserves

Cape Reinga

Poor Knights Island

WHANGAREI

Great Barrier Island

AUCKLAND

Coromandel Peninsula

Bay of Plenty

ROTORUA

Te Urewera National Park

Egmont National Park

Tongariro National Park

GISBORNE

Whanganui National Park

Hawke's Bay

NAPIER

Tasman Bay

WELLINGTON

Cape Palliser

Cook Strait

Waipoua Forest in Northland has the finest examples of kauri trees in the country *(see p115)*. Kauris are among the world's largest trees. The warmer climate in this region encourages their growth.

The Miranda Shorebird Centre is an information centre on the west coast of the Firth of Thames. The area's broad intertidal flats *(see p126)* are a magnet for thousands of migratory wading birds from home and abroad.

The Crater Lake of Mount Ruapehu in Tongariro National Park, a geological witch's cauldron, explodes periodically before settling into a semi-dormant state *(see pp68–9, 146–7)*.

Mount Taranaki/Egmont, the volcanic centrepiece of Egmont National Park, forms a dramatic backdrop to the nearby city of New Plymouth. It has been dormant since it last erupted in 1755 *(see pp186–7)*.

Architecture in New Zealand

Earthquake risk in New Zealand has limited the height and structure of buildings, giving towns and cities a somewhat uniform appearance, while abundant space has led to suburban sprawl. Interspersed with the country's ubiquitous wooden houses are gracious historic homes and buildings, well-preserved Māori meeting houses and impressive public and commercial buildings. The latter range from early European-style structures built in stone to modern glass and concrete towers. Contemporary architecture is an eclectic mix of "New Zealand" and imported styles.

Glass and concrete towers in Auckland

Māori Meeting Houses

Communal meeting houses and storehouses have single gable roofs supported on posts sunk in the ground, and are elaborately carved. The porch bargeboards symbolize the arms of the ancestors, the ridgepole the tribal backbone, and the rafters the ribs of family lineage. Many older houses have been restored and new ones built of modern materials (see p135).

The figures on wall and roof posts represent ancestors and chieftains

Gable roof · Carved bargeboard · Ochre-painted rafters · Plaited reed walls

Te Tokanganui-a-Noho at Te Kuiti, a well-preserved meeting house built in 1872.

Homesteads

From the mid-1800s, wealthy sheep or cattle farmers and rich merchants demonstrated their affluence with substantial, architect-designed mansions to which they added rooms as they prospered. Stylistically varied, most mansions reflect a Victorian flavour, and some are romantically nostalgic and grandiose. The interiors are usually richly panelled, with elaborately carved stair rails, balusters, moulded ceilings and cornices (see p269).

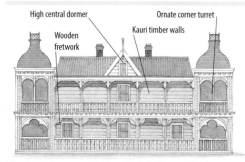

High central dormer · Ornate corner turret · Kauri timber walls · Wooden fretwork

Alberton, a two-storey residence built for farmer Allen Kerr in 1862, and later extended, now lies within Auckland city.

Public Buildings

Otago University (1878) in Dunedin, built in Gothic style after Scotland's Glasgow University (1870).

By the 1860s, the construction of public buildings reinforced links with "home", reflecting, for example, the Gothic Revival style in Britain. Sometimes timber was substituted for the customary stone. The emphasis is on verticality and repeated ornamentation.

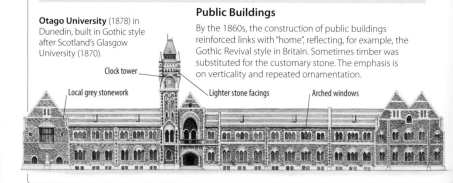

Clock tower · Local grey stonework · Lighter stone facings · Arched windows

Commercial Buildings

As New Zealand prospered, more permanent commercial buildings replaced temporary shops and warehouses. A wide range of styles, including Classical Renaissance, Edwardian Baroque and Neo-Classical, demonstrated the substance and affluence of successful commercial enterprise. Although façades are often splendid, with Roman or Greek columns, the structure behind uses more modern techniques of steel framing and reinforced concrete. As such techniques allowed varied exterior treatment, there is little consistency of style in city buildings.

Detail of Corinthian column

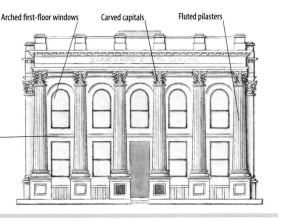

Arched first-floor windows

Carved capitals

Fluted pilasters

A floriated band of carved stonework marks the level of the first floor

Bank of New South Wales (Former) (1882) in Oamaru is Neo-Classical in style, with beautifully carved exterior ornamentation (see p272).

Bay Villas

In the early 1900s, bay-fronted villas became the standard domestic house, with often a street at a time being built to a stock design. Usually constructed of timber weatherboard with corrugated iron or clay tile roofs, they ranged from single bay villas decorated with crude sawn fretwork to more sophisticated and elaborate multistorey homes for the affluent (see p165).

Pierced wood fretwork decoration

Gable roof

Double-hung sash window

Projecting bays

Corrugated iron roofing

Balustraded verandah

Contemporary New Zealand Architecture

Although contemporary New Zealand architecture reflects international stylistic diversity, many architects are endeavouring to respond to the natural environment and to utilize ingredients from both Māori and European heritages.

Abstract art design on the exterior glazing

The Museum of New Zealand Te Papa Tongarewa, opened in 1998, incorporates elements of the gable forms of Māori meeting houses.

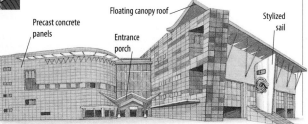

Precast concrete panels

Floating canopy roof

Entrance porch

Stylized sail

Māori Culture and Art

Māori have developed a complex culture derived from their Pacific Island inheritance. Climatic and seasonal conditions that differed from their former home, and a more extensive land area, permitted independent tribal development and variations in language, customs and art forms. Forests enabled them to build large canoes for transport and warfare, as well as meeting houses. Māori excel in wood, bone and stone carving, and in plaiting and weaving. Oratory, chant, song and dance are the means of passing on ancestral knowledge, and form an essential dimension of the rituals of challenge, welcome and farewell.

Moko (tattoo) involves incising lines into the skin and colouring them with pigment. The tradition has been revived and today, some Māori proudly wear moko.

Carving

The plentiful supply of large, straight-grained and durable timbers, and a variety of hard stones and obsidian that could be shaped into tools, enabled the early Māori to continue the Pacific tradition of carving. Today, an increasing awareness of Māori heritage has brought about a rebirth of traditional crafts. At Te Puia, a Māori arts and crafts centre in Rotorua, students learn to carve wood, bone and greenstone into exquisite and intricate Tiki pendants, combs and ceremonial objects *(see p142)*.

Carving in the Māori Affairs Select Committee Room of the Parliament Buildings in Wellington.

The eyes of figures are made of iridescent *paua* shell

Parallel ridges enclosing beaded lines are a distinctive feature of Māori carving

Taurapa (war canoe sternpost) of the mid-1800s, carved in the style of the Arawa tribes of Rotorua and adjacent areas

Māori motifs are mainly curvilinear in form

Song and Dance

Singing and dancing are an important feature of Māori life. They are performed on various occasions by both men and women. The *poi* dance, with its graceful movements is, however, restricted to women.

The *haka* is a war dance performed by men. Eyes and tongues protrude in a gesture of defiance.

Plaiting and weaving, using swamp flax, reeds or bird feathers, are women's arts. This 1880s *kete whakairo*, or decorated bag, was woven from flax, which was known as *harakeke* to Māori.

Cloaks and capes are a feature of traditional Māori dress and are made of various materials, including flax, feathers and dogskin. This engraving by Sydney Parkinson (1745–71) depicts a cloaked warrior.

Poi **balls** are stuffed with reeds and covered with woven flax fibre.

Songs are performed with the whole being; the body, hands, legs, arms and facial expressions all play their part.

Early Māori weapons were made of wood, stone and bone. Close hand-to-hand fighting was the main characteristic of Māori warfare. This *wahaika*, or short wooden hand club, from the early 1800s, is an example of a weapon used for striking.

Skirts consist of strips of flax hanging from a belt. The green leaves are scraped and dried so that they curl into tubes.

Contemporary Māori Artist

Very much a part of the remarkable renaissance in contemporary Māori art, artist Cliff Whiting celebrates his ancestral inheritance in this interpretation of the Māori legend of creation. Using a mixture of traditional and modern materials and processes, he depicts Tane Mahuta, God of the Forests, pushing apart Ranginui, his Sky Father, and Papatuanuku, his Earth Mother, to let light enter the world. The mural is in the National Library of New Zealand in Wellington.

Mural by Cliff Whiting (1974), depicting the separation of Ranginui and Papatuanuku

New Zealand Artists and Writers

From the time of first contact, botanists, navigators, surveyors and amateur painters recorded aspects of New Zealand's flora and fauna, the Māori people and early settlements. There were also many reports, diaries and commentaries in the British press which provided interesting descriptions and accounts of the new land, such as Lady Barker's *Station Life in New Zealand* (1870). The poetry, novels and paintings of the late 19th century were very much in the European tradition, but by the 1900s distinctive national elements began to emerge in writing and art.

Painting of a Māori chief, Charles Frederick Goldie (1870–1947)

Artists

The pioneer climate in New Zealand was not sympathetic to the arts. "Working class" settlers, struggling to survive in a strange and hostile land, had little knowledge of the arts. For the wealthy, the arts were largely a diversion for gentlewomen. Works of any substance were mainly by artists visiting New Zealand, such as William Hodges, whose work stylised the scenery into Romantic vistas. Italian Girolamo Pieri Nerli and Dutchman Petrus van der Velden, both also had a romantic European view of the untamed land.

A few New Zealanders sought training in European academies, such as Charles Frederick Goldie. By the 1900s art schools and societies had become established in New Zealand, but many artists, conscious of the Impressionist movement and other developments in Europe, escaped to that more exciting milieu. Frances Hodgkins left in 1901, and although some claim her as an eminent New Zealand artist, she achieved her reputation working in Britain and France.

In the 1920s, British-trained artists, such as Robert Field, Christopher Perkins and Roland Hipkins, came to teach and brought to their students the "radical" ideas of modernism, which were well established in Europe. Expressionist, Cubist and abstract influences began to appear in the works of John Weeks, Rhona Haszard and Louise Henderson, and by the 1940s a number of artists saw in modernism an opportunity to explore the "national" character of the land and its people. Much of the work of Eric Lee-Johnson, Sir Tosswill Woollaston, Russell Clark, Rita Angus and William Sutton seeks to define the substance or spirit of the land rather than give it superficial description.

In 1954 – late by world standards – the Auckland City Art Gallery presented New Zealand's first show of abstract paintings, "Object and Image", which caused a public outcry. However, artists such as Louise Henderson, Colin McCahon, Don Peebles and Rudy Gopas began to exhibit in the dealer galleries, which had become a feature of the larger cities.

Sculpture lagged behind painting, although Len Lye began his kinetic works as early as 1950. He moved to New York, but New Zealand is fortunate to have a substantial collection of his work at the Govett-Brewster Gallery in New Plymouth (*see p184*). From the 1960s, significant modern works were commissioned for public places from Jim Allen, Greer Twiss, Marte Szirmay, Terry Stringer, Neil Dawson and Paul Dibble.

Since the 1970s, there has been a substantial increase in the number of full-time professional artists, including outstanding Māori artists such as Para Matchett, Fred Graham and Shona Rapira Davies.

Dry September (1949), oil on canvas by William Sutton

Nga Morehu (The Survivors; 1988), a sculpture in mixed media by Shona Rapira Davies

Writers

New Zealand writing began to attract attention by the 1860s, but most of it was published in Britain as New Zealand lacked publishing houses. *Erewhon* (1872) by Samuel Butler is based upon his life in the high country of the South Island. *A History of New Zealand Birds* (1873) by Sir Walter Buller is still highly regarded for its careful documentation and illustrations. William Pember Reeves' *The Long White Cloud*, a romanticized version of New Zealand history, was published in 1898.

Jane Mander's *The Story of a New Zealand River* (1920) attracted some international attention for its depiction of colonial life. *Bliss*, Katherine Mansfield's first collection of short stories, marked the advent of New Zealand writing

Cover of *The Bone People*, a novel by Keri Hulme

of originality and substance. Born in Wellington, Mansfield was sent to London to further her education. Although she returned briefly to New Zealand, she spent most of her life in France and England. Though produced abroad, her work, which reveals her sharp observation of human behaviour, is based upon her memories of a New Zealand childhood. Mansfield died in 1923 at the age of 34.

By the 1930s, there emerged a conscious determination by novelists and poets to shape a New Zealand style, using local idioms, references to the raw landscape, and characterization of its settler inhabitants. Time spent overseas in the armed forces during both world wars also gave writers a new perspective of their homeland and added more pungency to their writing. Typical is poet Allen Curnow's *Landfall in Unknown Seas*, a powerful evocation of the visitor confronted by an alien but compelling land.

By the 1950s, Denis Glover, Robin Hyde, Frank Sargeson and Ruth Dallas, among others, ushered in a period of substantial productivity. Novelists such as John Mulgan, Dan Davin, Roderick Finlayson, and poet James K Baxter also cast a sharply critical eye upon what they saw as a conforming

and conventional society that concealed disturbing undercurrents.

Historian and poet Keith Sinclair, in his *A History of New Zealand* (1961), was one of the first to question prevailing versions of New Zealand history, which promoted colonial supremacy over "native" primitivism and biased interpretations of land settlement and the subsequent land wars. Dick Scott's research in *Ask that Mountain* (1975) revealed to New Zealanders a truer account of early settlement and relations with Māori. Writers such as Fiona Kidman, C K Stead, Maurice Gee, Fleur Adcock and historian Michael King have demonstrated a new maturity in their commentary upon racial and social issues.

A number of Māori writers are a voice for their people, among them Witi Ihimaera, Patricia Grace and Hone Tuwhare. In 1985, Keri Hulme, of Māori and Pakeha descent, won the British Booker Prize with *The Bone People*. Māori writer Alan Duff's *Once Were Warriors*, later made into a film of the same name, is a powerful exposure of the turbulence within the urban Māori people. Sylvia Ashton-Warner's novel *Spinster*, on provincial attitudes in a rural community, was made into a film in the US, as was Ian Cross's *God Boy*, an insight into adolescence and religion.

Katherine Mansfield

James K Baxter

Farming and Horticulture

Despite being so urbanized (85 per cent of New Zealanders live in cities or large towns), the country still depends heavily on its agricultural economy. Farming industries utilize around 40 per cent of the total land area of 268,000 sq km (103,500 sq miles) and produce 58 per cent of all export earnings, half of it from dairying. Traditionally, pastoral farming has centred on sheep and cattle but other types of livestock, such as deer, goats, pigs and poultry, are gaining in importance, with dairy products now a major contributor to the New Zealand economy. Pine trees cloak hills too steep to support livestock, while horticulture and crops dominate fertile coastal and inland areas.

Kiwifruit, grown primarily in the Bay of Plenty (see p133), is successfully marketed in more than 53 countries. New Zealand supplies about a quarter of world production.

Apples and pears, New Zealand's main pip fruits, are grown mostly in Hawke's Bay and Marlborough/Nelson. About 19.5 million cartons are exported annually.

Plastic sheeting protects rows of delicate berry fruits from frost.

Lines of trees between orchards serve as windbreaks.

Kiwifruit grow on vines supported by wooden trellises.

Peaches and other stone fruit, such as apricots, nectarines, plums and cherries, are concentrated in Hawke's Bay and Central Otago.

Horticulture

Although pastoral farming is the major land use in New Zealand, large areas are now planted with crops. The mild, sunny climate and fertile soils of the coastal regions of the Bay of Plenty, Gisborne, Hawke's Bay, Nelson and Otago have created a stunning mosaic of orchards producing a variety of traditional pip and stone fruit as well as citrus, berry and subtropical varieties.

Pastoral Agriculture

New Zealand's 27.6 million sheep and 10.6 million cattle are bred for their meat, wool, dairy produce and hides. Dairy herds are found on fairly flat land, while sheep and beef cattle are farmed in the rougher hill country. Deer, goats and other livestock are scattered throughout both islands.

The Romney Cross is the most common sheep in New Zealand and is bred for both meat and wool production.

The black and white Holstein-Friesian is the most common dairy cow, yielding more milk than other breeds.

Cereal and Other Crops

Wheat and garlic in Marlborough

Fields of traditional cereal crops are found on the plains of the South Island, especially in Canterbury and Southland. Here, wheat and oats are grown for home consumption and for milling, and barley and oats for the manufacture of stock feed; barley is also grown for malting at New Zealand breweries. Large-scale vegetable production has made inroads into fertile coastal regions in both the North and South islands, while new and distinct plant varieties, such as sunflowers, lavender and garlic, add colour and variety to the country's agricultural landscape.

Sunflowers, grown for their seeds, near Palmerston North

Sorting and packaging is done in packhouses.

Citrus trees are planted in long, straight lines.

Other fruits, such as the citrus grapefuit and subtropical varieties like avocados, tamarillos, persimmons and pepinos (in addition to kiwifruit), are grown in warmer North Island orchards – Northland, around Auckland, the Bay of Plenty and Hawke's Bay — while berry fruits such as raspberries thrive in the cooler South Island.

Grapefruit

Avocados

Pepinos

Persimmon

Tamarillos

Raspberries

Grapes are grown mainly for wine production (see pp40–41). Marlborough, Canterbury, Gisborne and Hawke's Bay are the major grape-producing areas. Few table grapes are grown.

Deer are bred on some 2,100 farms. Venison fetches premium prices worldwide, while deer velvet is popular in Asia.

Goats are farmed both domestically and commercially for their milk, meat and mohair as well as for weed control.

Ostriches (as shown here) and emus are among the other livestock breeds gaining in popularity.

The Wines of New Zealand

Although grapes were first planted in New Zealand as early as the 1830s, it was not until the 1980s when wine makers decided to concentrate on white wines, such as Sauvignon Blanc and Chardonnay, that the country's reputation as an excellent wine producer began. The number of wineries has since grown to almost 800, and export wine sales in 2016 reached 230 million litres (61 million gallons). In less than 20 years, the nation's wine makers went from producing wine of average quality to some of the best in the world. Wine drinking is popular in New Zealand. Many vineyards have restaurants, offer wine tastings and tours, and sell wine at the cellar door.

A visit to a vineyard for wine tasting or a meal is a popular weekend leisure activity.

James Busby

Appointed by the British Government as Resident or government representative to New Zealand in 1833, James Busby (1800–71) became the country's first recorded wine maker. He had earlier studied wine making in France and had also helped to establish a wine industry in the Hunter Valley in Australia. French explorer Dumont D'Urville confirmed the promise of viticulture in the country when he heaped praise on Busby's white wine, which he sampled during an 1840 visit to the Bay of Islands.

Marlborough is New Zealand's largest wine-growing region *(see pp210–11)*. The wide, flat Wairau Valley, dry, sunny climate and slow ripening conditions combine to produce the country's finest Sauvignon Blanc.

French settlers planted vines on Canterbury's picturesque Banks Peninsula as early as 1840 *(see pp234–5)*. Waipara, north of Christchurch *(see pp236–7)*, has become a more important wine-producing area.

● Christchurch

Gibbston Valley Winery in Central Otago *(see p282)* produces Pinot Noir, Chardonnay, Pinot Gris and Riesling. It has an underground cellar cut into the rock face behind the winery.

Central Otago's growing season is short, but it has become a world leader in Pinot Noir production.

● Dunedin

0 kilometres 100

0 miles 100

Dalmatian Croats living in the Henderson Valley close to downtown Auckland, were the pioneers of the modern wine industry (see pp90–91).

Grape Varieties of New Zealand

Northland's most notable wines are full-bodied reds, especially Merlot. The **Auckland** area is also primarily a red wine region, concentrating on Cabernet Sauvignon. The most prominent wines in **Waikato**, the **Bay of Plenty** and **Gisborne** are Chardonnays. **Hawke's Bay** has a reputation for high-quality Chardonnays and Cabernet blends. In **Wairarapa**, Pinot Noir is the most widely planted variety. **Marlborough** produces world-class Sauvignon Blanc, some Chardonnay and sparkling wines, while the small **Nelson** vineyards, like those in **Canterbury**, produce Chardonnay, Pinot Noir and Riesling. **Central Otago**, the world's southernmost wine area, produces Pinot Noir and other cold climate varieties.

Mills Reef Winery in Tauranga, in the Bay of Plenty, sells wines from its Art Deco-style winery building and restaurant.

Hastings is the venue for the annual Hawke's Bay Vintners' Charity Wine Auction (see pp154–5).

Te Mata Estate, a medium-sized winery using only Hawke's Bay grapes, is New Zealand's oldest winery (see pp154–5). Its Coleraine Cabernet Merlot is of world-class quality.

Wairarapa is one of New Zealand's newest wine areas. The original four wineries in 1980 have now grown to about 30.

Martinborough, the hub of wine-making in Wairarapa, is a popular week-end destination for people from Wellington. It is also the scene of the annual Toast Martinborough Wine, Food and Music Festival (see p176).

Key

■ Northland
■ Auckland
■ Waikato and Bay of Plenty
■ Gisborne
■ Hawke's Bay
■ Wairarapa
■ Marlborough
■ Nelson
■ Canterbury
■ Central Otago

New Zealand's Sporting Year

Sport has always been an important part of New Zealand cultural life. Māori were fond of running races, wrestling, surfing and canoe competitions, although nothing was formalized. European settlers found the relatively easy climate gave them a chance to play a variety of sports, and sporting events brought together isolated farming communities. The national passion for an active recreational life has contributed to New Zealanders carving out an international reputation for their sporting prowess, producing numerous world-class champions out of all proportion to the size of the country's population.

The Lake Taupo International Trout Fishing Contest attracts worldwide partici-pation to this Mecca of trout fishing.

The NZ Golf Open, held at a different golf course each year, attracts a world-class field.

The New Zealand Cup at Addington, Christchurch, is one of the important harness races on the racing calendar.

January	February	March	April	May	June

The Burt Munro Challenge, a large-scale motorcycle rally, is held in Invercargill (see p44).

The Auckland Anniversary Regatta, in which more than 600 yachts take part, is one of the largest yachting events in the world.

The NZ Rally Championship begins in April and attracts overseas competitors to race over some of the country's most difficult roads.

The Wellington Cup, like most of horse racing's premier events, is held during summer.

The National Dragon Boat Championships take place on Wellington's Lambton Harbour.

The Provincial Trophy is cricket's premier event in New Zealand. Cricket is the most popular summer sport and attracts large numbers of spectators.

The Adventure Racing World Series sees teams of three to five people competing in races held at various locations around the world. The climax of the series is the World Championship race in November. Teams cycle and use kayaks and rafts to cross lakes and rivers.

The New Zealand Women's Open golf championship is held at a different course each year and attracts keen players from around the world.

The Mitre 10 Cup, rugby's top domestic prize, is the climax of the rugby season.

⋅ly	August	September	October	November	December

The World Heli Challenge, at Wanaka, is just one of the many adventure sports events in New Zealand.

Black Magic

No sport has had such an effect on New Zealand life as rugby union. Imported from England in the 1870s, the sport was taken up with alacrity by New Zealanders, especially Māori and, in the last few decades, Polynesian Islanders. The standard bearers for rugby are the famous All Blacks, a name synonymous with the sport. In 1888, the Native team from New Zealand toured Britain, its uniform black with a silver fern on the chest. Known as the Blacks, they were the precursor to the first All Black team which conquered British teams in 1905.

Black attire was later adopted by other New Zealand sporting teams for international events. The national cricket team is dubbed the Black Caps and the basketball team, the Tall Blacks.

Former All Black Jonah Lomu

Key

- Cricket
- Golf
- Horse racing
- Lawn bowls
- Netball
- Rugby
- Skiing
- Surf life-saving

NEW ZEALAND THROUGH THE YEAR

New Zealand's seasons are opposite to those in the northern hemisphere. Spring arrives in September and summer comes in December, autumn is from March to May and the winter months are June, July and August. The South Island's temperatures are slightly lower than those in the North Island. Rain falls heaviest in winter in most areas, with the mid- to late summer months relatively dry. Visitors need to be prepared for sudden weather changes, a feature of the maritime climate. The country's latitudinal position opens it to prevailing westerly winds, plus the odd polar blast. Weather can change quickly and be extreme, especially around the mountains.

Spring

With the onset of finer weather, the rugby posts come down from the playing fields and cricketers start to practise their strokes. Blossom and food festivals, garden and fashion shows begin, and the horse racing season swings into gear.

September
World Heli Challenge *(mid-Sep)*, Wanaka. International snow-boarders as well as skiers take part in three days of heliskiing events.
Hastings Blossom Festival *(mid- to late Sep)*. The country's largest fruit-growing district ushers in a new season with this festival. Highlights include concerts and a blossom parade.
World of WearableArt Awards (WOW) *(late Sep)*, Wellington. A choreographed evening

Cattle on parade at Showtime Canterbury

in which art designs are worn. The competition began in Nelson where there is a museum of past winners.

October
Taranaki Garden Spectacular *(last week)*. More than 100 gardens are on view *(see p184)*.
Dunedin Rhododendron Festival *(late Oct–early Nov)*. Displays of rhododendrons set the Dunedin Botanic Garden and other gardens around Otago ablaze with colour in spring.

November
New Zealand Cup and Show Week , Christchurch. Features the region's main Agricultural & Pastoral Show, horse races, concerts, fashion shows as well as a diverse range of events.

F.A.W.C! Food and Wine Classic *(early Nov)*. Wineries in Hawke's Bay, North island open their doors to visitors for this three-day festival. Also held in mid-June.
Toast Martinborough Wine, Food and Music Festival *(mid-Nov)*, Martinborough Sq, Wairarapa. Showcases the wine and food of the region, along with entertainment by local artists.
Burt Munro Challenge *(late Nov)*, Invercargill New Zealand's most popular motorcyle event, first held in 2006, commemorates the life of racer Burt Munro. A series of rallies end in races at the Oreti beach.
Coromandel Pohutakawa Festival *(end-Nov–mid-Dec)*. This two-week festival celebrates the music, arts and outdoor culture of Coromandel.

Modelling designs in the World of WearableArt Awards

Average Daily Hours of Sunshine

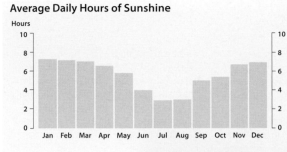

Hours

| | Jan | Feb | Mar | Apr | May | Jun | Jul | Aug | Sep | Oct | Nov | Dec |

Sunshine Chart

The chart gives figures for Wellington, but these are similar to other main centres. Nelson and Blenheim in the South Island, and Tauranga, Napier and Gisborne in the North Island, enjoy more sunshine hours than any other places. The least sunny region is the southern part of the South Island.

Summer

Although many New Zealanders head off for their annual visit to the beach, lake or high country during the summer school break, shops no longer "shut down" apart from Christmas day and New Year's day. Cities and towns have become increasingly lively places during the holiday season.

December

Kepler Challenge *(early Dec)*, Fiordland National Park, Te Anau. An annual endurance run that follows the 60-km- (37-mile-) Kepler Track *(see p287)* over mountains, swamps and rivers, through magnificent scenery.

TSB Festival of Lights *(Christmas to late Jan)*, New Plymouth. Special festive lighting in Pukekura Park and city streets. There are music and dance performances in the park each evening *(see p185)*.

January

Nelson Jazz Festival *(early Jan)*. A week-long festival featuring local and international talent (as part of the Summer in Nelson festival).

New Zealand Kite Festival *(late Jan)*. Hosted by various regions, this festival attracts top kite flyers from all over New Zealand as well as from other countries.

New Zealand Gliding Grand Prix *(late Jan)*, Omarama. The world's top glider pilots race head to head.

World Buskers Festival *(late Jan)*, Christchurch. Ten days of entertainment featuring street, circus and comedy acts.

Māori performing at the Waitangi Day celebrations

February

Waitangi Day *(6 Feb)*, Waitangi National Trust. Commemorates the signing of the Treaty of Waitangi *(see pp108–9)*.

Auckland Anniversary Regatta *(early Feb)*. Up to 600 yachts take part in one of the world's largest one-day

A yatch participating in the Anniversary Day Regatta in Auckland

regattas on Auckland's Waitemata Harbour *(see p76)*.

Aotearoa Traditional Māori Performing Arts Festival *(early Feb, even years)*, Waikato. Festival of Māori culture and art by New Zealand's best groups.

Marlborough Wine & Food Festival *(second Sat)*, Blenheim. Wines and food served under marquees in a vineyard setting *(see p212)*.

Art Deco Weekend *(third week)*, Napier. A celebration of Art Deco style with jazz-age dining and dancing, films, house tours, vintage cars and aeroplane rides.

Garden City Festival of Flowers *(late Feb–early Mar)*, Christchurch. Prestigious festival celebrates the beauty of flowers.

New Zealand International Arts Festival *(late Feb to mid-Mar, even years)*, Wellington. This renowned festival features some of the world's best talents *(see pp160–61)*.

Average Monthly Rainfall

Rainfall Chart
Rainfall is not evenly distributed throughout New Zealand. The west coast of the North Island and South Island is wetter than the east coast. More rain falls in winter and spring than in summer and autumn, in most areas. The figures given here are only for Wellington.

Autumn

Autumn often brings the most settled weather of the year, a time of mild, calm days still warm enough for most summer activities. This is harvest season, a good time to experience wine and food festivals. Hiking, fishing and hunting are also popular autumnal pursuits.

March

National Dragon Boat Championships (*Chinese New Year*), Wellington. Crews race on Lambton Harbour.

Golden Shears (*first week*), Masterton. The world's top sheep shearers are in action at this popular event (*see p177*).

Pasifika Festival (*second week*), Auckland. Cultural events and displays by Pacific Islanders (*see p97*).

Ellerslie Flower Show (*Mar*), Christchurch. Large floral exhibition located at Hagley Park (*see p231*).

Hokitika Wildfoods Festival (*mid-Mar*), Hokitika. Possum stew and huhu grub are some of the delicacies on the menu.

Round the Bays Run (*end-Mar*), Auckland. One of the world's

Balloons Over Waikato Festival in Hamilton

largest fun runs with 60,000 people taking part.

Ngaruawahia Regatta (*late Mar*), Ngaruawahia. Māori canoes compete on Waikato River in the hometown of the Māori monarch (*see p120*).

Ngongotaha Trout Festival (*late Mar–early Apr*). The annual trout fishing tournament and festival open the trout season.

Balloons Over Waikato (*late Mar–mid-Apr*), Hamilton. More than 30 balloons drift over the city and surrounding areas (*see p122*).

April

NZ Rally Championship (*early Apr*), Greater Auckland. Part of the World Rally Championships, in which drivers battle it out on the back country roads.

Bluff Oyster & Food Festival (*mid-Apr*). Features an array of seafood, fine wine and entertainment.

Royal Easter Show (*second week*), Auckland. Livestock competitions, art and craft awards, wine awards and the largest equestrian show in the country.

Lake Taupo International Trout Fishing Tournament (*third week*). Fishermen vie at this fine trout fishing location (*see p145*).

Warbirds Over Wanaka (*Easter weekend, even years*). Classic vintage and veteran warplanes take to the skies in this renowned world-class event (*see p274*).

May

Rotorua Tagged Trout Competition (*May*). Rotorua's premier fishing competition has a $10,000 trout waiting to be hooked.

Spectators at the Rally of New Zealand in Auckland

Average Monthly Temperature

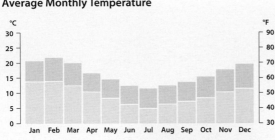

Temperature Chart
The chart gives the average maximum and minimum temperatures for the city of Wellington. The North Island has mild winters and humid summers. The South Island experiences the country's hottest summer temperatures, but in winter these can plunge to below freezing point.

Winter

Often the most spectacular time of the year to visit, winter also brings reduced rates on airfares, accommodation and activities. On the scenic west coast, rainfall is at its lowest and whales at Kaikoura can virtually be guaranteed to put in an appearance.

June

National Agricultural Fieldays *(mid-Jun)*, Mystery Creek, Hamilton. One of the world's largest agricultural events showcases the best of New Zealand's products, with an emphasis on innovative technology *(see p122)*.

Queenstown Winter Festival *(mid-late Jun)*. One of the highlights of the Queenstown calendar, this 10-day winter festival includes street parties, jazz and comedy performances, spectacular night skiing and firework displays.

Participants dressed up for the opening parade of the Queenstown Winter Festival

July

Hokonui Fashion Design Awards *(late Jul)*, Gore. A key national fashion event that attracts entries from all over New Zealand.

August

Bay of Islands Jazz and Blues Festival *(mid-Aug)*, Northland. A very popular event on the jazz calendar. More than 50 local and global bands take part.

Crater to Lake Challenge *(late Aug)*, Taupo. Multi-sport event featuring skiing, cycling, kayaking, water-skiing and

running from the slopes of Mount Ruapehu to Taupo.

Christchurch Arts Festival *(late Aug–mid-Sep, odd years)*. A biennial mid-winter festival of music, theatre, dance, film and the visual arts.

New Zealand Fashion Week *(late Aug–mid-Sep)*, Auckland. The country's top fashion designers showcase their latest collections to local and international buyers, media and guests.

Public Holidays

New Year's Day (1 Jan)
New Year Holiday (2 Jan)
Waitangi Day (6 Feb)
Good Friday (varies)
Easter Monday (varies)
Anzac Day (25 April)
Queen's Birthday (first Mon in Jun)
Labour Day (varies Oct)
Christmas Day (25 Dec)
Boxing Day (26 Dec)

Clydesdale horses and wagon at the National Agricultural Fieldays, Mystery Creek, Hamilton

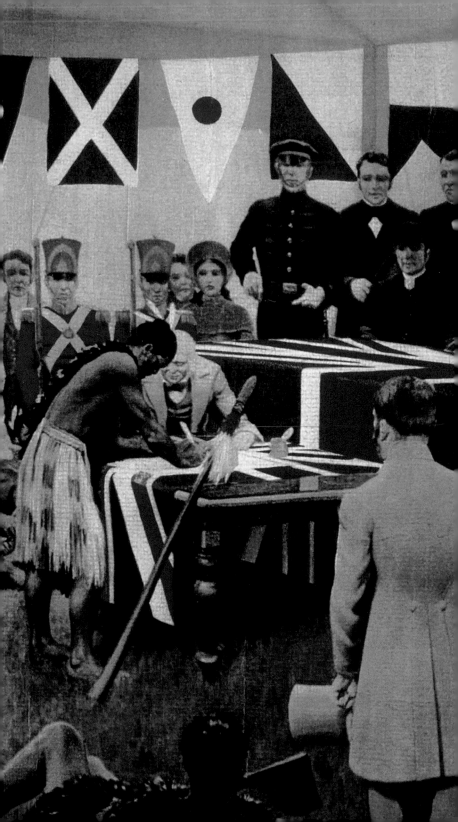

THE HISTORY OF NEW ZEALAND

The last of the world's significant landmasses to be colonized by people, New Zealand is a nation of immigrants. Māori settled in the country less than 1,000 years ago, while Europeans first arrived in 1642. Together, these two peoples have forged a unique identity out of their common experiences that reflects their Pacific environment.

The date the first Māori arrived in New Zealand has stirred much debate. According to legend, the first explorer to discover New Zealand was the Polynesian Kupe, around AD 950. He then returned to his ancestral homeland, Hawaiki. Three centuries later, a fleet of canoes set sail for New Zealand, guided by Kupe's directions on how to find land.

Basing their findings on radiocarbon dating of Māori middens, archaeologists believe that the first settlement was around AD 1200. Some scientists, however, believe that Māori arrived as long ago as 2,000 years, but these early settlers did not survive for long. Nonetheless, the rats that these first arrivals brought with them went on to devastate the native bird, lizard and frog populations.

Regardless of when they did arrive, Māori are known to have carried a number of plants and animals with them. The *kiore*, the Polynesian rat, was considered a great delicacy when fattened up on berries. Also known to have survived the journey was the native dog, the *kuri*. Root vegetables Māori brought with them were the yam,

kumara and *taro*. The *kumara* grew more successfully in the colder climate than the other two, and proved important in the development of Māori culture, enabling permanent settlement.

Abel Tasman

Since Greek times, there had been talk of a Terra Australis, or "great southern continent", to counterbalance the lands of the northern hemisphere. Such a landmass was necessary, it was argued, to offset the weight of the continents in the north and to balance the Earth on its axis. The mathematician Pythagoras speculated about the existence of such a land, but it was not until almost 2,000 years later that 17th-century Dutch explorers finally sighted Australia.

In 1642, the Dutch East India Company, a trading firm anxious to explore prospects for commerce beyond the East Indies, sent Abel Tasman south from Java in Indonesia. After sailing past Tasmania (then known as Van Diemen's Land), Tasman reached a point off present-day Hokitika on 13 December 1642, noting "a large high elevated land".

Moa skeleton

Double canoe

	1400–1500 Māori hunting drives moa to extinction	**1500** Māori develop fortified sites (*pa*) to defend themselves	
1300	**1400**	**1500**	**1600**
1300 First Polynesian inhabitants arrive from Cook and Society islands	**1400** Great fires on the South Island east coast destroy swathes of forest	**1531** Map drawn with Terra Australis on it	**1642** Dutch explorer Abel Tasman sights New Zealand

◄ Detail from *The Signing of the Treaty of Waitangi* by Marcus King (1939)

Māori Exploration and Voyage

It is now fairly well accepted that Polynesians, ancestors of the Māori, made planned voyages to New Zealand rather than simply drifting there by chance. Polynesians were skilled navigators who sailed long distances between the islands in the Pacific in large craft. Driven out of an island by starvation or intertribal warfare, some groups would have deliberately sailed to a far-off land, especially if they had been given directions by someone like Kupe who had been there *(see p49)*. With their vessels laden with plants and animals, they would have been guided by traditional navigation clues, such as the stars, migrating birds, cloud formations and even wave patterns.

Kupe's Anchor Stone
A 1912 photograph of a Māori elder standing beside what may be Kupe's anchor stone.

Canoe Prow
The prows of Māori *waka* (canoes), carved in intricate patterns, had forward-thrusting prows to improve the canoes' performance.

Fishing Net
Fish, a valuable part of Māori food supply, were caught using a variety of nets. This wood engraving (1840) by Joel Pollack is of a landing net.

Kuri
Māori brought the *kuri* (dog) with them on their migrations. It became extinct soon after European settlement.

Single Canoe
The single Māori canoe was used as a coastal vessel. It had decking made of long rods. Thwarts, lashed from one top edge to the other, served as seats. These evolved to be the longest and biggest craft in the Pacific due to the availability of enormous forest trees.

Polynesian Settlement

Archaeological discoveries indicate that Polynesians came from Southeast Asia to the eastern Pacific islands, settling the lands from Hawaii to Easter Island. In about 1250, expeditions from the islands of central Polynesia reached New Zealand where they established coastal tribal settlements.

Periods of Settlement

——— 30,000 years ago
——— 3,000 years ago
——— 1,500–2,000 years ago
——— 1,000 years ago
——— 500 years ago

Double Canoes
The largest of these craft, depicted here by William Hodges, artist on Cook's 1773 voyage, were capable of carrying up to 200 passengers and crew.

Taro Plant
Taro was brought over from Polynesia, but because it was not productive in New Zealand, it became a luxury food.

PACIFIC
OCEAN

HAWAII

NORTH
AMERICA

SOLOMON
ISLANDS

SAMOA

FIJI

NEW
CALEDONIA

TONGA

TAHITI

COOK
ISLANDS

EASTER
ISLAND

NEW
ZEALAND

0 kilometres 1,000

0 miles   1,000

Kiore
The *kiore* or Polynesian rat was introduced from Polynesia. It was a source of food for the early Māori, but killed native birds.

Canoe Regatta
Māori today celebrate their heritage of exploration and voyage in the annual Ngaruawahia Regatta, held on the Waikato River *(see p120)*.

Legend of Maui
An ink drawing (1907) by Wilhelm Dittmer depicts the legend of Maui, who created New Zealand by fishing the North Island out of the ocean.

Abel Tasman's ships, the *Heemskerck* and *Zeehaen*

Abel Tasman and the crews of the *Heemskerck* and *Zeehaen* had sighted the Southern Alps. Tasman wanted to land, but the rolling swell off the coastline convinced him to head north, where he found a relatively calm anchorage in what is now called Golden Bay. However, the provoked Māori rammed a pinnace (small boat) from the *Zeehaen*, and clubbed four of the Dutch sailors to death. The Dutch named the location Murderers' Bay. Tasman set sail north and left New Zealand waters on 6 January 1643 without further investigation.

Captain James Cook

There was a lull in European exploration of the New Zealand region for more than 100 years. No good commercial reason encouraged any visits; indeed, the reputation of the hostile Māori discouraged them. Then, in 1769, Englishman Captain James Cook set sail on a scientific expedition of discovery to the South Pacific, to observe the transit of the sun by the planet Venus. After having observed the rare phenomenon

in Tahiti, Cook sailed south until he sighted the east coast of New Zealand, on 9 October 1769.

Cook's ship, the *Endeavour*, was well equipped for its voyage, with botanists and artists on board. Besides documenting new scientific finds, Cook's mission was to assess the potential of the country as a colony. A master mariner, Cook mapped the coastline and the scientists on board made hundreds of discoveries. On this first of three visits to New Zealand, he claimed the country for England. Coincidentally, a French expedition led by explorer Jean de Surville sailed within a few kilometres of Cook at the end of 1769, but neither was aware of the other's presence.

Following Cook, Europeans trickled rather than flooded into New Zealand, working as whalers, sealers and timber traders. Few became permanent immigrants, and as soon as the resource they sought disappeared, so did they. By the early 1800s it had become uneconomic to send sealing gangs to New Zealand because most of the easy prey had been taken; whale numbers, too, plummeted.

Abel Tasman

The Treaty of Waitangi

The impact of these visitors on the traditional Māori way of life was enormous. Māori were exposed to a disastrous number of diseases, such as measles and smallpox, and their warlike instincts were incited by the purchase of guns. During the 1820s, at least 20,000 Māori were killed in intertribal "musket wars", which changed

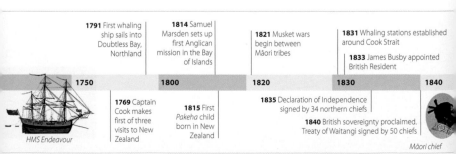

1791 First whaling ship sails into Doubtless Bay, Northland

1814 Samuel Marsden sets up first Anglican mission in the Bay of Islands

1821 Musket wars begin between Māori tribes

1831 Whaling stations established around Cook Strait

1833 James Busby appointed British Resident

| 1750 | 1800 | 1820 | 1830 | 1840 |

1769 Captain Cook makes first of three visits to New Zealand

1815 First *Pakeha* child born in New Zealand

1835 Declaration of Independence signed by 34 northern chiefs

1840 British sovereignty proclaimed. Treaty of Waitangi signed by 50 chiefs

HMS Endeavour

Māori chief

The Treaty House at Waitangi

the political face of Māori New Zealand as tribes invaded neighbouring territories, sometimes taking them permanently.

Another major influence for change was Christianity. Anglican missionary Samuel Marsden established New Zealand's first mission station in the Bay of Islands in 1814, and although progress was slow in converting Māori to Christianity, the faith had a significant foothold by 1840.

By then Māori numbered about 115,000 and European settlers (*Pakeha*) 2,000. While some Māori benefitted by trading with the Europeans and growing crops for them, there was concern about increasing lawlessness, the buying up of land by Europeans and the intertribal warfare. Leading chiefs asked Queen Victoria to provide a framework of law and order. Eventually Captain William Hobson obtained the signatures of Māori chiefs on the 1840 Treaty of Waitangi, giving sovereignty to Britain, although the Māori translation gave the chiefs a different understanding of the treaty.

Treaty of Waitangi

The Treaty of Waitangi is New Zealand's founding document, an agreement between the British Government and the Māori that is today the centrepiece of the country's race relations.

In return for giving Queen Victoria the right to buy land, Māori were granted all the rights and privileges of British subjects. A clause also gave them "full exclusive and undisturbed possession of their Lands and Estates Forests Fisheries and other properties". But misunderstanding arose because there were two different versions (Māori and English). The crucial difference was what was meant by the word sovereignty, translated by many as *kawanatanga*, suggesting a distant figure of authority. Controversy over the Treaty continues to this day. The Treaty of Waitangi is now on display at the National Library in Wellington.

Signatures on the Treaty

The New Zealand Wars

Unlike Australia, where some of the first immigrants were convicts, New Zealand settlers were freemen and many came in family groups. The New Zealand Company was set up in 1837 to transplant a cross-section of English society in the Antipodes. Planned settlements were established at Wellington, Wanganui, Nelson, New Plymouth, Christchurch and Dunedin.

Following the signing of the Treaty of Waitangi, Māori–Pakeha relations were relatively harmonious for some years. If there were conflicts, they were generally over land, and isolated skirmishes occurred until 1860, the year the New Zealand Wars began. The critical point was at Waitara, Taranaki. The cause was a land sale between the government and a minor chief of the

1844 Hone Heke chops down British flagpole and starts "War of the North"

1848 Dunedin settlement founded by Scottish pioneers

1850 Canterbury settlement founded by genteel English emigrants

1854 First session of General Assembly (Parliament)

Gold nugget

1860 New Zealand Wars begin between Māori and Europeans over land

1861 First New Zealand gold rush after discovery at Tuapeka, Central Otago

Te Kooti

1865 Capital moves from Auckland to Wellington

1867 Four Māori seats established in Parliament

1845   1850   1855   1860   1865

Te Ati Awa tribe who did not have the tribe's permission to sell, a prerequisite for communal property under Māori custom. When the tribe refused to accept the bogus deal, the government retaliated by marching troops onto the land, seizing it by force.

In response, most central North Island tribes backed the Te Ati Awa, intensifying the rebellion.

Passengers from the Cressy Landing at Port Lyttelton by William Fox (1851)

At the height of hostilities in the mid-1860s, British forces had increased to more than 20,000, against about 5,000 Māori warriors. On the British side were significant numbers of Māori who were either opportunists or had a score to settle with an enemy tribe.

United, the Māori would have easily been a match for the *Pakeha*. Even divided, they came close to persuading many settlers to flee the colony. In 1868, two chiefs, Titikowaru in the west and Te Kooti in the east, won a series of significant battles, but internal squabbles saw them lose the support of the wider Māori population. By 1869, the New Zealand Wars came to a halt as Māori opposition fell away. Land sales escalated, many of them under duress. The wars resulted in the government confiscating

12,000 sq km (4,630 sq miles) of prime land. Most of it was given to "friendly" Māori tribes, while some was handed to *Pakeha* settlers. It was a legacy that came back to haunt the country more than a century later, as Māori pursued their legitimate grievances through the Waitangi Tribunal.

Economic Expansion

The 1861 discovery of gold in Otago, and subsequent finds on the West Coast, set the South Island on its industrial feet. Up until then, the North Island had been outstripping the South economically and in population terms; it was not until 1896 that the North Island reasserted itself.

The late 19th century saw a time of great economic expansion, thanks to large-scale government borrowing. The rail network was established, telegraph lines were installed and emigrants were assisted to the country. During the 1870s, the population doubled. Good export prices for wool (which proved to be the mainstay of the economy for the next 100 years) underpinned the frenzy of economic activity. Technological advances

Te Henheu's Old Pa of Waitahanui at Lake Taupo by George F Angas (1847)

1869 New Zealand Wars end because of Māori disunity

1882 First refrigerated ship leaves Otago for the UK

1893 First country in the world to extend the vote to all women

1907 New Zealand becomes a Dominion

1870   1880   1890   1900   1910

1879 Vote given to every male over 21

1887 Tongariro National Park, the first in New Zealand, established

Māori weapon

Early transport

24c   New Zealand

NELSON-HORSE TRAM 1862

also played their part. The first shipload of frozen meat for Britain sailed from Otago in 1882; this technology was also vital later in shipping butter.

New Zealand soon gained a reputation for social innovation. In 1893, the Liberal Government granted the vote to all women, and in 1898 it introduced a means-tested old-age pension, both the first in the world.

The War Years

As New Zealand's population reached the one million mark in 1907, the country's status as a colony of Great Britain changed to that of the Dominion of New Zealand. In 1917, the title of governor (the representative of the Queen) became that of governor-general.

World War I poster

The Liberal Party, with its progressive tax policies, old-age pensions, votes for women and breaking up of large land holdings, was hailed domestically and externally for making New Zealand "the birthplace of the 20th century". Its hold on power lasted until 1912, by which time it had lost touch with

the public. It was replaced by the Reform Party, which was led by Bill Massey and gained most of its suppport from the farmers. The Reform Party remained in power until 1928 and served in a coalition with the Liberals until 1935 when a Labour government was elected.

World War I was a defining moment for the fledgling nation. In 1915, New Zealanders and Australians combined to form the Australian and New Zealand Army Corps (ANZAC). Ordered by the British to attack well-armed and better-placed Turkish defenders on the Gallipoli Peninsula, thousands were killed in eight months of action. The 25th of April (Anzac Day) has since been set aside as a national holiday to remember the soldiers' sacrifice.

For a small country, New Zealand suffered enormously during the war. Out of a total of 110,000 troops, 16,697 died and 41,262 were wounded – a massive casualty rate.

The period between the wars was one of mixed fortunes for New Zealand. While the 1920s were initially positive, the world's

New Zealand Expeditionary Force on the Hutt Road near Petone, Wellington, 1914

1915 New Zealand troops suffer heavy losses in the Gallipoli campaign against Turkey

1920 First Anzac Day commemoration

Elizabeth McCombs

1933 Elizabeth McCombs first female MP

1936 New Zealand pilot Jean Batten flies from England to Australia in world record time

| 1915 | 1920 | 1930 | 1935 | 1938 |

1914 New Zealand enters World War I on the Allied side

1918 End of World War I

1935 First Labour Government elected

1936 40-hour week introduced

Factory workers

Relief camp for unemployed workers at Akatarawa, Hutt Valley, in the 1930s

economic woes engulfed the country, and by 1932 it was in the depths of the Depression. The first Labour Government, elected in 1935, spent its way out of the Depression. New Zealand gained further accolades as the social laboratory of the world with its income-related health scheme and extended pension programme.

In 1939, for the second time in the century, New Zealand found itself embroiled in a world war. Prime Minister Michael Joseph Savage was in no doubt where the country's loyalty lay: "Where Britain goes we go, where she stands we stand." New Zealand

Interior of a Wellington clothing factory in the 1940s

soldiers served in Greece, the Middle East and Italy, even though the most serious threat to the country came from Japan. After the attack on Pearl Harbour (1941), troops were increasingly deployed in the Pacific and links were forged with the US. American soldiers spent time in New Zealand during the war and took New Zealand wives back home with them. In 1951, military ties between the US, Australia and New Zealand were formalized with the signing of the ANZUS military pact.

Moving away from Britain

After the war, while New Zealand looked to the US for its military security, its economy still remained firmly wedded to Britain. As Britain's "South Pacific farm", New Zealand had traditionally enjoyed easy access to UK's markets. As late as 1960, 55 per cent of its exports landed there. But the boom times came to an end once "the old country" joined the European Union (EU) in 1973 and its priorities shifted to the European continent. Within 20 years of joining the EU, Britain took only 6 per cent of New Zealand's exports. New markets were found, and Asia became important. Hong Kong, China, Japan, Taiwan and South Korea are now among the top ten countries with which New Zealand trades.

Mirroring countries in the West, New Zealand went through great social changes during the 1960s, as baby-boomers reached adulthood and challenged conservative society. The decision to support the US with a token force in the Vietnam War was

1939 New Zealand fights in World War II on Allied side

Sir Edmund Hillary

1953 Sir Edmund Hillary climbs Mount Everest with Sherpa Tenzing

1975 Waitangi Tribunal established to investigate Māori land claims following confiscations and compensate where justified

1985 *Rainbow Warrior* sunk

1984 Lange Government takes power

1981 First Māori language kindergarten opens

1940   1950   1960   1970   1980

1947 Statute of Westminster adopted by Parliament

1948 Protest against exclusion of Māori from All Black rugby tour to South Africa

1961 Capital punishment abolished

1965 Combat force sent to Vietnam

1973 Frigate sent to French Polynesia to protest against French nuclear testing

1981 Country divided by South African rugby tour with widespread protests

1987 Māori becomes official language

vigorously opposed, and in 1972 conscription was dropped by the new Labour Government. A year later, the government sent a frigate to French Polynesia to protest against nuclear weapons testing there.

In the mid-1970s, as imported oil price hikes affected the population, New Zealanders returned to the conservative politics of the National Party under the combative Robert Muldoon. Finally, weary of his interventionist economic policies, the electorate voted in a socially leftist but economically rightist Labour Government in 1984, headed by David Lange.

For the next six years, the country experienced a whirlwind of change as Labour floated the exchange rate, deregulated industries, removed tariffs, sold off state assets and made thousands of civil servants redundant in a quest for greater efficiency. At the same time, foreign relations were in upheaval: New Zealand had always maintained a strong antinuclear weapons policy, and in 1985 the US was told that nuclear-armed or powered warships were no longer welcome in New Zealand ports. The Americans suspended

The *Rainbow Warrior*, sunk in Auckland Harbour in 1985

ANZUS. In that same year, French saboteurs sank the Greenpeace vessel, the *Rainbow Warrior*, in Auckland.

The National Government, which came to power in 1990 led by Jim Bolger (succeeded in 1997 by Jenny Shipley), continued with economic reforms, albeit at a slower pace. However, many New Zealanders, disillusioned over a succession of unresponsive administrations, voted in a Mixed Member Proportional electoral system based on the German model. The system was first tested in 1997, which resulted in a vastly more representative parliament than before, and the emergence of the country's first directly elected woman prime minister, Helen Clark of the Labour Party, in 1999.

New Zealand society today has changed significantly, from a period when an overwhelming majority of the population was *Pakeha* to a point where Auckland is now the largest Polynesian city in the world, and an increasing number of Asians have become citizens. With its increasingly diverse cultures, New Zealand is carving out a confident and independent identity as a Pacific nation in the international community.

Representatives of the Ngai Tahu tribe and the government signing the Deed of Settlement in 1997

1990 Dame Catherine Tizard first woman Governor-General	**2004** Peter Jackson's *Lord of the Rings* wins 11 Oscars	
1990 National forms government	**2006** Māori Queen Te Atairangikaahu dies after a reign of 40 years	
1995 Team New Zealand wins America's Cup	**2008** National Party wins general election	
	2010 Earthquake hits Christchurch	**2017** New Zealand wins Americas Cup in Bermuda
		2020 Population expected to hit 5 million

1990	**2000**	**2010**	**2020**	**2030**

Jenny Shipley

1997 Jenny Shipley first woman prime minister	**2016** Earthquake hits Kaikoura on 14th November
1997 Government compensation to Ngai Tahu tribe for land confiscations	**2011** Christchurch hit by worst earthquake in the country's history, causing widespread damage
1997 First MMP Parliament elected	**2011** New Zealand hosts Rugby World Cup

The beautiful turquoise-coloured Lake Tekapo, Canterbury ▶

NEW ZEALAND AREA BY AREA

New Zealand at a Glance

Tucked away in the southwest corner of the Pacific Ocean, New Zealand is one of the most isolated and least populated countries in the world. It is also a land of contrasts: between the subtropical north and the more temperate south; the wet west and the drier east; the volcanoes of the central North Island and the fiords of the South Island. Powerful geological forces have created a landscape that is dominated by mountains, hills, lakes and rivers. These, in turn, have allowed New Zealand to become a paradise for nature lovers and outdoor enthusiasts. Sheep and cattle farming still cover large areas of the country, but increasingly the accent is on diversity. The more populated north is the centre of Māori and Pacific Island culture.

One of the many vineyards in Marlborough (see pp210–11)

The Pancake Rocks and blowholes at Punakaiki in Paparoa National Park (see p240)

The Gothic-style Canterbury Museum in Christchurch (see p230)

Lake Wakatipu from The Remarkables (see p280)

Larnach Castle, a century-old stone mansion (see p270)

Collingwood
Motueka
Karamea
Nelson
Westport
Blenhei
Murchison
Reefton
MARLBOROUG
AND NELSON
(See pp200–221)
Greymouth
Kaikoura
Hokitika
Arthur's Pass
Fox Glacier
Springfield
Waipara
Haast
CANTERBURY AND
THE WEST COAST
(See pp222–257)
Christchurch
Twizel
Geraldine
Ashburton
Milford Sound
Timaru
Wanaka
Oamaru
Alexandra
OTAGO AND
SOUTHLAND
(See pp258–295)
Palmerston
Manapouri
Gore
Dunedin
Invercargill
Balclutha
Oban

Te Kao

Mohutangi

Kaitaia

Russell

ᵒnoni

Kaihu

Whangarei

NORTHLAND
(See pp98–115)

Orewa

AUCKLAND
(See pp70–97)

Auckland

Thames

Hamilton

Cambridge

Otorohanga

Whakatane

Te Araroa

THE CENTRAL
NORTH ISLAND
(See pp116–155)

Matawai

New
ᵧmouth

Taupo

Turangi

Tolaga Bay

Gisborne

Eltham

Raetihi

ᵛera

Wanganui

Hastings

Napier

WELLINGTON
ND THE SOUTH
(See pp156–189)

Waipukurau

Palmerston
North

ᵣaparaumu

Levin

Masterton

Wellington

Wall carvings in the Māori meeting house at the
Waitangi Treaty Grounds *(see pp108–9)*

Boats moored at Westhaven Marina,
Auckland *(see p76)*

The Lady Knox Geyser erupting at Wai-o-Tapu Thermal
Wonderland *(see p144)*

0 kilometres	100	
0 miles		100

Māori meeting house at the Museum of New
Zealand Te Papa Tongarewa *(see pp170–71)*

Marina in Whitianga Harbour, Coromandel Peninsula on North Island ▶

THE NORTH ISLAND

Introducing the North Island

Blessed with a varied landscape, the North Island also offers a range of climates, from the "winterless" north to the snow-bound mountains of the Central Plateau and the blustery winds of the south. From the tip of Northland down to Taranaki on the west and Hawke's Bay on the east, the sea lends a distinct character to each coast. Although best known for its geothermal wonders around Rotorua and the Volcanic Plateau, the North Island is also a fertile land of lush dairy pastures, highly productive orchards and rolling sheep country. The country's largest city, Auckland, and its capital, Wellington, are both located in the North Island.

The Bay of Islands *(see pp106–7)* is one of New Zealand's most beautiful and historic areas. The warm, sparkling, aquamarine waters, year-round sunshine, sandy beaches and quiet coves make the area a paradise for deep-sea fishing, underwater diving, swimming and sailing.

Mount Taranaki/Egmont *(see pp186–7)*, a dormant, snow-capped volcanic peak, is the centrepiece of the agriculturally rich Taranaki region and the dominant feature of Egmont National Park.

The Parliament buildings in Wellington *(see p162)* are interesting for their varied architectural styles. The circular, copper-domed "Beehive", which houses Cabinet offices, is in complete contrast to the square marble Parliament Buildings, home to the House of Representatives.

NORTHLAND
(See pp98–115)

Te Kao

Mohutangi

Kaitaia

Kerikeri

Kaikohe

Opononi

Kaihu

Dargaville

Ruawai

New Plymouth

Inglewood

Eltham

Hawera

Wanganui

Collingwood

Takaka

Karamea

Motueka

Paraparaumu

Nelson Picton

Lev

Lower Hutt

Wellington

Murchison

Blenheim

St Arnaud

Locator Map

Sky Tower *(see p79)* is Auckland city's dominant landmark. From its four observation decks, visitors enjoy 360-degree views of the city centre, its sprawling suburbs, harbours, and the islands of Hauraki Gulf.

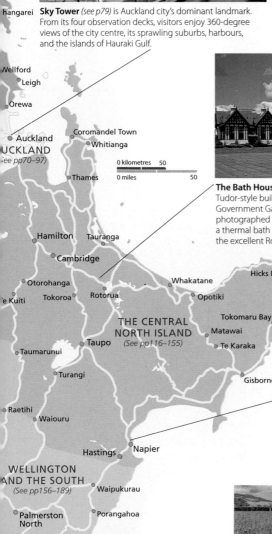

hangarei

Wellford
Leigh

Orewa

Auckland
UCKLAND
see pp70–97)

Coromandel Town
Whitianga

0 kilometres   50

0 miles   50

Thames

Hamilton   Tauranga

Cambridge

Otorohanga

e Kuiti   Tokoroa   Rotorua

Whakatane   Hicks Bay

Opotiki

THE CENTRAL NORTH ISLAND   Matawai
(See pp116–155)

Taumarunui   Taupo   Tokomaru Bay

Te Karaka

Turangi

Gisborne

Raetihi
Waiouru

Hastings   Napier

WELLINGTON AND THE SOUTH
(See pp156–189)   Waipukurau

Palmerston North   Porangahoa

Alfredton

Masterton

artinborough

The Bath House in Rotorua *(see p138)*, an elegant Tudor-style building situated in the English-style Government Gardens, is the town's most frequently photographed building. Originally constructed as a thermal bath house in 1908, it is now home to the excellent Rotorua Museum.

Napier's Art Deco buildings *(see pp150–51)*, such as the Rothmans Building, were constructed following a devastating earthquake in 1931. Napier sits in the wine-growing Hawke's Bay region.

Martinborough *(see p176)* is the hub of wine growing in Wairarapa, and its wineries have gained a reputation as producers of red wines. A good way to experience the area's wineries is to join one of the many vineyard tours that leave from Wellington.

Historic Northland

Between 700 and 800 years ago, the first Polynesian voyagers are believed to have come ashore on the northern coasts of the North Island. Northland is also sometimes referred to as "the birthplace of the nation". It was at Rangihoua in Northland that Samuel Marsden, the first missionary, set up an Anglican mission in 1814; at Waitangi that the Treaty of Waitangi was signed in 1840 *(see pp52–3)*; and at Russell that New Zealand's first capital was established in 1840 before shifting south. Here, too, were sown the first seeds of Māori rebellion against the British.

Kemp House
This Kerikeri Mission House, completed in 1822, is the oldest building in New Zealand. The house is associated with the Kemp family who lived in it for 142 years *(see p110)*.

Waipoa Bay, Moturoa Island
Captain Cook (in 1769) and French explorer Marion du Fresne (in 1772) took water on board here. Du Fresne buried in the sand a bottle with a document claiming New Zealand for France. The bottle, however, was never found.

Kauri trees are symbolic of Northland but much of the forest is now gone. Logging was at its height from 1870 to 1910.

Logging on the Hokianga

Charles Heaphy's painting *View of the Kahu-Kahu, Hokianga River* (1839) depicts the logging industry on the Hokianga River. The giant kauri trees made ideal ships' spars as well as timber for new settlements.

Hokianga Harbour was one of the main points of early Māori settlement. Kupe *(see p49)* left for Hawaiki from here.

Russell, Bay of Islands
This whaling and sealing town was dubbed the "Hell-hole of the Pacific" in the lawless days of the early 1800s *(see p106)*.

Hongi Hika

After Māori chief Hongi Hika met King George IV during a trip to England in 1820, he returned home determined to become king of New Zealand. In the 1820s, he led his Northland tribe, the Ngapuhi, in many conquests of other tribes.

Kauri Gum

Gum from kauri trees, used in paints and polishes, was an important export product from Northland until World War II.

Pohutukawa

The *pohutukawa* has an important place in Māori mythology. Māori believe that the spirits of the dead descend down the roots of a *pohutukawa* tree at Cape Reinga on their way to the homeland on Hawaiki.

Kauri logs being towed to a waiting ship.

Warrior Chiefs

Hone Heke is shown here with his wife, Harriet, and another chief, Kawiti. Unhappy with the Treaty of Waitangi, he was one of the first chiefs to fight the British.

Pa Site at Ruapekapeka

This *pa* (fortification) site was one of the most complex ever built. In 1846, British troops stormed it on a Sunday morning, catching the Māori inside by surprise. They did not expect the British to fight on a day traditionally given to rest and prayer.

Volcanic Heartland

From White Island in the northeast of the North Island to Mount Ruapehu in the centre lies the Taupo Volcanic Zone, which also includes Rotorua's geothermal wonders. Here, where the Pacific "ring of fire" begins, the clash of the Pacific Continental Plate and the Indo-Australian Plate has created the conditions for one of the most active volcanic regions in the world *(see p26)*. Beneath the Taupo Volcanic Zone, great slabs of crust are thrust down into the earth's mantle where they melt to form rhyolite magma. Every few thousand years, this magma reaches the surface, resulting in events like the Lake Taupo eruption of AD 186, when pumice was shot 50 km (30 miles) up into the air.

Mount Ruapehu
The North Island's tallest mountain is permanently snow-capped and cloaked by eight glaciers. Eruptions in 1995–6 emptied the crater of its lake and closed the mountain to skiers.

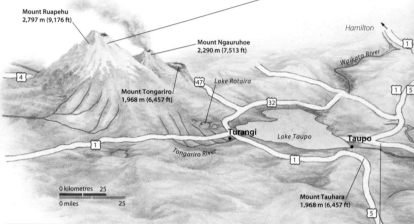

Mount Ruapehu
2,797 m (9,176 ft)

Mount Ngauruhoe
2,290 m (7,513 ft)

Mount Tongariro
1,968 m (6,457 ft)

Lake Rotaira

Turangi

Lake Taupo

Taupo

Hamilton

Waikato River

Tongariro River

Mount Tauhara
1,968 m (6,457 ft)

0 kilometres 25
0 miles 25

New Zealand's Main Volcanic Types

There are three major types of volcano in New Zealand: volcanic fields, such as Auckland, where each eruption builds a single small volcano in a different place; cone volcanoes, where a succession of eruptions occur close to a vent to form a large cone, which is the volcano itself; and caldera volcanoes, where eruptions are often so large that the ground surface collapses into the hole left behind. The Taupo Volcanic Zone contains three frequently active cone volcanoes (Ruapehu, Ngauruhoe and White Island) and the two most productive caldera in the world (Taupo and Tarawera). Mount Ngauruhoe is the vent for the adjacent Mount Tongariro.

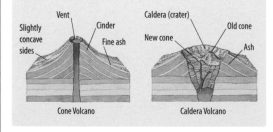

Slightly concave sides

Vent

Cinder

Fine ash

Caldera (crater)

New cone

Old cone

Ash

Cone Volcano

Caldera Volcano

Wairakei Geothermal Power Station
Almost 60 bores tap a vast underground water system, naturally heated by very hot rocks, to produce commercial quantities of steam.

Locator Map

Pohutu Geyser
One of only 12 geysers in New Zealand, Pohutu Geyser thunders to a height of more than 30 m (98 ft) *(see pp142–3)*.

White Island
This is an excellent active volcano to visit, by boat or by helicopter, because of its intense and daily changing thermal activity *(see p134)*.

Lake Rotoiti

Tauranga

5

Lake Rotorua

Bay of Plenty

Rotorua

2

Whakatane

5

Lake Trawera

Rangitaiki River

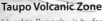

Taupo Volcanic Zone
The area from White Island to Ruapehu is by far the most frequently active of the North Island's five volcanic areas. Apart from its volcanoes, it has the greatest variety of volcanic features – geysers, cauldons, mineral pools, mud pools, silica terraces, lakes, rivers and waterfalls – making it one of New Zealand's most fascinating tourist destinations.

Wai-O-Tapu
The bubbling, hissing Champagne Pool, with its beautiful ochre-coloured petrified edge, is one of the many colourful attractions at Wai-O-Tapu *(see p144)*.

Mount Tarawera
In a volcanic explosion in 1886, a 6 km- (4 mile-) long, 250 m- (820 ft-) deep chasm was formed and the nearby Pink and White Terraces were buried *(see p141)*.

AUCKLAND

Every third New Zealander lives in the Auckland region, and the city, with its 1.5 million inhabitants, continues to expand faster than any other part of the country. Its population has increased by over 20 per cent since 1991, almost double the national rate. Auckland is the place to enjoy city life, but quiet beaches and bush tracks are within an hour's drive of the central business district.

Māori had settled in the Auckland area as early as 1350. Tribal wars and epidemics brought about the destruction of their settlements, and the area was almost deserted when European settlers arrived in 1840. Because of its central position, good harbour and fine soil, the site was chosen as New Zealand's capital, to replace Russell in the north, after the signing of the Treaty of Waitangi in 1840 (see pp52–3). However, in 1865 the capital moved south to Wellington.

Although Auckland was initially not a prosperous settlement, a gold rush in the Coromandel region and increased agricultural production in the late 19th century helped to develop it into what it is today – the largest and fastest growing city in New Zealand. The inner city has become more vibrant since the mid-1990s, due to the trend among some Aucklanders to trade in the traditional suburban villa for an inner-city apartment. Places such as Vulcan Lane, Viaduct Basin, Wynyard Quarter, Britomart and Ponsonby have become gathering points with cafés, bistros and up-market restaurants. The retail trade and performing arts have reaped the benefits of this migration.

Auckland is also attractive to New Zealand's Pacific Island neighbours and it now is the largest Polynesian city in the world. With Europeans, Māori, Polynesians and Asians complementing one another, the city's cultural diversity gives it a very cosmopolitan atmosphere. This is reflected in the variety of ethnic shops and restaurants, and can be observed at the local markets, such as those in Otara and Avondale.

Surfing at Piha, on the coast west of Auckland

◀ The illuminated Auckland Sky Tower at sunset

Exploring Auckland

Although the Auckland region is spread over more than 1,000 sq km (390 sq miles), many of its inner-city attractions are clustered near the waterfront and around the city's oldest parks. Panoramic views of the city, harbour and outer islands can be enjoyed from a number of extinct volcanic peaks, such as One Tree Hill *(see pp88–9)* and Mount Eden, and from the observation decks and restaurants of Sky Tower, the city's most distinctive landmark *(see p79)*. Queen Street, long known as Auckland's "golden mile", is a major business, entertainment and shopping area, complemented by Ponsonby, Parnell and Newmarket on the fringes of the city. Water is an important part of Auckland's magic, and no visit is complete without a trip to Rangitoto or one of the other islands in the Hauraki Gulf *(see pp92–3)*.

Yachts moored at Westhaven Marina, Auckland *(see p76)*

Sights at a Glance

1. Waitemata Harbour
2. Auckland Harbour Bridge
3. Westhaven Marina
4. Viaduct Harbour
5. New Zealand Maritime Museum
6. Ferry Building
7. Britomart Transport Centre
8. Old Customhouse
9. SKYCITY Auckland
10. Aotea Square and Aotea Centre at Auckland Live
11. Auckland Town Hall
12. Sky Tower
13. Old Government House
14. Old Arts Building and Clock Tower
15. Auckland Art Gallery
16. Auckland Domain and Winter Gardens
17. Auckland War Memorial Museum

0 metres   500
0 yards   500

For hotels and restaurants in this region see p302 and pp314–15

Getting Around

Auckland's city centre is compact and most places of interest are within walking distance. Alternatively, visitors can take the Auckland Explorer Bus, which leaves from Philips Corner/Princes Wharf every 30 minutes from 9am (hourly from 10am in winter) and stops at 14 tourist destinations. The tour includes taped commentary in various languages. For drivers, good motorways and internal roads link the northern, southern and western suburbs, which are also serviced by buses. Regular ferry services take visitors to the islands in the Hauraki Gulf.

Rollerblading along Tamaki Drive
(see p86)

Street-by-Street: The Waterfront

Excellent shops, historic buildings, top restaurants and bars, a superb view – Auckland's waterfront has something for everyone. Yet only 20 years ago, this area was of little interest to residents and visitors, and the inner city, traditionally reserved for offices, was almost deserted after dark. That trend has been reversed and downtown Auckland is now a hive of activity. New apartments, many on the water's edge and others in garden environments, along with numerous trendy bars and restaurants, have made the waterfront a prime living and entertainment area.

Britomart Transport Centre
Auckland's public transport hub is housed in the refurbished Chief Post Office building.

Old Customhouse
Formerly part of the city's financial district, this 1889 building houses a duty-free store (see p77, p94).

CUSTOMS STREET EAST

ALBERT ST

QUAY STREET

LOWER

QUEEN'S WHARF

QUAY STREET

★ **Ferry Building**
At the Ferry Building, visitors can buy tickets for ferries and harbour cruises or dine at its popular restaurants, located on the ground and first floors (see p77).

WAITEMATA HARBOUR

Boat Services
A variety of harbour cruises and ferry services to Devonport and the Hauraki Gulf islands operate from the back of the Ferry Building.

Locator Map

Princes Wharf, the departure point for overseas cruises, also attracts visitors to its restaurants and bars.

0 metres 100
0 yards 100

America's Cup

Viaduct Harbour was the home base for the yachts that participated in the 1999–2000 and 2002–2003 America's Cup. New Zealand successfully defended the cup it took off the Young America (USA) team led by Dennis Connor in 1995. In the 2002–2003 event nine challengers took on Team New Zealand and these syndicates came from all over the world. New Zealand will again host the challenge in 2021 as they won the cup back off the USA in Bermuda in 2017. The history of the cup goes back to the 1850s, but the intense emotion surrounding the challenge still remains.

New Zealand's *Black Magic* defeating its Italian challenger in the America's Cup 2000 final

Tepid Baths
Built in 1914 and refurbished, the baths now house modern aquatic and fitness facilities.

Viaduct Harbour
This former industrial area was developed as an entertainment precinct for the 1999–2000 America's Cup *(see p76)*.

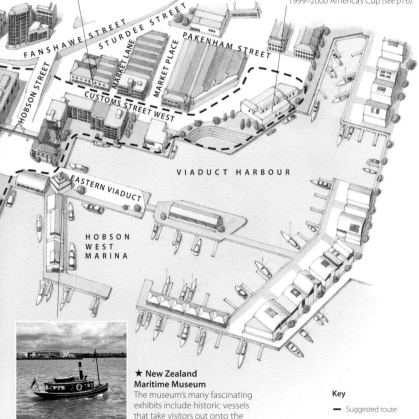

FANSHAWE STREET

STURDEE STREET

MARKET LANE

MARKET PLACE

PAKENHAM STREET

HOBSON STREET

CUSTOMS STREET WEST

VIADUCT HARBOUR

EASTERN VIADUCT

HOBSON
WEST
MARINA

★ **New Zealand Maritime Museum**
The museum's many fascinating exhibits include historic vessels that take visitors out onto the harbour *(see p77)*.

Key

— Suggested route

A forest of masts at Westhaven Marina, viewed from the Auckland Harbour Bridge

❶ Waitemata Harbour

This sparkling harbour, with the green volcanic cone of Rangitoto Island in the background, is one of Auckland's most cherished sights. Not only does the harbour add to the city's scenic beauty, it also forms a natural barrier between the central business district and the populous North Shore. Ferries and cruise boats, as well as commercial ships, use the harbour daily.

❷ Auckland Harbour Bridge

State Hwy 1.

In the late 19th century, ferries began taking passengers across the water from Auckland City to the north. In 1959, the Auckland Harbour Bridge was built and ten years later, the 43 m (141 ft) high steel bridge was widened, increasing the number of lanes from four to eight. Peak hour traffic across the 1,020 m (3,350 ft) bridge is slow. Concrete barriers marking the traffic lanes are shifted four times daily by a custom-built machine to accommodate the morning flow into the city and the late afternoon return to the northern suburbs. An electronic traffic light system at both ends of the bridge clearly indicates which lanes are accessible to traffic. Despite the traffic jams, the Harbour Bridge offers some of the best views in the city.

The bridge does not only link two large areas of Auckland; State Highway 1 is also the main arterial route for northbound traffic. Southbound travellers driving across the bridge will notice a forest of masts from the marina on their left.

❸ Westhaven Marina

Westhaven Drive.

Westhaven Marina reflects Aucklanders' passion for yachting. Operating for more than 70 years, it is one of the largest marinas in the southern hemisphere, accommodating 1,980 vessels. Among the facilities are Pier Z (the home of several major charter boat companies), launching ramps for trailer craft and a mast gantry. The premises of prominent yacht clubs are on the northern side of the marina.

❹ Viaduct Harbour

Cnr Halsey St and Viaduct Harbour.

Largely a legacy from the 1999–2000 America's Cup, the Viaduct Harbour's up-market apartments, shops and restaurants overlook a marina with mooring facilities for 150 yachts. The harbour is part of an extensive redevelopment of Auckland's waterfront, following the trend in cities such as Sydney, London and San Francisco, and the precinct has a vibrant atmosphere and a variety of restaurants. The Viaduct Events Centre is the focus for large conventions and trade shows, such as New Zealand Fashion Week.

Café at Viaduct Harbour

For hotels and restaurants in this region see p302 and pp314–15

❺ New Zealand Maritime Museum

Cnr Quay & Hobson sts. **Tel** (09) 373 0800. **Open** daily. **Closed** 25 Dec. 🖼️ ♿ 📷 ✏️ 🏪 📷 **W** maritime museum.co.nz

Boats have played a pivotal role in New Zealand's history, from those of the early Polynesian navigators who steered their canoes towards the country *(see pp50–1)*, to the whalers who made Russell *(see p106)* the centre of the whaling industry in the 1840s, and the thousands of immigrants who arrived in the 19th and 20th centuries. These aspects of the country's maritime past are highlighted in the museum. In Māori, the museum is called Te Huiteananui-a-Tangaroa, "the legendary house belonging to Tangaroa", god of the sea.

Even those with a limited interest in boats will enjoy the innovative exhibition galleries. One room is fitted out as a ship's interior, complete with a gently swaying floor and appropriate creaking noises. Several of the historic vessels berthed outside the museum take visitors for harbour trips.

The Ferry Building, a gateway to the harbour

of sandstone and brick, with a base of Coromandel granite and is registered with the Historic Places Trust. Not just a transport centre, it is also home to a number of cafés and restaurants with stunning harbour views.

❼ Britomart Transport Centre

Queen St.

The Britomart Transport Centre brings together Auckland's train, bus and ferry services in a single complex. The centre was the focus of an urban renewal project in 2009, construction for parts of which is ongoing, that included the redevelopment of surrounding streets, creating public spaces and Takutai Plaza, a precinct of shops and restaurants.

❽ Old Customhouse

Cnr Albert & Customs sts. **Open** daily. 📷

The old Customhouse replaces a building that was burned down in the 1880s. Designed by Thomas Mahoney, the 1889 French Renaissance-style building is said to have been modelled on the present Selfridge's department store in Oxford Street, London. It features intricate plasterwork and kauri joinery.

One of the oldest commercial buildings in the city, the Old Customhouse used to house the Customs Department, Audit Inspector, Sheep Inspector and Native Land Court. It is now home to the city's largest duty-free shop *(see p94)*.

Exhibit at the New Zealand Maritime Museum

❻ Ferry Building

Quay St. 🚢 **Open** daily. 📷 📷

This 1912 Edwardian Baroque building is the focal point for commuter ferries. A 10-minute ferry ride to Devonport leaves from here, as do boats to Waiheke Island *(see p92)*. Designed by Alex Wiseman, the ornate building is made

City of Sails

Auckland is purported to have the greatest number of pleasure boats per capita of any city in the world. The city's temperate climate also means that, on average, these are used more intensively than boats in Europe or on the east coast of America. Yachting has been a popular pastime in Auckland since the 1840s, when the first sailing regattas were held on Waitemata Harbour. Safe harbours and the nearby scenic islands make sailing attractive to overseas visitors as well. Charter company charges depend on the size of the yacht, the time of year and whether a skipper is hired. The highlight of the nautical year is the Auckland Anniversary Regatta *(see p45)*.

Yacht racing on Waitemata Harbour

Casino in the SKYCITY complex

⑨ SKYCITY Auckland

Cnr Victoria & Federal sts. **Tel** 0800 759 2489, (09) 363 6000. **Open** daily.
♿ 🚻 🅿 📷 **W** skycityauckland. co.nz

Lucky punters can win luxury cars at SKYCITY Auckland, New Zealand's biggest casino. Open 24 hours a day, 7 days a week, the complex offers a wide variety of entertainment and leisure options. More than 1,600 gaming machines feature all the latest stepper reel, video reel, poker and keno games offering cash prizes. The complex boasts 4 casinos and over 100 gaming tables with traditional games such as Caribbean stud poker, craps, blackjack, baccarat, roulette and money wheel. Chinese favourites include tai sai, played with three dice in a clear glass dome, and pai gow, played with 32 domino pieces.

Entertainment at SKYCITY is not limited to gaming. The complex is best known for the country's tallest structure, the Sky Tower, which has viewing levels and restaurants *(see p79)*. There are also two hotels, the four-star SKYCITY Hotel *(see p302)*, with 306 rooms and 38 suites, and the five-star Grand Hotel, which has 316 guest rooms and a spa. In addition, there are bars, cafés, restaurants, conference facilities, and a 700-seat theatre.

⑩ Aotea Square and Aotea Centre at Auckland Live

Aotea Square (upper Queen St). **Tel** (09) 309 2677. **W** aucklandlive.co.nz

In the late 1980s, several New Zealand souvenir shops began stocking a postcard that was entirely black except for a small heading, "Night Life in New Zealand". Things have since changed. Built in 1990, the Aotea Centre was designed by New Zealand architect Ewen Wainscott and is a hub of vibrant nightlife. On its opening night, the centre featured New Zealand-born Dame Kiri Te Kanawa, the world-renowned opera singer. It is a venue for dance, opera, classical music, theatre and shows. It is also used for festivals, such as the Aotearoa Hip Hop Summit.

Aotea Square, in front of the centre, houses a popular market as well as outdoor festivals. The wooden *waharoa* (gateway) at its entrance was created by Māori artist Selwyn Muru. The square is flanked on one side by the Metro Centre, which includes a 460-seat IMAX (widescreen) cinema *(see p97)*, a games centre, cafés, food court and shops. The Auckland Town Hall is situated on the other side of the square.

Collectively, all these locations – Aotea Centre, Aotea Square, Town Hall, The Civic, Bruce Mason Centre and

stadiums – are known as Auckland Live and promote performing arts, culture and entertainment.

⑪ Auckland Town Hall

Queen St. **Tel** (09) 309 2677. **Open** daily. **Closed** public hols. ♿

The wedge-shaped Edwardian Town Hall, built in 1911, is Auckland's prime historic building. It has been used extensively as an administrative and political centre, as well as a cultural venue. During work to restore it to its original design, the building was gutted (non-original materials were removed) and strengthened structurally.

The Concert Chamber, Council Chamber and main street foyer were meticulously restored, a process which included using vintage glass to reconstruct windows that had disappeared over the years. The Great Hall, an excellent concert facility, is a replica of the Neues Gewandhaus in Leipzig, Germany, which was destroyed by Allied bombing during World War II.

Auckland Town Hall

⑫ Sky Tower

Opened in August 1997, Auckland's 328 m (1,076 ft) Sky Tower, a splendid tourist, broadcasting and telecommunications facility, has taken over from Sydney's AMP Tower as the tallest tower in the southern hemisphere. Part of SKYCITY Auckland, the tower is visited by around 500,000 people per year. Its three observation levels offer 82 km (50 mile) views while the tower's SkyJump and 360° SkyWalk provide the ultimate in adrenaline adventure.

VISITORS' CHECKLIST

Practical Information
Cnr Victoria & Federal sts. **Tel** 0800 759 2489. **Open** 8:30am till late daily. 🅿 ♿ 🚻 🖥 🏛
🅦 skytower.co.nz

Observation Levels
Visitors enjoy fantastic views of the city of Auckland and its environs from the tower's indoor observation levels.

The 92 m- (302 ft-) high spire weighs 170 tonnes and is the main telecommunications and broadcasting mast in the region.

The Sky Deck offers 360-degree views through seamless glass, and is the country's highest public viewing area.

Orbit 360° Dining makes a full revolution every 60 minutes.

The Sugar Club on level 53 offers fine dining and a luxurious cocktail bar.

SkyJump is a 192 m (630 ft) cable controlled base jump.

The floors above and below the centre pod house telecommunications facilities.

The main observation level is the best spot to take in the views, with helpful diagrams to help you find all of Auckland's key spots and glass floor panels to test your nerves.

The structure of the tower has been designed to withstand winds gusting to 200 km/h (125 mph) and earthquakes measuring 8.0 on the Richter Scale.

The lower observation level contains the Sky Lounge Café.

Entrance to Tower
Entry to Sky Tower's lifts is through an underground gallery.

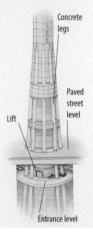

Concrete legs

Paved street level

Lift

Entrance level

The Sky Tower at Night
The Sky Tower is an even more visible landmark at night. At various times of year it is lit in different colours to mark a range of activities and celebrations.

Entrance to the Auckland Art Gallery (Toi o Tāmaki)

⑬ Old Government House

Cnr Waterloo Quadrant and Princes St.
Closed to public.

The Classical Old Government House was the seat of government until 1865 when the capital was moved to Wellington. It was also the residence of New Zealand's governor-general until 1969. Royalty used to stay here, and Queen Elizabeth II broadcast her Christmas speech from upstairs in 1953. It is now a part of the University of Auckland, housing the staff common room, council reception suite and apartments for visiting academics.

Located within walking distance of the central business district, Old Government House, designed by William Mason and completed in 1856, appears from a distance to be made of stone. Like its British prefabricated predecessor,

University of Auckland's Old Arts Building and Clock Tower

however, it is built from wood. A big coral tree and a Norfolk pine at the southern edge of the lawn are said to have been planted by Sir George Grey during his second term as governor from 1861 to 1867.

⑭ Old Arts Building and Clock Tower

Princes St. **Closed** to public.

Also part of the university buildings, the Old Arts Building and Clock Tower face Albert Park, a summer gathering place for students. Designed by Chicago-trained architect R A Lippincott, it was completed in 1926. Lippincott's brother-in-law, Walter Burley Griffin, was the designer of Canberra in Australia. The clock tower that crowns the building was inspired by the Tom Tower of Christ Church in Oxford, England, and has come to symbolize the university. The building's octagonal interior is vaulted and galleried with a mosaic floor and piers. A major reconstruction was undertaken between 1985 and 1988, which won an Institute of Architects award.

From the rear of the Old Arts Building, the Barracks Wall runs for 85 m (280 ft) to the back of the Old Choral Hall. Built in 1847, it is the only remnant of the wall which enclosed an area, including Albert Park, where British troops were stationed until 1870. The basalt stone wall was quarried from the slope of Mount Eden, now known as Eden Garden.

⑮ Auckland Art Gallery

Cnr Wellesley & Kitchener sts.
Tel (09) 307 7700. **Open** daily.
Closed Good Friday, 25 December.
🎨 some exhibits. ♿ 🚻 📷 🏛
🖥 aucklandartgallery.com

Visitors interested in art should add the Auckland Art Gallery (Toi o Tāmaki) to their itinerary. Designing the 1887 French Renaissance-style building must have been a challenge to the architectural firm of Grainger and D'Ebro, as it occupies a rising corner site. The gallery originally housed civic offices and the public library, but today it is solely a gallery, mainly devoted to showcasing the development of New Zealand art. The collection of around 12,500 works includes international as well as national art. The New Zealand collection contains works from many of the nation's most prominent artists, including Frances Hodgkins, Colin McCahon and Ralph Hotere. The Mackelvie Collection, named after a self-made man who lived in Auckland between 1865 and 1871, is mainly of non-New Zealand paintings, as is the Grey Collection.

The New Gallery, across the road from the Auckland Art Gallery, was a former telephone exchange. It focuses on contemporary art.

A multi-million dollar development next door has created a space where the gallery can compete with renowned collections, playing host to a wide array of international artists.

Entrance to the New Gallery, Auckland Art Gallery

For hotels and restaurants in this region see p302 and pp314–15

⑯ Auckland Domain and Winter Gardens

Auckland Domain: **Open** daily.
Winter Gardens: **Open** daily.
🏛 (War Memorial Museum).

Central Auckland has been built around a number of extinct volcanoes, including 14 volcanic cones, many of which are now parks. The oldest park is the Auckland Domain, situated within walking distance of both the city centre and the Parnell area. Tuff rings created by volcanic activity thousands of years ago can still be seen in its contours.

Land for the city's 1.35 sq km (0.50 sq mile) park was set aside in 1840, in the early years of European settlement. In 1940, a carved Māori memorial palisade was installed around a totara tree on Pukekaroa knoll. This enclosure commemorates Māori leader Potatu Te Whero Whero, who made peace with the neighbouring tribes on the site a hundred years earlier.

Nearby is a sports field where the tuff rings form a natural amphitheatre. The field is used

An evening event at the Auckland Domain

for free outdoor concerts over the summer that attract large crowds.

The large, shady Auckland Domain is also a popular place with walkers and picnickers. Several of the large trees in the park were seedlings from a nursery set up in 1841 to grow and distribute European plants and trees. The formal gardens feature many sculptures. The best known are the three bronze sculptures in the free-form pond.

The central, male figure represents Auckland and the two females represent wisdom and fertility of the soil.

The Winter Gardens, a legacy from the Auckland Exhibition of 1913, consist of two glasshouses

Statue at the Winter Gardens

joined by a courtyard that contains a large water lily and lotus pool. The dome-roofed areas contain a wide variety of plants. The scoria quarry behind the Winter Gardens has been converted into a fernery. Ferns are a dominant feature of the New Zealand landscape and there are more than 100 varieties in the fernery. The gardens are a popular venue for wedding and other photography.

The Domain's best-known structure is the Auckland War Memorial Museum *(see pp82–3)*. Made of reinforced concrete and faced with Portland stone, the museum has bronze detailing. The façade contains plaques that list the battles of World War I, while at the rear of the building, added by R F and M K Draffin in 1960, there are lists of World War II battles.

One of the two glasshouses at the Winter Gardens

⑰ Auckland War Memorial Museum

Built in 1929 to commemorate the end of World War I, in which 18,166 New Zealanders died, the museum is a Neo-Classical design that evokes the Greek temples that many servicemen saw from the decks of warships in the Mediterranean. The Cenotaph in front of the museum is based on Sir Edwin Lutyens first design, and mirrors the cenotaphs erected in London and around the Commonwealth. Besides providing visitors with an introduction to New Zealand's history, people and landscape, the museum also contains one of the world's greatest collection of Māori *taonga* (treasures) and holds Māori cultural performances.

Aerial view of the museum, located in the Auckland Domain

Museum Foyer
The foyer features tall columns reminiscent of the Parthenon in Greece. Light filters through the stained-glass ceiling above the foyer.

"Origins" features the skeletons of extinct animals, such as dinosaurs and moa, many of which were discovered in caves around the country.

Garden

Ground floor

The museum entrance evokes the temples of Greece.

Key to Floorplan

- ☐ Natural History Galleries
- ☐ Design & Decorative Arts
- ☐ Special Exhibition Hall
- ☐ Library
- ☐ Māori and Pacific
- ☐ Other exhibits
- ☐ Discovery Centres
- ☐ War exhibits

★ Māori Treasures
This gallery showcases a superb collection of Māori artifacts, such as the *waka* (canoe) in the foreground and a traditional carved meeting house.

Discovery Centre
The "Weird & Wonderful" area is the museum's interactive space for discovering the natural world. It is designed especially for children and families.

Top floor

Auditorium

VISITORS' CHECKLIST

Practical Information
The Domain, Parnell. **Tel** (09) 309 0443. **Open** 10am–5pm daily. **Closed** 25 Dec. 🅿 donation (none for war memorials); Māori cultural show. ♿ 🅿 🅿 🅿

Transport
🚌 Explorer bus or Link bus.

"Scars on the Heart"
contains exhibits depicting the two World Wars, including a re-creation of a World War I front trench.

Library

First floor

Spitfire Gallery
This area features an early fighter plane. A high percentage of Royal Air Force pilots during World War II came from New Zealand, including Air Chief Marshal Sir Keith Park.

★ **World War I Sanctuary**
The stained-glass ceiling above the entrance lobby shows the coat of arms of all British dominions and colonies during World War I. On the balcony are badges of the units, regiments and corps in which New Zealanders served.

Museum Guide

The museum's collections are housed across three levels. The ground level is dedicated to the people of New Zealand and their place in the Pacific region. On the first floor, natural history galleries trace New Zealand's ancient origins from the great lost continent of Gondwana, while the top floor tells the compelling story of its emergence as a nation through the loss and suffering of war. The Library is open 10am to 5pm Monday to Saturday. There is a shop in the foyer and a café in the atrium.

Auckland city and Sky Tower viewed from Devonport ▶

Further Afield

Beyond central Auckland, visitors are offered a range of places to visit and a variety of things to do. Harbours, beaches and islands are prime attractions, not only for their superb scenic views but also for sea sports, such as kayaking, surfing and sailing. The city is well known for its beautiful parks and gardens which provide peaceful retreats; some offer visitors a chance to walk through bush and wilderness. Families with young children will find Kelly Tarlton's Sea Life Aquarium, Rainbow's End and the Auckland Zoo enjoyable. Across the harbour by a short ferry ride, Devonport makes for a pleasant outing for the day, with its many restaurants and art and crafts shops. Its naval history is also of interest.

Tamaki Drive and the Auckland City skyline as seen from the shore

❶ Tamaki Drive

Tamaki Drive, east of the city, shows Auckland at its best. The road crosses Hobson Bay and closely follows the water's edge past Okahu Bay, Mission Bay and St Heliers Bay. The views across Waitemata Harbour towards Rangitoto Island and Devonport are stunning and should not be missed.

Many of the city's most prestigious homes are located on the slopes behind Tamaki Drive. Many tourist buses make a small detour to go through nearby Paritai Drive, which is the most expensive real estate in Auckland. Sandy beaches, such as the one at Mission Bay, are a major attraction along Tamaki Drive. These lovely beaches serve as a base for family outings, swimmers and sunbathers.

Mission Bay got its name from the Melanesian Mission House. Built in 1859, the house was part of Bishop Selwyn's Mission School. When the school was transferred to Norfolk Island in 1867, the house was used for different purposes. It is now an up-market restaurant. Tamaki Drive ends at St Heliers Bay.

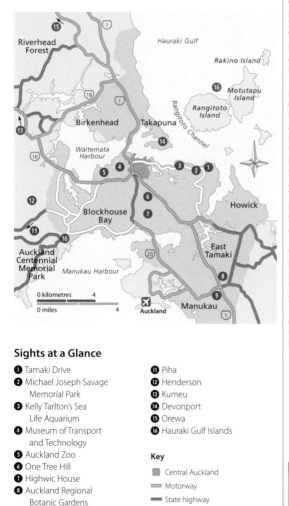

Hauraki Gulf
Riverhead Forest
Rakino Island
Motutapu Island
Rangitoto Island
Birkenhead
Takapuna
Rangitoto Channel
Waitemata Harbour
Howick
Blockhouse Bay
East Tamaki
Auckland Centennial Memorial Park
Manukau Harbour
Manukau
Auckland

0 kilometres 4
0 miles 4

Sights at a Glance

❶ Tamaki Drive
❷ Michael Joseph Savage Memorial Park
❸ Kelly Tarlton's Sea Life Aquarium
❹ Museum of Transport and Technology
❺ Auckland Zoo
❻ One Tree Hill
❼ Highwic House
❽ Auckland Regional Botanic Gardens
❾ Rainbow's End
❿ Titirangi
⓫ Piha
⓬ Henderson
⓭ Kumeu
⓮ Devonport
⓯ Orewa
⓰ Hauraki Gulf Islands

Key

▦ Central Auckland
▭ Motorway
▬ State highway
═ Other road
✈ Airport

Cyclists enjoying the sun on Tamaki Drive

For hotels and restaurants in this region see p302 and pp314–15

Rangitoto Island, dominating Auckland's harbour horizon

Instead of turning right into St Heliers Bay Road, it is worthwhile to continue along Cliff Road, leading to Ladies Bay. The viewing platform at the top of the cliff offers a superb panorama of the Hauraki Gulf. Directly below the platform, but far enough from viewers not to be intrusive, is one of New Zealand's few nudist beaches. At other beaches along Tamaki Drive, nudity is prohibited.

Learning to windsurf

❷ Michael Joseph Savage Memorial Park

Located off Tamaki Drive, the park was named after New Zealand's first Labour prime minister, Michael Joseph Savage (1871–1940). The gardens, which have formal arrangements, also contain concrete fortifications that date from World War II.

The area occupied by the gardens was originally a historic Māori *pa*, and its shoreline was renowned for its plentiful supply of mussels. Originally named Tokapurewha, Māori for "mussel rocks", the area has since been renamed Bastion Point.

It is best known for a Māori protest staged in 1977 after the government had razed a local Māori village to develop Bastion Point as a prime residential zone. A 506-day occupation was organized to protest against the appropriation of the site, followed by ten years of litigation. In 1990, the land was finally returned to the Ngati Whatua tribe. The nearby 900 sq m (9,690 sq ft) Orakei Marae is the tribe's meeting house. Smaller ones can be found around the Kaipara Harbour and at Helensville, at the southern extremity of the harbour.

❸ Kelly Tarlton's Sea Life Aquarium

23 Tamaki Drive. **Tel** (09) 528 0603 or 0800 805 050. 🚌 757, 767, 769. Free shuttle from Quay Station every hour from 9:30am–3:30pm daily. **Open** daily. 🐧 ✉ no flash. ♿
🌐 **kellytarltons.co.nz**

Tamaki Drive's best-known tourist attraction is Kelly Tarlton's Sea Life Aquarium. Visitors ride on a moving walkway through a Plexiglas tunnel inside a tank, with fish swimming around the sides. The tunnel winds past two marine aquariums, one devoted to reef fish and the other to sharks and stingrays. Exploration experiences on offer here include the Penguin Discovery, which consists of navigating an indoor colony of penguins on a snowboard, with plenty of time to interact with the creatures. Other attractions include the Shark Dive and the Shark Cage (not for the faint hearted), as well as behind-the-scenes tours of the fascinating aquarium complex.

Riding through the Plexiglas tube at Kelly Tarlton's Sea Life Aquarium

❹ Museum of Transport and Technology

Great North Rd, Western Springs (access via Meola St to MOTAT 2 entrance until 2019). 🚋 Customs St, 45. **Tel** (09) 815 5800, 0800 668 286. **Open** daily (last adm: 4:30pm). **Closed** 25 Dec. 🐾 ♿ 🖥 🌐 motat.org.nz

The Museum of Transport and Technology has a collection of about 300,000 items, some of which can be seen in various buildings on two sites within walking distance of Auckland Zoo. Exhibits vary from dental equipment and underwear to 19th-century houses and a pumphouse. An interactive gallery for under-5s offers hands-on play with pulleys, levers, diggers and wheelbarrows.

The focal point is a collection of 30 rare and historic aircraft. These include a replica of a home-made plane by New Zealander Richard Pearse, believed by many to have preceded the Wright brothers in being the first person to fly (see p252). Also of interest is the Solent flying boat ZK-AMO *Aranui*, a luxurious aircraft, the only one in the world of its kind, that flew around the South Pacific from 1949 until 1960. An electric tram runs about every 20 minutes from the entrance of MOTAT to the zoo gates.

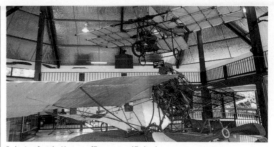

Early aircraft at the Museum of Transport and Technology

❺ Auckland Zoo

Motions Rd, Western Springs. 🚋 Customs St, 45. **Tel** (09) 360 3800. **Open** daily. **Closed** 25 Dec. 🐾 ♿ 🖊 🖥 🏠 🌐 aucklandzoo.co.nz

New Zealand's isolated geographical position means that its fauna has developed differently from that of most countries. A lack of predators, for example, has resulted in many flightless birds. With the exception of bats, there are no native mammals. The best place to learn about the country's varied and unusual wildlife is at Auckland Zoo. Established as a small private menagerie in 1912, the zoo opened in its current spot in 1922. It houses more than 700 animals covering 117 species, including saddlebacks, tui and kaka, besides the nocturnal kiwi.

The zoo's population, which is not limited to native animals, is presented in natural settings. Primates such as squirrel monkeys and macaques can be seen at close range in a rainforest. Zebras and giraffes roam on an African savanna with Zulu huts and inter-connected habitats. A wetlands environment features baboons as well as hippopotamuses.

❻ One Tree Hill

Manukau Rd.

One Tree Hill (Maungakiekie), a dormant volcanic cone and once the site of the largest prehistoric Māori settlement in the region, was named after the solitary tree which was planted on its summit in 1640. Since then, a succession of single trees have stood there. The last, a Monterey pine, was removed in October 2001 by city council workers as it was

One Tree Hill (Maungakiekie), formerly the site of a large Māori fortification

For hotels and restaurants in this region see p302 and pp314–15

unstable (a grove of native trees has now been planted, with a plan to thin them out to one). Its most famous predecessor was a native totara tree, cut down in 1852 by workmen angry at the non-arrival of rations.

Surrounding the hill is Cornwall Park, named after the Duke and Duchess of Cornwall, and donated to the city by Sir John Campbell during their royal tour in 1901.

Acacia Cottage, Auckland's oldest surviving wooden building, was built in 1841 by Sir John Campbell. It was relocated in 1920 from Shortland Street to Cornwall Park, where he once had a farm.

Near the entrance to the park, is the **Stardome Observatory and Planetarium**. It has telescopes for viewing the stars, and aspects of space and astronomy are shown at the Stardome Planetarium.

🏛 Acacia Cottage
Cornwall Park. **Tel** (09) 630 8485. **Open** 10am–4pm daily. **Closed** public hols. 🚌 302, 304, 305.

🏛 Stardome Observatory and Planetarium
One Tree Hill Domain (best accessed from Mortimer Pass). **Tel** (09) 624 1246. **Open** daily. **Closed** public hols. 🚸 ♿ 📷 Stardome and telescopes. 📷 🖥 **stardome.org.nz**

Acacia Cottage, in Cornwall Park

❼ Highwic House
40 Gillies Ave, Epsom. 🚌 Link bus. **Tel** (09) 524 5729. **Open** Wed–Sun. **Closed** Good Fri, 25 Dec. 🚸

Built in 1862, Highwic was the home of Alfred Buckland, a stock and station owner. The house was built in stages, with the front part showing more

Water ride at Rainbow's End

detail than the rest. The house, with its elaborate decoration and diamond pane windows, is an example of Carpenter Gothic Revival architecture. The extensive landscaped gardens are also worth a visit.

❽ Auckland Regional Botanic Gardens
Hill Rd, Manukau City. **Tel** (09) 267 1457. **Open** daily. ♿ 📷 🖥
🖥 **aucklandbotanicgardens.co.nz**

These gardens, which sprawl over 64 ha (158 acres), contain more than 10,000 species of New Zealand native and introduced plants, and a large collection of ornamental plants. Guided walks are held regularly. Surrounded by lush South Pacific vegetation and sweeping views, the award-winning Visitor Centre offers interpretative and themed plant displays.

❾ Rainbow's End
Cnr Great South & Wiri Station rds, Manukau City. 🚌 Central Auckland, 471, 472. **Tel** (09) 262 2030. **Open** daily. **Closed** 25 Dec. 🚸 ♿ 📷 🖥 📷 🖥 **rainbowsend.co.nz**

Lots of rides and entertainment are available at this amusement park, which is New Zealand's largest. The most popular attraction is a roller coaster that takes you up more than 30 m (98 ft) in the air, hurls you down through a complete loop, round a corner and through a double corkscrew. Other attractions include the Motion Master Virtual Theatre, featuring dinosaurs, an enchanted forest ride, family go-karts, Stratofear and The Invader rides, water rides and the Goldrush, which takes you on a thrilling ride through an abandoned gold mine in a runaway mining cart. Kidz Kingdom provides indoor amusements for small children.

Sir John Logan Campbell
Sir John Logan Campbell (1817–1912) was one of New Zealand's pioneering entrepreneurs. On 21 December 1840, he set up a tent at the bottom of Shortland Street that served as Auckland's first shop. When he died at the age of 95, he was the city's most prominent businessman. Apart from trading and farming, he was involved in shipping, brewing, timber, the export of kauri gum, flax and manganese, newspaper publishing and banking. He was also a member of New Zealand's parliament, captain of the militia, and a founding member of the Mechanics Institute and the Northern Club. Today, "the father of Auckland" is best remembered for donating his farm, Cornwall Park, to the city.

Totem pole at the entrance to the Arataki Visitors Centre

⑩ Titirangi

Road map E2. 🚗 3,400. 🚌

Situated to the west of Auckland city, the small settlement of Titirangi offers superb views of the Waitakere Ranges and the 390 sq km (150 sq mile) Manukau Harbour to the south. The village, which is home to a number of artists and writers, has a reputation for being trendy. Its main street is lined with cafés and restaurants. The main landmark is the Spanish-style Lopdell House, opened in 1930, which has a small theatre and restaurant with Te Uru Waitakere Contemporary Gallery next door. The square in front of the nearby library is transformed into an art and crafts market on the last Sunday of the month from 9am to noon.

Titirangi is the gateway to the Waitakere Ranges Regional Park. Formed by volcanic action about 1.7 million years ago, the park has about 250 km suitable for people of all levels of fitness. It attracts over two million visitors a year.

The **Arataki Visitors Centre**, 6 km (4 miles) beyond Titirangi, has well-organized displays on the area's logging history and attractions, and also stocks detailed maps of the ranges, books and posters. Large timber decks around the building offer good views of the harbour. Across the road from the centre is the Arataki Nature Trail, a self-guided walk, which provides a good introduction to native plants and wildlife.

🛈 **Arataki Visitors Centre**
Scenic Drive. **Tel** (09) 817 0077.
Open daily. **Closed** 25 Dec.

⑪ Piha

Road map E2. 🚗 2,500. 🚌

Prized by locals but not well known to tourists, Auckland's rugged, windswept west coast beaches are within easy reach of Auckland and are well worth visiting. Because they are exposed to the Tasman Sea, however, swimmers and surfers need to exercise care as the currents can be treacherous and conditions often change rapidly.

Piha is the most popular of the beaches because of its heavy surf. It is also the most gentrified. Here, many "baches", New Zealand's traditional ramshackle holiday homes, have made way for designer mansions. While the Piha Surf Life Saving Club serves as a community centre over the summer, the Piha Store and Piha Beach Café are also focal points on the beach.

Environs

The bleakest, yet perhaps grandest, stretch of coast is at **Whatipu**, south of Piha at the entrance to the Manukau Harbour. A sand bar visible from the beach partly blocks the harbour. It was here that the HMS *Orpheus* was shipwrecked on 7 February 1863. Of the 259 officers and crew of the 1,727-tonne corvette, only 70 survived.

Just south of Piha, **Karekare** has several idyllic picnic spots and a swimming hole at the base of a waterfall. Its beach achieved some fame as the location for the award-winning film *The Piano*.

To the north of Piha is **Bethells Beach**, inhabited by Māori for several centuries; some 75 sites have been recorded here by archaeologists. Ihumoana Island, just off the beach, is the area's best-preserved island *pa*. Although not as spectacular as Cape Kidnappers (*see p153*), a headland beyond Bethells, is home to a colony of around 2,000 Australasian gannets, which originally nested on offshore Motutara Island. Barriers and viewing platforms allow visitors to observe the birds without disturbing them. The best time to see the gannets is from October to February.

⑫ Henderson

Road map E2. 🚗 4,600. 🚌

The vineyards at Henderson, many dating back to the early 1900s, are a half-hour drive from Auckland city. They have

Piha as seen from the lookout at the top of the road

become a popular weekend destination for Aucklanders and visitors alike. Many of the wineries sell food, ranging from a snack to a complete meal, and offer free wine tastings.

Family-owned Babich Wines, founded in 1916, has a picnic and *pétanque* area overlooking its vineyards. The winery has a reputation for award-winning vintages, such as Babich Patriarch, but also produces inexpensive wines. New Zealand's second largest winery, Corbans Wine, established by Lebanese immigrants in 1902, is another popular destination, especially its Art Centre, which holds regular exhibitions and events. Montana Wines has the distinction of producing half of New Zealand's total output, making it the largest wine producer in the country. Its Deutz Marlborough Cuveé, made under an arrangement with Champagne Deutz, won the 1998 Sparkling Wine of the Year award at the International Wine Challenge in London. Visitors can obtain details of Henderson's vineyards at the Auckland visitor centre.

Locally grown fruit and vegetables for sale at Kumeu

the top 100 Wines of the World list of the United States *Wine Spectator* magazine five times. The House of Nobilo, with 4,000 tonnes of grapes crushed in 1998, is the country's fourth largest winery. It also sells wines from Selaks Wines, which it purchased in 1998. Soljans Estate Winery features a pleasant picnic area and offers visitors tours. Its premium varieties include Chardonnay.

Matua Valley Wines produces a broad range of good quality wines but specialise in Sauvignon Blanc. The winery also serves gourmet treats to accompany the wines. These may be enjoyed in the pleasant grounds, which have picnic and barbecue facilities, and where music events are staged regularly. Classes in wine blending are also offered, as are tailored group tastings.

Outdoor eating area at Babich Wines in Henderson

⓭ Kumeu

Road map E2. 🏔 1,800. 🚌

Another popular weekend pursuit of Aucklanders is lunch at a vineyard restaurant followed by shopping for fresh fruit and vegetables from a roadside stall on the way home. At Kumeu, a wine as well as fruit growing district, visitors are spoilt for choice. Kumeu River Wines should be included in every wine safari. Specializing in regionally grown grapes, Kumeu River's Chardonnay has made

Film Making in New Zealand

New Zealand's coastal scenery has not escaped the notice of location finders in the film industry. The beach scenes in Jane Campion's *The Piano*, winner of the 1994 Palme d'Or at Cannes and Oscars for Best Original Screenplay and Best Supporting Actress, were shot at Karekare. Bethells Beach features in *Xena: Warrior Princess* and *Hercules: The Legendary Journeys*. Numerous television series, such as *Black Beauty*, films and commercials have also been filmed along the New Zealand coast. International interest has spawned a burgeoning domestic film industry. Over 120 feature films have been produced in the country since 1940. Lee Tamahori's *Once Were Warriors* was released in 1994 in cinemas around the world. Local director Peter Jackson's Oscar-winning *Lord of The Rings* trilogy eclipsed all previous New Zealand film productions in terms of scale and budget. New Hollywood blockbusters being filmed in New Zealand, including *Avatar 2*, continue to put the industry on a sound footing.

Shooting a film on a New Zealand beach

Well-preserved Victorian buildings on Devonport's waterfront

⓮ Devonport

Road map E2. 🚗 18,000. 🚌 ⛴

In comparison to Auckland's less affluent southern and western (except Titirangi) quadrants, the eastern and northern quadrants are seen to be prosperous. Although over-simplified, this view is not a completely inaccurate one. The North Shore, the suburban area north of the Harbour Bridge, is relatively wealthy and blessed with a string of beaches that also function as launching pads for sailing boats and dinghies.

Devonport is a 10-minute ferry ride from Auckland's Ferry Building (see p75). It is the only North Shore suburb with a distinctly historical flavour. With many of its villas found along the waterfront, a stroll along King Edward Parade provides an impression of the suburb's Victorian architecture, as well as views of Auckland's central business district across Waitemata Harbour. From Victoria Wharf, where the ferries arrive, it is a 5-minute walk to the cafés, restaurants and book shops of Victoria Road. Mount Victoria and North Head, both extinct volcanoes, are accessible by car or by walking and offer good views.

Devonport has a long military history. Its association with the Royal New Zealand Navy dates back to 1941 and there are approximately 2,200 staff currently stationed at the local naval base. Devonport's naval heritage can be viewed at the

Navy Museum which houses a collection of photographs, uniforms, weapons and other related memorabilia.

Further north, **Takapuna** has its own popular beach. Restaurants, cafés and shops are found along Hurstmere Road and The Strand.

🏛 Navy Museum

64 King Edward Parade. **Tel** (09) 445 5186. **Open** daily. **Closed** Good Fri, 25 & 26 Dec. 🖼 donation. 🛈 on request. 🖼 🖵 navymuseum.co.nz

⓯ Orewa

Road map E2. 🚗 (including Hibiscus Coast) 28,000. 🚌 🛈 i-SITE 1A Baxter St, Warkworth, (09) 425 9081.

Beach houses and motels line the main road through this small seaside town, 30 minutes' drive north of Auckland. Orewa's main attraction is its beach, a 3 km- (2 mile-) long stretch of sand. The beach is suitable for swimming, surfing and boating. Easterly winds from the sea also attract windsurfers.

Environs

Just north of Orewa, a small road off State Highway 1 leads to **Puhoi**, New Zealand's earliest Bohemian settlement. A tiny calvary shrine beside the road leading to the settlement is a reminder of the settlers' background. The local pub also doubles as a museum of the pioneers of the area. The Church of St Peter and St Paul, built in 1881, features a Bohemian painting.

About 48 km (30 miles) north of Auckland, Waiwera is best known for its thermal resort, **Waiwera Infinity Hot Pools**. The complex has nine indoor and outdoor pools, spas, water slides, beauty therapies and picnic areas. The natural springs deliver up to 1 million litres (0.2 million gallons) of water per day.

🏊 Waiwera Infinity Hot Pools

State Hwy 1. **Tel** 0800 924 937. **Open** daily. 🖼 🖵 🖵 🖼 🖵 waiwera.co.nz

⓰ Hauraki Gulf Islands

Road map E2. ⛴ 🛈 Department of Conservation, 137 Quay St, Auckland, (09) 379 6476. 🖵 doc.govt.nz

The Hauraki Gulf Islands are among the most beautiful in the world. Some of the 65 islands are popular spots for recreational activities. Others, with their rare bird sanctuaries and unspoiled stands of native trees and plants, are protected for conservation. Waiheke is now home to many commuters, while Great Barrier and Kawau are preferred by those who

The beach at Orewa, popular with swimmers and windsurfers

For hotels and restaurants in this region see p302 and pp314–15

Sir George Grey's historic home, Mansion House, on Kawau Island, Hauraki Gulf

enjoy a somewhat slower lifestyle. **Waiheke Island** has gained an "alternative" reputation because of its organic farms and artisans. Apart from its white sand beaches, attractions include its vineyards, bush walks and olive groves.

Electricity on **Great Barrier Island**, the furthermost island in the Hauraki Gulf, is provided by diesel generators and solar panels, while some refrigerators still use kerosene. Drinking water comes from rain collected on roofs. The island is dominated by Mount Hobson, standing at 620 m (2,034 ft), and Ruahine, 410 m (1,345 ft). Visitors may spot a kaka, the New Zealand parrot, or a brown teal duck while on a tramping trip.

Regular boats to **Kawau Island** leave from Sandspit at Warkworth. The island is best known for Mansion House, built in 1846, the home of former New Zealand governor and prime minister Sir George Grey. Sir George imported a variety of animal species, such as kookaburras and peacocks. Several, such as the parma wallaby, thought to be extinct in Australia, can still be seen. **Rangitoto** has a highly visible

Brown kiwi with egg

presence in the gulf. The now-extinct volcano erupted about 600–700 years ago to form an island. Now, the 260 m- (850ft-) high lava slopes are covered in trees and shrubs including ferns, mangroves, tree daisies, orchids, coastal pohutukawa, manuka and rewa. There are good walks, including one to the summit. Alternatively, visitors can use a tractor-drawn train.

Rakino is popular with weekenders. A hotchpotch of houses sit perched on striking ridges. Its beaches are suitable for swimming and it is a favourite stop for yachts.

Little Barrier Island, a wildlife sanctuary, has 30 native and 19 introduced species of birds breeding on it. They include the brown kiwi, kaka and bellbird. Flora includes 370 native species, with 90 ferns. It is prohibited to land on Little Barrier but it is possible to visit the island with a permit obtained from Forest and Bird, a conservation organisation (www.forestandbird.org.nz).

Gazetted in 1975, **Goat Island Marine** Reserve is also known as the Leigh

Marine Reserve. The sheltered channel between Goat Island and the mainland provides an opportunity to see red moki, moray eel, snapper and blue cod, as well as marblefish and kelpfish.

The channel is only about 2 to 5 m (7 to 17 ft) deep and diving is possible straight from the beach. Underwater visibility fluctuates from 2 to 15 m (7 to 50 ft) and is at its best from January to June.

🦜 **Waiheke Island**
🗺 9,000. 🚢 ℹ 1 Sea View Rd, Waiheke. 🌐 waiheke.co.nz; tourismwaiheke.co.nz

🦜 **Great Barrier Island**
🗺 1,000. ✈ 🚢 🚌 ℹ Freephone (0800) 997 222. 🌐 greatbarrier islandtourism.co.nz

🦜 **Kawau Island**
🗺 80. 🚢

Visitors watching birds at the Leigh Marine Reserve

SHOPPING IN AUCKLAND

Shops in Auckland cater for the needs of most shoppers. However, the city is quite spread out and it pays to do some research first. Shops in downtown Auckland are predominantly European in character; in other areas they have a more Pacific or Asian flavour. Shoppers in search of local items should consider pure wool products, such as hand-knitted sweaters or cuddly toys made from possum fur. The New Zealand fashion scene is lively and creative, and local designers such as Zambesi, Karen Walker, Anne Mardell, and Trelise Cooper have outlets in all the smart shopping areas. Jewellery, pottery, glass and other crafts are of a high standard and are worth buying. Specialized retailers sell items such as crayfish, which they will package for outbound travellers.

Shopping Hours

Typical business hours are 9am to 6pm, with many stores open on Saturday and Sunday. Most large supermarkets are open until 9pm and some 24 hours. Dairies (convenience stores) are found throughout the suburbs and sell a wide range of groceries and other items, as do most petrol stations.

Duty-free Shopping

The New Zealand government adds 15 per cent Goods and Services Tax (GST) to sales items. Visitors to New Zealand can avoid paying this tax, as well as other government duty, by purchasing duty-free goods on arrival and departure at the airport or at the large duty-free shop, **DFS Galleria**, in the city. This results in savings of 30 per cent on average. Items purchased at the shop have to be collected at the airport. Besides the usual cigarettes and alcohol, sheepskin goods, *paua* shell jewellery, *paua* pearls, and finely crafted woodwork using local timbers are popular items with tourists.

Shopping Areas

With its Britomart transport hub, Queen Street is the major banking and commercial centre. However, the restoration of Charles Bohringer's Civic Theatre (1929), the Force Entertainment Centre and shopping areas such as **Atrium**

Interior of a Rodd and Gunn outlet in the city

on Elliott and the **Britomart** have revitalized the central business district as a shopping and entertainment centre. Book stores such as **Whitcoulls**, **Women's Bookshop** and **Unity Books**, CD and record shops such as **Marbecks Classical Shop**, woollen clothing and couture boutiques, and many souvenir stores are also found downtown. Nautical-type

The country's largest duty-free shop, DFS Galleria, located at the Old Customhouse

clothing and souvenirs, sought after since the 2000 America's Cup Regatta, can be bought at the **New Zealand Maritime Museum Shop**.

Newmarket is Auckland's prime shopping area and has hundreds of stores. Shops along Broadway include **Country Road, Rodd and Gunn**, and **Living and Giving**. Parnell and Ponsonby retailers specialize in luxury goods, such as delicatessen food, clothing, art, ceramics and glassware.

Fresh fruit on sale at one of Auckland's markets

Markets

Shoppers who are more interested in typically New Zealand goods at lower prices should go to **Victoria Park Market**, a former rubbish destructor building built in 1905. Today, the site houses shops and stalls selling anything from souvenirs to snacks. There are also five licensed restaurants and a food court at the complex. Saturday morning's **Otara Market**, open from 6am to noon, offers yams, green bananas, *hangi* (Māori food cooked on heated stones) and Pacific Island fashion.

DIRECTORY

Shopping Centres

Atrium on Elliott
21–25 Elliott St.
Tel (09) 375 4960.
W atriumonelliott.co.nz

Britomart
8–10 Queen St, Auckland.
Tel (09) 914 8431.

DFS Galleria
Old Customhouse, Cnr of Albert & Customs sts.
Tel 0800 388 937.

Dress-Smart Factory Outlet
151 Arthur St,
Onehunga.
Tel (09) 622 2400.

Queens Arcade
34–40 Queen St.
Tel (09) 358 1777.
W queensarcade.co.nz

Markets

Otara Market
Newbury St & Te Puke,
Otara Community Hall.
Tel (09) 274 0830.

Victoria Park Market
210 Victoria St West.
Tel (09) 309 6911.
W victoriapark market.co.nz

Food and Wine

Accent on Wine
347 Parnell Rd, Parnell.
Tel (09) 358 2552.

LaBy BritomartCigale Market
Takutai Square, 1010.
Tel (09) 366 9361.

Pandoro Panetteria
427 Parnell Rd, Parnell.
Tel (09) 358 1962.

Clothes

Country Road
164 Queen St.
Tel (09) 309 6862. 157 Broadway, Newmarket.
Tel (09) 529 1987.

Karen Walker
The Pavillions, 18 Te Ara Tahuhu Walking St,
Britomart.
Tel (09) 309 6299.
6 Balm St, Newmarket.
Tel (09) 522 4286.

New Zealand Maritime Museum Shop
Viaduct Basin.
Tel (09) 373 0800.

Rodd and Gunn
75 Queen St.
Tel (09) 309 6571.
277 Broadway, Newmarket.
Tel (09) 522 0607.

Workshop
Cnr of Vulcan Lane and High St. Tel (09) 303 3735.
18 Morrow St, Newmarket.
Tel (09) 524 6844.

Books and Music

Marbecks Classical Shop
28 Queen's Arcade.
Tel (09) 379 0444.
W marbecks.co.nz

Rare Books
6 High St (winters: open Tue & Thu only).
Tel (09) 379 0379.

Real Groovy Records
369 Queen St.
Tel (09) 302 3940.

Unity Books
19 High St.
Tel (09) 307 0731.
W unitybooks.co.nz

Whitcoulls
210 Queen St.
Tel (09) 984 5400.

Women's Bookshop
105 Ponsonby Rd.
Tel (09) 376 4399.
W womensbook shop.co.nz

Souvenirs and Others

Living and Giving
Westfield St Lukes,
St Lukes Road, St Lukes.
Tel (09) 846 6999.

OK Gift Shop
131 Quay St, Auckland.
Tel (09) 303 1951.

Opal and Jade World
105 Queens St.
Tel (09) 379 3739.

Smith and Caughey's
253–261 Queen St.
Tel (09) 377 4770.
255 Broadway,
Newmarket.
Tel (09) 524 8049.

The Sheepskin Store
7A Bassant Ave,
Penrose.
Tel (09) 622 2889

ENTERTAINMENT IN AUCKLAND

Reflecting Auckland's ethnic diversity, events staged in the city range from a Puccini opera to a Māori dance performance. Many of these take place at venues in the central business district. The Aotea Centre, Auckland Town Hall and several cinemas are all on Queen Street. The Civic Theatre is worth a visit for architectural reasons alone. Bordering Queen Street, Fort Street and Karangahape Road, commonly known as K-Road, offer alternative entertainment in the form of strip clubs and massage parlours. K-Road is also known for its funky atmosphere and its many nightclubs. SKYCITY Casino features more than 100 gaming tables and 1,000 machines. In the suburbs, multiplex cinemas, sports parks and nightclubs are the main entertainment venues.

Impressive interior of the Civic Theatre

Information

The entertainment section of *The New Zealand Herald* should be checked first for events in the city. It carries cinema listings and information about concerts, ballets and theatre performances. Several publications outlining what's on in Auckland are available from visitor information centres which can be found across the city. The country's two main booking agencies, **Ticketmaster** and **Ticketek**, list events on their websites. Reservations can be made online or by phone.

Theatre

The main venues, the **Aotea Centre**, **Auckland Town Hall** and the **Civic Theatre** are part of the complex known as Auckland Live *(see p78)*. This is where the biggest musicals and productions are staged. The Great Hall in the Auckland Town Hall *(see p78)* is renowned for its acoustics. Other theatres include the Maidment Theatre at the university, the Silo in Grey's Avenue and Q Theatre at Queens Street.

Dance

New Zealand has a small dance community. Its leading contemporary dance choreographers are Mary Jane O'Reilly, Michael Parmenter, and Douglas Wright.
At present, the Footnote Dance Company is the country's only full-time contemporary dance company. Based in Wellington, the troupe performs in Auckland, as does the classical Royal New Zealand Ballet, which also has its home in the capital. However, the Black Grace Dance Company is Auckland-based. There are regular tours by overseas dance and ballet companies.

Annabel Reid of the Royal New Zealand Ballet in *Raymonda*

Music

For classical music, the New Zealand Symphony Orchestra (NZSO) and the Auckland Philharmonia Orchestra (APO) have a good reputation. The 33-member APO is unusual in that the musicians own the orchestra. Most concerts are held in the Auckland Town Hall. Both NZSO and APO regularly pool resources to hold big concerts. More information about Auckland's music events including gigs, concerts and festivals can be found at www.heartofthecity.co.nz.
Many pubs in Auckland have live bands that play most nights, including the Powerstation, King's Arms and The Dogs Bollix, a popular Irish pub.

Fireworks during a symphony performance at the Auckland Domain

A traditional Māori dance at the Auckland War Memorial Museum

Cultural Performances

At the Auckland War Memorial Museum *(see pp82–3)*, visitors are able to witness authentic Māori ceremonies and dances. During the shows, which are staged three to four times daily, talented singers and dancers from the Manaia Cultural Performance Group present the *haka*, the fierce war dance of the men, the *poi* dances of the women *(see pp34–5)*, as well as various other traditional songs and dances. Each show lasts about 45 minutes.

Visitors can also get to see Pacific Island culture and events at the Pasifika Festival, held at Western Springs, in March every year *(see p46)*. The festival features the traditional arts and culture of the various Pacific Island communities.

Clubs

Although theatres throughout the country feature one-off performances by local and visiting comedians, the **Classic Comedy & Bar** claims to be the only venue in the whole of New Zealand that is dedicated to stand-up comedy.

The city's main night-club strip is on Karangahape Road. Venues that are popular with young people include **Stoners Lounge Nightclub** which has marble walls and leather couches unlike any other club in the city.

Zen, which features dance music such as hip hop and drum and bass, and **Ding Dong Bar**, a popular rock café with DJs willing to play any requests. Auckland's gay clubs include **Mea Culpa** on Ponsonby Road and Caluzzi Bar and Cabaret on Karangahape Road which hosts drag acts and other entertainment evenings.

Film

Multiplex cinemas are found throughout Auckland. The larger multiplexes, such as the **Event Cinemas**, show block-buster films, often before they are seen in Europe. New-market's refurbished **Rialto Cinema**, on the other hand, regularly screens foreign titles for more sophisticated film buffs.

The highlight of the cinematographic year is the New Zealand Film Festival, held in July. Auckland filmgoers get to enjoy a wide selection of local and international films over two weeks.

Façade of Event Cinemas

DIRECTORY

Booking Tickets

Ticketek
Tel (09) 307 5000, 0800 TICKETEK.
w ticketek.com

Ticketmaster
Tel (09) 970 9700.
w ticketmaster.co.nz

Theatres

Aotea Centre
Aotea Square. Tel (09) 309 2677.

Auckland Town Hall
Queen St. Tel (09) 309 2677.

Civic Theatre
Cnr Queen and Wellesley sts.

SKYCITY Theatre
Cnr Wellesley and Hobson sts.
Tel 0800 759 2489.

Clubs

1885 Britomart
27 Galway St, Britomart.
Tel (09) 551 3100.

Casette 9
9 Vulcan Lane.
Tel (09) 366 0196.

Classic Comedy & Bar
321 Queen St.
Tel (09) 373 4321.

Ding Dong Bar
26 Wyndham St.
Tel (09) 377 4712.

Mea Culpa
3/175 Ponsonby Rd.
Tel (09) 376 4460.

Ponsonby Social Club
152 Ponsonby Rd.
Tel (09) 361 2320.

S P Q R
150 Ponsonby Rd.
Tel (09) 360 1710.

Spy Bar
204 Quay St, Viaduct Basin.
Tel (09) 377 7811.

Stoners Lounge Nightclub
146 Karangahape Rd.
Tel (09) 379 7388.

Cinemas

Rialto Cinema
169 Broadway, Newmarket.
Tel (09) 369 2417.

Event Cinemas
Metro Building, 291–297
Queen St.
Tel (09) 369 2400.

NORTHLAND

Strong Māori roots, early European settlements, a subtropical climate and enchanting scenery – these make Northland both the cradle of the nation and one of its favourite playgrounds. Northland is where Europeans first made their presence felt in New Zealand. It is a region with a history of bloodshed and raw frontier emotions, but is today dominated by holiday fun.

The long history of Māori occupation in Northland is evident in the hillside *pa* sites and shellfishing grounds around the coast. Māori culture *(see pp34–5)* continues to be extensively practised in this region and many Māori tribes live here.

Early post-European history in Northland includes both the licentious whalers, who earned Russell its title of "hell-hole of the Pacific" *(see p106)*, and missionaries, who brought Christianity to the country. Buildings such as Pompallier House are reminders of early Christian influences.

Historically, Waitangi Treaty House, where the Treaty of Waitangi was signed *(see pp52–3, 108–9)*, is of major importance. Cape Reinga *(see p112)* is a draw, because of its location at the top of the country where the Pacific Ocean and Tasman Sea merge, and also because of its significance in Māori mythology as the place from where the spirits of the dead depart for Hawaiki.

Visitors to Northland will be impressed by its natural beauty: gently rolling farmland, white sand beaches, massive sand dunes and rock formations. In a world where scenic spots are often spoiled due to countless visitors, Northland stands out. In its forests, with gigantic kauris that are around 2,000 years old, it is still possible to walk for hours without encountering a single fellow hiker. The region also offers other activities, such as fishing, diving, kayaking, sand surfing and horse riding.

Diving near the wreck of the Rainbow Warrior *(see p57)* off Matauri Bay

◄ Matapouri Bay on the stunning Tutukaka Coast

Exploring Northland

Northland's charm lies in its unspoiled, simple character. The region is blessed with two contrasting coastlines, which offer endless scope for outdoor recreation. As the site of first permanent contact between Māori and Europeans, the region is also rich in history and has many well-preserved historic sites. There are many areas from which visitors can explore the region: Paihia, which has its own attractions but is close to historic Russell, Waitangi and Kerikeri, and the beautiful Bay of Islands; Kaitaia, which attracts day-trippers to the Aupori Peninsula, Mangonui and Ahipara; and Opononi and Omapere, which have wonderful beaches and are close to Rawene, a historic settlement on Hokianga Harbour.

Pohutukawa trees and bays around Whangarei Heads

0 kilometres 20
0 miles 20

Top Outdoor Activities

The places shown here have been selected for their recreational activities. Conditions vary depending on the weather and the time of year, so exercise caution and, if in doubt, seek local advice.

	Cruising	Game Fishing	Kayaking	Sailing	Scuba Diving	Snorkelling	Swimming	Hiking
Cape Reinga								●
Kai-Iwi Lakes			●	●			●	
Kaitaia								●
Ninety Mile Beach							●	●
Omapere	●	●	●				●	
Opononi	●	●	●				●	
Paihia	●	●	●	●	●	●	●	
Russell	●	●	●	●	●	●	●	●
Tutukaka	●	●	●	●	●	●	●	●
Waipoua Forest								●
Whangarei	●	●	●	●	●	●	●	●

Painting an ancestral figure on the meeting house at Waitangi

For hotels and restaurants in this region see pp302–3 and pp315–17

Fullers tour coach on Ninety Mile Beach

Sights at a Glance

1. Whangarei
2. Tutukaka
3. Poor Knights Islands
4. Matapouri
5. Russell
6. Paihia
7. *Waitangi Treaty Grounds pp108–9*
8. Kerikeri
9. Waimate North
10. Whangaroa
11. Doubtless Bay
12. Kaitaia
13. Cape Reinga
14. Ninety Mile Beach
16. Kaikohe
17. Rawene
18. Opononi
19. Waipoua Forest
20. Dargaville

Tour

15. Aupori Peninsula

Getting Around

The best way to see Northland is by car. The main road to the Aupori Peninsula is a 21 km (13 mile) section to Cape Reinga. Tour operators often return via Ninety Mile Beach, a trip not recommended for cars. Visitors can start either on the east or west coast, along the 800-km (497-mile) Northland Twin Coast Discovery touring route from Auckland.

Map labels

DOUBTLESS BAY
Cavalli Islands
Mangonui
10 WHANGAROA
Kaeo
10
WAITANGI TREATY GROUNDS
Mangamuka
KERIKERI 8
Bay of Islands
Cape Brett
PAIHIA 6
7
5 RUSSELL
WAIMATE NORTH 9
1
12
16 KAIKOHE
Kawakawa
Oakura
Whangaruru Harbour
RAWENE
Towai
Waima
NORTHLAND
Purua
Hikurangi
3 POOR KNIGHTS ISLANDS
4 MATAPOURI
2 TUTUKAKA
WAIPOUA FOREST
Tatamoe Range
Parakao
Maunu
1
PACIFIC OCEAN
12
Kaihu
Maungatapere
1 WHANGAREI
Kai-Iwi Lakes
14
Portland
McLeod Bay
Bream Head
DARGAVILLE 20
Ruakaka
Bream Bay
Waiotira
Waipu
12
Wairoa
Matakohe
Maungaturoto
TASMAN SEA
Ruawai
12
Mangawhai
Little Barrier Island
North Head
Wellsford
Leigh
Kaipara Harbour
16
Warkworth
Kawau Island
South Head
AUCKLAND
Hauraki Gulf
Orewa
Kaukapakapa
Auckland
Helensville

Key

— Major road
═ Minor road
▬ Toll road
— Scenic route
---- Minor railway
— Regional border

For keys to symbols *see back flap*

The Town Basin on the waterfront at Whangarei

● Whangarei

Road map E1. 🗺 47,000. 🚌 🚐
ℹ Tarewa Park, 92 Otaika Rd, (09) 438
1079. 🇼 **whangareinz.com**

The northernmost city in New
Zealand and the only one in
Northland, Whangarei is a two-
hour drive from Auckland. It lies
between forested hills and a deep
harbour. The combination of
fertile soil and temperate climate
is reflected in the city's lush
gardens and in the surrounding
farmlands and orchards.

Whangarei's historic Town
Basin, in the heart of the city, has
been redeveloped in a colonial
theme. Its cafés, restaurants,
art galleries, museums and
speciality shops make it a
popular gathering place for
locals and visitors. It is also one
of the most popular destinations

for yatchies sailing the world,
who come here to avoid the
cyclonic storms common in
the South Pacific over the
summer. The Town Basin
and local marinas are
often full with visiting
yachts coming to refit.

A giant sundial marks
the location of the Town
Basin's **Claphams National
Clock Museum**, which
houses more than
1,400 items, of which
400 were donated by
A Clapham, who
made many of the
clocks himself. The
oldest, an English
lantern clock, dates
from 1690. The collection also
includes Biedermeier wall clocks,
grandfather and Black Forest
clocks, and a *staartklok* (literally

Claphams National
Clock Museum exhibit

a "tail clock" after the shape
of its winding mechanism)
from Friesland in the
Netherlands. To avoid the
deafening sound of the
hundreds of time-pieces
marking the hour simul-
taneously, the clocks have
been set at different times.

Just to the west of
Whangarei is the **Quarry
Arts Centre**, offering local
arts and crafts for sale. Set
in a bush-clad quarry the
Trust is home to a number
of artists who live on-site,
some in adobe-style
dwellings. Further out is
Kiwi North, home to the
Whangarei Museum and
Kiwi House & Heritage
Park. The museum
displays a fine range of

Maori artifacts, and there is
a 1885 homestead. The Kiwi
House provides the chance
to view one of the country's
most endangered birds.

For those looking for more
challenging activities, there are
many hiking opportunities
around Whangarei. The
Parahaka Scenic Reserve, on
the eastern side of the city,
has good bush walks. The war
memorial at the summit of
Parihaka Mountain can be
reached via Memorial Drive
or by two tracks from Mair Park
or Dundas Road, for a superb
panoramic view of the city and
harbour. There are Maori pits
and old gum-digging workings
on all the walks, and a trail
leads to a historic Maori *pa*
site nearby. Whangarei
Falls, known as the most
photogenic waterfalls in
New Zealand, lie northeast
of the Parahaka Scenic Reserve
in the suburb of Tikipunga,
5 km (3 miles) north of the
town centre. The 26 m-
(86 ft-) high waterfall
drops over basalt cliffs.

There are natural pools
and picnic spots, plus
two viewing platforms
that provide excellent
views of the falls.

🏛 **Clapham Clock Museum**
Town Basin, Dent St. **Tel** (09) 438 3993.
Open daily. **Closed** 25 Dec. 🔲 🔲
🔲 🔲

🏛 **Quarry Arts Centre**
21 Selwyn Ave. **Tel** (09) 438 1215.
Open daily. 🔲 🔲

🏛 **Kiwi North (Whangarei
Museum and Kiwi House &
Heritage Park)**
Gate 1, 500 State Hwy 14, Heritage
Park, Maunu. Tel (09) 438 9630. **Open**
daily. **Closed** 25 & 26 Dec. 🔲 🔲

● Tutukaka

Road map E1. 🗺 520. 🚐 ℹ Dive!
Tutukaka, Marina Rd, (09) 434 3867.
🇼 **tutukakacoastnz.com**

On the coastal loop road, a
short distance from Whangarei,
Tutukaka is a well-known base
for diving trips to the Poor
Knights Islands and for big
game and deep-sea fishing.

The picturesque Whangarei Falls

Yachts moored at the marina in Tutukaka's sheltered harbour

Several diving companies are based here and the sheltered, natural harbour is alive with yachts and fishing boats.

One of the most popular diving sites off the coast between Tutukaka and Matapouri is an artificial reef created by the sinking of two former naval ships, the *Tui* and the *Waikato*. Several professional diving companies offer their services as guides to this underwater grave. For further information on diving trips available in the area, visit www.diving.co.nz.

❸ Poor Knights Islands

Road map E1. ℹ Tarewa Park, 92 Otaika Rd, Whangarei, (09) 438 1079. 🆆 whangareinz.com

About 24 km (15 miles) from the coast at Tutukaka are the Poor Knights Islands. Once a favourite spot for fishermen, the area around these two islands was established as a marine reserve in 1981. Although landing on the islands is prohibited without a special permit from the Department of Conservation, the surrounding waters are accessible to divers. Well-known mariner Jacques Cousteau considered the reserve one of the world's top five diving sites

because of its exceptional water clarity and the variety of its sea life. The area benefits from a subtropical current that makes it warmer than the surrounding coastal waters, and promotes a profusion of tropical and temperate marine life. Eroded volcanic rock has created a seascape of tunnels, arches and caves where divers can view fish and sponges. Scuba diving in this haven can be enjoyed all year round. Boats leave daily from Tutukaka Marina.

Reptiles such as geckos and tuataras can be found on both islands, which are thought to be the world's only nesting spot for Buller's shearwaters.

❹ Matapouri

Road map E1. 🆆 whangareinz.com

Located a short distance north of Tutukaka on the coastal loop road, Matapouri has one of Northland's most beautiful beaches. Tucked between headlands and dotted with islets, Matapouri's calm waters and white sands make it a popular place for swimming and snorkelling.

A walking track connects the beach with Whale Bay, 2 km (1.2 miles) north. Lookout points on the track offer magnificent views of the coastline and ocean.

Diving in the marine reserve at Poor Knights Islands

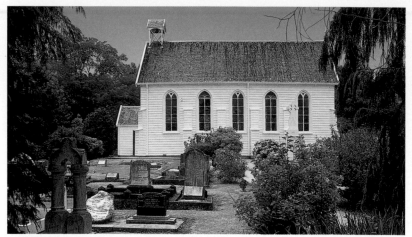

The churchyard, Christ Church, Russell

❺ Russell

Road map E1. 🗺 1,000. 🚍 🚢
ⓘ The Wharf, (09) 403 8020.
🖥 **northlandnz.com**

At the turn of the 19th century, Russell, then known as Kororareka, served as a shore station for whalers. It became a lawless town, earning the title "Hell-hole of the Pacific". It was renamed Russell in 1844 in honour of the British colonial secretary of the day. Today, the quiet town is involved in tourism, fishing, oyster farming and cottage industries.

Formerly known as the Captain Cook Memorial Museum, the **Russell Museum** features a working model of Captain Cook's *Endeavour* and memorabilia from American author Zane Grey, who helped establish the Bay of Islands as a game fishing centre in the late 1920s. There is also a collection of early settlers' relics.

Christ Church, built in 1836, is the country's oldest surviving church. One of the contributors to the church was Charles Darwin, author of *The Origin of Species*, who visited New Zealand in 1835.

Stately **Pompallier Mission** was built on the waterfront between 1841 and 1842 to house the Marist mission's Gaveaux printing press. The building later became much neglected, until it passed to the

New Zealand Historic Places Trust in 1968 and was restored to its original state in 1993. The country's oldest standing industrial building, it now houses a printing and bookbinding exhibition, which includes the original printing press.

Flagstaff Hill serves as a reminder of Russell's turbulent past. It was here that Hone Heke (1810–50) cut down the British shipping signal flagpole in 1844 *(see p67)*.

The waterfront is lined with chic cafés and the town is still a favoured spot for boaties who seek safe anchorage.

Paihia restaurant sign

🏛 Russell Museum
2 York St. **Tel** (09) 403 7701. **Open** daily. **Closed** 25 Dec. 🅿 ♿ 📷

⛪ Christ Church
Church Rd. **Tel** (09) 403 7696.
✝ 10:30am Sun.

🏛 Pompallier Mission
The Strand. **Tel** (09) 403 9015.
Open daily. **Closed** 25 Dec. 🅿
♿ garden only. 📷 📷

❻ Paihia

Road map E1. 🗺 1,850. 🚍 🚢
ⓘ Marsden Rd, (09) 402 7345.

Starting life as a mission post in 1823, Paihia now joins places

such as Russell and Tutukaka as a base for deep-sea game fishing. To the north of Paihia, on the road to Kerikeri is the **Lily Pond Farm Park**. The park gives visitors the chance to interact with a whole range of farm animals including sheep, pigs and goats. There are also more exotic species of animal, such as eels, alpaca and emus. It is a working farm that will appeal to families with small children. Located 3 km (2 miles) from Paihia, on the Waitangi River *(see pp108–9)*, are the **Haruru Falls**. There is a track from Waitangi to Haruru Falls. Visitors can also walk to the mangroves to see herons and nesting native shags. An alternative approach to the falls is by kayak along the river. Kayaks can be hired from **Coastal Kayakers**, who also take groups of kayakers on guided tours.

🚜 Lily Pond Farm Park
RD1 Puketona Rd. **Tel** (09) 402 6099. **Open** Fri–Tue. **Closed** 25 Dec.
🅿 ♿

🌿 Haruru Falls
Near Waitangi Treaty Grounds.
Tel (09) 402 7437. **Open** 9am–5pm daily. **Closed** 25 Dec. 🅿 📷 Coastal Kayakers: Te Karuwha Pde, Waitangi.
Tel (09) 402 8105. 📷
🖥 **coastalkayakers.co.nz**

Leisure Activities in the Bay of Islands

A favourable climate, an irregular coastline lapped by the Pacific Ocean and 144 islands dotted around its aquamarine waters, which are full of marine wildlife, combine to make the Bay of Islands one of New Zealand's most popular playgrounds. The region has been a favourite tourist destination since the 1930s when a road connecting Northland with Auckland to the south was built. The Bay of Islands' reputation is based primarily on deep-sea fishing, but today visitors also have the opportunity to experience other watersports, such as swimming, kayaking, sailing, diving and water-skiing. Tour operators tempt visitors by adding new attractions, such as scenic flights, paragliding and horse trekking.

Fishing

A number of fishing charters operate in the Bay of Islands all year round. Not only do these operators know exactly where to go for great fishing, but a charter fishing trip is also one of the best ways to see the natural beauty of the Bay of Islands.

The Rowe family, keen anglers of the Bay of Islands Swordfish Club, with their prize catch

Swimming with dolphins in the bay's warm waters is a popular activity. Licensed tour operators ensure that human attention does not scare the dolphins.

Kayaking guided tours range from paddling up sheltered waters to kayaking on the open sea.

Leisure cruises include Paihia's Cream Trip. The boat used to collect cream from outlying dairy farms but now drops off mail and takes visitors on cruises.

Paragliding, one of several airborne sports introduced in the Bay of Islands, is an excellent way to appreciate the beauty of the bay.

❼ Waitangi Treaty Grounds

Waitangi earned its pivotal place in New Zealand's history on 6 February 1840 when the Treaty of Waitangi was signed *(see p22, pp52–3)* in front of the house of James Busby (1800–71), the British Resident. The Residency, renamed the Treaty House, became a national memorial in 1932. The house and grounds are a gathering point for Māori and government leaders each year on 6 February, Waitangi Day. Visitors are recommended to take the guided tours.

Aerial View of Waitangi Treaty Grounds
The grounds are surrounded by a beautiful coastline, tidal estuary, mangrove, forest and native bush.

Visitor Centre
An audiovisual presentation every half hour describes the events surrounding the signing of the Treaty of Waitangi. There are also displays on the major personalities involved and copies of the Treaty documents. A shop sells souvenirs, Māori carvings and books.

Paihia

Waitan

Tai Henare Drive

Hobson Beach

0 metres 200
0 yards 200

KEY

① **Café**

② **Car Park**

③ **Canoe House**

④ **A coastal walk** takes visitors past unusual pillow lava rock, which fractured into hexagonal shapes as it erupted under water.

⑤ **Copthorne Hotel and Resort**

⑥ **Te Tii Marae**

⑦ **Bay of Islands Yacht Club**

⑧ **Waitangi Golf Course**

⑨ **Flagstaff**

★ **Māori War Canoe**
Carved from three kauri trees, this 35 m (114 ft) long canoe, named Ngatokimatawhaorua after the canoe in which Kupe discovered New Zealand *(see p49)*, carries up to 120 warriors. It is launched each year on Waitangi Day.

Mangrove Forest Boardwalk
A boardwalk takes visitors through a mature mangrove forest to the Haruru Falls at the end of the tidal Waitangi River.

VISITORS' CHECKLIST

Practical Information
Road map E1.
W waitangi.org.nz
i 1 Tau Henare Drive, Waitangi, (09) 402 7437. **Open** 9am–5pm daily. **Closed** 25 Dec.

Transport
from Kerikeri.

Hutia Creek

River

8

9

★ Treaty House
Prefabricated in Australia, the Treaty House *(see p53)*, was the home of the first British Resident, James Busby. It was the venue for important political events up to 1840.

★ Māori Meeting House
Opened on 6 February 1940 to commemorate the centennial of the Treaty, the meeting house (Te Whare Runanga) contains beautiful Māori wall carvings.

Treaty Grounds
A ceremonial celebration of the signing of the Treaty of Waitangi is held each year on the Treaty House each year.

The Stone Store, St James Church and Kerikeri Mission House

❽ Kerikeri

Road map E1. 🏔 4,200. 🚌 🚆
🅆 northlandnz.com

The pretty town of Kerikeri is noted for its subtropical climate, citrus and kiwifruit orchards, historic buildings, and an art and craft trail.

The Kerikeri Basin is home to **Kerikeri Mission Station**, one of New Zealand's earliest settlements. It was the second European mission station to be set up in New Zealand, in 1819, under the protection of Māori chief Hongi Hika (*see p67*); the first mission was established near the entrance to the Bay of Islands five years earlier. The mission station includes Kerikeri Mission House. Constructed in 1821, the building belonged to the Kemp family in 1832 and was left to the New Zealand Historic Places Trust in 1974. Restored, it looks much as it did in the 1840s. The mission station also encompasses New Zealand's oldest surviving stone building, the Stone Store, built in 1835 as part of the mission house. Intended as a storehouse, it gradually turned into a general store and, from the 1960s, a souvenir shop, selling merchandise such as hand-forged nails and other products in keeping with its history. On the slope behind the mission house is **St James Church**, constructed in 1878 of native timbers such as kauri and puriri.

Above the Basin are the remnants of Kororipo Pa, a Māori fortification. The strategic base of Hongi Hika, the *pa* is best known as an assembly point for war parties in the 1820s. Across the river from the *pa* is **Rewa's Village**, a reconstructed pre-European Māori fishing village built from native materials; those used before the missionaries came. It provides an introduction to traditional buildings such as *marae* (gathering place) and *pataka* (communal raised storehouse). There are two ancient canoes at the village and the Discoverers' Garden.

⊞ Kerikeri Mission Station
The Basin, 246 Kerikeri Rd.
Tel (09) 407 9236. **Open** daily.
Closed 25 Dec. 🏠 📷 📁

⛪ St James Church
The Basin. 🏠 daily.

🏛 Rewa's Village
1 Landing Rd. **Tel** (09) 407 6454.
Open daily. **Closed** Good Fri, 25 Dec.
🏠 ♿ 📷 by arrangement. 📁

❾ Waimate North

Road map E1. 🏔 700.

Not far from Kerikeri is Waimate North, a missionary community in the 1830s. It was also the site of New Zealand's first large English-style farm. It is now best known for **Te Waimate Mission**,

the sole survivor of three mission houses built in 1832 and first occupied by the Clarke family. It is furnished with missionary period furniture and early tools.

⊞ Te Waimate Mission
Te Ahu Ahu Rd. **Tel** (09) 405 9734.
Open May–Oct: Sat–Mon; Nov–Apr: daily. **Closed** 25 Dec. 🏠

❿ Whangaroa

Road map E1. 🏔 530. 🚌
🅆 northlandnz.com

A small, scenic settlement with a beautiful harbour, Whangaroa is best appreciated from the summit of St Paul, a rock formation that dominates the town. The surrounding hills were once covered in huge kauri trees, which have long since been turned into ship masts and timber. Croatians worked the Matauri Bay gum-fields in the late 19th century, extracting resin (*see p114*).

Today, Whangaroa Harbour has become well known for its big-game fishing, cruises, diving and snorkelling.

⓫ Doubtless Bay

Road map D1. 🚌
🅆 northlandnz.com

Said to be the first landfall for the explorer Kupe (*see pp49–50*), Doubtless Bay was an important base for whalers in the early days of European settlement. The bay encompasses a wide crescent of golden beaches, including Cable Bay and Cooper's Beach, popular with swimmers and snorkellers. The fishing village of Mangonui, situated on the bay's estuary, has many historic buildings.

Te Waimate Mission, one of New Zealand's oldest wooden buildings

Arts and Crafts

Art and crafts are well developed in Northland, often with a strong local flavour in the use of colours and motifs. Ironically, the best-known artist was not a New Zealander but Austrian architect and painter Hundertwasser, who spent much of his time in New Zealand until his death in March 2000. Visitors to Kawakawa, south of Paihia, and Russell can visit a grass-roofed Hundertwasser-designed toilet block. Local artist Chris Booth is known for sculptures that feature large stones – his best-known work is on the headland at Matauri Bay. There are many outlets in the area, however, that offer paintings, prints, bone carvings and traditional greenstone (jade) items. In Kerikeri, an art and craft trail leads visitors through shops selling a variety of individually handcrafted and decorated pieces of high quality.

Hundertwasser-designed, open, grass-roofed toilet block is a major tourist attraction.

Swamp Kauri Carving
Swamp kauri is turned by local artisans into items ranging from small bowls to dining sets. The timber is milled from the remnants of huge trees which fell into swamplands 30,000–50,000 years ago.

Part of a stone sculpture by Northland artist Chris Booth, which forms the entrance to Auckland's Albert Park.

Plaited floor mats, baskets and hats made from flax, a swamp plant, are popular souvenirs. Flax weaving is a traditional Māori skill.

Wood, bone or greenstone are carved by crafts people like Hohepa Renata, who use their own designs or traditional Māori ones.

Carved wooden mask

Pottery is produced in a variety of techniques, including glazing methods from Japan.

⑫ Kaitaia

Map D1. 🏔 5,300. 🚌 ℹ Cnr Matthews Ave and South Rd, (09) 408 0879. 🌐 **northlandnz.com**

The largest town in the Far North, Kaitaia is a good base for day trips in the area. It is home to the **Te Ahu Centre**, which has the earliest authenticated European artifact left in New Zealand – a 1,500 kg (3,300 lb) wrought-iron anchor, lost in a storm in Doubtless Bay in 1769 by J F M de Surville, the French explorer.

🏛 **Te Ahu Centre**
Cnr Matthews Ave and South Rd. **Tel** (09) 408 1403. **Open** daily. **Closed** Good Fri, 25 Dec. 🎫 📷 ♿ 🎁 on request. 📷 🌐 **farnorthmuseum.co.nz**

⑬ Cape Reinga

Map D1. 🌐 **northlandnz.com**

Reinga, meaning "underworld", refers to the Māori belief that this is where the spirits of the dead leave for the journey to Hawaiki. The roots of an old pohutukawa tree at the tip of the cape are said to be the departure point for these spirits. Looking out from Cape Reinga over the Columbia Bank, visitors can see the Tasman Sea converge with the Pacific Ocean. The cape is not the very end of the country; the northernmost point is on North Cape.

⑭ Ninety Mile Beach

Map D1. 🌐 **northlandnz.com**

A misnomer, Ninety Mile Beach is, in fact, only 96 km (60 miles) long. The longest beach in the country, this area is almost like a desert, with sand dunes that can reach 143 m (470 ft) high fringing the beach. It was once a forested region, but the kauri trees were destroyed by inundations of water during successive Ice Ages. Pine trees have been planted to stabilize the dunes. Surf fishing and digging for shellfish are popular activities.

⑮ Aupori Peninsula Driving Tour

Called "The Tail of The Fish" by Māori, Aupori Peninsula is a thin strip of land no more than 12 km (7 miles) wide between Ninety Mile Beach on the west coast and a number of beaches and bays along the east coast. The unspoilt beaches and coastline, together with high year-round temperatures, make this region an appealing holiday destination. The peninsula offers swimming, walking, sand tobogganing and fishing.

⑥ Ninety Mile Beach
The hard sand on the beach makes it a popular area for farm biking and coach tours, as well as for cycling and marathons.

0 kilometres 6
0 miles 6

Key
━ Tour route
━ Scenic route
═ Other roads

⑤ Cape Reinga Lighthouse
Visible from a distance of 48 km (26 nautical miles) offshore, the solitary, whitewashed Cape Reinga Lighthouse is New Zealand's northernmost lighthouse.

For hotels and restaurants in this region see pp302–3 and pp315–17

③ Spirits Bay
This sacred Māori area is the starting point for the 28 km (17 mile) walking track to Cape Reinga.

Digging for Shellfish

Gathering *kai moana* (seafood) – fishing from boats or the shore, diving for fish, or digging in the sand for shellfish – is a Kiwi tradition. At Ninety Mile Beach, people are likely to be searching for *tuatua*, a shellfish that is plentiful in the area. Visitors can collect 150 *tuatua* per person per day. They can also snorkel or free dive for *paua* (abalone), which are found in rocky areas including at the very top of Ninety Mile Beach. The limit for *paua* is ten per diver per day, and each must be over 125 mm (5 inches) in length.

Digging for *tuatua* at Ninety Mile Beach

② Rarawa Beach
Sparkling white silica sand makes Rarawa Beach one of the most attractive beaches on the east coast.

① Gumdiggers Park
Take a walk around this park and learn about the ecology of the Manuka regrowth forest and its inhabitants.

④ Te Paki Reserve
Tobogganing off the massive sand dunes is the main attraction here but there is also a pleasant 40-minute walk to the beach.

Tips for Drivers

Length: 210 km (130 miles).
Stopping-off points: There are places to stay and eat between Kaitaia and Waitaki Landing. There is a further 21 km (13 mile) drive to the lighthouse. As an alternative to returning on State Hwy 1, 4WD vehicles can access Ninety Mile Beach at Te Paki, 16 km (10 miles) south of Cape Reinga Lighthouse, and exit near Waipapakauri Beach. Trips should be made two hours before or after high tide. Visitors are advised to take a coach tour, as rental cars are not allowed on the beach.

Map labels:
North Cape
okaikai Scenic eserve
Great Exhibition Bay
Henderson Bay
Pukenui
Houhora Heads
Mohutangi
Hukatere
Waipapakauri Beach

For keys to symbols *see back flap*

Boatshed Café and Gallery at Rawene

⑯ Kaikohe

Road map E1. ⛰ 4,100. 🚍
W **northlandnz.com**

A service centre for farms in the area, Kaikohe is best known for the **Ngawha Hot Springs** (Waiaraki Pools). While such hot springs have been turned into major tourist attractions in places such as Rotorua (see pp138–9), they are mainly a local feature in Kaikohe, where most visitors and the attendant are on first-name terms. Outsiders are welcome, and if they can accept the springs' unadorned character, they will enjoy the hot spring waters with temperatures between 32 and 42 °C (90 and 108 °F).

Kaikohe's **Heritage Kaikohe** indoor and outdoor museum is a collection of houses and artifacts related to the district's early Māori and European history. A conducted tour takes visitors to attractions from the 1862 Old Courthouse to Maioha Cottage (1875), Utakura Settlers Hall (1891) and Alexander's Sawmill (1913). There are also vintage vehicles, a fire station, a bush railway and a small railway station. From a hillside monument to Chief Hone Heke (grand-nephew of the old chief), there are fine views of both coasts.

🏕 **Ngawha Hot Springs**
Ngawha Springs Rd, off SH 12.
Tel (09) 405 2245. **Open** daily.
Closed public hols. 🅿

🏛 **Pioneer Village Kaikohe**
1a Recreation Rd. **Tel** (09) 401 0816.
Open daily. **Closed** 1 Jan, Good Fri, 25 & 26 Dec. 🅿 🔥 🚻 📷

⑰ Rawene

Road map D1. ⛰ 520. 🚍
ℹ Boatshed Café and Gallery, Clendon Esplanade, (09) 405 7728.
W **northlandnz.com**

This quaint village, which has shops jutting out over the water, was home to James Reddy Clendon (1800–72), the first US Consul in New Zealand. He later became Hokianga's Resident Magistrate. **Clendon House**, now owned by the New Zealand Historic Places Trust, was probably built after 1866.

The ferry across Hokianga Harbour links with an alternative route to Kaitaia, via Broadwood and Herekino.

🏛 **Clendon House**
Clendon Esplanade. **Tel** (09) 405 7874.
Open Sat–Mon. **Closed** May–Oct & 25 Dec. 📷 W **historic.org.nz**

⑱ Opononi

Road map D1. ⛰ 600. 🚍 🚌
ℹ Hokianga i-SITE, State Hwy 12, (09) 405 8869. W **northlandnz.com**

In the minds of many New Zealanders, the small beach town of Opononi is forever linked to that of its most famous visitor, Opo. This dolphin became a national celebrity when it spent the summer of 1955 playing with children and performing tricks with beach balls. Sadly, it was killed by unknown dynamite fishers. A sculpture by Christchurch artist Russell Clark marked the dolphin's grave outside Opononi's pub. Although the statue has been removed, a video of Opo can be viewed at the Hokianga i-SITE information centre.

Diagonally across the road from where Opo's statue was loacted, is the wharf, which is the starting point for a short boat trip to see, at close range, the giant sand dunes on the far side of Hokianga Harbour.

Hokianga Harbour in Opononi

The Early Kauri Gum Industry

As the immigrants of the 19th century rapidly depleted the country's native forests of kauri trees, a new industry began to emerge. Resin, exuded by the trees, became a valuable commodity in the production of varnish. To reveal the location of lumps of resin, long rods were poked into the ground near dead trees, a job mostly carried out by Croatian immigrants. By 1885, 2,000 people were employed in this trade. Many of these people later turned to growing vegetables and to viticulture near Auckland.

Today, lumps of kauri gum, known as amber, are popular souvenir items. The gum is carved and polished and made into pendants and other small items. Sometimes insects or fern fragments can be seen trapped inside the finished items.

Polished kauri gum

Tane Mahuta, New Zealand's largest kauri tree

⑲ Waipoua Forest

Road map D1. 🛈 Waipoua Visitors' Centre, (09) 439 6445. **Open** daily.
🆆 **northlandnz.com**

Waipoua Forest is well worth a visit because of its magnificent kauri trees. Being in the presence of a tree that has entered its third millennium is a memorable experience, as photos seldom capture the grandeur of these trees. Local Māori have christened the country's largest living kauri Tane Mahuta, "Lord of the Forest". Reached by an easy 5-minute walk from the road through the park, the tree is 51 m (168 ft) high, has a girth of 14 m (46 ft) and a volume of 244.5 cu m (8,635 cu ft). Department of Conservation experts estimate the tree to be about 2,000 years old. Four other known giant trees in the forest are at least 1,000 years old. The forest also contains around 300 species of trees, palms and ferns.

⑳ Dargaville

Road map E1. 🏔 4,900. 🚌
🛈 4 Murdoch St, (09) 439 4975.
🆆 **northlandnz.com**

Dargaville is the nation's *kumara* capital and many road stalls with honesty boxes offer the opportunity to buy these sweet potatoes. The **Dargaville Museum** is not just of interest to sailors. Apart from Māori canoes, ship models and other nautical items, the displays range from old photos of the local Croatian Social Club to memorabilia from the Northern Wairoa Scottish Society and a pig skull from New Mexico.

🏛 **Dargaville Museum**
32 Mt Wesley Coast Rd, Harding Park. **Tel** (09) 439 7555. **Open** daily. **Closed** 25 Dec. 🅿🚹📷📹

Environs
Located 45 km (28 miles) south of Dargaville, the **Kauri Museum** in Matakohe gives visitors an insight into kauri trees, especially after a trip through Waipoua Forest Park. The museum illustrates the role these mammoth trees played in New Zealand's pioneering history. A steam sawmill, with mannequins representing local settler families, shows how the logs were milled.

Within the main museum there is also kauri furniture, carvings and timber panels as well as an extensive collection of carved and polished kauri gum. Outside is a kauri post office from 1909, a 6-room fully furnished early 20th-century home and an 1867 pioneer church.

The **Kai-Iwi Lakes**, 34 km (21 miles) north of Dargaville, are well worth a visit and are frequented by locals and visitors. Comprising the Waikere, Taharoa and Kai-Iwi, these brilliant blue lakes are popular with swimmers, water-skiers, fishermen, picnickers and campers.

🏛 **Kauri Museum**
5 Church Rd, Matakohe. **Tel** (09) 431 7417. **Open** daily. **Closed** 25 Dec. 🅿🚹📷 by arrangement. 📹
🆆 **kaurimuseum.com**

Boat exhibit in the Dargaville Museum

THE CENTRAL NORTH ISLAND

Stretching from Auckland down to Taranaki, Manawatu and Hawkes Bay, this area includes beautiful and varied natural and man-made sights: snow-capped volcanoes, geothermal features, trout-filled lakes and rivers, mountain ranges, sandy beaches, fertile farmlands, prolific orchards and vineyards, and extensive forests. It is also a major centre of Māori history and culture.

Cutting a swathe from White Island in the north to Mount Ruapehu in the south, the Taupo Volcanic Zone *(see pp68–9)*, is testimony to underground forces that have fashioned the central plateau. Rotorua has a range of thermal attractions: geysers, bubbling mud pools, multi-coloured silica terraces, steaming lakes and streams and hot mineral pools. Lakes dotting the plateau offer excellent fishing, while rivers flowing from them are used for white-water rafting and jet-boating. In winter there is downhill skiing on the slopes of Mount Ruapehu in Tongariro National Park. Steep, rugged, bush-clad ranges stretch 300 km (186 miles) from the volcanic plateau to the East Cape, separating the temperate area to the west from the warm, dry east coast region. Farming and forestry are well established in the Bay of Plenty, King Country and Waikato. Dairy farmers compete with horticulturists for the best land, while sheep, cattle and deer roam larger paddocks on hills clear-felled of their native forest in the 19th and early 20th centuries. The Coromandel Peninsula, gripped by gold fever in the latter half of the 19th century, is now home to alternative lifestylers and artists inspired by its natural beauty. The curving Bay of Plenty, the scenic East Cape and the beaches of Gisborne offer excellent swimming, fishing and surfing, while the Hobbiton™ Movie Set, as featured in *The Lord of the Rings* films, awaits you near Matamata.

The entire region is rich in Māori history, and Rotorua is the main centre for Māori cultural experiences. The Waikato-based Māori King Movement *(see p121)* began here in 1858, shortly before battles waged between the government and Māori over land.

Māori cultural performance at Rotorua

◀ The geothermal vents and stream at Waimangu, Rotorua

Exploring the Central North Island

The Central North Island contains a wide range of landscapes and activities. Hamilton, the region's metropolitan hub, is set among lush farmland close to the western surf beaches of Raglan and the magical Waitomo Caves. North of Hamilton, the rugged Coromandel Peninsula flows into sandy, unspoilt Bay of Plenty beaches, the East Cape and the east coast, all popular spots for fishing and watersports. Hawke's Bay is famous for its Art Deco buildings, orchards and vineyards. Geothermal attractions stretch from lunar-landscaped White Island to the volcano Ruapehu, the North Island's best skiing location. At the bottom of the region, Tongariro National Park offers a wilderness experience.

Hawke's Bay vineyard

Top Outdoor Activities. The places shown here have been selected for their recreational activities. Conditions vary depending on the weather and the time of year, so exercise caution and, if in doubt, seek local advice.	Game Fishing	Golf	Scuba Diving/ Snorkelling	Skiing	Surfing	Swimming	Hiking	Trout Fishing
Coromandel		●	●		●	●	●	
Gisborne	●	●	●		●	●	●	●
Mayor Island	●		●			●	●	
Mount Maunganui/Tauranga	●	●			●	●	●	
Opotiki		●			●	●	●	
Raglan		●	●		●	●	●	
Rotorua		●				●	●	●
Taupo		●				●	●	●
Te Urewera National Park						●	●	●
Tongariro National Park		●		●		●	●	
Turangi		●				●	●	●
Whitianga	●	●	●			●	●	

Cape Colville **12 PORT JACKSON**

COROMANDEL TOWN 11   **WHITIANGA 13**   14 HAHE

Firth of Thames   25   COROMANDEL FOREST PARK   Pauan

Auckland   THAMES   10   9   26   15
Waitakaruru   2   WHANGAMATA

Tuakau   Paeroa   16   WA
Te Kauwhata   Lake Waikare
22
Huntly   Te Aroha

Pukemiro   26   KATIKA
Waingaro Hot Springs   1 NGARUAWAHIA   Morrinsville   27
TASMAN SEA   2   5   Matamata
HAMILTON   6 CAMBRIDGE
RAGLAN   3   Tirau
PIRONGIA FOREST PARK   3   Te Awamutu   Putar
KAWHIA   4   WAIKATO

7 OTOROHANGA   Tokoroa
WAITOMO CAVES   8   Te Kuiti   32
Mangakino
Piopio   30   Whakamaru
New Plymouth   3   Benneydale
4

Okahukura   La   Ta
Taumarunui   32

Owhango   TURANGI 34
National Park   35   TONGARIRO NP   1
Mount Ruapehu 2797m
Wanganui   MANAWA   WANGANI
Ohakune
Waiouru

Key
— Major road
···· Minor road
══ Toll road
— Scenic route
⋯ Major railway
···· Minor railway
— Regional border
△ Summit

For hotels and restaurants in this region see pp302–3 and pp315–17

Sights at a Glance

Māori meeting house at Te Kaha, Bay of Plenty

Getting Around

The best way to tour the Central North Island is by car. State Highway 1 bisects the region, while the scenic Pacific Coast and Thermal Explorer highways hug the Coromandel Peninsula, Bay of Plenty and East Cape. Roads are usually in good repair, but in winter snow may close roads near Tongariro National Park. A passenger train service links Auckland with Wellington, with stops at Hamilton and other main towns. Local buses and tour companies operate throughout the region.

For keys to symbols *see back flap*

❶ Ngaruawahia

Road map E2. 🚩 6,500. 🚌
ℹ 156 Great South Rd, Huntly,
(07) 828 6406. 🎏 Ngaruawahia
Regatta (third Sat in March).
w hamiltonwaikato.com

Situated where the Waikato and Waipa rivers meet at the edge of the central Waikato Basin, Ngaruawahia is one of the oldest and most historic settlements in Waikato and an important centre of Māori culture. On the northeastern bank of the river, off River Road, is one of the Māori people's most important locations – Turangawaewae Marae, "the footstool" or home of the Waikato Tainui tribe. Turongo House, located within the *marae*, is the official residence of the reigning Māori monarch, Tuheitia Paki. Although Turangawaewae Marae is considered too sacred for tourism, and visitors are likely to be referred to Rotorua where Māori cultural experiences are widely available, the *marae* is open to the public for the annual Ngaruawahia Regatta on the river, which features *waka* (canoe) racing, *iwi* dance competitions and other activities *(see p46)*.

The 1863–64 Waikato War was a pivotal moment in New Zealand's history. Māori united to protect their land and formed a resistance movement known as Te Kingitanga. A look at the Waikato War Driving Tour on www.thewaikatowar.co.nz will reveal how this war unfolded and explain the events at these sites.

The single-plume Bridal Veil Falls in Raglan

In the Hakarimata Scenic Reserve on the slopes of the Hakarimata Range to the north of Ngaruawahia, native rimu and kauri trees grow beside three well-marked tracks, which offer excellent hiking and views of the Waikato Basin.

Environs
Waingaro Hot Springs, 30 km (19 miles) west of Ngaruawahia, features four open-air mineral water pools ranging in temperature from 32 to 42° C (89 to 107° F) as well as private spa pools. New Zealand's longest hot water hydroslide as well as bumper boats offer plenty of excitement. A range of accommodation options is available at the springs.

🏊 **Waingaro Hot Springs**
Waingaro Rd. **Tel** (07) 825 4761.
Open daily. 🎿

❷ Raglan

Road map E2. 🚩 3,100. 🚌
ℹ 13 Wainui Rd, (07) 825 0556.
🎏 Raglan Surf Classic (Nov).

A laid-back coastal town with friendly locals and a thriving arts scene, Raglan fills with visitors during summer who are drawn to the water-sports available in its tranquil harbour, its good swimming beaches and its excellent surfing. Te Kopua Beach and Te Aro Aro Bay, close to Raglan, are popular for swimming, while Manu and Whale Bays, a ten-minute drive south along the coast, are famous worldwide among surfers for their left-hand break, purportedly the longest in the world.

The 25 km (15 mile) drive south along Raglan's narrow coastal Whaanga Road provides

Turangawaewae Marae, Ngaruawahia, home of the Māori king

For hotels and restaurants in this region see pp303–4 and pp317–19

fantastic views of the coastline and the swells of the Tasman Sea.

About 21 km (13 miles) southeast of Raglan, an easy 10-minute walk through dense bush leads to the Bridal Veil Falls. The 55 m (180 ft) waterfall plunges in a single plume from a rock cleft to a deep pool below. A stepped track continues to the base of the falls and an even more dramatic vantage point with views across the pool and up at the falls.

Mount Pirongia, an extinct volcanic peak

Whale Bay, Raglan, world famous for its surfing

❸ Pirongia Forest Park

Road map E3. 🛈 Pirongia Heritage and Information Centre, 798 Franklin St, Pirongia, (07) 871 9018.

This park, comprising four separate forest areas south and southeast of Raglan, contains an extensive network of trails, from easy walks on the lower peaks to more strenuous hikes higher up. At 959 m (3,146 ft),

Mount Pirongia, an ancient volcano lying southeast of Raglan, is the most obvious landmark in the park; its dramatic skyline and dark green forest contrast strongly with the surrounding farmland. Closer to Raglan, 756 m (2,480 ft) Mt Karioi rises sharply from the coastline. Tracks lead to both peaks.

During the summer months it is advisable to carry drinking water when walking on the tracks. A number of native birds can be seen along the tracks and around the park's margins. Several native fish species and a huge variety of aquatic invertebrates can be found in the park's streams.

A hut on Mount Pirongia – Pahautea – sleeps six to eight people. Hut tickets are available from the Department of Conservation in Hamilton. There are picnic areas at the end of both Corcoran and Grey roads and a camping area alongside trout-filled Kaniwhaniwha Stream.

❹ Kawhia

Road map E3. 🚹 550. 🛈 Kawhia Museum & Information Centre, Kaora St, (07) 871 0161.

Located on the coast 55 km (34 miles) to the south of Raglan, along winding but scenic back roads, the small settlement of Kawhia comprises a jumble of cottages on the north side of Kawhia Harbour, 5 km (3 miles) from the Tasman Sea. The harbour is remote, splendid and huge, its shoreline twisting and turning for 57 km (35 miles).

In former times, Māori prized the harbour and the fertile valleys running down to it and fought over rights to the area. The Māori migration canoe Tainui, which plied the coastline eight centuries ago, is buried on the slopes behind the Makatu meeting house. Stones placed 23 m (75 ft) apart above the bow and stern mark its position. The canoe was once moored to a pohutukawa tree, Tangi te Korowhiti, on the shore at the end of Karewa Street. Now a large clump of pohutukawas, the tree is still revered by the Tainui people as signifying the beginning of their association with Aotearoa.

The large Kawhia harbour on the west coast

Māori King Movement

Queen Te Atairangikaahu

This movement grew in the 1850s out of a realization among Māori that intertribal feuding assisted the *Pakeha* (Europeans) to acquire Māori land. In 1858, several tribes chose a paramount king in the hope that the dignity and *mana* (respect) that would accrue to him would promote peaceful co-existence with the government and settle land conflicts. Instead, the government interpreted the Māori King Movement as a form of rebellion. Attitudes hardened and spawned the Waikato land wars of the 1860s *(see pp53–4)*. In 1966, Te Atairangikaahu was proclaimed queen. She was succeeded by King Tuheitia Paki in 2006, the seventh monarch. His role is mainly cultural and spiritual, though this is becoming more important as the place of the Māori in New Zealand society is reassessed.

❺ Hamilton

Road map E2. ⛰ 118,000. ✈ 10 km (6 miles) S of city. 🚌 ℹ Cnr Aro and Alexandra Sts, Garden Place, (07) 839 3580. 🎈 Balloons Over Waikato (Apr); National Agricultural Fieldays (Jun). 🅦 **hamiltonwaikato.com**

New Zealand's fourth largest metropolitan area and largest inland city, Hamilton straddles a meandering section of the mighty Waikato River, at 425 km (264 miles) the longest in the country. The city has grown from a 19th-century military settlement into a bustling centre servicing the Waikato region, a huge undulating plain. Attractive parks and gardens, dissected by footpaths, border the river, and bridges connect the east and west banks. The **Waikato River Explorer** cruises the river from its landing at Hamilton Gardens Jetty, offering the best views of the area.

Perched on five levels above the river, the **Waikato Museum** features a large collection of New Zealand art, Waikato history and history of the local Tainui people. On permanent display is an impressive war canoe, Te Winika.

The **Hamilton Gardens**, located at the southern end of the city, are Hamilton's most popular visitor attraction with over a million visitors a year. Set along a scenic stretch of the Waikato River, they have pavilions showcasing the history of gardens through time, including the Italian Renaissance, Indian Char Bagh, Modernist, and New Zealand's only traditional Māori garden, Te Parapara.

Hamilton hosts Balloons Over Waikato, a fiesta which attracts balloonists from around the world, and the National Agricultural Fieldays at nearby Mystery Creek, one of Australasia's largest agricultural trade shows (see p47).

🚢 Waikato River Explorer
Hamilton Gardens Jetty. **Tel** (0800) 139 756. **Open** Tue–Thu, Sat & Sun. 🚻 ♿ ✐ 🅦 **waikatoexplorer.co.nz**

🏛 Waikato Museum
1 Grantham St. **Tel** (07) 838 6606. **Open** 10am–5pm daily. **Closed** 25 Dec. 🚻 ♿ 🖵 📷 🅦 **waikatomuseum. co.nz**

🌿 Hamilton Gardens
Hungerford Crescent, SH1 off Cobham Drive. **Tel** (07) 838 6782. **Open** daily. ♿ 🖵 🅦 **hamiltongardens.co.nz**

❻ Cambridge

Road map E3. ⛰ 13,500. ✈ 15 km (9 miles) E of city. ℹ Cnr Queen & Victoria sts, (07) 823 3456.

Fifteen minutes' drive south of Hamilton, Cambridge lies amid farmland, home to New Zealand's thoroughbred horse industry. Known as "the town of trees" because of its avenues of oak and elm, the town has a charming village green and pretty gardens. The domain around Lake Koutu, fringed by exotic trees and native bush, is a popular place for walks and picnics.

Cambridge is also known for its contemporary art and crafts outlets. The town's numerous antique shops and galleries are another major attraction.

Visitors can also view a potpourri of architectural styles at St. Andrew's church and the public buildings along and adjacent to Victoria Street.

Bag End, one of the Hobbit Holes™ at the Hobbiton™ Movie Set, Matamata

Environs
The rolling hills just west of **Matamata**, 40 km (25 miles) from Cambridge, is home to the Hobbiton™ Movie Set where you step into the lush meadows of The Shire™, the same as when Peter Jackson filmed the *Lord of the Rings* and *The Hobbit* trilogies. Guests are guided around the movie set, taking in all the Hobbit Holes™, the Mill and into the Green Dragon™ Inn, where a beverage concludes the visit to Middle-earth. This is an extremely popular attraction, so booking is essential. The 2-hour tours run every 30 minutes between 8.30am and 3.30pm daily.

❼ Otorohanga

Road map E3. ⛰ 2,600. 🚉 🚌 ℹ 27 Turonga St, (07) 873 8951.

Fifty kilometres (31 miles) south of Hamilton lies Otorohanga, a small town whose main attraction is the **Otorohanga Kiwi House**. Three kiwi species are bred at the zoological park and 300 birds, representing 29 species, many of which can be viewed in a massive walk-through aviary. In addition to kiwi, these include native pigeons, tui, silvereyes, parakeets and saddlebacks. Geckos, weta, and tuataras (an ancient reptile) are also displayed.

Otorohanga is regarded as the gateway to the Waitomo Caves (see pp124–5).

🥝 Otorohanga Kiwi House
20 Alex Telfer Drive. **Tel** (07) 873 7391. **Open** daily. **Closed** 25 Dec. 🚻 ♿ 🌙 Nocturnal House. 📷 🅦 **kiwi house.org.nz**

The *Waikato River Explorer* cruising on the Waikato River

Stock–Stud Heartland

One of the most fascinating sights on the drive between Hamilton and Cambridge is the wooden-railed fences behind which young thoroughbred horses cavort, growing strong on the best pasture and supplementary feed their owners can provide. Set back from the road are signposted stud stables where the horses are housed and trained. Black and white cows grazing on dappled green fields can also be seen. New Zealand's thoroughbred racehorse and dairy cattle stud industries are concentrated in the Waikato region. Here a mild, wet climate produces lush cattle pasture and the rolling plains that are ideal for exercising and training racehorses.

Thoroughbred yearlings and foals on a Waikato stud farm

Thoroughbred Horses

Waikato is renowned internationally for its racing progeny, and the yearling export industry earns the country more than NZ$120 million annually. Some 60 stallions are available for breeding purposes at 18 Waikato commercial thoroughbred studs, the most sought after of these sires mating 100–150 mares.

New Zealand Horse Magic, 6 km (4 miles) south of Cambridge, showcases a collection of horse breeds and features an informative hour-long show. Thoroughbred stud tours are also available at other stud farms in the area.

Waikato-bred horses have won Australia's Melbourne Cup, the pinnacle of the Australasian racing season, 18 times.

New Zealand's main dairy breeds – Holstein-Friesian, Jersey and Ayrshire – can be found in Waikato, although the Holstein-Friesian predominates. The average New Zealand cow produces 3,420 litres (752 imperial gallons) of milk a year.

New Zealand's thoroughbred industry is showcased to the world each February at the yearling sale held at Karaka on the southern outskirts of Auckland.

❽ Waitomo Caves

The area known as Waitomo consists of a 45 km (28 mile) network of underground limestone caves and grottoes linked to the Waitomo Stream. A chamber of the Waitomo Glowworm Caves was first explored in 1887, but most caves remain the domain of cavers and speleologists. Apart from touring the Waitomo Glowworm, Ruakuri and Aranui caves, famous for their glowworm grottoes and fantastic limestone formations, visitors can enjoy a range of cave-based adventure activities, including abseiling into a limestone shaft and cave system, and black-water rafting, an adventure sport unique to New Zealand. The caves that are accessible to the public have superb lighting, good paths, handrails and informative local guides.

Waitomo Walkway
A 5 km (3 mile) walk over farmland and through native bush takes visitors past typical limestone karst features such as outcrops, small caves and sinkholes.

Black-water Rafting
Equipped with wet suits, lights and "cave rafts" (inner tubes), these black-water rafters drift in darkness, beneath millions of glowworms, along an underground river in the Ruakuri Cave.

Te Anga Road

Waitomo stream

Tumutumu Road

KEY

① **The Ruakuri Natural Tunnel**, a large U-shaped tunnel, is reached by a 30-minute walk up the Ruakuri Gorge. Ruakuri Cave is accessible to wheelchairs and guided tours are available.

② **The Tokikarpu meeting house**, off Te Anga Road, serves the needs of the local Māori people.

③ **The Waitomo Caves Hotel**, built in 1908, nestles among trees on a hill above Waitomo village. It has rooms to suit every traveller.

④ **Kiwi Paka YHA Waitomo hostel**

⑤ **The Museum of Caves**, which includes the Waitomo i-SITE Visitor Centre, has excellent displays on caves and natural history as well as a multi-media show about the New Zealand glowworms.

⑥ **Waitomo Top Ten Holiday Park camping ground**

Key

⸬ Road
═ River
▬ Walking track

0 metres 500
0 yards 500

★ Aranui Cave
The high chambers, magnificent formations and pale brown, pink and white shades of the huge stalactites are the finest to be seen in Waitomo's caves.

★ Waitomo Glowworm Caves
A walk through the three levels of the caves – the Banquet Chamber, Pipe Organ and Cathedral – is capped by a tranquil boat ride through the magical Glowworm Grotto.

VISITORS' CHECKLIST

Practical Information
Road map E3. *i* 21 Waitomo Caves Rd, (07) 878 7640. All sights: **Open** daily. **Closed** 25 Dec. Waitomo Museum of Caves: **Tel** (07) 878 7640. Waitomo Glowworm Caves: **Tel** (07) 878 8227. ✉ in Waitomo Caves. 🎬 Woodlyn Park: **Tel** (07) 878 6666. 🎭 Pioneer Show. Black Water "Rafting": **Tel** 0800 228 464. 🎬 Lost World: **Tel** 0800 924 866.

Transport
🚌 from Hamilton, Auckland and Rotorua.

State Highway 3 and Lost world →

Formation of the Waitomo Caves

Caves are formed through the erosion of layers of limestone by water flowing underground. The cave systems in the Waitomo area have developed in fractured limestone, up to 100 m (330 ft) thick, along or adjacent to major fault lines *(see p26)* where percolation of groundwater is particularly high. Surface water flowing down cracks in the limestone created an underground drainage system which gradually increased in size and complexity. Inside the Waitomo caves, dripping water containing dissolved limestone has formed stalactites on the cave roofs, stalagmites on the floors, and other fascinating formations.

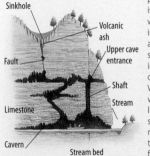

Sinkhole
Volcanic ash
Upper cave entrance
Fault
Shaft
Stream
Limestone
Cavern
Stream bed

Lost World
The Lost World involves a 100 m (330 ft) abseil descent into a huge limestone shaft followed by an amazing caving expedition through the Mangapu Cave system.

Karaka Bird Hide on the Firth of Thames

❾ Thames

Road Map E2. 🏙 10,000. ✈ 2 km (1.2 miles) S of town. 🚌
🛈 206 Pollen St, (07) 868 7284.
🎭 Pohutakawa Festival (Nov–Dec).
🆆 **thamesinfo.co.nz**

Located at the southeastern corner of the Firth of Thames, against hills that 100 years ago rang to the sound of battery stamps pounding quartz ore to extract gold, Thames is the principal town of the Coromandel region. It services surrounding farmland and a swelling coastal population. It is the gateway to the Coromandel Peninsula and an ideal base from which to explore the Coromandel Forest Park wilderness area. Many buildings in the town owe their grandeur to wealth created during the gold-mining era.

The **Thames Historical Museum** features relics from the town's past, including the pioneering foundries that sprang up to support the mining industry, while the **Thames School of Mines and Mineralogical Museum** features 5,000 mineral samples and equipment used to process quartz ore and extract gold. Mine managers were taught in the school's classroom from 1885 to 1954.

A large World War I memorial, off Waiotahi Creek Road, stands on a hill above the town to the north, and affords panoramic views of the town, the Firth of Thames, and the Hauraki Gulf

beyond. At the small Karaka Bird Hide, built among mangroves off Brown Street on the edge of town, migratory wading birds can be seen, especially between high and low tides.

🏛 **Thames Historical Museum**
Cnr Pollen & Cochrane sts. **Tel** (07) 868 8509. **Open** 1–4pm daily. 🎨 🏠
⛔ 🏠

🏛 **Thames School of Mines and Mineralogical Museum**
101 Cochrane St. **Tel** (07) 868 6227.
Open Jan–Feb: daily; Mar–Dec: Wed–Sun. **Closed** Good Fri, 25 Dec.
🎨 🏠 🏠

Environs
Along the Firth of Thames' southern edge, 85 sq km (33 sq miles) of rich, intertidal mud flats provide another excellent habitat for migratory wading birds, such as gulls, shags, oystercatchers and pied stilts, and opportunities to observe them. The **Miranda Shorebird**

Trampers in the Kauaeranga Valley, Coromandel Forest Park

Centre, established by the Miranda Naturalists' Trust, can arrange tours to see the birds as well as accommodation. Nearby is the Miranda Hot Springs, a thermal pool complex.

🐦 **Miranda Shorebird Centre**
285 East Coast Rd, Pokeno.
Tel (09) 232 2781. **Open** daily.
Closed 25 Dec. 🎨 donation. ⛔ 🏠
🆆 **miranda-shorebird.org.nz**

❿ Coromandel Forest Park

Road map E2. 🛈 Kauaeranga Valley, Thames, (07) 867 9080.

This park stretches for 100 km (62 miles) along the peninsula's interior, but the most accessible part is the forested Kauaeranga Valley, with its well-developed network of short walks, longer hikes and picnic areas.

The valley was a major source of kauri timber from the 1870s to the 1920s. Remains of dams, trestle bridges and river booms, used to flush kauri logs into the Kauaeranga River, are evident.

Anglers can fish for trout in the valley's streams where the keen-eyed may also find gemstones. A rocky ridge known as the Pinnacles offers fine views of both coastlines. The Kauaeranga Visitor Centre, 13 km (8 miles) northeast of Thames, provides details of walks and hikes that comprise the Kauaeranga Kauri Trail, a pack track made by kauri bushmen, as well as park accommodation.

Gold Fever in the Coromandel

The first significant gold find on the Coromandel Peninsula occurred in October 1852 near Coromandel Town. Three hundred diggers rushed to the area. Further discoveries near Thames in 1867 attracted 5,000 men into the surrounding hills. Soon Thames became a boom town and its population mushroomed to 18,000. Miners thronged the town on Saturdays, three live theatres were seldom closed, and more than 100 hotels sold liquor. However, by the 1870s the Thames goldfields were in decline and interest had shifted southeast to Karangahake Mountain and to Waihi. By 1912, Waihi's Martha Mine had become one of the world's largest *(see p130)*. The mines all closed eventually, but new goldbearing zones found within old fields prompted large-scale mining operations to begin once more at the open mining pit at Waihi from 1988 to 2007.

Candles provided light and indicated the presence of gas.

A mallet and pick were used to loosen gold-bearing rock.

Gold-Mining Relics

Old gold mines, shafts, mine dumps and abandoned mining machinery are dotted around Thames. The mining school and mineralogical museum, as well as the gold mine tours on offer, are further reminders of the town's gold-mining history. Coromandel gold had to be laboriously extracted from the ground with pick and shovel.

Canvas bags held any nuggets that were extracted.

Model of a miner at the Thames Gold Mine and Stamper Battery

Orange calcite

Goodlitite

Amethyst

Stitchtite

Pink tourmoline

Coromandel is also rich in semi-precious gemstones. It is still possible to stumble across agate on some of the beaches north of Thames.

This classroom in the Thames School of Mines provided practical instruction for gold-miners working the quartz fields.

Fossicking for gold in the old gold mines is a popular pastime but be sure when entering an old mine that it is structurally safe.

The Imperial Hotel, one of a number of fine colonial hotels in Thames built at the height of the town's gold-rush prosperity.

⑪ Coromandel Town

Road map E2. 🏔 1,500. ✈ 3 km (2 miles) S of town. 🚌 ⓘ 85 Kapanga Rd, (07) 866 8598. 🅦 **coromandel town.co.nz**

Coromandel Town, as it is referred to in order to distinguish it from the peninsula (referred to as The Coromandel), is a quiet fishing and crafts town about an hour's drive north of Thames. It owes its name to the 1820 visit of HMS *Coromandel*, which called to load kauri spars for the British Royal Navy. Mining featured prominently in the town's formative years (*see p127*), and fine examples of Victorian and colonial architecture are a legacy of that era. The laid-back atmosphere and beauty of the area make it a haven for artists and crafts people, and an ideal place in which to walk, swim, fish, sail or simply relax.

One of Coromandel Town's most popular attractions is the **Driving Creek Railway and Potteries**, built by New Zealand potter Barry Brickell to convey clay and wood to his kiln, and to service a kauri forest replanting project. The narrow-gauge mountain railway takes visitors in specially designed carriages on a 1-hour round trip through native forest and tunnels and across bridges to a viewpoint high above Coromandel.

The **Coromandel Gold Stamper Battery** and a 100-year-old gold-processing museum, featuring a working water wheel, lie at the end of Buffalo Road to the north.

Water-powered bicycle at the Waterworks, a fun-park set in lovely gardens

The **Coromandel School of Mines and Historical Museum** has displays of early gold-mining and kauri logging, and an old jailhouse.

🚂 **Driving Creek Railway and Potteries**
380 Driving Creek Rd. **Tel** (07) 866 8703. **Open** daily. **Closed** 25 April, 25 Dec. 🅿 🚻 📷
🅦 **drivingcreekrailway.co.nz**

⚒ **Coromandel Gold Stamper Battery**
Buffalo Rd. **Tel** (07) 866 7933. **Open** summer: daily; winter: Thu–Mon. **Closed** 25 Dec. 🅿 🚻

🏛 **Coromandel School of Mines and Historical Museum**
841 Rings Rd. **Tel** (07) 866 8039. **Open** summer: daily; winter: Sat & Sun. **Closed** 25 Dec. 🅿 🚻

Environs
The delightful **Waterworks**, 9 km (5.5 miles) from Coromandel Town, showcase artist Chris Ogilvie's genius for inventing water-powered art forms and gadgets that amaze both children and adults. One of Coromandel's most innovative attractions, The Water-works is set in park-like gardens.

Just east of the waterworks is a turn-off to Castle Rock. At 525 m (1,722 ft), it is the core of an old volcano on the "backbone" of the peninsula. A drive through pine forest takes visitors to the start of a 45-minute walk. The last few metres are a strenuous climb, but panoramic views make it worthwhile. Further along the road is the Waiau Kauri Grove where magnificent kauris, protected for more than 100 years, can be seen ten minutes' walk along a track on the left side of the road.

🌿 **The Waterworks**
471 The 309 Rd. **Tel** (07) 866 7191. **Open** daily. 🅿 🚻 📷
🅦 **waiauwaterworks.co.nz**

Coastline between Coromandel Town and Port Jackson

⑫ Port Jackson

Road map E2. 🏔 10. ⓘ 85 Kapanga Rd, Coromandel Town, (07) 866 8598.

At the tip of the peninsula, 56 km (35 miles) north of Coromandel Town, Port Jackson's long, lupin-backed beach comes as a surprise. The road, which is unsealed from the small settlement of Colville, the last supply point, ends at Fletcher's Bay, 6 km (4 miles) further on, a pretty pohutukawa-shaded cove with good fishing.

The Coastal Walkway, a 7 km (4.5 mile) track, leads from Fletcher's Bay to Stony Bay and takes about three hours to complete. Port Jackson, Fletcher Bay and Stony Bay all have camping grounds with toilets, cold showers and barbecue pits.

The unique Driving Creek Railway

Boats at sheltered Whitianga harbour

⓭ Whitianga

Road map E2. 🚗 3,500. ✈ 3 km (2 miles) SW of town. 🚌 ℹ 66 Albert St, (07) 866 5555. 🇼 **thecoromandel. com**

Whitianga sits on the innermost recess of Mercury Bay which was named by Captain Cook *(see p52)* when he observed a transit of the planet Mercury on his 1769 visit to the area. Whitianga provides safe boat launching, ideal during the big game fishing season from November to April. Major fishing contests occur in February and March. The tiny Mercury Bay Boating Club, at the west end of Buffalo Beach, earned world fame when it spearheaded Auckland financier Michael Fay's unsuccessful 1988 challenge to the San Diego Yacht Club for the America's Cup.

The **Mercury Bay Museum** occupies a disused dairy factory opposite the wharf on The Esplanade. It documents

Boating club logo

the Polynesian chief Kupe *(see p50)*, whose descendants are said to have occupied the town for more than 1,000 years. A short ferry ride across the narrow harbour entrance takes visitors to Ferry Landing, the original site of Whitianga, where there are walks, lookouts and craft outlets. Whitianga Rock, upstream of Ferry Landing, was formerly a *pa* site of the Ngati Hei tribe. Whitianga's Buffalo Beach is named after an 1840 shipwreck. The British ship *Buffalo*, which had delivered convicts to Australia and was to return to Britain with kauri spars, was blown by a storm onto the beach and destroyed. A cannon from the ship is mounted at the RSA Memorial Park in Albert Street.

At the northeast tip of the headland, 1.5 km (1 mile) from Ferry Landing, is Shakespeare Lookout, named after the bard. Here also, a memorial to Cook stands above Lonely Bay and Cooks Beach. Wave action at Flaxmill Bay, at the southwest

end of Front Bay, has undercut the rock to form a natural soundshell.

The **Te Whanganui-A-Hei Marine Reserve** at Cathedral Cove covers 9 sq km (4 sq miles) and extends from Cooks Bluff to Hahei Beach. It was established in 1992 to restore the area's marine environment to its former rich and varied condition. No fishing or gathering of shellfish is allowed, although visitors may swim, dive and sail in the reserve.

🏛 **Mercury Bay Museum**
11A The Esplanade. **Tel** (07) 866 0730. **Open** daily. **Closed** 25 Dec. 🚫 ♿ 🇼 mercurybaymuseum.co.nz

⓮ Hahei

Road map E2. 🚗 200. 🚌 General Store, Hahei Beach Rd.

Hahei is the start of a 2-hour return walk to Cathedral Cove, where a dramatic, cathedral-shaped cavern, accessible at low tide, cuts through a white headland. Reasonable fitness is required to reach the cove but panoramic clifftop views make the effort worthwhile. Hahei's beach is sheltered by offshore islands and tinged pink with broken shells. The area is popular with divers.

At Hot Water Beach, 6 km (4 miles) south of Hahei, visitors can dig their own thermal spa in the sand between low and mid-tides. Spades are available for hire.

Visitors soaking in hot springs in the sand at Hot Water Beach, south of Hahei

Whangamata Beach, one of New Zealand's best surf beaches

⑮ Whangamata

Road map E2. ⚑ 4,100. 🚌
ℹ 616 Port Rd, (07) 865 8340.
🌐 whangamatainfo.co.nz

The town of Whangamata, meaning "obsidian harbour", was named after the dark, glass-like volcanic rock that has washed ashore from Mayor Island, 30 km (19 miles) from the mainland. The town is often referred to as "the surfing capital of New Zealand" because of the size of the waves in the area, particularly its sandbank surf break known as "the bar". Its surf is also popular with swimmers who enjoy large waves and with surf-fishers. Other superb surfing beaches in the vicinity include Onemana and Opoutere to the north of the town and Whiritoa on the coast to the south.

The hills and valleys behind Whangamata, a short drive from the town, offer many outdoor activities. Within the Tairua Forest lie the Wentworth Valley, Taungatara Recreation Reserve and Parakiwai Valley. These are crisscrossed with walking tracks that make the most of stony streams and pockets of native bush. A popular walk takes in the "Luck at Last" gold mine and the remains of ore processors, water races, buildings and even a baker's oven. Walk details are available from the Whangamata information centre and forestry company Matariki Forests, which may close access when it is conducting forestry operations. Wharekawa Wildlife Refuge, 15 km (10 miles) north of Whangamata, is a conservation area based on the Opoutere sandspit. It is home to oyster-catchers and dotterels.

⑯ Waihi

Road map E2. ⚑ 4,500. 🚌
ℹ Seddon St, (07) 863 6715.
🌐 waihi.org.nz

The history of Waihi has been linked with gold since Robert Lee and John McCrombie discovered a gold-bearing quartz reef in 1878. The **Martha Mine**, established on the site in 1882 and worked until 1952, was the most successful of many in the district (*see pp126–7*). In 1988, the Martha Mine reopened, with concessions to operate until 2007, and substantial amounts of gold were extracted from the mine during that period of time. The mine is undergoing further exploration, with a likelihood that mining will resume in the future.

Learn about the development of gold mining in Waihi at the nearby **Gold Discovery Centre**, located opposite the iconic Cornish Pumphouse. Visitors can operate mining equipment and watch pioneer miners come alive in the Ghost Theatre.

The **Goldfields Railway** operates vintage diesel and steam trains on 7 km (4 miles) of track between Waihi and Waikino, gateway to the Karangahake gold fields.

The Karangahake Gorge Historic Walkway, a 5 km (3 mile) loop along the gorge past old bridges, abandoned mining equipment and shafts, is signposted from the road. Waihi Beach, 11 km (7 miles) east of the town, is one of the most popular along the coast.

🏛 **Gold Discovery Centre**
126 Seddon St, Waihi. **Tel** (07) 863 9015. **Open** daily. **Closed** 25 Dec.
🌿 📷 10:30am and 12:30pm daily.
🌐 golddiscoverycentre.co.nz

🚆 **Goldfields Railway**
30 Wrigley St. **Tel** (07) 863 9020. **Open** daily. **Closed** 25 Dec. 🌿 ♿ 🚻 📷

⑰ Katikati

Road map E2. ⚑ 4,000. ℹ 36 Main Rd, (07) 549 1658. 🌐 katikati.co.nz

Enthusiastic Irish colonizer George Vesey Stewart bought Katikati and its surrounding land in the 1870s and sold it to 406 "refined and educated" Ulster families. Unfamiliar with the hard work needed to break in their land, these immigrants initially resented Stewart, but the district has since proved itself ideal for horticulture and dairy farming. Today, Katikati is thought of as an open-air "art gallery". More than 35 murals and other artworks decorate its buildings, streets and parks, all produced by local artists.
Sapphire Springs & Motor Camp, set in a bush reserve 6 km (4 miles) from the town, has warm freshwater thermal springs for swimming or soaking.

🏕 **Sapphire Springs & Motor Camp**
274 Hot Springs Rd. **Tel** (07) 549 0768. **Open** daily. 🌿 📷

Mural on a building at Katikati

Coromandel's Artisan Lifestyle

The ever-changing sea, beautiful valleys and rugged forest interior of the Coromandel Peninsula not only offer a quiet alternative to city life but also provide constant inspiration to a large number of artists and crafts people. Here painters farm, potters paint and raise silkworms, and weavers rear their own sheep for wool. Since their arrival in the early 1960s, many of these "alternative lifestylers" have turned to art and crafts to support their nature-based lifestyle, honing their talents to produce a large number of items for sale in retail outlets throughout New Zealand. The Coromandel Craft Trail leaflet, available at visitor's centres, directs visitors to tucked-away studios where they can see artists at work and buy items direct at studio prices.

Bone and greenstone are popular materials for carving pendants with Māori designs.

Retail outlets in Thames and Coromandel Town, such as Weta Art, sell a wide range of Coromandel and other New Zealand-made crafts.

Barry Brickell at Driving Creek Potteries *(see p128)*

Pottery items are either thrown on a wheel or, like these pieces, hand-sculpted and glazed in a multitude of colours.

Coromandel's Crafts

Although the initial surge of artistic pursuits on the peninsula in the early 1960s focused on clay, crafts quickly diversified to include carving (in wood, bone and greenstone), kauri furniture, weaving, knitting, jewellery, leadlight glass work, hand-made knives and garden décor.

Colville Store, one of the peninsula's most unusual retail outlets, 26 km (16 miles) north of Coromandel Town, is owned by an 80-member co-operative.

Alternative lifestylers often choose to raise young children in supportive community environments where they grow organic produce, paint, sculpt and make crafts.

⑱ Tauranga

Road map E2. 🏙 including
Mount Maunganui, 120,000.
✈ 3 km (2 miles) E of town. 🚌
ℹ 95 Willow St, (07) 578 8103.
🌐 bayofplentynz.com

The largest city in the western
Bay of Plenty and an important
commercial centre and port,
Tauranga lies along a section of
the sprawling Tauranga Harbour,
a plain thought to have been
flooded at the end of the last
Ice Age. On its seaward side, the
city is sheltered by Matakana
Island and to the west by the
Kaimai Ranges.

Tauranga is a popular city.
Its benign climate and coastal
location are attractive to retired
New Zealanders and to anyone
who enjoys year-round outdoor
activities. Recreational and
competitive boating, surfing
and deep-sea fishing are among
its major attractions. It is also a
popular venue for jet-skiing,
water-skiing, windsurfing,
parasailing and diving. The
Strand, in the centre of town,
is the main shopping and
restaurant area.

Originally a flax-trading
and missionary town, Tauranga
was the scene of fierce fighting
during the New Zealand land
wars in the 1860s *(see pp53–4)*.
Many of the troops involved in
a significant battle at Gate Pa,

5 km (3 miles) south of the city,
were stationed at Monmouth
Redoubt, a military camp built
by British troops in 1864 to stop
supplies reaching the Waikato
Māori King Movement *(see p121)*.
Well-preserved earthworks and
heavy artillery, are still in place.

The Elms Mission Station,
built in stages between 1838
and 1847 by the Reverend
Alfred Brown, is one of New
Zealand's oldest homes. The
grounds contain gardens and
several buildings, including an
1839 free-standing library.

Tauranga's other attractions
include 50 km (31 miles) of
beach and foreshore reserve
and 27 km (17 miles) of public
walkways around the coast,
estuary and inland reserves.

🏛 **The Elms Mission Station**
Cnr Mission & Chapel sts. **Tel** (07) 577
9772. **Open** grounds: daily; house &
library: 2–4pm Wed, Sat, Sun & public
hols (tours by arrangement). 🎟
house & library. 🌐 theelms.org.nz

Environs
McLaren Falls Park, off State
Highway 29 on the road to
Hamilton, has walks through
picturesque native bush
interspersed with thousands
of introduced trees. A river and
Lake McLaren offer swimming.
On scheduled days throughout
the year, top white-water action

occurs downstream on the
Wairoa River when floodgates
on the hydro-controlled waterway are opened. The park has
three backpacker hostels.

🌳 **McLaren Falls Park**
McLaren Falls Rd. **Tel** Tauranga
District Council, (07) 577 7000.
Open daily. ♿

Beach at Mount Maunganui
from "The Mount"

⑲ Mount Maunganui

Road map E2. 🏙 including Tauranga,
120,000. ✈ 3 km (2 miles) S of town.
🚌 ℹ 95 Willow St, (07) 578 8103.

The town of Mount Maunganui,
built on a narrow peninsula at
the mouth of Tauranga Harbour,
is the main port for the central
North Island timber industry.
Overshadowing the town is
the 232 m (761 ft) cone-shaped
Mount Maunganui. A walk
to the summit and back takes
90 minutes and provides views
of Māori fortifications dating
from when "The Mount", as it is
commonly called, was a *pa* site.
At the top, unobstructed views
up and down the coast can be
seen. At the bottom are the
Mount Hot Pools, which are
saltwater pools heated by
natural thermal water and make
a great way to relax after a walk.

Magnificent Ocean Beach
extends east from The Mount to
Papamoa and beyond, creating
an ideal summer playground for
surfers and swimmers. In high
seas, a blowhole at Moturiki
Island, off Marine Parade, shoots
spray skywards.

♨ **Mount Hot Pools**
Adams Ave. **Tel** (07) 575 0868.
Open daily. 🎟 ♿ 📷

Game fishing competition, Tauranga

⑳ Mayor Island

Road map F2. 35 km (22 miles) from Tauranga Harbour. 🚢 from Tauranga or Whangamata. 🚹 95 Willow St, Tauranga, (07) 578 8103.

Mayor Island (Tuhua) is rather hilly and bush-clad and there are very few landing places around its steep cliffs. The highest peak, Opauhau, reaches 354 m (1,161 ft) above a roughly circular island 4 km (3 miles) across. Two lakes lie within a crater crowning the summit of what is a dormant volcano rising from the sea floor.

The island's most striking feature is black obsidian, a natural glass formed by rapid cooling of silica-rich lava. In pre-European times, Māori prized obsidian and fought battles over the island.

An 18 km (11 mile) walking track circles the island while other paths cross the interior. All sea life is protected within a marine reserve on the northern coastline. A camping ground and cabins provide accommodation, but visitors must take adequate food and water as supplies on the island are limited. Game fish in the vicinity of the island include tuna, marlin, kingfish and mako sharks. Several companies run diving and sightseeing trips to the island.

School of Splendid Perch swim over a kelp forest off Mayor Island

㉑ Te Puke

Road map F3. 🏔 6,800. 🚌
🚹 130 Jellicoe St, (07) 571 8008.
🌐 tepuke.co.nz

Te Puke is another town originally settled with Irish folk by Ulsterman George Vesey Stewart (*see p130*) in the 1880s. Early farming of sheep and cattle in the area was hampered by "bush sickness," a cobalt deficiency that dogged farming in many central North Island regions until it was identified in the 1930s and corrected with cobaltized fertilizers. With an ideal climate for sheep, cattle and dairy farming, these land uses predominated until interest in horticulture strengthened in the 1960s.

Pioneering horticulturists experimented with what was then known as the Chinese gooseberry, and developed an international market for it under a new name – kiwifruit. Since then Te Puke has been hailed as "the kiwifruit capital of the world". All aspects of the industry are displayed at the export kiwifruit orchard and horticultural park **Kiwifruit Country**. Situated alongside State Highway 33 at Paengaroa, the attraction showcases the story of the fruit with creative exhibits. There is an orchard of kiwifruit vines on site, as well as a café and retail areas.

Tours that run from the area explore the extraordinary productivity and abundance of the Bay of Plenty region, taking in spectacular horticultural estates which most tourists don't get to see. Longer trips include either the coastlines of the Bay of Plenty or other highlights of Tauranga.

🈂 **Kiwifruit Country**
State Highway 33, Paengaroa. **Tel** (07) 573 6340. **Open** daily. **Closed** 25 Dec.
🈂 🈺 💳 obligatory. 🈂 📷 🈷
🌐 kiwifruitcountrytours.co.nz

Kiwifruit

Before kiwifruit (*Actinidia chinensis*) became an international marketing success, it was known in New Zealand as the Chinese gooseberry after its country of origin. The first plant was grown in Te Puke in 1918, but it was not until the mid-1930s that Te Puke grower Jim McLoughlin planted the first orchard and sold fruit on the local market. Offshore markets were sought as more kiwifruit were grown. In the late 1960s, the industry was propelled to success by a combination of good marketing and the discovery that refrigerated kiwifruit remains in good condition for up to six months. In the late 1970s, many horticulturists became millionaires almost overnight. Since 1998, the yellow-fleshed, tropical-flavoured Zespri Gold variety has supplemented the traditional emerald green-centred Hayward variety.

Kiwifruit from Te Puke

Fishing at the mouth of the Whakatane River

㉒ Whakatane

Road map F3. 🚶 19,000. 🚌 ℹ️ Cnr Quay St & Kakahoroa Dr, (07) 306 2030, 0800 942 528. 🌐 whakatane.com

Resting in the coastal heart of the eastern Bay of Plenty, Whakatane is one of New Zealand's sunniest locations. The town enjoys more than 2,500 sunshine hours a year, making it ideal for a wide range of marine activities. These include fishing and viewing and swimming with dolphins. Whales and Dolphin Watch NZ takes visitors on a voyage out into the Bay of Plenty to swim with dolphins.

The **Whakatane Museum and Art** gives an insight into the lifestyles of early Māori and European settlers. It contains a pictorial history of the district as well as displays of Māori artifacts.

There are several excellent local walkways. One, the Nga Tapuwae O Toi Walkway, provides beautiful views of the sea and coastal pohutukawa trees. Access to the route, which takes 7 hours to complete, is from Seaview Road above the town. The first landmark is Kapu

te Rangi ("ridge of heaven"), with some of the country's oldest earthworks.

🏛️ **Whakatane Museum and Art**
51–55 Boon St. **Tel** (07) 306 0505. **Open** daily. **Closed** 1 Jan, Good Fri, 25 & 26 Dec. 🎟️ donation. ♿
🌐 whakatanemuseum.org.nz

Environs
Whale Island, 10 km (6 miles) north of the harbour entrance, is a wildlife refuge. Excursions are organized by the Whakatane Coastguard over the Christmas–New Year period. Bookings can be made at the Whakatane Visitor Centre.

East of Whakatane, idyllic **Ohope Beach** stretches 12 km (7.5 miles) from Otarawairere, its western extremity, to the mouth of tidal Ohiwa Harbour.

㉓ White Island

Road map F2. 50 km (31 miles) from Whakatane. ℹ️ White Island Tours: 15 The Strand East 0800 733 529 (freephone), 07 308 9588. 🌐 whiteisland.co.nz

New Zealand's most active volcano, White Island lies at the northern end of the Taupo–Rotorua volcanic fault line *(see pp68–9)*. It can be reached by boat or helicopter or simply viewed from the air. The island's terrain is likened to that of the moon or Mars and many visitors rate it as one of the country's best attractions. The island was mined for sulphur until 1914, when a night-time eruption killed all the miners. Remains of mining activities can be seen.

There is a large gannet colony on the island and it suffers no ill-effects from the ash fall-out. The island also offers excellent diving.

Old sulphur mining equipment on White Island

㉔ Opotiki

Road map F3. 🚶 4,150. 🚌
ℹ️ 70 Bridge St, (07) 315 3031.
🌐 opotikinz.com

Situated at the confluence of the Waioeka and Otara rivers, Opotiki is the gateway to the East Cape and the last major town before Gisborne. In 1865, at Opotiki, the Reverend Carl Sylvius Völkner was hanged and then decapitated by the Māori convinced he had passed information about their movements and fortifications to Governor George Grey *(see p80)*. Hiona St Stephen's Anglican Church, where the incident took place, lies at the northern end of the Church Street business area. A key is held across the road at the **Opotiki Museum**, which is full of early settlers' items and has a separate grocery and hardware store museum nearby.

An excellent example of a warm, temperate rainforest is Hukutaia Domain, which can be reached from the western end of Waioeka Bridge along Woodlands Road. The reserve is home to more than 2,000 native tree species, including a 2,000-year-old hollow puriri *(Vitex lucens)* where the bodies of important Māori were once exposed.

🏛️ **Opotiki Museum**
123 Church St. **Tel** (07) 315 5193. **Open** Mon–Sat. **Closed** Good Fri, 25 Dec. 🎟️ ♿ 🏛️

Ohope Beach, Whakatane's best surf beach

Māori Migration and Settlement

According to legend, three migration canoes travelling from Hawaiki landed in the eastern Bay of Plenty in the 14th century *(see p49)*: the Mataatua at Whakatane, the Arawa at Maketu and Tainui at Whangaparaoa Bay, west of East Cape. Muriwai's Cave at Whakatane is testament to Muriwai's arrival on the Mataatua: she is believed to have had supernatural powers and lived hermit-like in the cave. Mild weather and abundant seafood encouraged Māori to settle along the coastal margins. Māori continue to form a high proportion of the population in the Bay of Plenty area, and red-framed Māori meeting houses, important spiritually and as decision-making centres, dot the countryside.

Māori Art and Culture

The meeting houses and other Māori works of art seen along the coast reflect Māori history, belief in gods and ancestral spirits, and a hierarchical, tribal social structure. Māori culture was primarily a wood culture. Wood was crafted into objects for economic, social and religious purposes, and embellished with symbols and motifs (see pp34–5).

Meeting houses, like the beautifully carved Tukaki at Te Kaha, are usually symbolic of a male tribal ancestor. His head is represented by the mask below the gable figure, while the wide, sloping bargeboards represent his arms.

Elements of Māori artistry have been incorporated into Christian churches, such as the intricate woven panels, carved wooden wall panels and rafter patterns at St Mary's Church at Tikitiki.

The *haka*, a vigorous rhythmic posture dance formerly performed by warriors to steel their resolve for war, is taught in schools along the coast.

This ornately carved gateway guards the entrance to coastal Omaio Marae.

A prominent carving in the main street of Opotiki is indicative of a renaissance in Māori arts, culture and traditions that took hold in the 1980s and 1990s.

㉕ East Cape Tour

Skirting the rugged hills of the East Cape peninsula, this section of the Pacific Coast Highway offers exceptional scenery. From Opotiki northeast to East Cape, the road clings to rocky coastline cloaked with pohutukawa trees. The second part of the route heads south to Gisborne along an inland farming route with secondary roads providing access to the coast. Most beaches and bays are suitable for swimming, fishing and diving. There are also opportunities for jet-boating, horse trekking and hiking. Māori *marae* and churches dot the route.

③ Te Araroa Pohutukawa
On the foreshore at Te Araroa grows Te Waha-o-Rerekohu ("the mouth of Rerekohu"), believed to be the largest pohutukawa tree in the country. It has 22 trunks.

② Raukokore Church
Built in 1894, this small, wooden Anglican church, with its distinctive roofline, stands lonely sentinel between road and sea.

① Motu River
The Motu River, banked by steep hills and forest, is a magnificent setting for rafting and jet-boating. There is also excellent fishing at its mouth.

Cape Runaway

Hicks Bay

Te Kaha

Raukumara Ranges

Bay of Plenty

Motu River

Mata River

Hikuwai River

Opotiki

35

Waipaoa River

Waimata River

Gisborne

Poverty Bay

0 kilometres   20

0 miles   20

⑧ Tolaga Bay
The site of New Zealand's longest wharf, Tolaga Bay is excellent for swimming and fishing. A 5 km (3 mile) walk leads to Cooks Cove and a fascinating rock archway.

⑦ Tokomaru Bay
This attractive, cliff-framed bay is popular with swimmers and surfers. Old buildings at the bay house crayfishermen and craft workers.

Tips for Drivers

Length: 334 km (207 miles)
Stopping-off points: There is a spectacular view from the Maraenui Hill Lookout 36 km (22 miles) from Opotiki. Towns on the route are small, but most offer food. Accommodation is available at Hicks Bay. Permission to climb Mount Hikurangi must be obtained from Ngati Porou Outdoor Pursuits, Gisborne (06) 876 9960. Bookings for jet-boating on the Motu River can be made at the Opotiki Information Centre (see p134).

④ East Cape Lighthouse
A gravel road along a picturesque coastline leads to New Zealand's most easterly lighthouse. The view from the lighthouse is well worth the climb up the 700 steps to reach it.

⑤ Tikitiki's St Mary's Church
Built in 1924 to commemorate Māori servicemen killed in World War I, St Mary's Church at Tikitiki is one of the most ornate Māori churches in the country (see p135).

⑥ Mount Hikurangi
The first place in mainland New Zealand to see the sun each day, Mount Hikurangi is sacred to Māori and permission must be obtained to climb it.

Key
◼ Tour route
⎯ Other roads
⩵ River

Star of Canada wheelhouse, Gisborne Museum

㉖ Te Urewera National Park

Road map F3. 🚐 ℹ️ Aniwaniwa Visitor Centre, State Hwy 38, Wairoa, (06) 837 3803. 🌐 doc.govt.nz

This is New Zealand's fourth largest national park and the biggest tract of untouched native forest remaining in the North Island. For centuries its dense rainforest sheltered the industrious and resilient Tuhoe people. At the centre of Te Urewera lies the 243 m (797 ft) deep Lake Waikaremoana ("the lake of rippling waters"), formed 2,200 years ago by a landslide. A 46 km (28 mile) track around the lake, one of the country's Great Walks (see p334), takes three to four days to complete. Booking through the Aniwaniwa Visitor Centre is essential. There are also many beautiful short walks into the park from the main road, which is partly gravel.

㉗ Gisborne

Road map F3. 🚗 35,000. ✈️ 4 km (2.5 miles) NW of town. 🚌 ℹ️ 209 Grey St, (06) 868 6139. 🍷 Wine and Food Festival (last week of Oct). 🌐 gisbornenz.com

Gisborne is renowned for its warm summers, its farming, viticulture and horticulture, its surf beaches at Midway, Wainui and Makorori, and its history. A monument and reserve on Kaiti Hill are named in honour of Captain James Cook who made his first New Zealand landfall at Gisborne's Kaiti Beach (see p52) on 9 October 1769.

The **Gisborne Museum**, also known as the **Tairawhiti Museum**, houses fine Māori and European artifacts and an extensive photographic collection. On the bank of the Taruheru River, but part of the museum complex, rests the salvaged wheelhouse from the *Star of Canada*, which sank off Kaiti Beach in 1912. Statues of Captain Cook and Young Nick, at the mouth of the Turanganui River, commemorate cabin boy Nicholas Young, the first crewman on board Cook's ship, the *Endeavour*, to sight New Zealand.

🏛 Gisborne/Tairawhiti Museum
Kelvin Park, Stout St. **Tel** (06) 867 3832. **Open** daily. **Closed** Good Fri, 25 & 26 Dec. ♿ except in Star of Canada. 📷 🌐 tairawhitimuseum.org.nz

Environs
Eastwoodhill Arboretum, 35 km (22 miles) west of Gisborne, contains a world-renowned collection of exotic trees and shrubs. Set among lush native bush and abundant birdlife, **Morere Hot Springs**, 60 km (37 miles) south of Gisborne, has both hot and cold pools.

🌳 Eastwoodhill Arboretum
2392 Wharekopae Rd. **Tel** (06) 863 9003. **Open** daily. **Closed** 25 Dec. 🎫 ♿ 🛍 by arrangement.

♨ Morere Hot Springs
State Hwy 2, Morere. **Tel** (06) 837 8856. **Open** daily. **Closed** 24 & 25 Dec. 🎫 ♿ 📷

Tall trees in the Eastwoodhill Arboretum, Gisborne

㉘ Rotorua

Situated on the southern shore of a lake of the same name, Rotorua is the North Island's most popular tourist destination. The city's hot and steamy thermal activity (evident from countless bores, spectacular geysers and bubbling mud pools), healing mineral pools, adventure activities and surrounding lakes, rivers and crystal springs are major attractions. Rotorua is known as the heartland of Māori culture and offers visitors the chance to experience Māori art, architecture, song and dance and cultural performances.

Government Gardens and the Rotorua Museum

🔘 Government Gardens
Queens Drive.

The formal Government Gardens are laid out in front of the stately Tudor-style Rotorua Museum. They comprise a series of trimmed croquet and bowling greens and formal flower gardens dotted with steaming thermal pools. The 1927 Arawa Soldiers' Memorial, a short distance north of the museum, symbolizes the history of contact between Pakeha and local tribes. At its base is the Arawa migration canoe, from which Rotorua's Te Arawa people trace their descent.

🏛 Rotorua Museum
Government Gardens, Oruawhata Drive. **Tel** (07) 350 1814. **Open** daily. **Closed** 25 Dec. 🚻 🦽 ground level. 🎞 📷 📱 🎧 **w** rotoruamuseum.co.nz

Māori artifacts are plentiful in Rotorua's museum, situated within a magnificent Elizabethan building that opened as the Great Spa of the South Pacific in 1908. Some of the most important of these are bargeboards from Rotoiti's

Houmaitawhiti meeting house, carved in 1860. Also on display is 19th-century palisading from the Māori settlement of Ohinemutu and a female pumice figure, Pani, a *kumara* goddess depicted in the act of giving birth; most Māori fertility gods are male.

The story of the building itself is shown in "Taking the Cure", in a section of the building painstakingly restored to its original condition. History, mythology and geology are combined in a dramatic 15-minute film to explain Rotorua's geothermal activity and Māori history. The film also shows a re-enactment of the 1886 Tarawera eruption.

🔘 The Blue Baths
Queens Drive. **Tel** (07) 350 2119. **Open** daily. **Closed** 25 Dec. 🚻 📱 **w** bluebaths.co.nz

These heated pools were built in the 1930s and offered the then-novel attraction of mixed bathing. Housed in a Spanish mission-style building, they were once a symbol of New Zealand's ambitions to become the premier spa of the British Empire. A museum documents the social history associated with the construction and use of the baths.

🔘 Polynesian Spa
Hinemoa St. **Tel** (07) 348 1328. **Open** daily. 🚻 🦽 📱 **w** polynesianspa.co.nz

People from around the world visit the Polynesian Spa's mineral waters, which vary in temperature from 33 °C (92 °F) to 42 °C (107 °F). Radium and Priest waters, both acidic and cloudy, are sourced from an underground spring while alkaline Rachel water is piped to the spa from nearby. Adults have access to a mineral pool overlooking a large, heated, freshwater pool, with a shallow end for toddlers. Users can regulate the temperature in the spa's private pools. Aix massage (under jets of water) and other therapies are available in the luxury spa area.

Spa City

"Cripples throw away their crutches and the gouty man regains his health," a government report proclaimed in 1903, referring to Rotorua's mineral waters. Two mineral waters were used in a succession of 19th-century and early 20th-century spas, the largest being the Bath House, opened in 1908. The waters were considered "stimulating and tonic in reaction". Today, on the shores of Lake Rotorua, QE Health uses hot mineral waters to relieve pain, relax muscles and stimulate joint movement.

Mineral pool at Polynesian Spa complex

St Faith's Anglican Church

🏛 St Faith's Anglican Church

Ohinemutu. **Open** daily. 🏛 9am Sun.

Built in 1910, the Tudor-style St Faith's is the second church built at Ohinemutu, a Māori village on the shores of the lake around which Rotorua grew. An etched-glass window in the chapel at the far end of the church depicts Christ dressed in a *korowai* (chief's cloak) and appearing to walk on the waters of Lake Rotorua. The interior is richly embellished with Māori carvings, woven wall panels and painted scrollwork. There are a few graves of interest next to the church, including that of Seymour Mills Spencer (1810–98) who preached to the Arawa for 50 years, and Captain Gilbert Mair (1843–1923) of the Arawa Flying Column, a guerilla unit of local Māori who fought for the British army in the New Zealand wars.

🏛 Tamatekapua

Ohinemutu.

The magnificent Tamatekapua meeting house, built in 1873, is the main gathering place of the Arawa tribe. Located opposite St Faith's, it was named for an earlier house that stood on Mokoia Island and the captain of the *Arawa*, one of the canoes that brought the ancestors of Māori to New Zealand. The figure at the base of the centre post is Ngatoroirangi, the canoe's navigator, whom mythology credits with bringing thermal activity to the region.

Carving at Tamatekapua

🏛 Kuirau Park

Kuirau Rd.

Within Kuirau Park there are a number of boiling mud pools, steam vents and small geysers. Free thermal foot pools, picnic areas, well-kept gardens, a children's playground and a small, warm lake are other attractions within the domain. Visitors will also appreciate a scented garden in the park.

Rotorua City Centre

① Government Gardens
② Rotorua Museum
③ The Blue Baths
④ Polynesian Spa
⑤ St Faith's Anglican Church
⑥ Tamatekapua
⑦ Kuirau Park

0 metres 500
0 yards 500

For keys to symbols *see back flap*

Greater Rotorua

Many of Rotorua's best attractions lie outside the city centre, around Lake Rotorua and the 17 other magnificent bush-fringed lakes that make up the Rotorua Lakes district. Complementing the lakes are geothermal wonders, bubbling springs, crystal-clear trout streams and unspoiled native forests. The rivers and lakes are renowned for their trout, and make a beautiful setting for boating, camping and hiking. Thrill-seekers can take four-wheel drive tours and ride horses to remote forest locations. Visitors can also enjoy Māori cultural experiences and observe the farming and livestock displays.

Visitors viewing trout at Rainbow Springs Nature Park

Lake Rotorua and Mokoia Island from Mount Ngongotaha

🦆 Lake Rotorua

This nearly circular lake is the largest of the lakes around Rotorua and is a popular venue for fishing, windsurfing and kayaking. It can be enjoyed by paddle steamer, kayak, jetboat or water scooter. Mokoia Island, in the centre of the lake, is famous for the love story of Hinemoa, who defied her family's wishes and swam at night to the island to be with the chief Tutanekai, who played his flute to guide her. The island is rich in native bird life and offers 4 km (2.5 miles) of walking tracks as well as Hinemoa's thermal pool.

🏛 Skyline Rotorua

185 Fairy Springs Rd. **Tel** (07) 347 0027. **Open** daily. 🅿 🅱 🅒 🅕
W skyline.co.nz/en/rotorua

Mount Ngongotaha towers 778 m (2,552 ft) above the city and lake. The Skyline lookout, at 487 m (1,598 ft), can be reached by gondola, and gives stunning views. An exciting way to descend the mountain, by day or night, is by luge (a short, raised toboggan on wheels). A gondola assisted bike lift allows access to 10.5-km (6.5-miles) of mountain biking trails. A 2 km (1 mile) scenic ride suits most people, while two steeper rides provide an adrenalin rush. Chairlifts return riders to the start.

🦆 Rainbow Springs Nature Park

Fairy Springs Rd. **Tel** (07) 350 0440. **Open** daily. 🅿 🅱 🅒 🅒 🅕 🅕
W rainbowsprings.co.nz

Visitors can feed some of the thousands of rainbow, brown, brook and tiger trout in the crystal-clear freshwater streams and fern-fringed pools here, and view tuataras and kiwi in a walk-through aviary. Rainbow Springs is also home to Kiwi Encounter, a conservation-in-action attraction, combining natural history with wildlife conservation. Staff prepare, incubate and hand-raise kiwi chicks taken as eggs from the wild. Once at maximum weight, they are returned to the wild.

🔵 Agrodome

Western Rd, Ngongotaha. **Tel** (07) 357 1050. **Open** daily. 🅿 🅱 🅒 🅒 🅕
W agrodome.co.nz

Founded in 1972, this family business offers a broad range of farming-related and adventure activities. There are three live sheep shows daily, at which champion rams are introduced on stage, and sheep shearing and sheep dog trials are demonstrated. Visitors can also tour the organic farm and feed the animals. The shop specializes in quality woollens and sheepskin rugs.

Nearby is ZORB® Rotorua, which offers a chance to roll downhill inside a large plastic ball.

🔵 Agroventures

1335, Paradise Valley Rd. **Tel** (07) 357 4747. **Open** daily. 🅿 🅱 🅒 🅒 🅕
W agroventures.co.nz

Adventure activities include jet-boating, bungy jumping, the Swoop

Live sheep show at the Agrodome Agricultural Theme Park

swing and the Shweeb (the world's first human-powered monorail racetrack, consisting of two overhead rail circuits from which hang high performance pedal powered vehicles).

Hells Gate

State Hwy 33. **Tel** (07) 345 3151. Open daily. 🎭 🕉 📷 🗂 🖥 📷
W **hellsgate.co.nz**

Sixteen kilometres (10 miles) from Rotorua, at Tikitere, Hells Gate is famous for its ferocious volcanic activity. Drifting, wraith-like mists part to reveal a fierce and spectacular thermal valley that includes the Kakahi Falls, the largest hot waterfall in the southern hemisphere, and New Zealand's largest boiling whirlpool. Another cauldron of water, the Sulphur Bath, is purported to cure septic cuts, bites and skin ailments. The area is well signposted, with good pathways and barriers. Traditional Māori massage is on offer at the Wai Ora Spa.

Horse riding in The Redwoods – Whakarewarewa Forest

The Redwoods – Whakarewarewa Forest

Off State Hwy 5. W **redwoods.co.nz**
This 40 sq km (15 sq mile) forest adjoining the Whakarewarewa thermal area *(see pp142–3)* contains majestic groves of redwoods, firs and other plantation trees. Forest walks can take from 30 minutes to all day. There are also 180 km (112 miles) of mountain biking and horse tracks, a nature trail and picnic area.

Tamaki Māori Village

State Hwy 5. **Tel** (07) 349 2999. **Open** daily. **Closed** 25 Dec. 🎭 🕉 📷 🖥
📷 W **tamakimaorivillage.co.nz**

Visitors are introduced to Māori customs and traditions at this

A Māori "warrior" greets visitors at the Tamaki Māori Village

replica of a pre-European Māori village. Sampling a full *hangi* feast, in which selected foods are cooked on hot rocks in an authentic earth oven, is part of the cultural experience. This daily highlight starts at 6:30pm to 10pm. Educational workshops are also held regularly on traditional Māori carving and weaving, performing arts, weaponry and warfare, and Māori food and health.

Blue and Green Lakes

Tarawera Rd.
Eleven km (7 miles) southeast of Rotorua are the stunning Blue and Green Lakes (Tikitapu and Rotokakahi). The narrow isthmus that divides the lakes provides a good vantage point to compare their contrasting hues. Lake Rotokakahi is sacred to Māori and is not accessible, but Lake Tikitapu is the scene of many summer activities.

The Buried Village

Tarawera Rd. **Tel** (07) 362 8287. **Open** daily. **Closed** 25 Dec. 🎭 🕉
🗂 🖥 📷 W **buriedvillage.co.nz**

Fifteen minutes' drive from Rotorua and 2.5 km (1.5 miles) from Lake Tarawera is what remains of the village of Te Wairoa, devastated by the eruption of Mount Tarawera in 1886. A walk through parkland takes in the excavations of several sites and an interactive museum explains the eruption. A bush walk leads to the Te Wairoa waterfalls, while a walkway offers clifftop views.

Tarawera Eruption

Months of underground rumbling culminated early in the morning of 10 June 1886 with the eruption of Mount Tarawera, which left a deep crater *(see pp68–9)*. Lasting about three hours, the blast spread along a 17 km (10 mile) rift and killed 153 people. The eruption hurled red-hot volcanic bombs and pieces of solidified lava 14 km (8.5 miles), and the Māori villages of Te Ariki, Te Wairoa and Moura were buried under 20 m (65 ft) of mud. The explosion's roar was heard in Christchurch and Auckland. The famous Pink and White Terraces, massive fan-like silica terraces, regarded as the eighth wonder of the world, were completely obliterated. Information on guided walks and 4WD tours to the crater, and on scenic flights over it, can be obtained from the Rotorua information centre *(see p139)*.

Painting by Charles Blomfield of the Pink Terraces, around 1890

Whakarewarewa Thermal Area

The geothermal area at Rotorua's southern edge, commonly referred to as Whaka, comprises two separate areas – Te Puia, once known as the New Zealand Māori Arts and Crafts Institute, and Whakarewarewa Thermal Village. Te Puia's attractions include Māori carving and weaving, cultural performances, examples of Māori buildings and fortifications, and the geysers Pohutu and Prince of Wales Feathers. At the Thermal Village, visitors can see a meeting house, cooking and bathing pools and a cemetery. At both venues, guides take visitors on an educational journey that unravels the mystery of Māori ways.

★ **Te Aronui-a-Rua Meeting House**
Visitors are greeted with a Māori "challenge" at Te Aronui-a-Rua meeting house at Te Puia.

★ **Carving School**
Ancient carving skills are passed to younger generations at Te Puia's carving school.

HEMO ROAD

④

⑤

Te Puia

③

②

①

Pataka
Storehouses like this were used by pre-European Māori to store food. However, *kumara* (sweet potato), their staple carbohydrate, was stored in pits in the ground.

VISITORS' CHECKLIST

Practical Information
Te Puia: Hemo Rd. **Tel** (07) 348 9047. **W** tepuia.com
Open 8am–6pm daily (to 5pm winter). ⚡ ♿ 🎫 hourly. ✏ 🖥
🎭 Māori concerts: 10:15am, 12:15pm, 3:15pm. Cultural show: 6:15pm. Whakarewarewa Thermal Village: 17 Tryon St. **Tel** (07) 349 3463. **W** whakarewarewa.com
Open 8:30am–5pm daily. **Closed** 25 Dec. ⚡ 🎫 ♿ 🖥 ✏ ⚡ 🖥 🎭
Cultural show: 11:15am & 2pm.

Transport
🚌 No. 2 CityRide bus from main depot in Rotorua.

★ Pohutu Geyser
Pohutu ("Big Splash") is the largest geyser and typically erupts 10–25 times a day up to 30 m (98 ft) high, depending on wind strength and direction.

★ Wahiao Meeting House
Tourists, including children, join in a cultural performance outside Wahiao meeting house.

TRYON ST

0 metres 100
0 yards 100

KEY

① **Lake Waikaukau**

② **Cooking Pool**

③ **At the Weaving House**, broad native flax is transformed into functional items.

④ **Kiwi House**

⑤ **Leaping Frog Mud Pool**

⑥ **At Puarenga Stream**, village children dive for coins thrown from a bridge by tourists.

⑦ **Whakarewarewa Thermal Village**

⑧ **Prince of Wales Feathers Geyser**

⑨ **Geyser Flat**, a 1 sq km (0.4 sq mile) silica terrace, is home to more than 500 thermal features, including seven geysers.

⑩ **At the Cemetery** at Whakarewarewa Thermal Village, the dead are buried above ground in vaults to keep the remains out of the steaming earth.

⑪ **The Brainpot**, a symmetrical silica basin, is said to have been used to cook the heads of enemies.

Volcanic Features

The volcanic activity at Whakarewarewa is a reminder of how the earth is still changing and how the pressure of volcanic gases and heat below the surface can break through in spectacular and often dangerous ways. Here, superheated steam escapes from a vast chamber of boiling water through narrow vents in roaring towers of spray; mud pools boil and heave as gas and hot water seek to escape through the surface, and steam and gases are discharged in hot pools beside mineral-coloured silica flats.

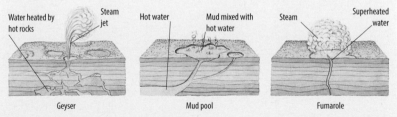

Water heated by hot rocks — Steam jet

Geyser

Hot water — Mud mixed with hot water

Mud pool

Steam — Superheated water

Fumarole

㉙ Waimangu Volcanic Valley

Road map E3. **Tel** (07) 366 6137.
Open daily. 🅿 🚌 to bus stop &
boat cruise (assisted). 🚻 📷
🌐 waimangu.co.nz

Created on 10 June 1886 as a
result of the Tarawera Eruption
(see p141), Waimangu is the only
hydrothermal system in the
world wholly formed within
historic times. It offers an easy,
mostly downhill, 90-minute
walk past a succession of
geothermal features at the
southern end of the 17 km (10
mile) rift created by the eruption.

The 38,000 sq m (409,032
sq ft) Frying Pan Lake, claimed
to be the world's largest hot
water spring, emits steam over
its entire area and is dominated
by the red-streaked Cathedral
Rocks. The lake was formed by
an eruption in 1917 that buried
a nearby tourist hotel.

The pale blue steaming water
and delicate silica clay terracing
of the Inferno Crater should not
be missed, even though it
requires a short detour from the
main path. The water reaches
80° C (176° F) in the lake and
rises and falls 8 m (26 ft) over
a 38-day cycle.

At the end of the walk lies
Lake Rotomahana, submerging
what remains of the Pink and
White Terraces (see p141).
Across the water stands Mount
Tarawera. A boat excursion
follows a shoreline scarred by
craters, fumaroles and geysers.
Unusual thermal plants grow
along the lake's edge. Visitors
need to allow two to three
hours for the volcanic valley
walk and the boat cruise.

Inferno Crater at Waimangu
Volcanic Valley

Champagne Pool at Wai-o-Tapu Thermal Wonderland

㉚ Wai-O-Tapu Thermal Wonderland

Road map E3. **Tel** (07) 366 6333.
Open daily. 🅿 🚻 main area. 🚽 🛒
📷 🌐 waiotapu.co.nz

This is the country's most
colourful and diverse
geothermal area and is home
to the reliable Lady Knox
Geyser, named in 1904 after
Governor-General Lord
Ranfurly's daughter. The geyser
shoots water and steam up
to 21 m (69 ft) into the air at
10:15am daily.

Other main attractions
include the Artist's Palette,
a panorama of hot and cold
pools, boiling mud pools and
hissing fumaroles in a variety
of ever-changing colours, and
the Champagne Pool, with its
ochre-coloured petrified edge.
The Primrose Terraces are also
naturally tinted and have
delicately formed lacework
patterns. Walks through the
geothermal area, over boardwalks and along signposted
paths, take 30 to 75 minutes.

㉛ Orakei Korako Geyserland

Road map E3. **Tel** (07) 378 3131.
Open daily. 🛒 📷 🚌 (includes boat
ride). 🌐 orakeikorako.co.nz

Orakei Korako, or "The Hidden
Valley", as it is known, lies at the
southern end of Lake Ohakuri,
fed by the Waikato River as it
flows northward from Lake

Taupo. Reaching the valley's
geothermal attractions requires
a boat trip across the lake to the
imposing Emerald Terrace, the
largest silica feature of its kind
in the country. Beyond is a
60-minute walk taking in a
geyser, more silica terraces, hot
springs, a cave and mud pools.
A café with a large deck
overlooking the lake serves
snacks and drinks.

Jet-boating rapids on the
Waikato River

㉜ Wairakei Park

Road map E3.

Ten kilometres (6 miles) north
of Taupo is the area loosely
referred to as Wairakei Park.
The star attraction is the Huka
("foam") Falls, where the Waikato
River is channelled through
a narrow rock chute before
hurtling over an 11 m (36 ft)
bluff to a foaming cauldron
below. Access down the
Waikato River from Taupo to
the Huka Falls is possible by

jet-boat, or by the more sedate paddlewheeler, built in 1908. A 7 km (4 mile) path leads from the falls down the right-hand side of the river to the Aratiatia Rapids, also accessible by road. Floodgates to the dam above the rapids are opened several times a day to allow kayaking and jet-boating.

At **Craters of the Moon**, at the end of Karapiti Road, 2 km (1.2 miles) south of Wairakei, steaming craters and boiling mud pits can be viewed for a charge ($8 for adults) among a bush-covered landscape.

The country's only prawn farm, off Huka Falls Road, uses geothermally heated river water to raise giant prawns for its restaurant, Huka Prawn Park Restaurant. Tours of the farm are conducted hourly.

㉝ Taupo

Road map E3. 🏔 21,300. ✈ 8 km (5 miles) S of town. 🚍 Gascoigne St Travel Centre. **Tel** (07) 378 9005. 🛈 30 Tongariro St, (07) 376 0027. 🎣 Lake Taupo International Fishing Tournament (late Apr). 🌐 **laketauponz.com**

The town of Taupo lies at the northeastern end of Lake Taupo, New Zealand's largest lake, formed by a volcanic explosion in AD 186 (see pp68–9). White pumice beaches and sheltered rocky coves surround the lake, which covers 619 sq km (239 sq miles). On a clear day, the distant volcanic peaks of Mounts Tongariro and Ngauruhoe and the snow-capped Ruapehu provide a spectacular backdrop to the lake.

Taupo services surrounding farms and forests and an important tourist industry. All year round the town attracts large numbers of holiday-makers who come for its excellent lake and river fishing, sailing and water-sports, and local geothermal attractions. There is a wealth of accommodation in the town, much of it with lakeside views, and good dining and shopping. Many hotels have their own hot pools.

The wide selection of outdoor activities includes bungy jumping, boating and rafting, horse riding, mountain biking, tandem skydiving, flightseeing and golf. The bungy, set in majestic surroundings above the Waikato River off Spa Road, is a big draw. Details of the operators offering outdoor recreation may be obtained from the information centre in Taupo.

㉞ Turangi

Road map E3. 🏔 5,500. 🚍 🛈 Ngwaka Place, (07) 386 8999.

Located at the southeastern end of Lake Taupo on the banks of the Tongariro River, Turangi was a small fishing retreat until it was developed into a town in 1964 to accommodate workers for the Tongariro Hydro-Electricity Scheme. It remains an excellent resort area for anglers, and is also a popular base for hikers, white-water rafters, kayakers and skiers.

South of Turangi is the **Tongariro National Trout Centre**, a hatchery and research facility. Ova collected from wild female trout are fertilized to

Trimming pine trees in a pine forest near Turangi

breed trout for research purposes and to release into the lake. A self-guided 15-minute walk takes you through the hatchery and by a stream to an underwater viewing chamber to see trout in their natural environment.

🐟 **Tongariro National Trout Centre**
State Hwy 1. **Tel** (07) 386 9254. **Open** 10am–3pm daily. **Closed** 1 Jan, 25 Dec. ♿

Trout Fishing Paradise

World-famous Lake Taupo and its surrounding lakes – Kuratau, Hinemaia, Rotoaira and Otamangakau – are fed by numerous rivers and streams well-stocked with rainbow and brown trout. Fishermen frequently stand shoulder to shoulder at the mouth of the Waitahanui River to form the "picket fence" fishing phenomenon. Line fishing from boats on Lake Taupo or from the shore is effective from November until March, as trout feed on smelt spawning close to shore. In late summer, trout congregate after dark where streams flow into the lake, providing excellent fly-fishing. River fishing is best from May till October. A special fishing licence, available from sports shops and information centres, is required in the Taupo Fishing District.

Fishing at the mouth of the Waitahanui River

㉟ Tongariro National Park

At the southern end of Lake Taupo lies the magnificent 7,600 sq km (2,930 sq m) Tongariro National Park. The peaks of the three active volcanic mountains which form its nucleus, Ruapehu, Ngauruhoe and Tongariro *(see pp68–9)*, were a gift to the government in 1887 by Tukino Te Heuheu IV, a Ngati Tuwharetoa chief. The park, which is surrounded by access roads, is a winter playground for skiers and snowboarders and a year-round wilderness walking, hiking and mountain-climbing area. The park was the first in the world to achieve UNESCO World Heritage status for both its natural (1990) and Māori spiritual and cultural (1993) value.

★ Whakapapa Ski Area
The largest developed ski area in New Zealand, Whakapapa has a sophisticated chairlift system and more than 30 groomed trails catering to all levels of skiers and snowboarders.

Chateau Tongariro
This luxury hotel, built in 1929 on the lower slopes of Mount Ruapehu, offers outstanding mountain and valley views.

★ Mount Ruapehu
In summer, visitors can climb to the crater of Mount Ruapehu, the North Island's tallest mountain, from the highest Whakapapa chairlift.

Manga

National Park

47

48

4

Whakapapa Village

Makatote River

Mount Ruapehu
2,797 m (9,174 ft)

Round the Mountain Track

Mangawhero River

Ohakune Mountain Road

Crate

3

Mangawhero Falls

Ohakune

Rangataua Forest

49

Dreadnought Rd

KEY

① **The Turoa Ski Area** is renowned for its expansive ski areas, long runs and vertical drops.

② **Mountain biking** is prohibited in the park but is allowed in the Rangataua, Erua and Tongariro Forest Areas.

③ **Round the Mountain** is a four- to five-day hike around Ruapehu for those seeking solitude, magnificent mountain views and a back-country experience.

④ **Ketetahi Hot Springs**, consisting of 40 fumaroles, boiling springs and mud pools, is located on private property but can be viewed from the walking track.

⑤ **Lake Rotopounamu**, "the greenstone lake", is a picturesque lake on the side of Mount Pihanga, 20 minutes' walk from State Highway 47.

⑥ **Mount Ngauruhoe** is the youngest of the three volcanoes, and is a vent of Tongariro.

⑦ **Tukino Skifield**, accessible by 4WD from the Desert Road, is a small club-run field which operates rope tows only.

Key

━━━ State highway
━━━ Minor road
〜〜 River
– – 4 WD track
- - Walking track
━ ━ Park boundary
— — Restricted area

VISITORS' CHECKLIST

Practical Information
Road map E3. Ohakune. ℹ️ 54 Clyde St, (06) 385 8427. **Open** 9am–5pm daily. Whakapapa ℹ️ behind Bayview Chateau Tongariro, (07) 892 3729. **Open** 8am–5pm daily. 🌐 doc.govt.nz

Transport
🚆 National Park. 🚌 National Park Store, Carroll St.

★ **Emerald Lakes**
The uneven summit of Mount Tongariro, the lowest of the three volcanoes, comprises a maze of craters, including the beautiful, mineral-tinted Emerald Lakes.

Tongariro Alpine Crossing
The Tongariro Alpine Crossing, from Mangatepopo to Ketetahi, covers 18.5 km (11.5 miles) of varied and spectacular volcanic terrain and is often described as the best one-day trek in New Zealand.

Volcanic Hazards

The volcanoes of Tongariro National Park are unique because of the frequency of eruptions, their highly explosive nature and the high density of active vents. Volcanic activity can occur in the park at any time and with little or no warning. Anyone intending to hike or climb on the upper slopes of the volcanoes needs to check the current volcanic alert status and exclusion zones with the nearest visitor centre and read any recommended safety information for the area before starting out.

Rangipo Desert
Temperature extremes on the eastern side of the volcanoes have produced a desolate landscape of gravel fields and hardy alpine vegetation. The area is used mainly for army training.

⚛ Street-by-Street: Napier

Perched on the edge of the Pacific Ocean, this elegant
city is a memorial to a 1931 earthquake and fire that
destroyed most buildings and killed many people. The
quake raised marshland and the harbour bed, providing
new farmland and room for urban development. During
rebuilding, an earthquake-proof building code was
enforced and architects adopted the then fashionable
Art Deco style. Today, the city's Art Deco buildings, with
their pastel colours, bold lines and elaborate motifs, are
internationally renowned.

Napier Mall
Traffic bollards and seats topped
with Art Deco motifs enhance
pedestrian-friendly Emerson Street.

★ Deco Centre
Purpose-built in 1922 as Napier's Central
Fire Station, and refurbished in Art Deco
style after the earthquake, it now houses
the Art Deco Trust and Art Deco Shop.

The Municipal Theatre, built in
1938, is noted for its Egyptian-style
columns and door lintels, and for
the leaping nude wall panels
flanking the stage in the
auditorium.

The Public Trust Building's
massive columns and internal
oak fittings escaped
earthquake damage.

Countrywide Bank
This 1932 building has charming
balcony windows framed by
angular arches decorated with
sunbursts and zigzags.

Art Deco Trust

The Art Deco Trust is responsible for protecting, enhancing and
promoting Napier's Art Deco
buildings, keeping a register of
them and maintaining worldwide
links with other Art Deco groups. It
also organizes Art Deco walks and
publishes information on tours. A
highlight is the annual Art Deco
Weekend. Held in February, this
celebration of Art Deco style
attracts more than 40,000 visitors.

**A couple dressed for an
Art Deco Weekend**

0 metres   50
0 yards   50

Key

— Suggested route

For hotels and restaurants in this region see pp303–4 and pp317–19

The Napier Antique Centre, built in 1932, is one of four buildings in Napier ornamented with Maori designs.

Daily Telegraph Building
Built in 1932, this building is well endowed with Art Deco details – sunbursts, zigzags, ziggurats and fountain-like flowers.

Criterion Hotel
Leadlight glass was a favourite form of decoration in the 1930s, as shown in the window in the hotel's stairwell.

The ASB Bank's
interior features fine examples of Maori carving and rafter patterns.

Masonic Hotel
Completed in 1932, the hotel features an unusual first-floor loggia built over the street.

CATHEDRAL LANE

STREET

HASTINGS STREET

BROWNING STREET

HERSCHELL ST

MARINE PARADE

★ **The Dome**
This Napier landmark, built in 1936 to house the Silver Slipper Nightclub, has a beautifully restored elevator.

Exploring Napier

Within easy walking distance of Napier's inner-city Art Deco buildings is the ocean front Marine Parade, fringed by Norfolk pines. The floral clock, Tom Parker Fountain, statue of Pania (a maiden of local legend), Soundshell, Colonnade, Sunken Gardens, and the Viewing Platform extending out along the Marine Parade's waterfront, add to the city's charm. To the north, Bluff Hill, notable for its steep roads and lovely old wooden homes, is the city's only high ground. Beyond it is the bustling port of Ahuriri, the site of the region's first European settlement.

tunnel, and is home to sharks, stingrays, seahorses and east coast native fish. Visitors can watch divers hand-feed the fish at 10am and 2pm every day, and there are even daily opportunities to take part in a supervised swim with the sharks. The aquarium is also involved in many conservation programmes and was the first to hatch a turtle egg in 1975.

⊠ The National Aquarium of New Zealand

Marine Parade. **Tel** (06) 834 1404. **Open** daily. **Closed** 25 Dec. 🔲🖥🏠Ⓦ nationalaquarium. co.nz

The aquarium is located in a stingray-shaped building on Napier's foreshore, and its proximity to the ocean means that fresh seawater can be pumped directly to its tanks and enclosures. The ground floor has native marine life and other species such as the tuatara (the New Zealand lizard), while the upper floor is dedicated to

Visitors at the National Aquarium of New Zealand

creatures from different parts of the world. The Oceanarium is viewed from an underwater

MTG Hawke's Bay

1 Tennyson St. **Tel** (06) 835 7781. **Open** daily. **Closed** 25 Dec. 🔲 🔲🖥🏠Ⓦ mtghawkesbay.com

MTG Hawke's Bay occupies three buildings that are home to a museum, a theatre, and an art gallery. The museum has extensive collections of Māori treasures, fine art, applied and decorative arts and textiles, as well as artifacts relating to the daily lives of Hawke's Bay's early settlers. Through audiovisual displays and ephemera, visitors can also experience the devastation of the 1931 earthquake.

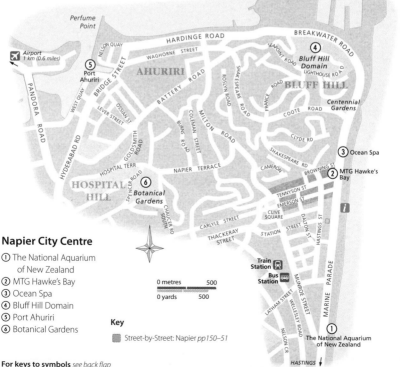

Napier City Centre

① The National Aquarium of New Zealand
② MTG Hawke's Bay
③ Ocean Spa
④ Bluff Hill Domain
⑤ Port Ahuriri
⑥ Botanical Gardens

0 metres   500
0 yards   500

Key

Street-by-Street: Napier *pp150–51*

🏠 Ocean Spa
42 Marine Parade. **Tel** (06) 835 8553.
Open daily. **Closed** 25 Dec. 🈂️ 🚻
🖥️ 🏠 🚾 **oceanspa.co.nz**

This attractively landscaped open-air pool and spa complex has vast ocean views and is a great place to relax and recharge. Visitors can enjoy heated saltwater pools at various temperatures, a lap pool, two leisure pools, a toddler pool, outdoor and indoor private spas, as well as a sauna, steam room, massage facility and the well-equipped Ocean Club gym.

🅱️ Bluff Hill Domain
Lighthouse Rd.

Prior to the 1931 earthquake, Napier comprised an oblong mass of hills (Scinde Island) surrounded almost entirely by water. A stroll or drive to the 102 m- (335 ft-) high lookout within Bluff Hill Domain will recreate this feeling if visitors imagine much of the low-lying area south of the hill covered in water. What were gun emplacements are now vantage points from which to view the Kaweka and Ruahine ranges to the west, the Mahia Peninsula to the northeast, and Cape Kidnappers to the southeast, as well as the spectacular sight of the commercial port below.

🅿️ Port Ahuriri
At Port Ahuriri, 4 km (2.5 miles) from Napier's centre, visitors can watch boys fishing and fishing fleets being unloaded or enjoy the port's many lively bars and restaurants, which are among the finest in Napier. A beach boardwalk meanders to the harbour entrance at Perfume Point. The Rothmans Building, one of the most beautiful Art Deco buildings in Napier, is in nearby Ossian Street.

🅱️ Botanical Gardens
Spencer Rd.

Located on a hill in the middle of the city, the gardens form a charming oasis. Apart from a spacious aviary, there are well-kept lawns bordered by flower beds, groves of stately trees, and a stream with

View north towards Napier from Te Mata Peak

🔢 Hastings
Road map F4. 🏔️ 28,400. ✈️ 25 km (15 miles) N of town. 🚌 🚏 Caroline Rd. 🅿️ Cnr Russel St North & Heretaunga St, (06) 873 5526. 🍷 Hawke's Bay Wine and Food Festival (first weekend of Feb); Hastings Blossom Festival (Sep).

Situated on the Heretaunga Plains, 20 km (12 miles) south of Napier, Hastings is the centre of a large fruit growing and processing industry, including wine making (see pp154–5). Rebuilt after the 1931 earthquake, it is the only city in New Zealand with streets laid out on the American block system. It has some fine Spanish Mission buildings, the most notable being the Hawke's Bay Opera House.

Hawke's Bay apples

Between Hastings and the eastern coastline, Te Mata Peak rises 399 m (1,309 ft). Māori legend describes the Te Mata

ridgeline as the body of chief Te Mata O Rongokako, who choked and died eating his way through the hill, a task set him by the beautiful daughter of another chief. From Hastings the "bite" that killed him can be clearly seen, as can his body, which forms the skyline.

🔢 Cape Kidnappers
Road map F4.

The Māori believe that the crescent-shaped bay and jagged promontory of Cape Kidnappers, 30 km (19 miles) south of Napier, represent the magical jawbone hook used by Maui to pull the North Island from the sea like a fish. In October 1769, Captain Cook anchored off the headland (see p52) naming it Cape Kidnappers after some Māori attempted to carry off his Tahitian translator.

At the cape, up to 20,000 young and mature yellow-headed Australasian gannets surf wind currents metres from onlookers. The best time to see them is from November to February. Access is closed during the early nesting phase between July and October. At low tide, visitors can walk 8 km (5 miles) along the beach to the colony – check walking times with the local i-SITE Visitor Centre. Guided tours by coach and tractor-trailer are also available.

Australasian gannets at Cape Kidnappers Gannet Reserve

㊳ Hawke's Bay Vineyard Tour

Hawke's Bay's long sunshine hours, wide range of growing microclimates, and variety of soil types have allowed more than 70 wineries to develop all the classical grape varieties to a high standard. Traditionally a fruit-growing area, Hawke's Bay's fruit is sourced from varied vineyard and orchard sites, and wines are made using both modern and traditional techniques. The success of the region's wine is not only evident in its international awards, but in one of New Zealand's most important wine events, the Hawke's Bay F.A.W.C! Food and Wine Classic festival, held every June and November.

① Mission Estate Winery
Established in 1851 by a group of French Catholic missionaries, early vintages were produced for sacramental purposes. Today, New Zealand's oldest winery, nestled on a hill overlooking sweeping vineyards, offers wine sales, winery tours, a gourmet restaurant and a craft gallery.

⑨ Clearview Estate Winery
Established in 1989 by Tim Turvey and Helma van den Berg, this gently sloping coastal vineyard produces small quantities of hand-made wines sold only from the winery or by mail order.

⑧ Te Mata Estate Winery
One of the oldest wineries operating in New Zealand (vines were planted on the lower slopes of Te Mata peak in 1892) and one of its most prestigious and successful, Te Mata produces mainly red wines, which can be bought at its winery or by mail order.

⑦ Vidal Wines
Anthony Vidal, an immigrant from Spain, established his winery in a stable in 1905. Urban development has encompassed the site but Vidals continues to produce good wines. Sales, tastings and a brasserie are available.

⑥ Sileni Estates
Located within an area of red-metal soils, massive investment has produced a showcase winery incorporating a gourmet food store, wine education centre and restaurant/café.

Palmerston North

0 kilometres   4

0 miles

Key

■ Tour route

═ Other roads

▬ River

② Park Estate Winery

Formerly a traditional orchard, Park Estate has established niche markets for three very different beverages: grape wines, fruit wines from feijoa, boysenberry, kiwifruit and apple, and natural fruit juices. Orchard and winery tours, wine tasting and dining are available. A shop sells fresh fruit and homemade produce.

Fruitbowl of New Zealand

Hawke's Bay's warm, sunny summers and crisp winter frosts have been exploited by generations of horticulturists, who have earned the region its unofficial title of "fruitbowl of New Zealand". While apples are the largest crop, pears, kiwifruit, peaches and other stone fruits are also important. However, increased world production of apples and falling prices have begun to affect export levels.

At Pernel Fruitworld, a large orchard on the outskirts of Hastings with its own packhouse, some 90 varieties of pip and stone fruits are grown. Tours are conducted hourly, fruit is available to taste, and a museum traces the history of the fruit industry.

Orchard tour at Pernel Fruitworld

③ C J Pask Winery

This Mediterranean-style winery, located in a stony, silt-covered river bed, produces grapes with very ripe fruit flavours across a range of premium varieties. It is one of the region's best wineries.

④ Te Awa Winery

Named "River of God" for the enormous aquifer beneath the Hawke's Bay plains that is tapped to irrigate crops, Te Awa makes fine Bordeaux-blend red wines, which can be savoured at its restaurant.

Tips for Drivers

Visiting three or four wineries in one day will allow time to taste and discuss the wines. Many wineries offer tours and most offer tastings and sales. Some have indoor and outdoor eating facilities, although booking is advisable. Information on the facilities at each listed winery can be obtained at the Napier Visitor Information centre (see p151).

Visitors planning to visit a greater number of wineries and make the most of tasting opportunities may prefer to take one of the many tours available.

⑤ Ngatarawa Wines

A large rectangular lily pond and stable buildings housing the winery make an attractive setting that is more than matched by Ngatarawa's wines. The vineyard also has a pleasant picnic area and a *pétanque* court.

WELLINGTON AND THE SOUTH

European settlers arriving in the mid-1800s and making their way north of Wellington, New Zealand's capital city from 1865, quickly found themselves in the middle of virgin rainforest. The recent history of much of the area covered by Wellington and the South is linked to the massive clearance of the land through the milling and burning of forest during the late 19th and early 20th centuries.

In their thousands, giant ancient trees covered potentially rich pastoral land acquired from the Māori. Between the 1870s and 1910s, the area became the site of the country's biggest forest clearance programme as settlers poured in from overseas and demand for farmland grew. Sawmills, closely linked with the new rail network, sprang up throughout the district. Small towns along the railway enjoyed periods of importance before the sawmillers moved on. By 1907, however, milling output in the lower half of the North Island had passed its peak, to be superseded by the rich, rolling farmlands and rural lifestyles that have been a feature of the area ever since.

Although Taranaki, Wanganui and Manawatu are among the most productive and intensively farmed areas in New Zealand, these days diversity is the rule rather than the exception for the lower North Island. The exploitation of natural gas fields off the Taranaki coast, for example, has added to the economic mix of the region.

Tourists are drawn to the compact lower North Island because of its mild climate, wild coastline, stunning beaches, scenic rivers, national parks, mountain ranges, ski fields, vineyards, and rich Māori heritage.

Harbour-fringed Wellington, situated at the bottom of the North Island, is the area's main city, and the centre of government, business, and the performing arts. The numerous small towns that radiate from it to the north, servicing local farms, are charming, friendly stopover points for travellers.

The Beehive and Parliament Buildings in Wellington, New Zealand's capital city

◀ The rocky coastal landscape in Wellington

Exploring Wellington and the South

Wairarapa, the Kapiti Coast, Horowhenua, Manawatu, Wanganui and Taranaki are all within a day's drive of Wellington. The contrast between the arty, political capital city and the areas immediately to its north is striking. Within an hour, the country's rural heartland reveals itself with the numerous small, sleepy towns. Dairy and sheep farms continue to feature strongly in the region, but visitors can also see newer forms of land use, such as ostrich farms and vineyards. The Egmont and Whanganui national parks await the more adventurous.

Sheep farm near Martinborough

Top Outdoor Activities

The places shown here have been selected for their recreational activities. Conditions vary depending on the weather and the time of year, so exercise caution and, if in doubt, seek local advice.

	Golf	Jet-Boating	Kayaking	Sailing	Surfing	Swimming	Hiking	Windsurfing
Egmont National Park						●	●	
Te Apiti – Manawatu Gorge			●				●	
Masterton	●		●			●	●	
New Plymouth	●	●	●	●	●	●	●	●
Oakura					●	●		●
Opunake					●	●		●
Palmerston North	●					●		
Paraparaumu	●	●	●	●		●	●	
Sugar Loaf Islands						●		
Waikanae	●	●	●			●	●	
Wanganui	●	●	●			●		
Wellington	●			●	●	●		●
Whanganui National Park			●			●	●	
Whanganui River			●	●		●	●	

Sights at a Glance

Key

═══ Motorway
─── Major road
····· Minor road
∽∽∽ Major railway
──── Minor railway
─── Regional border
△ Summit

Getting Around

The area is well served by rail, bus and air services, and an extensive, well-maintained road network. The country's mild climate ensures roads in the region are usually passable throughout the year. Wellington's state-of-the-art airport serves both international and domestic travellers, while international cruise liners make use of the city's port. Several times a day, ferries, including those carrying cars, trucks and railway freight wagons, take travellers from Wellington across Cook Strait to the South Island and back again.

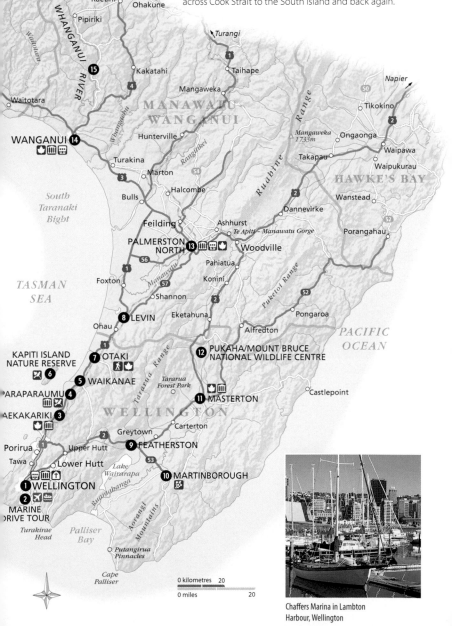

WHANGANUI NATIONAL PARK

16

Taumarunui

Raetihi

Ohakune

Pipiriki

WHANGANUI RIVER

15

Kakatahi

Waitotara

Turangi

Taihape

1

Mangaweka

4

Napier

50

Tikokino

WANGANUI **14**

MANAWATU-WANGANUI

Hunterville

Mangaweka
1733m

Ongaonga

2

Waipawa

Waipukurau

Turakina

Marton

56

Takapau

HAWKE'S BAY

3

Bulls

Halcombe

2

Wanstead

Porangahau

52

South Taranaki Bight

Feilding

Ashhurst

Te Apiti – Manawatu Gorge

Woodville

Dannevirke

PALMERSTON NORTH **13**

Ruahine Range

TASMAN SEA

1 **56**

Foxton

57

Pahiatua

Konini

Shannon

2

LEVIN **8**

Eketahuna

Pongaroa

52

Puketoi Range

Ohau

Alfredton

PACIFIC OCEAN

KAPITI ISLAND NATURE RESERVE

6

OTAKI **7**

PUKAHA/MOUNT BRUCE NATIONAL WILDLIFE CENTRE **12**

WAIKANAE **5**

Tararua Forest Park

Tararua Range

PARAPARAUMU **4**

MASTERTON **11**

Castlepoint

PAEKAKARIKI **3**

WELLINGTON

Carterton

Porirua

1

Greytown

2

Upper Hutt

FEATHERSTON **9**

Tawa

Lower Hutt

Lake Wairarapa

53

WELLINGTON **1**

2

MARINE DRIVE TOUR

MARTINBOROUGH **10**

Turakirae Head

Palliser Bay

Ruamahanga

Aorangi Mountains

Putangirua Pinnacles

Cape Palliser

0 kilometres   20

0 miles   20

Chaffers Marina in Lambton Harbour, Wellington

For keys to symbols *see back flap*

Wellington: Cultural Capital

Known primarily as the home of New Zealand's parliament and its public servant population, Wellington transformed itself during the 1980s and 1990s into a vibrant, culture-driven hot spot. Tucked around one of the world's most picturesque harbours, the capital city is intimate, sophisticated, arty and packed with national treasures. It is home to the Museum of New Zealand Te Papa Tongarewa *(see pp170–71)*, the Royal New Zealand Ballet, the New Zealand Symphony Orchestra, the New Zealand Opera, the Chamber Music New Zealand and the New Zealand School of Dance. The city's strong arts scene combines an international flavour with an intrinsic Pacific identity.

Professional theatre, strongly supported by Wellingtonians, can be enjoyed at several venues, including Downtown, Circa and Bats.

The numerous public and private galleries in Wellington are well patronized and exhibit local and international works of art. Dealer galleries, such as the Peter McLeavey Gallery, play a significant role in bringing the best of New Zealand art onto the market.

The kiwi and the fern, both symbols of New Zealand, form the logo for the New Zealand International Arts Festival.

New Zealand's Film Industry

Film making in New Zealand began on a large scale only in the 1960s and 1970s. Today, film production is a multimillion dollar industry in New Zealand, with much of it based in studios around Wellington. The International Film Festival, held every July, attracts large crowds.

Wellington is home to Sir Peter Jackson (director of *The Lord of the Rings* and *The Hobbit*) and to Weta Workshop, which created many of the special effects and props for these films. Behind-the-scenes tours, starting every 30 minutes from 9:30am to 5pm, give an opportunity to see the props and models created by the workshop. Tickets can be purchased in the Weta Cave on the corner of Camperdown Road and Weka Street in Miramar (www.wetanz.com).

Film making at one of the many locations around the city

The New Zealand Symphony Orchestra, based in Wellington, performs regularly throughout the country. The orchestra accompanied New Zealand-born diva, Dame Kiri Te Kanawa, to welcome the dawn of the new millennium at Gisborne.

Books and Writers

The emphasis on formal education, especially by Scottish immigrants who settled in Dunedin in the late 1800s, resulted in the demand that education in the new country be "free, secular and compulsory". Today, the early value placed on book learning by those settlers, many of them barely literate, has resulted in a national literacy rate of around 99 per cent. New Zealand-based reading programmes and books for children are exported around the world.

In Wellington, annual literary festivals, writers and readers programmes, and readings by local and visiting authors, are able to attract sponsorship as well as big audiences. Internationally recognized writers from Wellington include UK-based poet Fleur Adcock and novelists Maurice Gee, Elizabeth Knox and Vincent O'Sullivan *(see p37)*.

Author Linda Burgess at her book launch

Percussion instruments, including assorted percussive junk, are drummed in a high-energy performance of rhythmic power.

A scaffold "cube" formed the setting for the band's players and instruments.

International Arts Festival

Held biennially in Wellington in early autumn, the New Zealand International Arts Festival is the country's largest performing arts festival. The New Zealand percussion group, Strike, is among the local and international artistes who have performed at the festival.

The Royal New Zealand Ballet conducts national and international tours from its base in the capital city. Stephen Wellington and Nadine Tyson are shown here in a pas de deux from *Raymonda*.

The Westpac Stadium is the leading venue for one of the mainstays of New Zealand culture – sport. Rugby, cricket and soccer, as well as concerts, are held in the 40,000-seat state-of-the-art stadium.

❶ Wellington

Wellington's compact central business district lies between the city's foothills and its mountain-encircled harbour. Partly built on land developed during reclamation projects begun in the mid-19th century, the area today is the working environment of the country's politicians and the national government infrastructure. Foreign embassies, the Court of Appeal, National Archives, National Library, Museum of New Zealand Te Papa Tongarewa and the head offices of local and international businesses are among the institutions and organizations in its precincts. The city is known for its stylish shops, café culture, restaurants and galleries, with an atmosphere that is both stimulating and unhurried.

🏛 Cathedral Church of St Paul
34 Mulgrave St. **Tel** (04) 473 6722. **Open** daily. **Closed** to tourists Good Fri, 25 Dec. 🛒 🎫 🚻 donation welcomed. **W** oldsaintpauls.co.nz

Known as Old St Paul's, the Cathedral Church of St Paul is an outstanding example of an early English Gothic-style cathedral adapted to colonial conditions and materials. Built on the site of Pipitea Pā, a Māori settlement on the waterfront, the church was consecrated in 1866, and is made entirely of native timber, including its nails.

🏛 Wellington Cathedral of St Paul
Cnr Molesworth and Hill sts. **Tel** (04) 472 0286. **Open** daily. 🎫 🏠 behind church. 🏠 **W** wellingtoncathedral.org.nz

After a building programme spread over several decades, including a number of exterior and interior design changes and reversals, the Wellington Cathedral of St Paul was finally completed in 1998. Standing in the parliamentary precinct opposite the Law Courts and the National Library, the Romanesque-style cathedral houses various unique etched and stained-glass windows, memorials to historic events, and a 4,000-pipe organ. The Lady Chapel, which was formerly a parish church on the Kapiti coast north of Wellington, was relocated to the site in 1998 to complete the cathedral complex.

🏛 Parliament Buildings
Molesworth St. **Tel** (04) 817 9503. **Open** daily. **Closed** 1 & 2 Jan, 6 Feb, Good Fri, 25 & 26 Dec. 🎫 🛒 🎫 🏠 **W** parliament.govt.nz

New Zealand's Parliament is made up of three main buildings: the Edwardian Neo-Classical style Parliament Building (1922); the Parliamentary Library (1899); and the Beehive, occupied since 1979. Free guided tours take in all three buildings. They stand next to each other on a site that has housed the country's parliament since 1865, 400 m (1,300 ft) away from the earthquake fault line which runs through Wellington. Historic trees have been retained in the grounds, which also feature a rose garden.

Art in the Galleria of the Parliament Buildings

🏛 Old Government Buildings
15 Lambton Quay. **Tel** (04) 472 7356. **Open** daily. **Closed** 1 & 2 Jan, Easter Sun, 25 Apr, 25 & 26 Dec. 🛒 🎫 🚻 🏠 🏠

The largest wooden building in the southern hemisphere, and one of the largest such buildings in the world, the Old Government Buildings was built in the 1870s in a style imitating stone. Used in the early 20th century by New Zealand's parliamentary cabinet and then by government departments until 1990, the restored buildings are now filled with law school students. The original cabinet room on the first floor and historic displays on the ground floor are open to the public.

0 metres 500
0 yards 500

Key

◼ Street-by-Street: The Harbourfront
pp166–7

Old Government Buildings

Wellington City Centre

VISITORS' CHECKLIST

Practical Information
Road map D5. ⯑ 499,000.
🆆 wellingtonnz.com
ℹ️ i-SITE, Cnr of Wakefield
and Victoria sts, (04) 802 4860.
🎭 New Zealand Inter-national
Arts Festival (Feb–Mar).

Transport
✈️ 8 km (5 miles) S of city.
🚌 Bunny St (between
Featherston St & Waterloo Quay).
🚆 Platform 9, Wellington
Railway Station, Waterloo Quay.
⛴️ Aotea Quay Terminal.

🏢 Lambton Quay

Wellington's premier
shopping street, Lambton
Quay runs through the heart
of New Zealand's political
and commercial life. Its lively
1,100 m (3,600 ft) route is lined
with arcades, plazas and
elevated walkways. Most
of Lambton Quay and its
seaward parts are sited on
reclaimed land. Plaques set
at intervals along its footpaths
identify the lay of the shoreline
before the mid-1800s. While
steep steps lead up to the
slopes on the west, the side
streets on the east offer flat
access to the redeveloped
harbourfront (see pp166–7).

Items for sale in the Katherine Mansfield
Birthplace

🏛️ Katherine Mansfield House and Garden

25 Tinakori Rd. **Tel** (04) 473 7268.
Open 10am–4pm Tue–Sun.
Closed Good Fri, 25 Dec. 🔖 🔖
📷 by appt. 📷

This 1888 villa is the birthplace
and childhood home of the
famous author Katherine
Mansfield (see p37). It contains
period photographs, excerpts
from Mansfield's writing, and
antique furniture.

For keys to symbols see back flap

Exploring Wellington

A vibrant, inner-city area bordered to the north by a green belt, central Wellington encompasses late Victorian mansions, student flats, tiny former workers' cottages, the Prime Minister's residence, an historic cemetery and the main motorway in and out of the city. At the end of the 19th century, as the number of overseas settlers increased, land near the foreshore became scarce, and steeper, less accessible land above the city was utilized for housing. Today, a walk around the suburb of Thorndon up to some higher view-points shows how a community has spread onwards and upwards from its original concentration in the port area.

Cable car climbing to the top of the Botanic Garden

🚋 Wellington Cable Car
Cable Car Lane, 280 Lambton Quay. **Tel** (04) 472 2199. Museum: **Open** daily. **Closed** 25 Dec. 🅿️
W wellingtoncablecar.co.nz

New Zealand's only historic cable cars opened in 1902 to link the hill suburbs with the city. They have been electrically powered since 1933. Stops on the way include Victoria University, with access to the Botanic Garden and Space Place at Carter Observatory at the top. The Kelburn terminus has fine views over the city and harbour.

🌿 Wellington Botanic Garden
Tinakori Rd. **Tel** (04) 499 1400. **Open** daily. 📷 🖥️ 🏛️
W wellington.govt.nz

Established in 1868, the garden is a mix of protected native forest, conifer plantings and plant collections. A major seasonal bedding programme includes a massed display of 30,000 tulips in spring and early summer. The Lady Norwood Rose Garden has 106 formal beds, including recent introductions and old favourites. The Begonia House features tropical and temperate plants, a lily pond, seasonal displays of orchids, and a collection of epiphytic and carnivorous plants. The garden's information hub, the Treehouse Visitor Centre, can be accessed via a tower lift. The more hardy can get to the centre via a steep path.

The **Space Place at Carter Observatory**, New Zealand's national observatory, stands in the Botanic Garden complex near the terminus of the cable car. Astronomical displays, audiovisual shows and a planetarium are special features.

🏛️ Space Place at Carter Observatory
40 Salamanca Rd, Kelburn. **Tel** (04) 910 3140. **Open** daily. 🅿️
W museumswellington.org.nz

The ivy-covered Hunter Building at Victoria University

🏛️ Victoria University
Kelburn Parade. **Tel** (04) 472 1000. With 21,500 students enrolled in over 50 departments and schools, Victoria University is the fourth largest of New Zealand's eight universities. Opened in 1897, Victoria University's main campus has occupied its Kelburn site over-looking downtown Wellington since 1904. The Faculties of Law and Commerce, as well as the School of Architecture and Design, are among the campuses located in the city.

Lady Norwood Rose Garden in the Wellington Botanic Garden

For hotels and restaurants in this region see pp304–5 and pp319–21

Suburban Hillside Villas

Often appearing to cling precariously to the sides of hills, accessible only by cable car or long flights of steep steps, hillside villas are a striking feature of Wellington's older city suburbs such as Oriental Bay, Mount Victoria, Thorndon and Kelburn. These ubiquitous New Zealand homes evolved during the late 19th and early 20th centuries from simple, flat-fronted single-storey colonial cottages with verandahs running across the front, to two-storey houses with projecting faceted bay windows. The villas were traditionally made of timber from New Zealand's kauri forests, roofed with corrugated iron, and decorated with mass-produced components ordered from catalogues. Other features included the use of stained glass, large double-hung sash windows and balustraded porches or verandahs.

Harbourfront Suburbs

Wellington's early settlers were forced by a shortage of flat land to build on the hills bordering the harbour. Many original villas, as well as those restored and adapted as family homes, can be seen during a walk or drive through Wellington's harbourfront suburbs.

Wooden villas on the hillside overlooking Oriental Bay

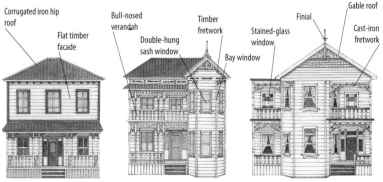

Corrugated iron hip roof

Flat timber facade

Bull-nosed verandah

Double-hung sash window

Timber fretwork

Stained-glass window

Bay window

Finial

Gable roof

Cast-iron fretwork

Flat-fronted, hip-roofed villa with long verandah

Gabled hip-roofed villa with faceted bay window

Gable-roofed villa with ornate cast-iron decoration

Late 19th-century villas constructed for middle-income families usually had a living area (the "parlour"), three or four bedrooms and a central hallway, with a single bathroom and kitchen area to the rear. The toilet (often referred to as the "long drop") and laundry ("wash house") facilities were usually located at the back of the house.

Parlour at the 1888 villa in Thorndon where Katherine Mansfield was born *(see p163)*

Street-by-Street: The Harbourfront

The area between Lambton Harbour and Clyde Quay Wharf on Wellington's harbourfront stands entirely on reclaimed land. It covers a site once central to Wellington's waterfront industry, and can be covered on foot within an hour. Echoes of the commercial sailing ships and liners that once dominated the area remain in the Wellington Museum. In spring and summer, dragon boat competitions are held opposite the Museum of New Zealand Te Papa Tongarewa. The Civic Square, with its open spaces and nearby public buildings, such as the Town Hall, is a favourite meeting place for Wellingtonians and visitors alike.

Courtenay Place
Lined with bars, clubs, restaurants and theatres, Courtenay Place provides a taste of the city's nightlife *(see p169)*.

Key

— Suggested route

Circa Theatre
This refurbished building is one of the focal points of the city's contemporary theatre scene *(see p160)*.

Waitangi Park, next to Te Papa Tongarewa, is an award-winning urban park with a beach and boardwalk promenade – a popular spot on a summer's day.

The Overseas Terminal provides berths for yachts and other small vessels. It also houses facilities for conferences and exhibitions.

★ **Museum of New Zealand Te Papa Tongarewa**
The museum offers visitors interactive experiences of New Zealand's Maori heritage, national history and natural environment as well as art treasures *(see pp170–71)*.

0 metres 100
0 yards 100

For hotels and restaurants in this region see pp304–5 and pp319–21

City-to-Sea Bridge
Linking Civic Square and Frank Kitts Park, the bridge is decorated with large, Pacific-style woodcarvings.

The Civic Square is an open space bounded by the Michael Fowler Centre, Town Hall and City Gallery Wellington *(see p168)*.

Frank Kitts Park contains a children's playground with lighthouse and slide. An overhead bridge beside the park provides access to the city's business district.

★ **Wellington Museum**
Housed in an 1892 building, the museum focuses on Wellington's social and maritime history *(see p169)*.

Town Hall
A mainstay of entertainment for decades, the Town Hall is one of several international standard concert venues in the city *(see p169)*.

Queens Wharf
The complex of cafés, restaurants and bars on Queens Wharf is a popular entertainment hub for nearby office workers.

The Harbourfront

The Harbourfront is dominated by the City-to-Sea bridge, a pedestrian-only right of way above one of Wellington's main roads. Bordered on one side by Wellington's wharves and on the other by office blocks, the bridge leads from steps within the Civic Square complex to Frank Kitts Park and the waterfront, a lagoon and further on to the Museum of New Zealand Te Papa Tongarewa *(see pp170–71)*. The bridge is a public art space in its own right, featuring works by leading New Zealand sculptors.

Contemporary exhibit at the City Gallery Wellington

✪ Civic Square

Wakefield St. **Tel** (04) 802 4860. **Open** daily. ♿ 🅦 wellingtonnz.com

The heart of the city's cultural scene, this extensive paved, plaza-style courtyard was opened in the early 1990s, making use of an area that was previously a busy street. The pink and beige square is an open space that features various sculptures and provides a link to a number of institutions bordering it. These include the Public Library, Visitor Information Centre, City Council Buildings, City Gallery Wellington and the capital's main concert venues, the Town Hall and Michael Fowler Centre.

The square harkens back to its previous role as a thoroughfare. It brings together Wellington's central business district with the city's cultural and social side: the Museum of New Zealand Te Papa Tongarewa, the Opera House, theatres, cinemas and shops, as well as the bars and restaurants of the city's main night-time entertainment area, Courtenay Place. The square has become a well-used and central meeting place for Wellingtonians. Visitors to the square will often find themselves among street theatre performers and at outdoor concerts, exhibitions and rallies of all kinds.

🏛 City Gallery Wellington

Civic Square. **Tel** (04) 801 3021. **Open** 10am–5pm daily. **Closed** 25 Dec. 🎨 international exhibitions. ♿ ▣ 🅦 citygallery.org.nz

Housed in a striking Art Deco building fitted with original kauri doors, marble finishes, handrails and steel windows, the building that for decades served as the city's Public Library is now home to the country's leading, and often most controversial, art gallery.

Primarily an exhibition space, with no permanent collection of its own, the gallery has nonetheless developed a distinctive character, specializing in bringing to Wellington the best contemporary art and design shows from within New Zealand and around the world. Exhibitions held at the gallery have covered a diverse range of media and subjects, including painting, sculpture, film and video, industrial and graphic design and architecture.

The building has been expanded to include an auditorium, a gallery of Māori and Pacific art, and an enlarged Michael Hirschfield Gallery, which is dedicated to exhibiting works by Wellington artists.

Neil Dawson's ferns sculpture suspended in the Civic Square

For hotels and restaurants in this region see pp304–5 and pp319–21

🎹 Michael Fowler Centre

Wakefield St. **Tel** (04) 801 4231.
Open daily. 🎵 for concerts. ♿
🎥 by arrangement. 💻

Designed by Christchurch's
Sir Miles Warren and named
after a former mayor and
prominent architect, the
semicircular complex is internationally renowned for its
ability to distribute sound
throughout its 2,550-plus seat
concert chamber. Rock
concerts, conventions and even
political rallies are staged in
what has become the city's
premier concert hall. Many
events associated with the
increasingly popular biennial
New Zealand International Arts
Festival *(see pp46, 160–61)*,
which attracts thousands of
local and overseas visitors to
Wellington, are held here.

The Victorian-tiled lobby of the
Town Hall

🎹 Town Hall

Wakefield St. **Tel** (04) 801 4231.
Open daily. 🎵 for concerts.
♿ 🎥 by arrangement. 💻

Restoration of the Town Hall,
a sedate 1904 Edwardian brick
building with a Roman-style
portico, has returned the hall
to much of its former glory.
Restoration work included
seismic strengthening of the
building, restoring the floor's
Victorian tiles, uncovering
wrought-iron balustrades,
manufacturing lights and
fittings from original samples,
and repairing the auditorium's
pressed zinc ceiling. The hall's
magnificent main staircase is
now a major attraction. The
2,000-seat "shoe box" auditorium
is regarded as one of the world's
leading venues for the performance of classical music.

Courtenay Place, a prime night-time entertainment area

🎹 Courtenay Place

Lined with a concentrated strip
of sophisticated night-clubs,
trendy cafés and restaurants,
and professional theatres,
Courtenay Place and the
streets leading from it form
the night-time entertainment
heart of the city.

With nearly every cuisine style
and price range available, from
budget eating outlets to award-
winning restaurants, Courtenay
Place is the venue to meet
visitors, mix with locals, and eat
and dance the night away.
Live music inside cafés and bars
is matched by a lively street
scene, where crowds thread
their way through buskers and
performers that add to the
area's relaxed atmosphere.

🏛 Wellington Museum

Queens Wharf. **Tel** (04) 472 8904.
Open 10am–5pm daily.
Closed 25 Dec. ♿ 🎥 📷
🌐 **wellingtonmuseum.org.nz**

Housed in the former
customs house which
was constructed in
1892, the Wellington
Museum gives an
insight into the capital's
rich cultural and social
history. The museum
uses model ships, ships'
instruments, relics from
wrecks, maritime
paintings, old maps and
sea journals, as well as
holographic re-creations
and videos to tell the
story of Wellington
in the context of its

harbour and surrounding coast.
One of the most interesting
exhibits in the museum's
collection of ship models
is the inter-island ferry, the
Wahine. This vessal sank
off the Wellington suburb of
Seatoun in April 1968 during
a storm. A photograph exhibit
documents the tragedy.
The Plimmer's Ark Gallery
displays part of the excavated
remains of the ship *Inconstant*,
built in 1848.

The museum also features
a 12-minute show on Māori
creation legends and looks
at early Māori and European
settlement. A 20th century
gallery explores how the city
has changed. There is also an
education room for children.

Façade of the historic Wellington Museum located
on the city's waterfront

Museum of New Zealand Te Papa Tongarewa

With exhibition space equivalent to three football pitches, the Museum of New Zealand Te Papa Tongarewa ("Place of Treasures") is one of the largest museums in the world. Committed to telling the stories of all cultures in New Zealand, home to the National Art Collection, and with ample gallery space for touring international exhibitions, the museum opened on its waterfront site in 1998. Te Papa's collections include a number of significant Māori works of art and treasures, as well as a unique 21st-century carved meeting house.

Gallipoli: The scale of our war
This exhibition explores the eight-month Gallipoli Campaign of World War I using the stories of eight New Zealanders. The Weta Workshop *(see p160)* helped bring this interactive exhibit to life.

★ Te Marae
The contemporary meeting house is the focal point of a Māori *marae*. Named Te Hono ki Hawaiki ("the link back to Hawaiki"), Te Papa's *marae* recalls the ancestral land of Māori.

Level 2

Level 1

Bush City
Visitors step into the open air to experience native bush, wetlands, a volcanic landscape, a waterfall and a lagoon right in the centre of the city. They can also explore a glowworm cave.

"Awesome Forces" help visitors experience the powerful forces shaping the country's landscape.

★ Mākōtukutuku Wharepuni

Go back 600 years on entering this *wharepuni* (sleeping house) reconstructed using traditional methods and tools.

VISITORS' CHECKLIST

Practical Information
Cable St. **Tel** (04) 381 7000.
W **tepapa.govt.nz**
Open 10am–6pm daily (10am–9pm Thu). 🎫 for Introducing Te Papa Tour and some temporary exhibitions. ♿ 📷 ✏️ 🖥️ 🎒 🅿️

Transport
🚌 Courtney Place.

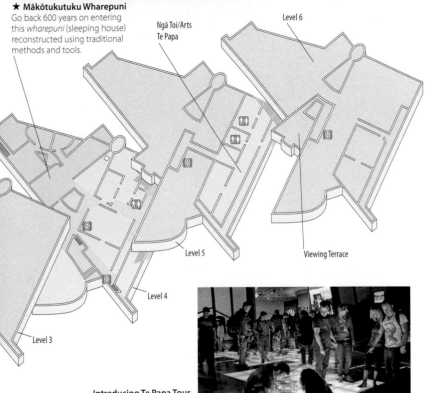

Ngā Toi/Arts
Te Papa

Level 6

Level 5

Viewing Terrace

Level 4

Level 3

Introducing Te Papa Tour

This 60-minute tour takes visitors to see the museum's main highlights and various Māori treasures that are on display. The tour departs every hour and is ideal for those pressed for time.

Key to Floorplan

- ▢ Art
- ▢ History
- ▢ Māori
- ▢ Nature

Gallery Guide

The first of the high-tech interactive exhibitions begins on Level 2, which also provides access to Bush City. Level 3 features an exhibition called Blood, Earth, Fire, *which tells the story of human impact on New Zealand's flora and fauna. Māori, Pacific Island and European multi-cultural exhibits are on Level 4. Ngā Toi/Arts Te Papa, works from the national art collection, can be found on Levels 4 and 5, but are also spread throughout the museum. Level 6 has an outdoor terrace, with sweeping views of the city and harbour. Note that in 2019, the layout of the museum is due to change completely.*

❷ Marine Drive Tour

Hugging the coastline from Oriental Bay, southeast of the city centre on the inner harbour, to Owhiro Bay on the outer shoreline facing Cook Strait, this route is one of New Zealand's great coastal drives. It is both picturesque on cloudless days and awe-inspiring when Wellington's famous southerly gales whip up pounding waves. The route takes visitors past numerous small bays and sheltered, sandy beaches. It also passes through several suburbs where wooden villas *(see p165)* perch on what seem precarious sites high above the road, and around steep, uninhabited hillsides covered with trees that come down to the water's edge.

⑩ Owhiro Bay
Tourers can turn right at this bay and return to the city via Happy Valley Road or continue onto the 4 km (2.5 mile) Red Rocks Coastal Walk, where 80–150 male seals take up residence each year.

⑨ Island Bay
Descendants of Italian immigrants, who settled here in the early 20th century, are among those seen fishing in Cook Strait and beyond.

⑧ Lyall Bay
Bordered by Wellington's airport, this bay is used all year round by surfers and swimmers. On a clear day, the South Island's snow-covered mountain ranges can be seen.

Key
■ Tour route
— Other road

0 kilometres   1
0 miles   1

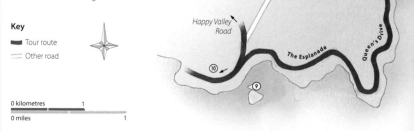

City Centre
Cambridge Tce
Kent Tce
Government House
Rongotai
Adelaide Road
Wellington Zoo
Municipal Golf Links
Lyall Parade
Happy Valley Road
Queen's Drive
The Esplanade
⑩
⑨

① Oriental Bay
This is an area of cafés and fashionable restaurants and a favourite spot for joggers and swimmers. Across from the sandy beach, stately Victorian villas share the hillside with modern apartment blocks.

Tips for Drivers

Length: 30 km (19 miles).
Stopping-off points: There are glorious views at all points along the route. Several parking areas allow visitors to leave their cars and stroll along the bays. Eating places include Scorch-O-Rama at Scorching Bay, whose staff have permission to serve customers seated across the road on the waterfront.

③ Mahanga Bay
One of the smallest and most sheltered bays along the route, Mahanga Bay is fringed with pine trees.

② Evans Bay
This sheltered bay is a popular spot for yachting. It also contains a marina.

Mount Victoria

Oriental Parade
Evans Bay Parade
Shelly Bay Road
Massey Road
Karaka Bay Road
Marine Parade
Calabar Rd
Broadway
Miramar Golf Course
Wellington International Airport
Breaker Bay Road
Moa Point Road

④ Scorching Bay
Popular with swimmers, this beach allows good views towards Somes and Ward islands and Cook Strait. The seaside suburb of Eastbourne is opposite.

⑤ Karaka Bay
This bay is named after the native orange-berried karaka trees found along its edge. It has a pier and a number of wooden summer houses built in the early 20th century by wealthy people from out of town.

⑥ Worser Bay
The eastern suburbs are home to the city's thriving film industry, including Peter Jackson's workshops *(see p160).*

⑦ Breaker Bay
Little blue penguins can sometimes be seen crossing the road here to nest noisily under nearby houses.

Old trams at the Tramway Museum, Paekakariki

❸ Paekakariki

Road map E4. 🏔 1,700. 🚉 🚌
ℹ️ i-SITE, Rimu Rd, Paraparaumu, (04)
298 8195. 🇼 **naturecoast.co.nz**

Situated on the Kapiti Coast,
40 minutes' drive north of
Wellington on State Highway 1,
Paekakariki is the first of four
townships on 40 km (25 miles)
of sandy coastline known as the
"nature coast". A main attraction
at Paekakariki is Queen Elizabeth
Park, which encompasses a
stunning coastline, sand dunes,
streams, peat swamps and bush
walks. A tram ride from MacKays
Crossing north of Paekakariki
takes in the 6.4 sq km (2.5 sq
mile) park.

At the **Wellington Tramway
Museum** in the park, visitors
can view displays of some of
the forerunners of the trolley
buses that still run on
Wellington's streets.

🏛 **Wellington Tramway Museum**
Queen Elizabeth Park. **Tel** (04) 292
8361. **Open** summer: daily; winter:
Sat & Sun. **Closed** 25 Dec. 🚫 ♿

❹ Paraparaumu

Road map E4. 🏔 12,000. 🚉 🚌
🚌 ℹ️ Coastlands, (04) 298 8195.

The main centre on the Kapiti
Coast, Paraparaumu has
shorefront shops, cafés and
restaurants. It also has a
developed beach, with a park
and playgrounds. The town is
the departure point for boat
trips to Kapiti Island.

The area's major attraction is the
Southward Car Museum, which
holds the largest collection of
vintage and veteran vehicles
in the southern hemisphere. The
collection of bicycles
includes an 1863 boneshaker.
Marlene Dietrich's limousine is
one of more than 250 classic
and quirky vehicles dating
from 1895. Racing boats,
homemade vehicles, motor-
cycles, early motoring curios
and traction engines are also
housed on the site. A highlight
is a 1950 Cadillac Gangster
Special, once owned by an
employee of Al Capone and

Lucky Luciano. It boasts a bomb
proof floor, armour-plated
doors, bullet-proof windows,
and a hinged windscreen to
enable firing from inside.

The **Lindale Tourist Centre**,
set around a New Zealand farm,
is a good place to bring children.
The centre offers sheep shearing
demonstrations as well as hands-
on opportunities to milk a cow,
bottle-feed lambs and goats,
play with chickens and baby
deer, and observe exotic species
like llama and emu. There are
farm walks taking in the animal
barn, where visitors can handle
and feed smaller animals.

A shop showcasing the
award-winning gourmet Kapiti
Cheese and Kapiti Ice Cream,
is located on the site, along
with galleries, shops and eating
places. There are also places
to picnic and have a barbecue.

🏛 **Southward Car Museum**
Otaihanga Rd, Paraparaumu.
Tel (04) 297 1221. **Open** daily.
Closed Good Fri, 25 Apr, 25 Dec.
🚫 ♿ 📷 🍴 🛍 🚻
🇼 **southward.org.nz**

🎫 **Lindale Tourist Centre**
State Hwy 1, Paraparaumu. **Tel** (04)
297 0916. **Open** daily. **Closed** Good
Fri, 25 Dec. 🚫 ♿ 📷 🛍 🚻
🇼 **lindale.co.nz**

Vintage cars at the Southward Car Museum

⑤ Waikanae

Road map E4. 🏔 8,600. 🚌 🚏
ℹ️ i-SITE, Rimu Rd, Paraparaumu (04)
298 8195. **w** naturecoast.co.nz

Nestled between the foothills of the Tararua Range and the Kapiti Coast, Waikanae is primarily a retirement centre, known for its craft shops and magnificent gardens. Burnard Gardens, recognized as one of New Zealand's most formally designed English-style gardens, is located here and viewings can be arranged.

The **Waikanae Estuary Scientific Reserve** is home to over 63 species of birds (though some are migratory), such as shags, dabchicks, Caspian terns, royal spoonbills and pukeko. Fires, hunting and mountain and trail biking are forbidden.

The unspoilt Kapiti Island as seen from the mainland

⑥ Kapiti Island Nature Reserve

Road map E4. 🚌 Paraparaumu.
ℹ️ Department of Conservation, Waikanae Field Centre, 10 Parata St, Waikanae, (04) 296 1112.

Kapiti Island, lying about 6 km (4 miles) from the mainland, dominates the Kapiti Coast. The 10-km- (6-mile-) long island has been a protected wildlife reserve since 1897. Access to the island is very limited although a permit to visit by charter boat can be obtained from the Department of Conservation in Wellington. All parties are met by the resident ranger. Trips around the island, and diving or fishing in the surrounding waters can be done at any time. Making their home on the island are birds rare or absent from the mainland, such as saddlebacks and takahe. Less rare, but twice as cheeky, are the kakas, which are likely to steal anything that is left unattended.

⑦ Otaki

Road map E4. 🏔 7,600. 🚌 🚏 🚏
ℹ️ State Hwy 1, (06) 364 7620.

Before the European settlers' arrival in 1840, Otaki was heavily populated by Māori. It had the finest Māori church, Rangiatea Church, in New Zealand. Built in 1851, it was destroyed by fire in 1995. A replica of the Māori church has been open to visitors here since 2003.

Environs
Just south of Otaki is the **Hyde Park Museum**. The museum has Māori artifacts from pre-European days, colonial memorabilia and exhibits from present-day New Zealand. Included are a Royal Room with displays from the 1953 visit of Queen Elizabeth and Prince Phillip, old farm machinery and a grocery shop with over 3,000 items marked at 1937 prices.

South of the town, the 19 km (12 mile) Gorge Road leads to Otaki Forks and the Tararua Forest Park. Along the way are walking tracks.

Entrance to the Hyde Park Museum, Otaki, which houses heritage displays

🏛 **Hyde Park Museum**
State Hwy 1, Te Horo. **Tel** (04) 298 4515.
Open Tue–Sun. 🎁 donation. ♿

⑧ Levin

Road map E4. 🏔 15,400.
🚌 🚏 🚏

Levin sits on a fertile plain that is one of the largest vegetable-producing areas in the country. Its main street, lined with shops that service its farming hinterland, epitomizes much of traditional small-town New Zealand. Owner-operated outlets on the outskirts of the town offer "pick-your-own" freshly grown produce direct from the fields and orchards.

Te Rauparaha

Kapiti Island was once the base of Te Rauparaha (1768–1849), chief of the Ngati Toa tribe and one of the greatest Māori generals of his era. After years of warfare in the Waikato and Taranaki areas, he moved to Kapiti Island in the 1820s, dominating the southwestern part of the North Island and the north of the South Island until the 1840s. He is credited with composing the well-known *haka* (war chant) often performed by the All Blacks before international rugby matches.

Watercolour (1840)
by Isaac Coates

Kamate. Kamate.
Ka Ora. Ka Ora.
Tenei te tangata
*   puhuruhuru*
Nana nei i tiki mai
I whakawhiti te ra.
Upane. Upane.
Whiti te ra.

It is death. It is death.
It is life. It is life.
This is the hairy person
Who caused the sun to
    shine.
Abreast. Keep abreast.
The rank. Hold fast.
Into the sun that shines.

A cyclist on the South Coast Rimutaka Cycle Trail, which runs from Wellington to Wairarapa

❾ Featherston

Road map E4. 🏔 2,600. 🚌 🚲 ℹ️
Old Courthouse, Main St, (06) 308 8051, 10am–1pm. **W** wairarapanz.com

Situated at the foot of the Rimutaka Range, Featherston, is the southern gateway to the Wairarapa area for those arriving from the Wellington side of the divide. Known for its antique shops and colonial buildings, it also houses the **Fell Locomotive Museum**, home to the world's only surviving Fell engine. Running on three rails, these ingenious locomotives used to climb up and over the Rimutaka Range.

🏛 **Fell Locomotive Museum**
Cnr SH2 and Lyon sts. **Tel** (06) 308 9379. **Open** daily. **Closed** Anzac Day (am only), 25 Dec. 🚫 📷 ♿
W fellmuseum.org.nz

Environs
On the right side of the road from Wellington, before reaching Featherston, a signpost points the way to a lookout. There are also terrific walks that enable visitors to enjoy splendid views across **Lake Wairarapa** to the ranges of Haurangi (Aorangi) Forest Park and Palliser Bay. The lake is home to internationally recognized wetlands that are the third largest in New Zealand. Both native and migratory breeds of bird gather at the lake.
Southeast of the lake is **Cape Palliser** where, next to a public road, visitors can find one of the country's largest breeding colonies for the New Zealand fur seal, one of nine fur seal species found worldwide. Seals can be seen throughout the year, with breeding from November to January.
Another spectacular sight in the area is the **Putangirua Pinnacles**, formed in the past 120,000 years by heavy rain eroding an ancient gravel deposit. Some of the pinnacles may be 1,000 years old.
Wairarapa has myriad cycle routes along the region's expansive rural landscape and rugged coastlines. The 115 km (71 mile) **Rimutaka Cycle Trail** begins in Wellington and takes riders through the Rimutaka Ranges to Wairarapa Valley and ends at Orongorongo.

❿ Martinborough

Road map E5. 🏔 1,500. ℹ️ 18 Kitchener St, (06) 306 5010. 🎡 Martinborough Country Fair (Feb & Mar), Toast Martinborough Wine, Food and Music Festival (Nov). **W** wairarapanz.com

Established in 1881 by Irish immigrant John Martin, Martin-borough was once reliant for its prosperity on the surrounding farming community. Since the late 1970s, the town has become internationally known for its grape growing and wine making (see pp40–41). It is now a fashionable weekend destination for those attracted by its premium wines, vineyard cafés, boutique stores, quality accommodation, olive groves and award-winning restaurants. Most of the town's boutique wineries are within walking or cycling distance of its picturesque town square.

Environs
New Zealand's first commercial wind farm, **Hau Hei Wind Farm**, is 21 km (13 miles) southeast of Martinborough. Operated by Wairarapa Electricity, the farm's turbines are ranged along a 540 m (1,770 ft) ridge. Although on private land, they can be seen from a public viewing area.

Visitors enjoying the wine at the Grapevine in Martinborough

⓫ Masterton

Road map E4. 🏛 22,800. 🚗 🚌 🚆
ℹ Cnr Dixon & Bruce sts (at Aratoi),
(06) 370 0900. 🏆 Golden Shears
(Mar). 🌐 **wairarapanz.com**

Ninety minutes' drive from both
Wellington and Palmerston
North, Masterton is Wairarapa's
largest town. It hosts a number
of events during the summer,
including a biennial air show
and also a traditional shearing
competition known as the
Golden Shears which is held
every year.

Masterton is home to **The
Wool Shed**, a national museum
dedicated to New Zealand's
shearing heritage with live
sheep-shearing displays for
groups of ten or more. The town
also has a recreation centre with
swimming pools, and the
region's art and history musem,
Aratoi. Queen Elizabeth Park
has a children's playground, a
miniature train, mini-golf and
a skatepark.

🏛 The Wool Shed
12 Dixon St. **Tel** (06) 378 8008.
Open 10am–4pm daily. **Closed** Anzac
Day, Good Fri, 25 Dec. 🅿 ♿ 📷
🌐 thewoolshednz.com

Environs
Masterton is close to the beach
resorts of **Castlepoint** and
Riversdale, which are popular
for surfing, fishing and walking.
State Highway 2 runs through
the village of **Greytown**. Settled
in 1854, it is the oldest town in

Agricultural implements at the
Cobblestones Museum

Wairarapa and has a restored
Victorian main street. It is home
to the **Cobblestones Museum**.
Located on the site of coach
stables built in 1856 for the
Wellington mail service, the
museum houses colonial
buildings, vehicles, agricultural
equipment and a working
print shop. It has relocated
and restored buildings,
complete with
memorabilia of
the days of the
early settlers.

The **Tararua Forest
Park**, located within the
rugged Tararua Range,
can be accessed at Holdsworth,
15 km (9 miles) from State
Highway 2, via Norfolk Road just
south of Masterton. The park

has bush walks ranging from
easy to difficult, while Grassy
Flats beside the Atiwhakatu
Stream are ideal for picnics
and barbecues.

🏛 Cobblestones Museum
169 Main St, Greytown. **Tel** (06) 304
9687. **Open** daily. 🅿 ♿ 📷

⓬ Pukaha Mount Bruce National Wildlife Centre

Road map E4. **Tel** (06) 375 8004. **Open**
9am–4:30pm daily. **Closed** 25 Dec. 🅿
♿ 🖥 📷 🌐 pukaha.org.nz

Located 30 km (19 miles)
north of Masterton, this
centre conserves some of
New Zealand's most rare and
endangered wildlife. Most
famously, it is home to three
white kiwi and features a Kiwi
House where the birds are
hatched, hand-raised and fed
from October to
April. Other bird
species include the
stitchbird, kokako and
takahe. Visitors can take
a walking tour through
native bush, including a last
remnant of forest once
known as "Forty Mile
Bush", containing native
rimu, rata and kamahi
trees, nocturnal kiwi and
tuatara. It is also possible to
watch eels being fed near the
centre's river bridge and kaka
being fed each afternoon.

Kokako at
Mount Bruce

Golden Shears Competition

One of the biggest sheep-shearing competitions in the world,
the Golden Shears competition is held in Masterton from the
Thursday to the first Saturday of March each year. Initiated by
the Wairarapa District Young Farmers' Club, the competition was
originally envisaged to form part of the local Agricultural and
Pastoral Show. Since the inaugural competition in 1961, the
Golden Shears has become a national institution, attracting
hundreds of competitors from around the world and thousands
of observers. The competition reached its peak during the 1960s
and 1970s when seats to the event were sold out 12 months in
advance. Although several smaller shearing competitions are
now held around the country, the Golden Shears remains the
pre-eminent show in New Zealand. Sheep shearing has also
entered the world of professionalism: prize money has risen
over the years, corporate sponsorship has become the norm,
and many shearers adopt fitness and training programmes not
dreamed of in the early days of the event.

Sheep shearer in competition

⑬ Palmerston North

Manawatu's largest city, Palmerston North lies in the centre of a broad, fertile coastal plain that stretches from the Tasman Sea across to the Tararua and Ruahine ranges and encompasses a varied landscape of valleys, plateaus and rivers. The city is a growing hub for the lower North Island, with three main roads converging near it. New Zealand's largest university, Massey University, and several colleges and research institutes are based here, giving Palmerston North a pleasant and diverse university city atmosphere.

1926 poster in the New Zealand Rugby Museum

♦ The Square

ℹ️ (06) 350 1922. 🌐 manawatunz.co.nz

Laid out in 1866, this tranquil, garden zone at the heart of the city provides welcome relief to the busy commercial centre. Originally bisected by New Zealand's main trunk railway, The Square's clipped lawns, flower beds, trees and shrubs, ornamental ponds and fountains, war memorial and chiming clock tower attract hoards of visitors all year round. The surrounding shops and buildings reflect the diversity of styles in New Zealand's architectural history.

🏛️ Te Manawa Art Gallery

326 Main St. **Tel** (06) 355 5000. **Open** 10am–5pm daily. **Closed** 1 Jan, Good Fri, 25 & 26 Dec. 🌐 temanawa.co.nz

First opened in 1959 as the Palmerston North Art Gallery, the gallery was renamed and rehoused in a modern, spacious building near The Square in 1977. Visitors are greeted at the entrance by local artist Paul Dibble's striking sculpture, *Pacific Monarch*, reputedly the largest bronze work cast in New Zealand.

The gallery's strength lies in its collection of contemporary art, particularly that from the 1970s, but it also houses a permanent collection of paintings, sculpture, prints, drawings, photographs and ceramics by prominent New Zealand artists. There is a regularly changing programme of exhibitions of New Zealand and international art and crafts. The gallery is part of the Te Manawa complex, which also includes a museum and science centre.

🏛️ New Zealand Rugby Museum

326 Main St. **Tel** (06) 358 6974. **Open** 10am–5pm daily. **Closed** 1 Jan, Good Fri, 25 & 26 Dec. ♿ 📞 phone to book. 🌐 rugbymuseum.co.nz

Founded in 1968, the museum relocated to the Te Manawa complex in 2011. It contains exhibits and memorabilia relating to the history of rugby in New Zealand from the first game played in the country, at Nelson in 1870, to the present. There are also exhibits from other rugby-playing countries. The paraphernalia on display includes caps, jerseys, trophies, badges, autographed balls, ties, posters and photographs.

Interactive exhibits allow visitors to explore the aspects of rugby that interest them most, and famous international games can be watched on screen. Also on display is a broken protestor's shield, a legacy of the bitter 1981 tour to New Zealand by the South African Springbok rugby team. The tour divided the country and caused bloody protests.

Environs

East of the city, the Manawatu River runs through the imposing **Te Apiti – Manawatu Gorge**. Offering one of North Island's most well-known day walks, Te Apiti is a stunning, culturally rich, structure formed over time. The river seems to defy geographical logic by rising on the eastern slopes of the Tararua Range, then turning back on itself to reach the Tasman Sea to the west. The gorge is popular with jet-boaters, kayakers, walkers and campers. Visitors can also marvel at the sculpture of Whatonga, an ancient Māori warrior who has been immortalized as a 6-m- (20-ft-) tall sculpture along one of the walking tracks.

There are a number of beautiful gardens around the city and region. One of these is the Cross Hill Gardens, a 45-minute drive north, has one of New Zealand's largest and most varied collections of rhododendrons.

🌿 **Te Apiti – Manawatu Gorge**
1631 Napier Rd, Ashhurst. **Tel** 0800 626 292. 🌐 teapiti.com

Sculpture by Paul Dibble in front of Te Manawa Art Gallery

For hotels and restaurants in this region see pp304–5 and pp319–21

Te Manawa

At the heart of the Manawatu region, Te Manawa is the only institution of its kind in New Zealand to unite a museum, art gallery *(see p178)* and interactive science centre. The constantly changing exhibition programme features nationally significant collections as well as innovative hands-on shows. The museum forms the heart of the complex and recalls the long occupation of the region by the Māori, as well as exploring the history of the Manawatu. The interactive science centre features changing exhibitions that are popular with children. The New Zealand Rugby Museum *(see p178)* is also part of the Te Manawa complex.

VISITORS' CHECKLIST

Practical Information
326 Main St. **Tel** (06) 355 5000.
🅦 temanawa.co.nz
Open 10am–5pm daily
(including some public hols).
Closed 1 Jan, Good Fri, 25 &
26 Dec. ♿ 📷 📧

★ Te Awa – The River
Live cave weta insects are among the creatures in an exhibition on the impact of the Manawatu River.

Manawatu Journeys
The area's history is explored via domestic items.

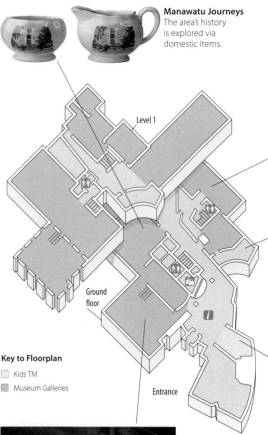

Level 1

**AgResearch
Conservatory** features samples of exotic and native plant species.

Ground
floor

Key to Floorplan
◻ Kids TM
▨ Museum Galleries

Entrance

Kids TM
This exciting area for the under-8s lets children explore and learn about the world through dressing up and role play.

★ Tangata Whenua Gallery
These 19th-century carved palisade posts are among the Māori treasures exhibited in the gallery.

Lush hills in front of Mount Egmont ▶

⑭ Wanganui

The area around Wanganui was first settled by Māori about AD 1100. By 1840 the New Zealand Company, unable to provide sufficient land in the Wellington district for the steady flow of new colonists, began to negotiate with the Māori for land in Wanganui. The town became a distribution centre for the area extending to Waitotara in the west, Marton in the east and up the Whanganui River Valley in the north. Less than an hour by road to Palmerston North and only two and a half hours to Wellington, Wanganui's thriving arts scene sits alongside a variety of export-oriented industries.

Wanganui and the city bridge as seen from Durie Hill

🎋 Cooks Gardens

Maria Place.
A leading outdoor venue, Cooks Gardens contain a wooden velodrome and an attractive old bell tower. It was here, in 1962, that New Zealander Peter Snell ran the mile in under four minutes, breaking the record held by Roger Bannister of Great Britain.

🏛 Victoria Avenue

The preserved buildings, cinema, gaslights, wrought-iron street furniture and palm trees make Victoria Avenue, Wanganui's central city shopping area, a charming spot for visitors. From December to March, around 1,000 floral baskets are hung on streetlights and verandahs to celebrate the Wanganui in Bloom festival.

🏛 Whanganui Regional Museum

Queens Park. **Tel** (06) 349 1110.
Open daily. **Closed** Good Fri, 25 Dec.
🖼 📧 ♿ 📷 W wanganui-museum.org.nz
Among the treasures displayed in the Whanganui Regional Museum, visitors will find paintings of the Māori by Gottfried Lindauer (1839–1926), who managed to avoid service in the Austro-Hungarian army by settling in New Zealand, and Te Mata-o-Hoturoa, a *waka* (Māori war canoe) carved from a single totara tree. Established in 1895, the museum is concerned with the geology and natural and social history of the city and surrounding region.

🏛 Sarjeant Gallery

Queens Park. **Tel** (06) 349 0506.
Open daily. **Closed** Good Fri, 25 Dec.
♿ 📷 W sarjeant.org.nz
This gallery features a highly regarded collection of New Zealand oil paintings, water-colours and prints from the 19th and 20th centuries. It houses the Denton photo-graphy collection and World War I posters and cartoons.

🎋 Moutoa Gardens

Market Place.
Located at the site of the settling of Wanganui as a town,

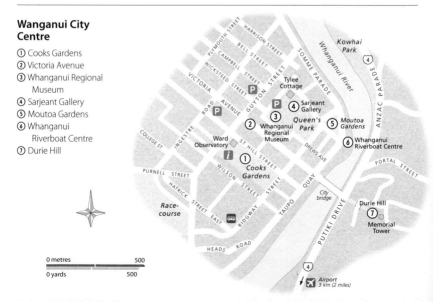

Wanganui City Centre

① Cooks Gardens
② Victoria Avenue
③ Whanganui Regional Museum
④ Sarjeant Gallery
⑤ Moutoa Gardens
⑥ Whanganui Riverboat Centre
⑦ Durie Hill

0 metres 500
0 yards 500

For keys to symbols *see back flap*

The *Waimarie* on the Whanganui River

the beautiful Moutoa Gardens feature monuments set within mature specimen trees and flower beds. Since the early 1990s, the gardens have been a political rallying point. In 1995, Māori tribes protesting about land and river rights occupied the gardens for 79 days.

🚢 Whanganui Riverboat Centre

Taupo Quay. **Tel** (06) 347 1863.
Open daily. 🅿️ 🖼️ inside. ♿ 📷
🌐 **riverboats.co.nz**

This centre houses the salvaged and restored paddle steamer *Waimarie*. Built in London in 1899, it plied the Whanganui River for 50 years. Cruises on the restored steamer leave from here.

🏛️ Durie Hill

2 Blyth St, via Anzac Parade.
Tel (06) 345 8525. **Open** daily. 🅿️
Located opposite the city bridge at the end of Victoria Avenue, Durie Hill is known for an historic elevator, which rises 66 m (216 ft) inside the hill to the summit. Opened in 1919, it is one of several such elevators in the world. A pedestrian tunnel leads to the elevator. It takes about a minute to rise to the summit.

A climb up the 176 steps of the spiral staircase inside the 34 m (110 ft) Durie Hill Memorial Tower, a short distance from the top of the elevator, allows panoramic views of Wanganui, Mount Taranaki/Egmont to the northwest *(see pp186–7)*, Mount Ruapehu to the east *(see pp147–8)*, and the Tasman Sea. The World War I memorial, opened in 1925, is constructed from blocks of fossilized seashell rock taken from quarries up the river.

⑮ Whanganui River

Road map E3–E4. ℹ️ Wanganui Department of Conservation, Taupo Quay, (06) 349 2100.
🌐 **whanganuiriver.co.nz**

The Whanganui River is the longest navigable and the third longest river in New Zealand. The 290 km (180 mile) river begins its journey high up on Mount Tongariro in the centre of the North Island, and meanders its way down through the Whanganui National Park to Wanganui and the Tasman Sea.

Up until the 1920s a regular riverboat service carried passengers, mail and freight into the interior, and a thriving tourist trade operated between Mount Ruapehu and Wanganui. Today, the river, with its deep gorges, sheer cliffs and 239 listed rapids, is New Zealand's most canoed waterway. The main entry and exit points for journeys on the river by canoe, raft or jet-boat are Taumarunui, Pipiriki and Wanganui. The 145 km (90 mile) journey from Taumarunui to Pipiriki takes about five days by canoe. From October to April, visitors must obtain hut and camp-site passes from the local Department of Conservation or other sales outlets.

The river can also be followed by road from Wanganui to Pipiriki. Good side tracks lead to historic sites, early Māori villages, waterfalls and lookouts.

⑯ Whanganui National Park

Road map E3. ℹ️ Department of Conservation, 74 Ingestre St, Wanganui, (06) 349 2100.

Established in 1987, the three main sections of the park lie within the catchment of the Whanganui River, which eroded through mudstone to form striking gorges, bluffs, ridges and valleys. Broadleaf podocarp forest surrounding the river forms the heart of the park. Tree ferns and riverside plants are also a feature, as is the birdlife. The river is rich in fish and contains 18 native species, as well as non-native fish.

Visitors can choose from a variety of energetic activities, including canoeing, kayaking, rafting, jet-boating, mountain biking and hiking. There is also fishing and hunting for deer and goats. For a more leisurely trip, visitors can enjoy a cruise on the 19th-century paddle steamer *Waimarie*.

The Whanganui River flowing through Whanganui National Park

⓱ New Plymouth

The principal centre of the Taranaki region, New Plymouth is situated around the only deep-water port on New Zealand's west coast, surrounded by surfing beaches along the North Taranaki Bight. The massive cone of Mount Taranaki/Egmont towers behind the city. Agriculture, with a strong emphasis on dairying, as well as heavy engineering, the marine industry and forestry are among the mainstays of the local economy. The area is also the base for the country's major oil, gas and petrochemical industries. One of the best ways to explore the inner city is to go on a walking tour. The city is recognized for its many beautiful parks, gardens and reserves, and is an ideal base from which to explore Egmont National Park *(see pp186–7)*.

Altar and stained-glass window in Taranaki Cathedral Church of St Mary

⌂ Taranaki Cathedral Church of St Mary
37 Vivian St. **Tel** (06) 758 3111.
Open daily. ⌂ most days. ⬤
Consecrated in 1848, this Anglican church is the oldest stone church in New Zealand. It is a fine example of 19th-century architecture, and has some outstanding stained-glass windows, an impressive vaulted timber ceiling and historic artifacts. In the grounds, headstones of children, settlers and soldiers, who died in the Taranaki Land Wars, poignantly recall the difficulties faced by early settlers. Several Maori chiefs are also buried there.

▥ Len Lye Art Centre
40 Queen St. **Tel** (06) 759 6060.
Open 10am–5pm daily.
Closed 25 Dec. ▨ specific exhibits.
⬤ ▣ ▢ ▥ govettbrewster.com/Len-Lye/Centre

Opened in 1970 as a contemporary art museum – a novel concept in New Zealand at the time – the Govett-Brewster Art Gallery was the gift of local benefactor Monica Brewster. She stipulated in her deed of gift that the gallery must always have a director of national standing and the ability to acquire art works with "minimal influence from local politicians".

Its main strengths lie in its collection of abstract art from the 1970s and 1980s, including works by Patrick Hanly, Michael Illingworth and Colin McCahon, and in its contemporary sculpture. It became the site of the Len Lye Archive containing the kinetic sculptures, paintings and films of this internationally renowned New Zealand multimedia artist, painter and film-maker (1901–80). After substantial refurbishment, the gallery reopened in 2015 and was renamed in his honour. It holds 20 exhibitions a year, conducts art lectures and has a comprehensive research library.

▦ Puke Ariki
1 Ariki St. **Tel** (06) 759 6060. **Open** daily. ⬤ ▣ ▢ ▥ pukeariki.com
Built on what was originally the most significant Maori site in Taranaki, Puke Ariki is an integrated library, museum and i-SITE. The centre provides a venue for the display of the museum's heritage collection, including 6,000 nationally important Māori *taonga* (treasures), such as paintings, photographs, cartoons, maps and coins. Puke Ariki overlooks a 12 km (7 miles) New Plymouth coastal walkway.

▤ Richmond Cottage
Ariki St. **Tel** (06) 759 6060.
Open 11am–3:30pm weekends and public hols. ▨ ⬤
Richmond Cottage, constructed in 1853 of stone instead of the customary timber, was the residence of the Richmond family. Many of the artifacts and furnishings on display in the beautifully restored cottage belonged to these former owners. During the 1880s, the cottage offered accommodation to seaside holiday-makers.

◘ Puke Ariki Landing
Ariki St. **Open** daily.
An oasis of green in the central city, Puke Ariki Landing opened in 1990 when train tracks previously fronting the coastline were removed. This attractive park stands where surfboats, which carried people and supplies from ships, used to come ashore.

Taranaki's Gardens and Parks

Taranaki's parks, reserves and gardens are a highlight of the district and a draw for visitors. Long hours of sunshine, high rainfall, a mild climate, rich volcanic soils and shelter from prevailing winds combine to create ideal gardening conditions. Rhododendrons, azaleas and camellias suit Taranaki's conditions perfectly, and this is reflected in the large numbers of such species grown successfully throughout the region, along with roses, magnolias, irises and various native plants. From the end of October until the end of the first week of November, about 100 home gardens, both small and large, open their gates for public viewing in two separate floral festivals. Visitors may enjoy tea at some of these gardens and buy plants. Visit www.gardens.org.nz for more information.

Rhododendrons in bloom

Fernery at Pukekura Park

🌸 Pukekura Park

Liardet St. **Open** daily. ♿

Opened in 1876 and only a ten-minute walk from the city centre, the dominant theme of Pukekura Park is water. Paths lead through dense native bushland, native and exotic trees, and fern gullies beside freshwater lakes and streams. A fernery, fountain, waterfall, water wheel, playground and boats for hire are other attractions. From the Tea House there is a dramatic view of Mount Taranaki/Egmont. During the Festival of Lights, held from mid-December to late January, Pukekura Park is transformed at night into a fairyland by thousands of coloured lights strung through its walkways and plantings.

🎭 Brooklands Park

Brooklands Park Drive. **Open** daily. ♿

Adjoining Pukekura Park, Brooklands is an English-style park with sweeping lawns and formal gardens. Originally a private family estate, it was bequeathed to the city in 1934. Highlights include an enormous 2,000-year-old puriri tree, 300 varieties of rhododendron, and a children's zoo. The Bowl of Brooklands, an outdoor soundshell in a bush and lake setting, is the site of concerts and other entertainment.

The park also contains a colonial hospital, the Gables, built in 1847. The beautiful beach stone building failed as a hospital, attracting only 55 patients, and is now an art gallery and medical museum.

New Plymouth City Centre

① Taranaki Cathedral
   Church of St Mary
② Len Lye Art Centre
③ Puke Ariki
④ Richmond Cottage
⑤ Puke Ariki Landing
⑥ Pukekura Park

For keys to symbols *see back flap*

⑱ Egmont National Park

Egmont National Park is one of the most easily accessed parks in New Zealand. The centrepiece is the solitary 2,518 m (8,261 ft) Mount Taranaki/Egmont, a dormant volcano. Almost all year round, snow and ice cover the peak and upper slopes of this near-symmetrical mountain. The park's 193 km (119 mile) network of tracks offers excellent climbing, hiking and some skiing for the fit and well prepared. Other tracks are suitable for the average walker. Weather conditions can change rapidly so hikers should be prepared for all conditions.

Huts
Walking tracks link the huts in the park. Hut passes can be bought from information centres and Department of Conservation offices.

Native trees
The wet mountain climate, combined with periods of dry, hot weather, promote luxurious vegetation. Native trees are abundant on the lower slopes.

```
0 kilometres          3
0 miles               3
```

KEY

① **The North Egmont Visitor Centre** has interesting displays on the park and the mountain, an audiovisual show and café.

② **The Dawson Falls/Te Rere O Noke Visitor Centre** has exhibits on the park's flora and fauna, and a model of its volcanic features.

Oakura River

Mangorei Track

Dover Track

Pouaka

Pouakai Range

Stony River

Puniho Track

Ho

Kahui

Kahui Track

Oaonui Track

Waiaua Gorge

Ihaia Track

Brames Falls Track

Waiaua River

Taungatara Track

Lake Dive T

Walks in Egmont National Park

The park includes an extensive network of walking tracks leading to the summit or around the mountain. Shorter tracks start off from the three roads heading up the mountain. These range from easy to difficult and take from 30 minutes to several hours. The popular two-day Pouaki circuit offers walkers a taste of what Egmont has to offer: rainforest, tussock land, an alpine swamp and volcanic features. This track can be accessed from North Egmont. Vegetation in the park ranges from tall rimu and kamahi trees at lower altitudes, to dense subalpine shrubs and an alpine herbfield complete with plants unique to the park.

Walker on one of the park's tracks

Key

═══ Minor road

〰 River

-- Park boundary

- - Walking track

For hotels and restaurants in this region see pp304–5 and pp319–21

Mount Taranaki/Egmont

Mount Taranaki/Egmont is believed to have formed after a volcanic eruption more than 70,000 years ago. Sacred to local Māori, the mountain last erupted in 1775.

VISITORS' CHECKLIST

Practical Information
Road map D3. W doc.govt.nz.
🛈 North Egmont Visitor Centre,
(06) 756 0990; Dawson Falls
Visitor Centre, (027) 443 0248;
egmontvc@doc.govt.nz

Transport
🚌 Stratford Depot.

Egmont Road

Signs at Egmont Village point to the 16 km (10 mile) Egmont Road, which brings visitors into the northern area of the park. There are picnic areas along the way within the park.

Winter Climbing

Several ice and snow routes lead to the summit from the northern slopes. Climbers must always be properly equipped.

Dawson Falls/ Te Rere O Noke

Dropping 18 m (60 ft) down an ancient lava flow, the waterfall is a 20-minute walk from the visitor centre.

For keys to symbols *see back flap*

One of the Sugar Loaf Islands

⑲ Oakura

Road map D3. 🏔 1,000.

Situated on a beautiful stretch of Taranaki coastline 15 km (9 miles) west of New Plymouth, Oakura is one of a number of small, scenic towns typifying the rural aspect of New Zealand. It has the traditional fixtures of such towns – the main street row of shops, service station, recreation grounds, churches, pubs and a war memorial. A train carriage restaurant in the main street is a novelty. The Crafty Fox, a neighbouring shop, sells works by the many artists and crafts people who live in the area.

The beach at Oakura is well known for its beautiful sunsets (in Māori, Oakura means "the bright red colour of an enchanted cloak"). It is also a prime spot for swimming, windsurfing and surfboarding.

⑳ Sugar Loaf Islands Marine Park

Road map D3. 🚢 from Lee Breakwater, New Plymouth.

Established as a marine protected area in 1991, the Sugar Loaf Islands lie between 700 m (2,300 ft) and 1.5 km (1 mile) off New Plymouth's Port Taranaki breakwater. The stacks and spectacular reefs that make up the islands are the oldest volcanic features in Taranaki. They consist of eroded andesitic domes produced around 1.75 million years ago, lying at depths of between 5 m (16 ft) and 30 m (98 ft). Of the eleven islands, or groupings of islands,

the two largest are Motuma-hanga and Moturoa, located at the northern end of the park. They are often referred to as the "outer islands". Four rocky islets close to the mainland at Paritutu are known as the "inner islands".

The islands support a wealth of wildlife and plants. Among them are 80 recorded types of fish, at least 19 species of birdlife, rare and endangered native and introduced plants and 33 species of sponge. Fur seals are present on the islands all year round, with common and Maui's dolphins and killer, pilot and humpback whales also seen at times.

Although the best way to explore the islands is by charter boat, Round Rock, one of the "inner islands", can be accessed on foot from the beach during mid- to low tide. Snapper Rock, another "inner island", is accessible from the shore only when the spring tides are very low.

The relatively deep water, wide variety of marine life and spectacular underwater scenery make the park a popular venue for divers. Visibility often reaches 20 m (65 ft) during the summer and autumn months. Recreational fishing is also very popular in the park, although it is restricted to small, defined areas. Blue cod, kingfish and snapper are among the most frequently caught species. Game fishing further offshore for tuna, marlin and mako shark usually takes place during summer and early autumn.

㉑ Cape Egmont

Road map D3.

Taranaki's most westerly point, Cape Egmont is characterized by strong winds and choppy seas. The solitary landmark is the Cape Egmont lighthouse, transferred from Mana Island near Wellington in 1881. Powered by diesel generators until 1951, it now operates on electricity.

Located 30 km (19 miles) offshore from the cape, the Maui field produces gas, which is processed at Oaonui, 9 km (6 miles) northwest of the town of Opunake. At the site of the processing plant, a visitor centre provides details of the history of oil exploration in the Taranaki region. There are also scale models of ships and oil rigs. Visitors can use the binoculars at the centre to get a good view of one of the platforms, Maui A, 35 km (21.5 miles) offshore.

Steps leading up to the Cape Egmont lighthouse

㉒ Opunake

Road map D3. 🏔 1,600. 🚌
🛈 55 High St, (06) 278 8599.
🎭 Opunake Beach Carnival (Jan).

The thriving centre of a rich dairy-farming district, Opunake is the largest town on the west side of Mount Taranaki/Egmont. The beach at Opunake, situated along from small, sheltered Middleton Bay, is regarded as one of Taranaki's best beaches. It teems with tourists attracted to its safe swimming and its surfing during the summer months. The Opunake Walkway

Opunake Beach, a picturesque swimming spot on the Taranaki coast

takes visitors around the beautiful coastline and beach front, as well as around the nearby Opunake Lake, an excellent spot for canoeing, yachting and other watersports. Other points along the way include two old cemeteries. The 7 km (4 mile) route can be accessed from a number of points along the way.

㉓ Hawera

Road map D3. 🏛 9,000. 🚌
ℹ 55 High St, (06) 278 8599.

Part of Taranaki's rural heartland, Hawera boasts many interesting places. The 38,000 sq m (409,000 sq ft) **Hollard Gardens** were laid out in the late 1920s by farmer Bernard Hollard and presented to the Queen Elizabeth II National Trust in 1982. The gardens are at their most colourful from September to November.

Near Hawera is the Fontera Dairy Factory, which is the world's largest single-site, multi-product milk-processing plant. It is closed to the public.

Hawera and its surroundings can be viewed from the top of the town's water tower, built after a series of fires in the 1880s, one of which razed most of the main street. In 1914, a month after the tower was erected, an earthquake caused it to list 0.75 m (2.5 ft) to the south. The fault has now been reduced to 8 cm (3 inches).

The **Tawhiti Museum**, claimed to be the best

private museum in the country, recreates many aspects of early life in South Taranaki. Exhibits range from the early land wars to the development of the dairy industry, and there is a traders and whalers experience, where visitors may take an underground canal boat to explore the region's history. The life-like figures in the exhibits, modelled on the faces of local volunteers, were cast at the museum's on-site workshops. A bush railway takes passengers on a reconstruction of the logging railways that used to operate in Taranaki.

Cow statue outside Fontera Dairy

🐾 **Hollard Gardens**
Manaia Rd, N of Kaponga. **Tel** (06) 765 7127. **Open** daily. 🅿 donation. 🚻
🌐 www.trc.govt.nz/gardens

🏛 **Tawhiti Museum**
401 Ohangai Rd. **Tel** (06) 278 6837. **Open** variable. 🅿 🚻 🌐 by arrangement. 🅿 📷 📖 🌐 www. tawhitimuseum.co.nz

㉔ Stratford

Road map D3. 🏛 5,700. 🚌
ℹ 61–63 Miranda St, (06) 765 6708.

Lying to the east of Mount Taranaki/Egmont, 40 km (25 miles) south of New Plymouth, Stratford is named after Shakespeare's birthplace, Stratford-upon-Avon, and many of its streets are named after Shakespearean characters. The **Taranaki Pioneer Village** in the town comprises restored or recreated buildings, including a school house, jail, railway station and about 50 other buildings that relate the area's local and provincial history.

Perhaps one of the best ways to appreciate this region is to drive the 150-km- (93-mile-) long Forgotton World Highway, which connects Stratford to the small town of Taumarinuione. Following colonial bridle tracks, the route travels through a truly memorable landscape and includes four mountain saddles, an eerie one-lane tunnel, and a sinuous journey through a river gorge. Fifteen kilometres (9 miles) of this road is unsealed gravel, and the only significant settlement here is Whangamomona. On the way, the historic Whangamomona Hotel is well known for its hospitality, and makes for the perfect halfway stop.

🏛 **Taranaki Pioneer Village**
State Hwy 3, Stratford South. **Tel** (06) 765 5399. **Open** daily. **Closed** 25 Dec. 🅿 📷 📖 🚻 some exhibits only.
🌐 pioneervillage.co.nz

Life-size exhibits in the Tawhiti Museum, Hawera

THE SOUTH ISLAND

Introducing the South Island

Unparalleled scenic variety awaits the visitor to the South Island. The snow-capped Southern Alps dominate the island, dividing it in two and creating a vast adventure playground of mountains, glaciers, lakes, rivers and fiords. Golden sand beaches, waterways and vineyards dominate the sun-soaked north. Along the narrow West Coast, waves from the Tasman Sea pound wild beaches. To the east is the patchwork Canterbury Plains and the rich, rolling farmland of Otago and Southland. Christchurch, known as the gateway to the South Island, and Picton in the picturesque Marlborough Sounds, are the two main entry points to the region.

Locator Map

In Aoraki/Mount Cook National Park *(see pp256–7)*, the highest peaks in New Zealand soar above the crest of the Southern Alps and over the surrounding subalpine park. The park is one of the country's most popular centres for walkers, climbers and photographers.

Fox Glacier

Mount Cook

Haast

Tek

Twizel

Omarama

Milford Sound

Wanaka

Queenstown

Cromwell

Alexandra

Lake Te Anau *(see p285)*, facing the glacier-carved mountains of Fiordland National Park, is one of the longest lakes in New Zealand and is popular with trout and salmon anglers.

Te Anau

Manapouri

OTAGO AND SOUTHLAND *(See pp258–295)*

Palme

Lumsden

Waitati

Gore

Dunedin

Invercargill

Balclutha

Bluff

Oban

The Octagon *(see pp262 & 265)*, an attractive eight-sided garden area in the centre of Dunedin, is surrounded by imposing public buildings and a statue of the Scottish poet Robert Burns.

◀ Canterbury Plains with snow-covered mountains in the background

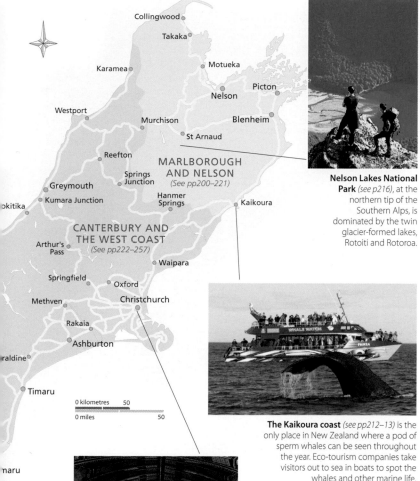

Collingwood
Takaka
Karamea
Motueka
Picton
Nelson
Westport
Murchison
Blenheim
St Arnaud
Reefton
MARLBOROUGH
Springs
Junction
AND NELSON
(See pp200–221)
Greymouth
Hanmer
Springs
okitika
Kumara Junction
Kaikoura
CANTERBURY AND
THE WEST COAST
(See pp222–257)
Arthur's
Pass
Waipara
Springfield
Oxford
Methven
Christchurch
Rakaia
Ashburton
raldine
Timaru

0 kilometres   50
0 miles   50

naru

**Nelson Lakes National
Park** *(see p216)*, at the
northern tip of the
Southern Alps, is
dominated by the twin
glacier-formed lakes,
Rotoiti and Rotoroa.

The Kaikoura coast *(see pp212–13)* is the
only place in New Zealand where a pod of
sperm whales can be seen throughout
the year. Eco-tourism companies take
visitors out to sea in boats to spot the
whales and other marine life.

The Provincial Council Buildings in
Christchurch *(see p230)* are considered the
finest example of secular Gothic architecture in New Zealand and are the city's most
historic buildings. They were damaged in
the earthquake of 2011, but are being
repaired and rebuilt.

The Moeraki Boulders *(see p271)*, a group of
perfectly round, smooth, grey boulders of various
sizes, are scattered haphazardly along the seashore
and near the cliffs behind the beach.

Southern Splendour

The overwhelming impression a visitor has of the South Island is its scenic diversity: the bush-clad inlets of the Marlborough Sounds, golden sand beaches of Nelson, sweeping plains of Canterbury, snow-covered mountains of the alpine chain, dripping rainforests of the West Coast, rugged tussocklands and rolling farmland of Otago and Southland and the fiords of the southwest. No less varied is the climate. Only three hours of driving separate the wetter west coast and the drier east coast.

Mitre Peak, the centrepiece of Fiordland National Park, is the world's highest sea cliff.

Abel Tasman National Park's golden sand beaches contrast with the deep green of the forest *(see pp218–19)*. The coastal walk in this park is one of the most popular in New Zealand.

Sheep need supplementary feed, such as hay, during the coldest winter months.

Southern Alps

Stretching almost the entire length of the South Island, the mighty Southern Alps and its various alpine environments were formed by the upward thrust of the Pacific Continental Plate (see p26).

The West Coast, occupying a narrow strip of land between the Tasman Sea and the Southern Alps, has the highest rainfall in New Zealand. It also has some of the best examples of untouched rainforest, as shown here on the Milford Track in Fiordland *(see p287)*.

On Banks Peninsula, the craters of past volcanoes, created by lava flows, are today's harbours of Lyttelton and Akaroa.

The Marlborough Sounds, in the north of the South Island, were produced by the drowning of an extensive river system (*see pp206–7*).

Mountains and glaciers combine to produce spectacular scenery and numerous opportunites for outdoor activities.

The rocks of the Southern Alps, folded and raised by titanic forces, and eroded by wind, rain and ice, are a striking sight from the air or road.

The Sutherland Falls in Fiordland, once thought to be the highest in the world, plunge 580 m (1,900 ft) in three cascades.

The lakes on the eastern side of the Alps, such as Lake Ohau shown here, are the direct result of glacial gouging.

Lake Tekapo and other eastern lakes are a milky blue, caused by ice rasping against rocks to produce fine powder.

Braided Rivers

Weaving sinuous strands of water from the mountains to the sea, the braided rivers of the South Island's east coast are, globally, rare ecosystems. Over thousands of years the largest rivers, among them the Rakaia, Waimakariri, Rangitata and Waitaki, have carried rocks and shingle from the Southern Alps and deposited this debris to create the fertile Canterbury Plains. On the river flats lives the wrybill, the only bird in the world with a sideways turning beak. The world's rarest wader, the black stilt, breeds on shingle "islands" in the rivers of the Mackenzie Basin (*see p255*).

The sinuous strands of the Waimakariri River cross the Canterbury Plains

Wildlife Colonies

With a smaller population, there is less human pressure on wildlife in the South Island than in the North Island, and this is reflected in the number of wildlife colonies scattered around the mainland which are accessible to tourists. New Zealand has been described as "the seabird capital of the world" because of the number of species that either visit or breed along its coasts. A lack of predators has also led inland birds to be more fearless, and therefore more visible, than birds in most other countries. Marine mammals abound and tour operators guarantee an almost 100 per cent chance of seeing these animals in their natural habitat.

The white heron breeds only in a coastal swamp near Okarito in September–October but is often seen in other estuaries along the coast.

The royal albatross has one of the greatest wingspans – up to 3 m (10 ft) – of any seabird. The world's only mainland breeding colony is at Taiaroa Head on the Otago Peninsula (see p270). Here a four-month-old chick is being weighed.

The kaki/black stilt, an endangered wader, can be seen along the braided rivers of the Mackenzie Basin and at visitor hides (see p255).

The blue penguin, the smallest of all penguins, can survive near populated areas, such as Oamaru (see p273), feeding on fish close to shore.

Bottlenose dolphins, known to swim as fast as 40 km/h (25 mph), prey on inshore bottom-dwelling species. A pod has taken up year-round residence in Doubtful Sound (see p288).

The Fiordland crested penguin, a rare native species, has a yellow crest over each eye. It comes ashore each June to build nests in caves beneath the roots of trees in coastal rainforests.

Okarito Lagoon
Okarito
La Te
Lake Puna
Haast
Milford Sound
Lake Wanaka
Twizel
Lake Hawea
Queenstown
Doubtful Sound
Lake Wakatipu
Oamaru
DUNEDIN
Otago Peninsula
Invercargill
STEWART ISLAND

The kiwi, although primarily nocturnal, can be seen during twilight hours foraging in the forest on Stewart Island (see pp292–3).

The yellow-eyed penguin, the world's rarest species, is mostly concentrated on the Otago Peninsula (see p271). In the evening, they can be seen patrolling the beach.

Fur seals haul out on rocky shorelines at several sites. At Cape Foulwind *(see p238)* there is a breeding colony where pups can be seen in spring and summer.

Wading birds, such as pied stilts (shown here), congregate in large numbers to methodically feed on rich tidal mud flats around the coastline.

Farewell Spit

Marlborough Sounds

Cape
ulwind
• Westport

Nelson

Blenheim •

kitika

Kaikoura •

Sperm whales, which can be viewed off the Kaikoura coast *(see p213)*, are specialized for hunting the deep sea, diving to depths of 1,000 m (3,280 ft) to feed mainly on large squid.

CHRISTCHURCH •

Akaroa •

Banks
Peninsula

Hector's dolphin, a small species found exclusively in New Zealand, spends most of its time close to the shore, in pairs or small groups.

Wildlife Watching

It is important to cause as little disturbance as possible, especially when animals are breeding, and to be very patient. Seals can attack if people get between them and the sea, yellow-eyed penguins will not come ashore to feed their young if disturbed, and dolphins do not always welcome people swimming with them. It is best to view wildlife with an experienced guide who is well versed in wildlife etiquette, skilled at finding the animals and who can provide interesting and informative commentary.

0 kilometres   75

0 miles   75

Adventure Sports Paradise

Queenstown is tagged as New Zealand's top adventure tourism destination because of the many adrenaline-pumping sports on offer in and around the town. The area's mountains, lakes and rivers and generally dry climate combine to create conditions ideal for outdoor pursuits, while daredevil New Zealanders continue to pioneer ever more thrilling sports for the enjoyment of visitors. Strict regulations and highly trained operators reduce the risks involved in speeding through inches of water, leaping off bridges, skiing at remote sites and free-falling from airplanes, and explain New Zealand's excellent safety record.

Jet-boats – propellerless power boats specially designed in New Zealand for use in 10 cm (4 inch) deep water – take visitors at breakneck speed down narrow river gorges.

Queenstown and Surroundings

Key

━━ State highway
═══ Minor road
≈≈≈ River

Adventure Sports Around Queenstown

These places are all within 115 km (70 miles) of Queenstown and offer a range of activities. Adventure sports tour operators provide transport, equipment and qualified instructors.

	Bungy Jumping	Hang-Gliding	Jet Boating	Mountain Biking	Skiing	Tandem Parapenting	Tandem skydiving	White-Water Rafting
Cardrona Alpine Resort				●	●			
Coronet Peak		●			●			
Kawarau Bridge	●		●					
Kawarau River			●					●
Queenstown (see pp280–81)	●			●		●	●	
Remarkables		●		●	●	●		
Shotover River			●					●
Skippers Canyon	●	●						
Trebble Cone					●	●		
Waiorau Snow Farm					●			
Wanaka (see pp274–5)				●	●	●	●	●

Downhill skiing at the commercial ski fields near Queenstown is rated some of the best in the country.

Mountain biking allows riders, either independently or as part of a guided tour, to explore off-road routes that were traditionally walked.

Queenstown, Lake Wakatipu and the Remarkables from the Skyline Gondola lookout on Bob's Peak.

White-water rafting through the narrow gorges and thundering rapids of the Kawarau and Shotover rivers is a heart-pounding, exhilarating and drenching experience.

The preparation area where ankles are strapped and adjustments made to the length of the cord to suit the weight of the bungy jumper.

Bungy Jumping

This was made famous by New Zealander A J Hackett, who dived from the Eiffel Tower in 1986 suspended by a rubber cord strapped to his ankles. Bungy jumping options now range from plummeting 134 m (440 ft) from a suspended "jump pod" over a gorge, dipping in at Kawarau Bridge, to hurtling earthward from "The Ledge" on Bob's Peak above Queenstown.

A jumper dives off the platform before soaring upwards again at the end of the bungy cord.

Cross-country skiing is a speciality of the Waiorau Snow Farm in the Pisa Range near Wanaka, which also hosts cross-country racing and ski-jumping competitions during the ski season.

Tandem parapenting (or paragliding) – plunging off a hill with a guide, strapped to a rectangular parachute – is a safer option than the "ultimate" tandem activity, tandem skydiving – jumping out of an airplane with an instructor attached to one's back followed by a parachute descent to ground.

MARLBOROUGH AND NELSON

The warm climate of the Marlborough and Nelson region has always attracted visitors. Landscapes vary from wild coast, golden beaches, drowned valleys and dry inland mountains to lush, forested ranges. Known for its horticulture, the area is also a major source of fresh seafood. Along with heritage sites, its national parks are an added attraction. Marlborough is New Zealand's largest wine producer.

Archaeological evidence dates Māori occupation of the region to at least AD 1250. Early Polynesian navigators, Kupe *(see p49)* and Rakaihautu, are also known to have spent time here. In 1642, Dutch explorer Abel Tasman sailed into Golden Bay *(see p52)*. A confused and ultimately fatal confrontation with Māori that left four of the crew dead, made the Dutch sail off without ever making landfall in the country. James Cook's later visits to Queen Charlotte Sound in the 1770s fortunately proved more successful *(see p52)*.

Following the signing of the Treaty of Waitangi in 1840 *(see pp52–3)*, the New Zealand Company established its Nelson settlement in 1842 *(see pp214–15)*. In 1858, Nelson was declared New Zealand's second city, a year before Marlborough gained identity as a separate province. The region splits neatly into halves, Marlborough in the east and Nelson in the west. Marlborough's contrasts are perhaps greater, from the sinuous waterways of the Marlborough Sounds in the north, to the sheep farms and grape-growing region around Blenheim. Further south is the coastal area of Kaikoura.

In northern Nelson is the Golden Bay region, sheltered from the open sea by Farewell Spit and isolated behind the national parks of Abel Tasman and Kahurangi. Nelson city and Motueka sit on the shores of Tasman Bay. The rich hinterland, peopled by artists, vintners and horticulturists, extends south to the Southern Alps and the region's third national park, Nelson Lakes.

The weekend market at Nelson

◄ Brancott Estate Vineyard, Marlborough

Exploring Marlborough and Nelson

The northern region of the South Island beckons visitors with its sunny climate, inviting coastline, food, wines, marine reserves and three national parks: Nelson Lakes, Abel Tasman and Kahurangi. Watching marine life at Kaikoura *(see p213)*, winery tours *(see pp210–11)* and Nelson's Suter Art Gallery *(see p214)* are well-known attractions. Nelson is home to craft artisans and is an excellent base for boating and adventure tours. Walking, hiking and cycling tracks are spread throughout the national parks and other areas, including the Marlborough Sounds, a unique geographical feature of the region *(see pp206–7)*.

Yachts anchored in a bay near Picton, a seaside town on South Island

Sights at a Glance

1 Picton
2 *Marlborough Sounds pp206–7*
3 Queen Charlotte Drive
4 Havelock
6 Blenheim
7 Kaikoura
8 *Nelson pp214–15*
9 Richmond
10 St Arnaud
11 Nelson Lakes National Park
12 Motueka
13 Kahurangi National Park
14 *Abel Tasman National Park pp218–19*
15 Takaka Hill
16 Takaka
17 Waikoropupu Springs Scenic Reserve
18 Collingwood
19 Farewell Spit

Tour

5 Wairau Valley Vineyards

Kaiteriteri Beach near Motueka, a popular beach resort

Map labels:
Cape Farewell
Puponga
FAREWELL SPIT 19
COLLINGWOOD 18
Golden Bay
60
WAIKOROPUPU SPRINGS SCENIC RESERVE 17
Totaranui
TAKAKA 16
KAHURANGI NATIONAL PARK
ABEL TASMAN NP 14
Marahau
TAKAKA HILL 15
Kaiteriteri
MOTUEKA 12
13
Cobb Reservoir
Karamea
Karamea
Upper Moutere
60
Woodstock
Brightwater
Mount Kendall 1810m
Tapawera
WEST COAST
Mount Owen 1875m
TASMAN
6
Owen River
Buller
Westport
Murchison
63
ST ARNAUD 10
Inangahua
Lake Rotoroa
Lake Rotoiti
Maruia
11
NELSON LAKES NATIONAL PARK
St Arnaud Range
65
Mount Travers 2338m
Mount Una 2301m
Clarence
Springs Junction
Hanmer Springs

Key

— Major road

::::: Minor road

— Scenic route

⊶⊶ Major railway

⎯⎯ Minor railway

— Regional border

△ Summit

Getting Around

Beyond the highways of the Marlborough and Nelson region many roads are narrow and unsealed, particularly those into Molesworth Station *(see p212)*. A proliferation of water taxi-services in the Marlborough Sounds, are now used by locals and tourists alike. A scenic journey by rail follows the east coast from Picton to Kaikoura and on to Christchurch, but there are no rail services to Nelson. Domestic airlines fly to Nelson city and Blenheim and private companies operate services from Wellington to Golden Bay and some locations in the Sounds. Bus and boat services at Nelson, Motueka, Marahau and Kaiteriteri provide access to all three national parks.

Vineyards at Blenheim in the Wairau Valley, New Zealand's largest wine-producing area

Top Outdoor Activities

The places shown here have been selected for their recreational activities. Conditions vary depending on the weather and the time of year, so exercise caution and, if in doubt, seek local advice.

	Birdwatching	Boating	Marine Life Watching	Mountain Biking	Sea Kayaking	Swimming	Hiking/Walking
Abel Tasman National Park	●		●	●	●	●	●
Blenheim	●			●			●
Collingwood	●			●			●
Farewell Spit		●		●			●
Havelock		●			●		●
Kahurangi National Park	●						●
Kaikoura	●	●	●	●	●	●	●
Marlborough Sounds	●	●	●	●	●	●	●
Motueka	●					●	●
Nelson		●		●		●	●
Nelson Lakes National Park	●	●				●	●
Picton		●	●			●	●
Queen Charlotte Drive						●	●
St Arnaud	●	●		●		●	●

For keys to symbols *see back flap*

● Picton

Road map D4. ⚑ 4,000. ✈
Koromiko, 9 km (6 miles) S of town.
🚌 🚢 🚢 *i* The Foreshore, (03) 520
3113. **W** marlboroughnz.com

Set in the upper reaches of
Queen Charlotte Sound, Picton
is the South Island terminus for
ferries that cross Cook Strait. The
buzz of port and railway activity
dominates this town nestled
between the sea and the hills.
Ferries and water taxis mingle
with pleasure boats in the region,
popular for its safe anchorages.

Picton's wide streets and
historic buildings along the
waterfront reflect its European
beginnings. Formerly known as
Waitohi, Picton was chosen to
become the port for the Wairau
district, and in 1859 became the
capital of the newly formed
province of Marlborough. That
status shifted to Blenheim in
1866. An inter-island
ferry service was first
mooted in 1899 and
the first rail and car ferry
began operating in 1962.

Picton is a good base to
explore the history of the
Marlborough region. The **Picton
Museum** tells stories of the
whaling era, beginning in
the 1820s, and of the 1770s
visit of Captain James Cook
to Queen Charlotte Sound.

At one end of the foreshore,
the sailing ship **Edwin Fox**
provides a fascinating look at
New Zealand's shipping history.
The *Edwin Fox* is the last Australian
convict ship and the last East
Indiaman clipper in existence.
It is therefore an internationally

The *Edwin Fox*, formerly a convict
transport ship

Whaling exhibits at Picton Museum

significant link to the era of
colonial settlement, having
brought convicts to Australia
and migrants to New Zealand.
Built in 1853, the ship is now
being preserved in a dry dock
beside a purpose-built museum.

Along the Picton Waterfront
is **EcoWorld Aquarium**, featuring the local species to
be seen throughout
Marlborough Sounds.
A number of walks
and cycling tracks in
Picton begin near
Shelly Beach on
Picton Harbour
where a lookout
affords excellent
views of the town.

A short uphill walk from here
leads to Victoria Domain, a
bushy reserve named after
Queen Victoria. A longer walk
past Bob's Bay passes a panoramic view of Queen Charlotte
Sound and leads to The Snout,
the headland between Picton
and Waikawa bays. Māori know
the Snout as Te Ihumoeoneihu
(nose of the sand worm). The
Tirohanga and Essons Valley
tracks allow exploration of
the forest behind the town.

Wildlife enthusiasts and
walkers will enjoy visiting **Kaipupu Wildlife Sanctuary**, an
island located in Picton Harbour.
There is a 3-km (2-mile) circular
track around the island offering
great views and birdwatching
opportunities. The circuit takes
an hour and a half to walk. The
island is reached by a 10 minute
boat ride from Picton Harbour.

Māori club, Picton
Museum

🐟 **EcoWorld Aquarium**
Picton Waterfront. **Tel** (03) 573 6030.
Open daily. **Closed** 25 Dec.
🅿 🏛

🏛 **Picton Museum**
9 London Quay. **Tel** (03) 573 8283.
Open daily. **Closed** 25 Dec. 🅿

🏛 **Edwin Fox**
Dunbar Wharf. **Tel** (03) 573 6868.
Open daily. **Closed** Good Fri, 25 Dec.
🅿 🏛

⚑ **Kaipupu Wildlife Sanctuary**
Kaipupu Point. **Tel** (027) 692 3488.
Open daily. **W** kaipupupoint.co.nz

Environs
A 20-minute drive northeast
of Picton leads to Karaka
Point, a narrow peninsula
once occupied by a *pa*. A short
walk leads down to the water
with signs explaining the
earthworks encountered
on the way.

● Marlborough Sounds

See pp206–7.

● Queen Charlotte Drive

Road map D4.

The best-known road in the
Marlborough Sounds, Queen
Charlotte Drive is a scenic
route connecting Picton and
Havelock. With stopovers, it
can take up to half a day to
complete the 35 km (21.5 mile)
journey on the sealed but narrow and winding road. Leaving

Picton, the Queen Charlotte Drive passes lookout points above the town and at Governors Bay, 8 km (5 miles) from Picton, with excellent views up and down Queen Charlotte Sound. Beaches and pleasant picnic and swimming areas can be found along the route that passes through the picturesque settlements of Ngakuta and Momorangi bays. At Ngakuta Bay, **Sirpa Alalääkkölä's Art Studio** showcases her large, bright paintings, many of them inspired by the Sounds.

Continuing west, a turn-off 12 km (8 miles) from Governors Bay leads to historic Anakiwa, where the Queen Charlotte Track begins (see pp206–7). A shelter and picnic area are provided and an easy stroll along the track leads through beech forest to Davies Bay.

The Queen Charlotte Drive route continues through Linkwater with the road following the waters of the Mahakipawa Arm, the innermost reaches of Pelorus Sound. The walking tracks and viewpoint at Cullen Point provide another perspective on the waterways below, before the road's final descent into Havelock.

🏛 **Sirpa Alalääkkölä Art Studio**
Phillips Rd, Ngakuta Bay. **Tel** (03) 573 7775. **Open** by appointment.

❹ Havelock

Road map D4. 🏔 500. 🚌 🚢
ℹ️ 46 Main Rd, (03) 574 2104.
🌐 **marlboroughnz.com**

The self-styled green lip mussel capital of the world, the village of Havelock receives a growing number of visitors attracted by its history and the success of its mussel-farming industry. Havelock was established in the 1850s on the Nelson–Blenheim track near the uppermost navigable reaches of Pelorus Sound. Timber milling and gold mining were its first industries,

A restaurant in Havelock advertising green lip mussels

while today fishing and aquaculture (the cultivation of shellfish) are major industries. The main street still retains something of its pioneer character. Highlights of a walk around the waterfront are the stately 1880s home of timber miller William Brownlee, the stone St Peter's Church, and the old primary school (now a hostel) attended by Lord Ernest Rutherford (see pp25, 216) in the 1870s. A number of cafés can be found in the town along with many interesting shops selling antiques, jewellery, carvings, crafts, and Māori art.

Greenstone carved in Havelock

Tours and activities such as sea kayaking begin in Havelock, with the scenic mail run (where mail is delivered by boat) being perhaps the easiest and most popular way to get to the outer sounds. The **Havelock Museum** preserves relics from the pioneer era and Rutherford's time. The annual Mussel Festival takes place in March.

🏛 **Havelock Museum**
Main St. **Tel** (03) 574 2176. **Open** daily. 💰 donation.

Environs

Canvastown, 9 km (6 miles) west of Havelock, was established in 1864 following the region's first gold rush.

A tent city grew here, attracting several thousand miners. Flood-prone fields and severe over-crowding meant many miners left shortly after the gold fields in the West Coast were opened.

A further 11 km (7.5 miles) west, along State Highway 6, the road crosses the Pelorus River at **Pelorus Bridge Scenic Reserve**. Spared destruction after development of a town failed to proceed, the reserve is the last remnant of riverplain forest that formerly covered much of lowland Marlborough. A network of tracks allows visitors to explore the rich forest and river banks, with a suspension bridge, swimming holes and waterfalls. Other facilities include a shop, café, cabins and caravan park with electric powered sites. River cruises and nature tours are also available. Some of the walks are accessible by wheelchair.

Pelorus Bridge Scenic Reserve, a popular swimming and picnic area

❷ Marlborough Sounds

The Marlborough Sounds region is a mass of bays, inlets and hidden coves with numerous walking tracks, wildlife, historical sites and unsurpassed views. Picton and Havelock are the Sounds' main towns *(see pp204–5)*. Launch services from these two towns provide the best access to the secluded bays and accommodation by the sea. The best ways to explore the Sounds are by bicycle, sea kayak, or on foot.

Cyclists on the road exploring the Sounds

D'Urville Island
Accessible by water taxi, the island was once an important source of argillite, a hard sandstone used in tool making by Māori. Today, farming is the main occupation with fishing, diving, kayaking and mountain biking popular pursuits.

French Pass
This picturesque fishing and farming village takes its name from the narrow and treacherous strait between the mainland and D'Urville Island.

0 km   5

0 miles   5

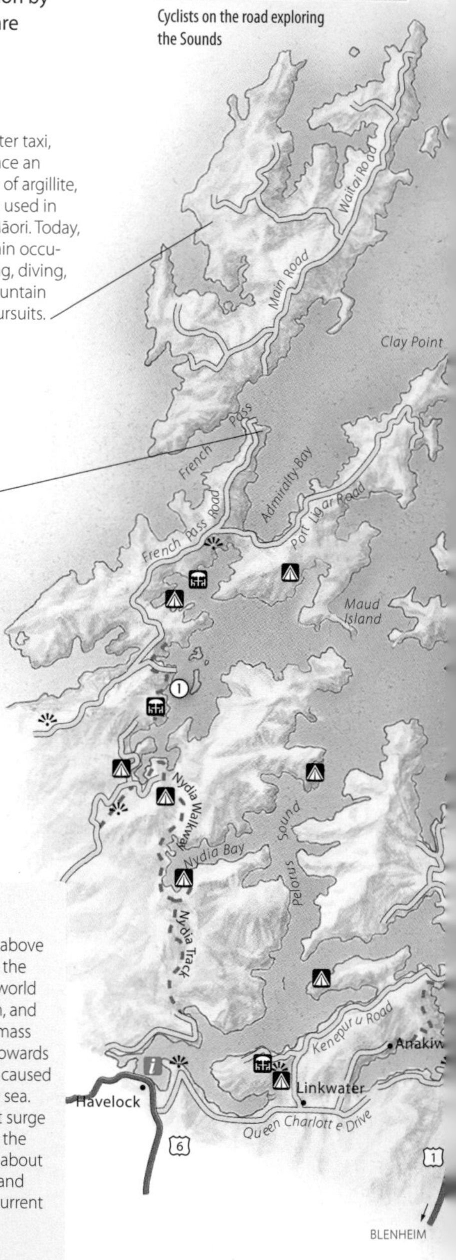

How the Sounds were Formed

The Sounds region appears as a series of ridges rising above the water but is, in fact, a series of valleys drowned by the ocean. A combination of changing sea levels (due to world climate changes), movement along faults in the region, and tilting of the landmass downwards and towards the northeast has caused inundation by the sea. The last significant surge in sea level was at the end of an Ice Age about 12,000 years ago, and gives the area its current sinuous coastline.

Drowned valleys at Elaine Bay, Tennyson Inlet

Walter Peak

Clay Point

French Pass Road

Main Road

French Pass

Admiralty Bay

Port Ligar Road

Maud Island

Nydia Walkway

Nydia Bay

Nydia Track

Pelorus Sound

Kenepuru Road

Anakiwa

Linkwater

Havelock

Queen Charlotte Drive

6

1

BLENHEIM

Kenepuru Sound
Numerous accommodation styles are available in this quiet waterway where walking, fishing and camping are popular.

VISITORS' CHECKLIST

Practical Information
Road map D4. **W** doc.govt.nz
i **Picton** The Foreshore, (03) 520 3113; **Havelock** 61 Main Rd, (03) 574 2161. **Open** Oct–Apr: daily. **Closed** Good Fri, 25 Dec.

Transport
Picton to Anakiwa.
from Picton and Havelock.

★ Queen Charlotte Track
This 71 km (44 mile) scenic walk (or mountain-bike ride), begins at Ship Cove and ends at Anakiwa. A well-marked track, it is suitable for moderately fit people. Stout shoes are necessary.

★ Motuara Island
The open sanctuary of Motuara Island Scenic and Historic Reserve is host to myriad birdlife and can be explored via a walkway.

★ Outer Queen Charlotte Sound
The outer sound provides an enticing combination of open water, islands and wildlife. It is best visited by water taxi, sea kayak or wildlife tour.

KEY

① **Tennyson Inlet** is cloaked in native forest. Natural beauty abounds in this quiet inlet where picnic areas and campsites are found along the shoreline.

② **Titirangi Bay**, one of the few bays in the Sounds with a sandy beach, has a recreation reserve and farm park.

③ **Tory Channel** was the site of New Zealand's first shore-based whaling stations, beginning in 1827. Closed in 1964, the remnants of the last station, Perano's, can still be seen.

④ **Port Underwood** was a strategic whaling station in the 1830s. Today, its main attraction is White's Bay, with its swimming beach and old cable station.

Forsyth Island
Titi Island
②
Cape Lambert
Cape Jackson
Ship Cove
Long Island
East Bay
Arapawa Island
Titirangi Road
Queen Charlotte Track
Sound
③
Portage
Charlotte
Queen
Port Underwood
①
④
-ton
Whites Bay

Key
State highway
Minor road
Walking track

For keys to symbols *see back flap*

❺ Wairau Valley Vineyard Tour

Well known for its Sauvignon Blanc, the Wairau valley is New Zealand's largest and best-known wine region. In the early 1970s, grape planting was begun by Montana Wines (see p212). Now, 130 wineries operate in the area. The wines of the Wairau are celebrated with the annual Marlborough Wine and Food Festival each February. West of Blenheim is the Brancott Estate Cellar Door and Restaurant, a visitor's centre covering all aspects of the wine experience.

Vineyards in the Blenheim region backed by the Richmond Range

⑨ Cloudy Bay
This is one of Marlborough's most successful exporting wineries, with a reputation for fine Sauvignon Blanc, Chardonnay and Pinot Noir. Tastings and sales are available daily.

⑧ Allan Scott Wines and Estates
One of the pioneers of grape growing in Marlborough, this vineyard offers wines characteristic of the region: Chardonnay, Sauvignon Blanc and Riesling.

⑦ Stoneleigh Vineyards
Built on a former riverbed, the vineyard is named after the stones covering the area. Sunlight reflected from the stones speeds the ripening process of the grapes. Chardonnay, Riesling, Sauvignon Blanc and Pinot Noir wines are produced here.

⑥ Hunters Wines
This is one of the region's most awarded wineries. Red, white and sparkling wines are available, including Sauvignon Blanc, Pinot Noir, Cabernet/Merlot, sparkling Brut and Chardonnay.

Key

■ Tour route
— Other roads
⌁ River

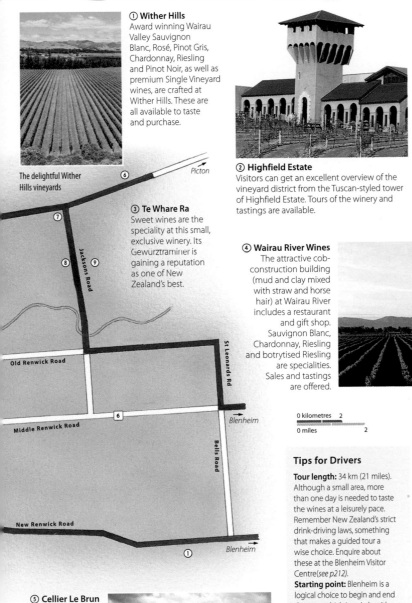

① Wither Hills
Award winning Wairau Valley Sauvignon Blanc, Rosé, Pinot Gris, Chardonnay, Riesling and Pinot Noir, as well as premium Single Vineyard wines, are crafted at Wither Hills. These are all available to taste and purchase.

The delightful Wither Hills vineyards

Picton

② Highfield Estate
Visitors can get an excellent overview of the vineyard district from the Tuscan-styled tower of Highfield Estate. Tours of the winery and tastings are available.

③ Te Whare Ra
Sweet wines are the speciality at this small, exclusive winery. Its Gewurztraminer is gaining a reputation as one of New Zealand's best.

④ Wairau River Wines
The attractive cob-construction building (mud and clay mixed with straw and horse hair) at Wairau River includes a restaurant and gift shop. Sauvignon Blanc, Chardonnay, Riesling and botrytised Riesling are specialities. Sales and tastings are offered.

Jacksons Road

Old Renwick Road

St Leonards Rd

Blenheim

Middle Renwick Road

Bells Road

New Renwick Road

Blenheim

0 kilometres 2
0 miles 2

⑤ Cellier Le Brun
This winery specializes in *méthode traditionelle* sparkling wines. Tours of the winery and underground cellar are available. Wine can be purchased at the wine shop.

Tips for Drivers

Tour length: 34 km (21 miles). Although a small area, more than one day is needed to taste the wines at a leisurely pace. Remember New Zealand's strict drink-driving laws, something that makes a guided tour a wise choice. Enquire about these at the Blenheim Visitor Centre(*see p212*).

Starting point: Blenheim is a logical choice to begin and end the tour, which is a circle with a short side trip. Road conditions are good throughout.

Stopping-off points: Besides restaurants at the wineries, Renwick and Blenheim offer many eating choices. Fruit stalls abound in summer, with December a good time for cherries.

The Clock Tower in Seymour Square, Blenheim

❻ Blenheim

Road map D5. 🏛 29,500. ✈ 6 km (4 miles) W of city. 🚌 🚌 *i* Railway Station, Sinclair St, (03) 577 8080. 🎷 Marlborough Wine & Food Festival (2nd Sat of Feb); Classic Fighters Air Show (Easter); Hunters Garden Marlborough (2nd weekend of Nov).

The largest town in the Marlborough region, Blenheim's importance in the Wairau Valley has grown along with the development of the wine industry in Marlborough *(see pp210–11)*. The annual food and wine festival is a major draw. A number of art and crafts people live and work in Blenheim and its environs.

In the city centre, Seymour Square has a fountain, pretty gardens and the Clock Tower. Blenheim's only public art gallery, the **Millennium Art Gallery** houses works by local artists and sculptors, while the **Marlborough Museum** is set beside the heritage streetscape of Brayshaw Park on the southern edge of town. The park has a miniature railway, boating pond and reconstructed colonial village, giving some insight into the way of life in Blenheim during that period. Nearby is **Wither Hills Farm Park** where a network of foot and cycling tracks have been developed for visitors within the working farm. The tracks are well marked and require average fitness.

🏛 Millennium Art Gallery
Cnr Seymour and Alfred sts. **Tel** (03) 579 2001. **Open** 1–4pm Sat & Sun. **Closed** public holidays. 🎷 donation. ♿ 📷

🏛 Marlborough Museum
Brayshaw Park, 26 Arthur Baker Place. **Tel** (03) 578 1712. **Open** daily (archive Tue & Thu only). **Closed** 25 Dec. 🎷 ♿

🌱 Wither Hills Farm Park
Redwood St. **Tel** Blenheim i-SITE Visitor Centre, (03) 577 8080. **Open** daily.

Environs
West of Blenheim is the **Brancott Estate Cellar Door and Restaurant**. Tours offer insights into the wine process, tutored tastings, vineyard cycle trips, and even helicopter flights over the estate.

Further south, in the Awatere valley, **Molesworth Station**, New Zealand's largest farm, can be explored when the road through it opens each summer. The 59 km (37 mile) road journey through high country, passes historic cob houses, wide river valleys and mountains.

🔲 Brancott Estate Cellar Door and Restaurant
180 Brancott Road, Marlborough. **Tel** (03) 520 6975. **Open** daily. **Closed** Good Fri, 25 & 26 Dec. ♿ 📷 🚫 📷

🔲 Molesworth Station
i Department of Conservation, (03) 572 9100. **Open** Dec–Feb. 🎷

❼ Kaikoura

Road map D5. 🏛 3,700. 🚉 🚌 *i* Westend, (03) 319 5641. 🎷 Kaikoura Seafest (first Sat in Oct); Kaikoura Races (Mon after Labour Day).

The name Kaikoura means "meal of crayfish" and reflects the importance of the sea throughout the area. Captain Cook sailed past the Kaikoura Peninsula in 1770, naming the place "Lookers On" because of the reticence of local Māori.

The first European settlers and whalers arrived in 1842. The town's current tourism boom is also based on whales and other marine wildlife. The visitor centre has extensive displays and an audiovisual show. Whale tooth carvings can be seen at historic **Fyffe House**, a colonial cottage from the whaling days and Kaikoura's oldest dwelling. Nearby, at the beachfront, is the Garden of Memories with a walkway encased with pairs of whale ribs.

Whale tooth carving

Above town, Scarborough Street has a lookout point, a remnant *pa* and the Gold Gallery with wall sculptures gilded with gold leaf.

On the southern edge of town, guided tours can be taken at the **Kaikoura Winery** and at **Māori Leap Cave**, a limestone cave full of stalagmites and stalactites. 6 km (4 miles) south of town is Fyffe Country Lodge which has pleasant gardens. Inland roads lead to Mount Fyffe, where superb views can be obtained from the walking tracks through the forest and mountains.

🏠 Fyffe House
62 Avoca St. **Tel** (03) 319 5835. **Open** summer: daily; winter: Thu–Mon. **Closed** Good Fri, 25 Dec. 🎷 Adults.

🔲 Kaikoura Winery
State Hwy 1. **Tel** (03) 319 7966. **Open** daily. **Closed** Good Fri, 25 Dec. 📷

🦇 Māori Leap Cave
State Hwy 1. **Tel** (03) 319 5023. **Open** daily. **Closed** 25 Dec. 🎷 📷 obligatory. 🚫 📱

Picnickers on the Kaikoura coast

Watching Marine Life at Kaikoura

In the late 1980s, the popularity of observing marine life in Kaikoura led to a tourism boom that transformed the town into one of New Zealand's premier visitor destinations. The main attraction is sperm whales, seen as they rest on the surface between dives, as well as orca and numerous dolphin species. Through the services of several eco-tourism companies in Kaikoura, the habits of whales and seals and the antics of the acrobatic dusky dolphins can be observed from the shore or air and both in and on the water. The special richness of Kaikoura's marine life is explained by the presence of very deep water and the mixing of warm and cold ocean currents there, which forces nutrients to the surface. Species of seabirds found in Kaikoura include the royal albatross, wandering albatross, grey petrel, Antarctic fulmer, and black-browed mollymawk.

Tourists get a close-up view from the Whale Watch® boat

Whale Watching

Most whales seen at Kaikoura are toothed whales, quite often sperm whales. Unlike baleen whales, which feed by filtering plankton, toothed whales hunt their prey, including fish, krill and giant squid, sometimes at great depths.

Tour operators offer opportunities to visitors to get close to the marine life.

Swimming with dusky dolphins, inquisitve, playful creatures, is a memorable experience.

New Zealand fur seals can be observed at a colony at Ohau Point, 23 km (14 miles) north of Kaikoura.

Fresh seafood is a speciality of Kaikoura's restaurants. The abundance of scallops, fish, crayfish and prawns is celebrated annually in October with the Kaikoura Seafest.

Mollymawks are one of the marine bird species to be seen within easy reach of the shores of Kaikoura.

❶ Nelson

Nelson was the second settlement developed by the New Zealand Company. The first settlers arrived in February 1842, but in 1844 the company failed. Some settlers persisted, and in 1853 Nelson became the capital of a province of the same name. A royal decree in 1858 made the small town New Zealand's second city. Today, Nelson is renowned as a vibrant art, crafts and festival centre with a superb climate and boutique hotels. The compact city centre includes many galleries, craft shops and heritage attractions. A memorial to Dutch navigator Abel Tasman can be seen at Tahunanui, a popular swimming beach close to the centre of the city.

Nelson as seen from Auckland Point

🏞 Centre of New Zealand
Cnr Milton & Hardy sts.

An easy walk beginning at the Botanical Reserve – where the country's first rugby game was played in 1870 – leads up Botanical Hill to a lookout known locally as "the centre of New Zealand". The hill provides good views of the city, harbour, Maitai Valley and the Maitai River, which flows through the city into the harbour. A path follows the river downstream through a pleasant park and past Riverside Pool, a modern heated pool with a historic façade.

🏞 Queens Gardens and Albion Square

The main focus of the city's heritage precincts remains the Queens Gardens. Some of the trees date back to the 1850s although the gardens were formally established in 1887. Albion Square borders the gardens and was once the political centre of Nelson when provincial government buildings dominated the square. Some historic buildings remain, such

as a powder magazine, trout hatchery and fire station. A still-in-service 1864 post box and surveyors' test chain complete the picture.

🏛 Suter Art Gallery
208 Bridge St. **Tel** (03) 548 4699. **Open** daily. **Closed** 1 Jan, Good Fri, 25 Dec. 🐾 🔒 🏠 📷 🖥 **w** thesuter.org.nz

One of New Zealand's oldest galleries (1899), the Suter Art Gallery holds a nationally important permanent collection, including paintings by Sir Tosswill Woollaston (one of the founders of New Zealand modern art), Frances Hodgkins, Colin McCahon, (see p36) and contemporary Nelson painter, Jane Evans. It also houses the collection of Andrew Suter, the city's bishop from 1866 to 1891. He donated early colonial paintings, including many by the colonial watercolourist John Gully, to the people of Nelson.

🏞 Anzac Park
Cnr Rutherford and Halifax sts.

The beautifully landscaped Anzac Park, with its pretty flowerbeds,

tall palms and cenotaph, is Nelson's main war memorial. A horse-drawn passenger carriage ran alongside the park until 1901, using a section of New Zealand's first railway line. Auckland Point nearby was once the site of Matangi Awhio Pa, a fortification. The site is now being revegetated and a winding track to the summit provides excellent views over the city.

🏛 The Nelson Provincial Museum
Cnr Trafalgar & Hardy sts. **Tel** (03) 548 9588. **Open** daily. **Closed** Good Fri, 25 Dec. 🐾 donation; charge for special exhibitions.

The lower gallery focuses on the natural and social history of the Nelson and Tasman region. Māori artifacts and *taonga* (treasures such as weapons and ornaments) form a large part of the collection, along with photographs, ceramics, glass and silverware, and textiles from colonial times to the present. The upper gallery hosts special exhibitions.

🏢 Nelson Market
Montgomery Square. **Tel** (03) 546-6454. **Open** 8am–1pm Sat, 9am–1pm Sun. **Closed** 1 Jan, 25 Dec. 🔒 📷

On weekends the car park at Montgomery Square is transformed into a colourful market-place. Vendors of plants, toys, crafts, organic produce and foods, ranging from sushi to Dutch cheeses, set up their stalls. Shoppers and buskers bring the market to life, creating a busy spectacle that has become a key part of life in Nelson, for locals and visitors alike.

Fresh flowers for sale at the Nelson weekend market

The facade of Christ Church Cathedral on Church Hill

🏛 Church Hill
Trafalgar Square.

Church Hill is dominated by the Anglican Christ Church Cathedral, the third church built on a site which has also been a survey base, *pa*, fort and immigration barracks. Church Hill is linked to Trafalgar Street by the impressive granite Cathedral Steps, one of many gifts to the city by Thomas Cawthron, a philanthropist. Panels explain the history of Church Hill and some of its notable trees, while the remains of the old fort are visible near the cathedral entrance.

🏛 Trafalgar Street South
Nelson's main street, Trafalgar, extends south of the cathedral to Trafalgar Street South. It leads to Fairfield Park and a small cemetery with the graves of some early settlers.

Close by are two colonial era houses, Melrose and Fairfield. Melrose House (around 1878) is a truly grand home in the Italianate style. A feature of Fairfield House (1873) is its viewing tower, a replica of one used by its original owner, Arthur Atkinson, for astrological purposes. The garden contains some plantings made by the Dalai Lama during his 1996 visit to New Zealand.

🏛 South Street
To the west of Church Hill is the historic precinct of South Street comprising a collection of workers' cottages built between 1863 and about 1867. Sixteen cottages remain intact and many have been restored for use as accommodation or to house craft galleries.

VISITORS' CHECKLIST

Road map D4. 🚗 43,500.
🌐 **nelsonnz.com**
ℹ i-SITE, 77 Trafalgar St, (03) 548 2304. 🎭 Nelson Jazz Festival (Jan); School of Music Winter Festival (Jul); Nelson Arts Festival (Oct); Sealord Summer Festival (Dec–Jan).

Transport
✈ 15 km (9 miles) SW of city.
🚌 27 Bridge St.

Former workers' cottages in the historic South Street precinct

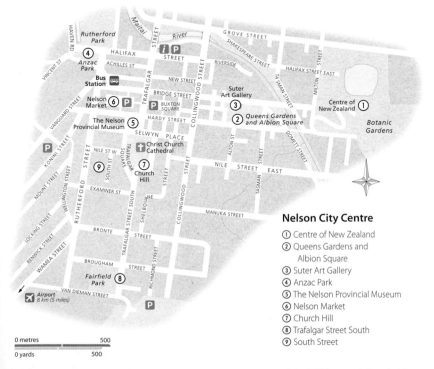

Nelson City Centre
① Centre of New Zealand
② Queens Gardens and Albion Square
③ Suter Art Gallery
④ Anzac Park
⑤ The Nelson Provincial Museum
⑥ Nelson Market
⑦ Church Hill
⑧ Trafalgar Street South
⑨ South Street

0 metres   500
0 yards   500

For keys to symbols *see back flap*

9 Richmond

Road map D4. 11,000.
Nelson, 8 km (5 miles) W of town.
22 Gladstone Rd, (03) 543 9521.

This busy town serves the productive horticultural lands to its south and west. Highlights are the Washbourne Gardens, complete with 1862 jailhouse, and the Redwood Stables restaurant, built using bricks from New Zealand's first racing stables. Visitors can observe the art of glass making at **Höglund Art Glass** where Ola and Marie Höglund create their renowned colourful glassware, including goblets, birds and jewellery.

Environs
Six km (4 miles) southwest of Richmond, at Brightwater, is a memorial to New Zealand's best known scientist, atom-splitting Lord Ernest Rutherford (see p25), born here in 1871. Also at Brightwater is the **McGlashen Pottery** (see p217). Continuing southwest to Wakefield is a historic church, St John's (1846).

Höglund Art Glass
52 Lansdowne Rd. **Tel** (03) 544 6500.
Open daily. **Closed** Good Fri, 25 Dec.

McGlashen Pottery
128 Ellis St, Brightwater. **Tel** (03) 542 3585. **Open** daily. **Closed** 1 Jan, Good Fri, 25 Apr, 25 Dec.

The South Island's oldest church, St John's, at Wakefield

10 St Arnaud

Road map D5. 200. View Rd, (03) 521 1806. Antique & Classic Boat Show (Mar); Rainbow Mountain Bike Race (Mar).

Approximately 90 minutes' drive from Blenheim or Nelson is the small town of St Arnaud, nestled on the shore of Lake Rotoiti, a trout fishing, boating and

Lake Rotoiti in Nelson Lakes National Park

water-skiing paradise. The nearby Lake Rotoroa also has good trout fishing but is more secluded and quiet. St Arnaud is the gateway to Nelson Lakes National Park and the closest town to the **Rainbow Ski Area**, where the terrain is suitable for novice and intermediate snow-boarders and skiers. In summer, the ski field access road continues through to Hanmer Springs (see p237) through Rainbow Station.

Rainbow Ski Area
Wairau Valley. **Tel** (03) 521 1861.
Open June–Oct daily.

11 Nelson Lakes National Park

Road map C5. View Rd, (03) 521 1806.

The twin, glacier-formed lakes Rotoiti and Rotoroa dominate the 1,017 sq km (393 sq miles) of this park at the northern tip of the Southern Alps. A water taxi is the easiest form of access to the area of high passes, forests, valleys and basins. The lakes and rivers are popular for kayaking, sailing, boating, swimming and trout fishing. Winter pastimes include ski touring. There are many trails for trampers and walkers, including the well-known 80 km (50 mile) Travers–Sabine Circuit that includes two major valleys, an alpine pass, the wetland Speargrass area and both main lakes. The two-day return walk along Robert Ridge to the beautiful Lake Angelus is also very pleasant but with high altitudes, caution is advised.

12 Motueka

Road map D4. 6,600. 20 Wallace St, (03) 528 6543.

Motueka has a diverse horti-cultural industry and is the country's most prolific orcharding area. Kiwifruit, apples, berries, hops, pears, and grapes are some of the produce grown here. The town is also a base for trips to the Abel Tasman and Kahurangi national parks.

Environs
Kaiteriteri, 14 km (9 miles) north of Motueka, is known for its stunning golden beaches. South of Motueka are the coastal villages of Tasman and Mapua. Inland is Upper Moutere village, established in the 1840s by German settlers. Each village has its own artists, shops, wineries, eating places and boutique accommodation.

13 Kahurangi National Park

Road map C4. 20 Wallace St, Motueka, (03) 528 6543.

A great variety of native animals and plants live in the 4,510 sq km (1,740 sq mile) park. A highlight is the Heaphy Track, a four- to five-day walking track. Kayaking, hunting, caving, hiking, rafting and fishing are all popular activities here. Alpine plants can be seen growing near the Cobb Reservoir. The major gateway is Motueka, but access is also possible from Karamea (see p238), Murchison and Golden Bay.

The Nelson Arts Scene

A combination of a warm climate and a relaxed environment has attracted many artists to Nelson, making it one of New Zealand's most vibrant arts regions. Its history of artistic endeavour is long. Today, Nelson abounds with opportunities to explore art in the many galleries and studios of glass-blowers, painters, jewellers, textile artists, woodworkers and ceramic artists. The Suter Art Gallery *(see p214)* is noted for its extensive collection of historical and contemporary works. The Nelson region is also becoming known for music and performance events, such as the Nelson Jazz Festival and the Nelson School of Music Winter Festival. Nelson's Provincial Museum houses a photographic display chronicling Nelson and New Zealand's early colonial beginnings.

Ron McGlashen at work in his ceramic studio at Brightwater

Ceramics

A variety of fine raw clays and glaze materials has long attracted ceramic artists to Nelson. A large number of pottery outlets showcase the work of talented potters, and many nationally recognized crafts people choose Nelson as a living and working base.

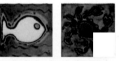

Handmade tiles adorn the doorway of a tile shop in Mapua

Glassware in Nelson is made by combining modern design ideas with traditional glass-blowing methods *(see p216)*. The results are colourful creations, each one hand-crafted and unique.

Art and craft galleries are a common sight in the region

Artists in Nelson have long been inspired by their surroundings. A nationally important collection can be seen at The Suter Art Gallery *(see p214)*.

Three-dimensional art, designed to be viewed from many sides, is popular in Nelson. Some pieces are practical, others whimsical. Local sculptors have been commissioned to provide works for public areas.

⑭ Abel Tasman National Park

New Zealand's smallest national park, at 225 sq km (87 sq miles), Abel Tasman has a mild climate, golden beaches and sandy estuaries fringed by natural forest. The park is best known for its coast track, which can be walked either way, with the return trip made on a launch or water taxi. There are huts and a large number of campsites on the coast track to break the journey. Due to the park's popularity, it is necessary to book walks and huts before visiting. Abel Tasman is also one of New Zealand's better sea kayaking destinations and a day spent drifting in a slowly filling estuary or watching seals, penguins, dolphins or bird-life from these quiet craft will not be forgotten.

Aerial view of Abel Tasman National Park

★ Wainui Falls
Nelson's finest accessible falls are reached via an easy 30-minute walk from a small car park off the road to Totaranui.

★ Harwoods Hole
A 1-hour walk from Canaan car park (see p220) leads to the entrance of the 176 m (577 ft) vertical marble shaft known as Harwoods Hole. It is dangerous to get too close to the chasm as the sides may be unstable.

0 kilometres   4
0 miles   4

VISITORS' CHECKLIST

Practical Information
Road map D4. W doc.govt.nz
i i-SITE, 79 Trafalgar St, Nelson,
(03) 546 9339.

Transport
to Marahau and Totaranui
daily from Nelson and Motueka.
water taxi and launch services
from Kaiteriteri and Marahau.

★ Totaranui
A main arrival point for visitors to northern Abel
Tasman National Park, Totaranui's sandy beaches and
azure waters are a prime attraction *(see p220)*.

Coast Track
The 51-km- (32-mile-) long Coast Track
from Marahau to Wainui crosses four
estuaries, two negotiable only at low
tide. Two have high tide tracks and a
bridge crosses the inlet at Onetahuti.

KEY

① **The Inland Track**, more rugged
than its coastal counterpart, is a
three-day walk from Tinline Bay to
Wainui Bay. Drinking water should
be carried on the track.

② **The Tonga Island Marine
Reserve** covers 12 km (8 miles) of
coastline. Established to restore the
marine environment to its natural
state, all animals, plants and sea life
here are completely protected.

③ **Granite Rocks** are a common
feature of the park, and were once
extracted at Tonga Quarry.

④ **Falls River** is about a 1-hour
walk from Torrent Bay. The track
follows Tregidga Stream and
passes Cascade Falls before ending
at Falls River. A further 15-minute
walk up rocks leads to the main falls.

Key

━━━ State highway
━━━ Minor road
〜〜 River
•••• Walking track
-••- Park boundary
•••• Marine Reserve boundary

Marahau
The southern gateway to Abel
Tasman National Park, Marahau is
the base for water taxis serving the
coast. Outdoor pursuits available
at Marahau include sea kayaking,
walking and swimming with seals.

For keys to symbols *see back flap*

View from Takaka Hill looking towards Motueka and Nelson

⑮ Takaka Hill

Road map D4.

Takaka Hill is commonly referred to as "the marble mountain" because of its large marble deposits that contrast sharply with the granite hills and headlands of adjoining Abel Tasman National Park. There are many caves and sinkholes to explore in the area, including **Ngarua Caves** near the summit of Takaka Hill, where a lookout offers views north to D'Urville Island and east towards Nelson city. Tours of the only cave open to visitors are available and bones of moa *(see p29)* can be seen. Visible below the caves is Marahau's golden beach *(see p219)*, where marble from a local quarry was shipped to Wellington for use in New Zealand's Parliament Building.

To the west of Ngarua Caves, Canaan Road leads to Canaan car park, the starting point for walking tracks, including the Rameka Track, one of Nelson's better mountain-bike rides.

An easy walk leads to the impressive Harwoods Hole *(see p218)*, a 176 m (577 ft) vertical shaft. A short steep side track leads to the Harwood Lookout with a fine viewpoint inland to the Tablelands in Kahurangi National Park *(see p217)*.

To the east of Ngarua Caves is Hawkes Lookout. A short walk leads to a platform perched over a precipitous 500 m (1,640 ft) drop to the forest at Riwaka Resurgence.

Ngarua Caves
Tel (03) 528 8093. **Open** summer: daily; winter: school hols.

⑯ Takaka

Road map D4. 1,500. 6 km (4 miles) N of town. Willow St, (03) 525 9136. **nelsonnz.com**

Takaka is the main shopping and business area for the Golden Bay region and an access point to Abel Tasman

National Park *(see pp218–19)*. The townspeople are a mix of "alternative life-stylers" and farming folk. Dairy farming is one of the largest industries in the region. The **Golden Bay Museum** is excellent, and best known for its displays on Abel Tasman and the story of Golden Bay's many extractive industries. Several galleries operate in the area and many artists near Takaka show their work – painted gourds, pottery and wood or stone sculptures – to visitors.

At **Anatoki Salmon**, visitors can catch Chinook salmon and get it smoked to eat or take it away. It is also home to tame eels and farm animals. Riverside walking and picnics in a valley at the park are other attractions.

Golden Bay Museum
Commercial St. **Tel** (03) 525 6268. **Open** 10am–4pm daily. **Closed** Sun in winter, public hols.

Anatoki Salmon
230 McCallum's Rd. **Tel** (03) 525 7251. **Open** daily. **Closed** 25 Dec. limited.

Painted gourd

Environs
Beyond the beach at Pohara, 10 km (6 miles) from Takaka, is a memorial to Dutch navigator Abel Tasman, with a lookout platform and display. After the memorial, the road leads to **Wainui Bay**. Several coastal walks and one to Wainui Falls *(see p218)* begin there. Beyond Wainui Bay the road climbs to Abel Tasman National Park, descending finally to the sea and golden sands of Totaranui. A camp ground and visitor centre with a shop operate here over the summer.

Scenic beauty of the Takaka River in autumn

For hotels and restaurants in this region see pp305–6 and pp321–2

The clear waters of Waikoropupu Springs Scenic Reserve

⓱ Waikoropupu Springs Scenic Reserve

Road map D4.

Seven km (4 miles) north of Takaka on State Highway 60, a turnoff leads to the Waikoropupu Springs Scenic Reserve. The waters here at New Zealand's largest freshwater springs are exceptionally clear, coming from an underground cave system that is connected to the kaarst features on Takaka Hill (see p220) and at Riwaka Resurgence. The springs are best viewed from the curved viewing platform, reached by an easy walk through beautiful forest. Swimming is prohibited as the water is considered *wahi tapu* (sacred).

Beyond the springs (at the end of the road), the Pupu Walkway is a track that follows the line of a water race originally built to serve a gold-mining claim. An impressive piece of engineering, the water race was later used (and still is) to generate electric power. The loop walk is about 5 km (3 miles) long and is Golden Bay's most popular day walk.

⓲ Collingwood

Road map D4. 250.

A quiet village at the mouth of the Aorere River, Collingwood was designated a port of entry in the 1850s gold rush and was considered as the site for New Zealand's capital city. Despite several devastating fires, the courthouse, post office, original cemetery and Anglican St Cuthbert's Church remain to remind visitors of the town's fleeting moment of glory.

Collingwood acts as a base for tours to Farewell Spit and for buses serving the Heaphy Track in Kahurangi National Park (see p216).

Environs
Within 20 km (12 miles) of Collingwood is the beautiful Kaituna Track with river views and lush forest, the Te Anaroa Caves, a 350 m (1,148 ft) limestone cave system with glowworms and shellfish fossils, and the Aorere, New Zealand's first major gold field. Quartz, silver and gold were mined here. The workings can be explored by a walking track with views over the valley.

⓳ Farewell Spit

Road map D4. 🚹 Farewell Spit Information Centre (03) 524 8454. **Open** daily. 🚫 💻 📷

At the northern tip of the South Island, a 35 km (22 mile) sandspit sweeps eastward into the sea. Farewell Spit is a nature reserve with restricted access and has been desig-nated a Wetland of International Importance.

In late spring, tens of thousands of migratory waders arrive from the northern hemisphere, joining the year-round residents before returning home in autumn to breed. Black swans, Canada geese, Australasian gannets, Caspian

Early gold workings at Aorere, near Collingwood

terns, oystercatchers, black shags and eastern bartailed godwits are amongst the species to be seen in summer. As the region is a protected area, the only way to visit the spit is on a guided tour with one of the licensed tour operators based in Collingwood.

Environs
Immediately to the west of the spit is **Puponga Farm Park**, with walking tracks and viewpoints. A short walk from the Farewell Spit visitor centre and café leads to Fossil Point on the wild ocean beach. Further west is the easy climb to Pillar Point lighthouse and the Old Man Range, while at the end of the road a shorttrack crosses a series of dunes to the spectacular Wharariki Beach, with rock pools, birds, seals and the towering Archway Islands nearby.

🏕 **Puponga Farm Park**
Collingwood–Puponga Main Rd. **Tel** (03) 525 8026. **Open** daily. 💻

Tourists climbing the sand dunes at Farewell Spit

CANTERBURY AND THE WEST COAST

Canterbury and the West Coast, stretching from the Tasman Sea in the west to the Pacific Ocean in the east, is characterized by sharp and sudden distinctions of geology, flora and climate. The combined area contains five national parks and New Zealand's highest mountain. Christchurch, the largest city in the South Island, is an ideal base from which to explore the various subregions.

When large-scale European settlement of Canterbury began in 1850, both Canterbury and the West Coast were dominated by the Ngai Tahu tribe. By 1860, the bulk of the tribe's land had been acquired by the government in a series of dubious sales transactions, leaving the Ngai Tahu impoverished and unable to participate equally in the new settler economy. It was not until 1997 that the Ngai Tahu received compensation from the New Zealand Government.

While pastoral farming was the key to the development of Canterbury in the 1850s, it was the discovery of gold in the 1860s that brought European settlement to the West Coast. Today, "the Coast" retains a rustic mystique, a product of its mining heritage, powerful landscapes of rugged mountains and glaciers, lush rainforest, rushing rivers and sombre lakes, as well as its isolation from the rest of New Zealand. The West Coast climate is wet, with prevailing westerly air-flows bringing frequent heavy rain as moisture-laden air is forced up and over the Southern Alps. By contrast, Canterbury is relatively dry, with warm, blustery winds commonly sweeping down the eastern side of the alps and over the Canterbury Plains.

The plains are carved into a patchwork of grazing and crop paddocks, backed by tussock vegetation and forest-covered mountain ranges. They merge to the north and south with rolling farmland, interspersed with wide, braided rivers. The inland region is a large, dry, open basin of austere beauty, over which New Zealand's highest mountains loom.

Climbers on the summit of Aoraki/Mount Cook

◀ Scenic view of Maruia River from Lewis Pass

Exploring Canterbury and the West Coast

Canterbury and the West Coast's distinctive landscapes are dominated by the Southern Alps through which there are only two roads and one railway line. To get the best out of the region, and particularly to appreciate the beauty of its varied geology, flora and fauna, a willingness to don sturdy shoes and set out on foot is necessary. For the independent outdoor enthusiast, the opportunities are enormous, and for those who prefer to be guided through the wilderness, commercially run adventure activities are available at most key locations.

Vintage-style tram, a classic mode of transport in Christchurch

Sights at a Glance

Top Outdoor Activities

The places shown here have been selected for their recreational activities. Conditions vary depending on the weather and the time of year, so exercise caution and, if in doubt, seek local advice.

	Fishing	Golf	Mountain Biking	Mountain Climbing	Skiing/Heli-Skiing	Hiking	Walking	White-Water Rafting
Arthur's Pass National Park				●	●	●	●	
Banks Peninsula	●	●	●			●	●	
Franz Josef Glacier				●	●	●	●	●
Hanmer Springs	●	●	●		●	●	●	●
Hokitika	●	●	●		●			
Karamea	●	●	●			●	●	●
Lake Ohau	●	●	●		●	●	●	
Lake Tekapo	●	●	●		●	●	●	
Lewis Pass			●	●	●	●	●	
Aoraki/Mount Cook		●		●	●	●	●	
Methven/Mount Hutt	●			●	●	●	●	
Paparoa National Park	●					●	●	
Port Hills			●			●	●	
Rakaia	●	●				●	●	
Reefton	●		●			●	●	●
Westport	●	●	●			●	●	

Abut Head
Hariha
Whataroa
Franz Josef Glacier
Fox Glacier
WESTLAND TAI POUTINI NATIONAL PARK
AORAKI / MT COOK NATIONAL PARK
Mount Cook 3755m
Haast
Mount Ward 2644m
Mount Cook
LAKE TEKAPO
Mount Huxley 2499m
LAKE PUKAKI
Lake Tekapo
Ben Ohau Range
Obau Forest
LAKE OHAU
TWIZEL
Lake Benmore
Clay Cliffs
Omarama
Queenstown
Kurow

Key

- ▬▬ Motorway
- ▬▬ Major road
- ▭▭▭ Minor road
- ▬▬ Scenic route
- ▬▪▬ Major railway
- ▬▬ Minor railway
- ▬▬ Regional border
- △ Summit

Getting Around

Numerous bus operators link all parts of the region, but the most convenient way to get around is by car. The roads are good, but care is needed in winter on the alpine routes, and some sights are accessible only via gravel roads. Day trips from Christchurch include Banks Peninsula, Hanmer Springs, Arthur's Pass and mid-Canterbury's ski fields. The four-and-a-half hour trip from Christchurch to Greymouth on the TranzAlpine railway is a relaxing way to see the region's diverse scenery. Air New Zealand links the east and west coasts with daily flights between Hokitika and Christchurch.

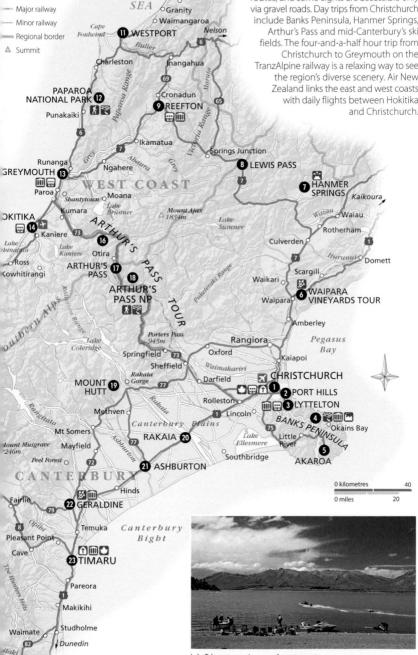

KARAMEA **10**

Karamea Bight

67

TASMAN SEA

Seddonville

Granity

Waimangaroa

Nelson

Cape Foulwind **11** WESTPORT

Buller

6

Charleston

Inangahua

PAPAROA NATIONAL PARK **12**

69

Cronadun

9 REEFTON

Punakaiki

Paparoa Range

6

Ikamatua

7

Springs Junction

8 LEWIS PASS

Runanga

Grey

Ngahere

7

GREYMOUTH **13**

Paroa

WEST COAST

Shantytown

Moana

Lake Brunner

Mount Ajax *1834m*

Lake Sumner

7 HANMER SPRINGS

Kaikoura

Waiau

Waiau

HOKITIKA **14**

Kaniere

73

Kumara

16

Otira

Lake Kaniere

Ross

Kowhitirangi

ARTHUR'S PASS **17**

18

ARTHUR'S PASS NP

Rotherham

Culverden

Hurunui

Domett

Scargill

Waikari

7

Waipara

6 WAIPARA VINEYARDS TOUR

Amberley

Pegasus Bay

Porters Pass 945m

Springfield

Sheffield

73

Rangiora

Oxford

Waimakariri

Kaiapoi

CHRISTCHURCH **1**

2 PORT HILLS

3 LYTTELTON

4 BANKS PENINSULA

Okains Bay

MOUNT HUTT **19**

Rakaia Gorge

77

Darfield

Rolleston

Lincoln

1

75

Little River

5

AKAROA

Methven

Canterbury Plains

Rakaia

RAKAIA **20**

Lake Ellesmere

Southbridge

Mt Somers

Mayfield

77

21 ASHBURTON

Ashburton

Mount Musgrave *246m*

Peel Forest

72

Hinds

Fairlie

79

22 GERALDINE

Canterbury Bight

Pleasant Point

Temuka

Cave

8

Makikihi

Studholme

82

↓Dunedin

TIMARU **23**

Pareora

Waimate

Lake Tekapo, a popular venue for watersports

For keys to symbols *see back flap*

① Christchurch

Canterbury's provincial capital, Christchurch, is the largest city in the South Island and the principal gateway to its scenic wonders. Laid out as the capital of the Canterbury Settlement in 1850, the city has many notable buildings and monuments that recall its colonial heritage, as well as many parks and gardens. It is often thought of as a conservative city, a reflection of its origins as a Church of England settlement modelled on 19th-century English society. During the 20th century the city became increasingly industrialized and is today a centre for IT. A rebuilding programme is underway to repair the damage caused by earthquakes in 2010 and 2011.

Old Government Building, built in Italian Renaissance style, now a Heritage Hotel

🏛 Cathedral Square

In the heart of the city, amid the worst of the earthquake devastation, Cathedral Square is still dominated by the ruins of Christchurch Cathedral. Other historic buildings include the sturdy Old Government Building (1911), which survived relatively intact, as well as the Renaissance-style Old Chief Post Office (1897), both of which are undergoing repairs. Completely demolished are the Edwardian Regent Theatre and the Gothic Press Building, which housed the city's daily newspaper. The 1867 statue of Robert Godley, which suffered damage in the 2011 earthquake, has been restored and returned to its plinth in the square. The fenced-off ruins of the Cathedral are still off limits but the reopened Square with vibrant art works and installations, daily markets and cultural performances, is drawing tourists again.

⛪ Ruins of Christchurch Cathedral

Cathedral Square. ℹ (03) 366 0046. **Closed** due to earthquake damage.

Begun in 1864 and completed in 1904, Christchurch Cathedral was built as the focal point of the new Anglican settlement of Canterbury and remains the city's most important landmark, particularly following the earthquakes. It was designed by English architect George Gilbert Scott in the Gothic Revival style. Noted local architect Benjamin Mountfort supervised the completion and also had considerable influence over the design. Built of Canterbury stone and native timbers, this impressive building had many notable features, including detailed wood and stone carvings around the high altar and main pulpit.

The cathedral had survived the earthquake of September 2010 with only minor damage, but during 2011's quake the iconic spire toppled into Cathedral Square, leaving the main entrance surrounded by deep drifts of broken masonry. The final fate of the cathedral ruins has yet to be decided and a new cathedral may still be built here.

Godley and the Canterbury Settlement

John Robert Godley (1814–61) is regarded as the founder of Canterbury although he spent only three years in the new province. With Edward Gibbon Wakefield, founder of the New Zealand Company (see p53), he formed the Canterbury Association in 1848, which then purchased 1,210 sq km (470 sq miles) of land for the creation of a Church of England-dominated province in New Zealand. A slice of England was to be transplanted on Canterbury's far shores. English newspapers commented on the "respectability" of the so-called "Canterbury Pilgrims" who set sail on four ships, the *Randolph, Charlotte Jane, Cressy* and *Sir George Seymour*, in September 1850. Within three years of its founding, Canterbury was governing itself as one of New Zealand's six provinces. Godley returned to England in 1852.

Statue of John Robert Godley

Key

▦ Street-by-Street: Christchurch pp228–9

– – Inner-city tram route

VISITORS' CHECKLIST

Practical Information
Road map C6. 316,000.
christchurch.com
i-SITE, Christchurch Arts
Centre, Worcester Boulevard,
(03) 379 9629. Showtime
Canterbury (Nov); Summertimes
Festivals (Dec–Mar).

Transport
10 km (6 miles) NW of city.
Troup Dr. 123 Worcester
St; Cathedral Square.

Punting on the Avon River in Christchurch

A transitional 700-seat
Cardboard Cathedral, designed
by architect Shigeru Ban, opened
in 2013 on Latimer Square. A
steel-and timber-clad A-frame
structure supported by 90 cardboard tubes, it is expected to
have a lifespan of about 50 years.

🔷 Avon River
Cashel St & Oxford Terrace.
The Avon River, which gently
meanders through the city,
is Christchurch's greatest
natural asset and one of its
main attractions. Its grassy
banks, weeping willows, old
oak trees, ducks, and bridges
linking the city's main streets
lure office workers and visitors

alike to its banks in summer.
A walk along the Avon River
bank from Victoria Square
to the Bridge of Remembrance
takes visitors past the Law
Courts, the Floral Clock, the
Provincial Council Buildings
and a 1917 statue of Antarctic
explorer Robert Scott sculpted
by his widow, Kathleen.

Another great way to enjoy
the river is to take a boat trip.
Punts operate from various
landings along the river,
including near the Town
Hall (see p228) and Antigua
Boat Sheds.

🔷 Victoria Square
Victoria Square is a beautifully
landscaped expanse of green
north of Cathedral Square.
Focal points are the Floral
Clock (see p228), statues of
Queen Victoria (1901) and
James Cook (1932), and the
much-photographed Bowker
and Ferrier fountains. The Town
Hall, built in 1972, was badly
damaged by the earthquakes
in 2010 and 2011 and is
being repaired. A block
away, on Victoria Street, is
the Christchurch Casino,
recognizable by its stylized
roulette wheel façade.

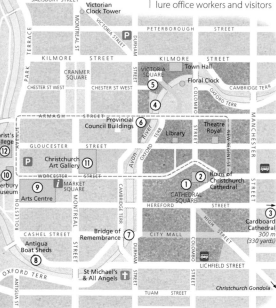

Christchurch City Centre

1. Cathedral Square
2. Ruins of Christchurch Cathedral
3. Cardboard Cathedral
4. Avon River
5. Victoria Square
6. Provincial Council Buildings
7. Bridge of Remembrance
8. Antigua Boat Sheds
9. Arts Centre
10. Canterbury Museum
11. Christchurch Art Gallery
12. Christ's College
13. Botanic Gardens pp232–3
14. Hagley Park
15. Mona Vale

Victoria Square, a park north of
Cathedral Square

For keys to symbols see back flap

Street-by-Street: Christchurch

The streets surrounding Cathedral Square are laid out in a grid pattern bordered by four broad avenues. The formality of the layout is broken by the quaint Avon River which winds serpentine through the inner city and adjacent parks. Christchurch's many Gothic Revival and Edwardian buildings, pretty parks and landscaped river bank support the oft-repeated description of Christchurch as the most English of cities outside England. As a result of earthquake damage, many of the city's buildings have been demolished and a programme of rebuilding is ongoing.

New Regent Street
This charming pedestrian-only area was built in the Spanish Mission style in 1932.

Floral Clock
Established in 1955, the clock was destroyed in the earthquake, but is in the process of being replaced.

Victoria Square, with its Avon River boundary, clipped lawns, formal plantings and many trees, is a peaceful oasis in the city.

The Town Hall, built in 1972 by noted local architects Warren and Mahoney, was badly damaged in the earthquakes, and is being repaired.

Earthquake Damage

Many notable Christchurch structures suffered extensive earthquake damage and are closed for repairs. These include: Bridge of Remembrance; Provincial Council Buildings; and the Town Hall. Those damaged beyond repair include: Christchurch Cathedral; Edwardian Regent Theatre; Gothic Press Building (demolished); Old Chief Post Office; and Oxford Terrace, which is being rebuilt.

Parkroyal Hotel

Law Courts

★ Provincial Council Buildings
These buildings, built 1858–1865, feature fine stained-glass windows, a ridge-and-furrow ceiling and mosaic tile work. They suffered extensive earthquake damage but will be repaired.

For hotels and restaurants in this region see pp306–7 and pp322–4

★ Transitional Cardboard Cathedral
The world's only cathedral made primarily of cardboard was designed by Japanese architect Shigeru Ban and serves as a temporary replacement for the Christchurch Cathedral that was damaged in the quake. Located at the southern end of Latimer Square, the cathedral seats 700.

Christchurch Tram
Taken off the tracks after the earthquake, the iconic trams now take the passengers on a shortened route past some of the city centre sights.

Old Government Building

COLOMBO STREET

HEREFORD STREET

CITY MALL

WORCESTER STREET

OXFORD TERRACE

STREET

Key

— Suggested route

| 0 metres | 100 |
| 0 yards | 100 |

Avon River

Bridge of Remembrance
The bridge's stone archway commemorates the gunners from Canterbury who served in World Wars I and II and subsequent conflicts.

City Mall, a pedestrian-only precinct spanning parts of High and Cashel streets, is a diverse complex including a department store (Ballantynes), shopping arcades and fashion boutiques. New shops are being constantly added.

Stone legislative chamber of the Provincial Council Buildings before the earthquakes

🏛 Provincial Council Buildings

Cnr of Armagh & Durham sts. **Tel** (03) 941 7680. **Closed** until further notice for repairs to earthquake damage.

Designed by Christchurch architect Benjamin Mountfort, the Provincial Council Buildings are claimed to be the finest example of secular Gothic Revival architecture in New Zealand. The buildings were constructed in three stages. The first two, from 1858 to 1861, saw the creation of a mainly wooden building. The third involved the construction of a stone council chamber, completed in 1865, the high point of the complex.

All of the buildings were severely damaged in the earthquakes, but their status as a UNESCO World Heritage Site ensures that they will be fully repaired and rebuilt.

🏛 Bridge of Remembrance

Cnr of Cashel St & Oxford Terrace.

A commemoration of New Zealand soldiers who served in various arenas of war, the bridge stands at the head of City Mall, the city's central shopping area. Structurally damaged during the earthquakes, the Bridge of Remembrance underwent extensive repair work.

🏛 Canterbury Museum

Rolleston Ave. **Tel** (03) 366 5000. **Open** Apr–Sep: 9am–5pm daily; Oct–Mar: 9am–5:30pm daily. **Closed** 25 Dec. 🔗 donation. ♿ 🌐 canterburymuseum.com

Built between 1869 and 1876, Canterbury Museum is considered to be one of Mountfort's most successful adaptations of the Gothic style for secular purposes. The museum has a comprehensive selection of genuine Antarctic relics as well as one of the finest mounted bird displays in the southern hemisphere. Other halls feature oriental art, a reconstruction of a 19th-century Christchurch street, and a Māori cultural section, including displays of the extinct moa and the bird's early Polynesian hunters.

Moa skeleton, Canterbury Museum

🏛 Christ's College

Rolleston Ave. **Tel** (03) 366 8705. **Open** daily. **Closed** during school hols. 📷 by arrangement. ♿ partial.

At Christ's College, a modern-day reminder of Christchurch's English heritage, the sons of Canterbury's élite are educated in black and white striped blazers along English public school lines amid Gothic Revival buildings dating back to 1863. There are tours of the grounds and buildings.

🏛 Arts Centre

Cnr of Rolleston Ave & Worcester Boulevard. **Tel** (03) 366 0989. **Open** in parts; check website for latest information. 🌐 artscentre.org.nz

Located in the old University of Canterbury buildings, the Arts Centre was Christchurch's art and crafts hub until it sustained substantial damage during the 2011 earthquake. The complex housed more than 40 galleries, studios and shops, as well as theatre, film and ballet venues and eateries. Construction of the Gothic Revival-style buildings began in 1877. It was designed by a succession of architects, including Mountfort, who was responsible for the Clock Tower building, Great Hall and Classics block.

The Clock Tower building was the early focus of earthquake repair work, but the entire complex is expected to be eventually repaired and rebuilt.

Canterbury Museum, housed in a beautiful stone building in Gothic Revival style

For hotels and restaurants in this region see pp306–7 and pp322–4

🏛 Christchurch Art Gallery (Te Puna o Waiwhetu)

Corner of Montreal St & Worcester Blvd. **Tel** (03) 941 7300. **Open** 10am–5pm daily. **Closed** 25 Dec. 🎟 for some exhibitions. ⚅ 🖺 🖵 🖾
🅦 **christchurchartgallery.org.nz**

Situated close to Cathedral Square, this is the city's principal art gallery. It houses a collection of 5,000 New Zealand and international works of art, which are complemented by touring exhibitions. The gallery's large, permanent display features Dutch, French, Italian and British paintings, drawings, prints, sculpture and ceramics.

The New Zealand collection, especially of Canterbury works, is one of the most comprehensive in the country. The collection displays works by Canterbury landscape artist William Sutton (see p36), as well as other prominent New Zealand painters, including Doris Lusk, Colin McCahon, Rita Angus, Charles Goldie, Frances Hodgkins, Dick Frizzell and Seraphine Pick.

🚣 Antigua Boat Sheds

2 Cambridge Terrace. **Tel** (03) 366 5885. **Open** daily. **Closed** 25 Dec. 🎟 🖵 🅦 **boatsheds.co.nz**

The Antigua Boat Sheds, on the banks of the Avon River, have been providing people with river recreation since 1882. Here, canoes, punts and paddle boats can be hired for trips through the city or upstream to the Botanic Gardens. They are the only surviving commercial boat sheds of the five or six that once offered boats for hire.

🏠 Mona Vale

63 Fendalton Rd. **Tel** (03) 348 9660. House: **Open** 9am–late afternoon daily. 🅦 **monavale.nz**

Mona Vale, one of Christchurch's historic homes, built between 1899 and 1900, is situated among sweeping lawns, mature trees and landscaped gardens to the northwest of Hagley Park. The Avon River meanders through the property. Visitors are invited to stroll through the gardens and feed the ducks. The imposing homestead was almost demolished in the 1960s,

Antigua Boat Sheds

but a public appeal for funds led to its purchase by the city. Mona Vale suffered substantial damage in the Christchurch earthquakes but it reopened in 2017 following extensive restoration work.

🌳 Hagley Park

Tel (03) 941 6840. **Open** daily. ⚅
Hagley Park, a vast green expanse in the heart of Christchurch, serves as the city's lungs. Within its boundaries are a golf course, sports grounds, tree-lined walking and cycling tracks, artificial lakes, and the Botanic Gardens (see pp232–3). When the early colonists laid out the site for their new town, they set aside 2 sq km (0.80 sq mile) for a public park, and in 1856 an ordinance was passed declaring it "reserved forever" for public recreation and enjoyment. By the early 1870s, the settlers had replaced the park's native flora with European plants, grasses and trees.

🏛 International Antarctic Centre

38 Orchard Rd. **Tel** (03) 353 7798. **Open** 9am–5:30pm daily. 🎟 ⚅ 🖵 🖾 🅦 **iceberg.co.nz**

About 20 minutes from the city centre, near the airport to the west, is the International Antarctic Centre, the base for the New Zealand, United States and Italian Antarctic programmes. Its visitor centre has a range of exhibits on the exploration and geology of Antarctica. Visitors can also take rides on Antarctic vehicles.

🚠 Christchurch Gondola

10 Bridle Path Rd. **Tel** (03) 384 0700. **Open** daily. 🎟 ⚅ 🖉 🖵 🖾 🅦 **gondola.co.nz**

Southeast of the city, the Christchurch Gondola takes passengers from a terminal in the Heathcote Valley to the rim of an extinct volcano at the top of the Port Hills. From the top there are amazing 360-degree views of the city, Banks Peninsula, Canterbury Plains and the distant Southern Alps.

Christchurch Gondola souring above the area's stunning landscape

Botanic Gardens

The Botanic Gardens, founded in 1863, include conservatories, rose and bulb beds, rock and water gardens, English lawns and woodland, all largely enclosed in the loop of the Avon River. Trees damaged during the 2011 earthquake have been replanted and the gardens restored to their former glory, but some buildings are still closed for repairs. The area fringing the eastern side of the Botanic Gardens is Christchurch's creative and artistic heart. The city's museum, civic art gallery, ballet company, professional theatre and Arts Centre are located here. A visitor centre featuring interactive plant displays, a gift shop and a café opened in 2014.

★ Conservatory Complex
Cuningham House (1923) and the complex's five other glasshouses remain closed for ongoing earthquake repairs.

★ Water Garden
This is enclosed by herbaceous perennials and exotic trees and shrubs, creating a cool and tranquil setting.

KEY

① **The Rose Garden** is a formal garden in front of the Conservatory Complex. Roses are symbolic of the city's English heritage.

② **In the New Zealand Garden** native plants are displayed in an authentic mixed forest setting.

③ **The Cockayne Memorial Garden** has specimen plantings of native trees and shrubs.

④ **Children's Playground**

⑤ **The Victoria and Albert lakes**, both artificial, attract large numbers of ducks and other bird life, including shags and swans, and are often used for model boat racing.

⑥ **Christ's College** (see p230)

⑦ **Rolleston Avenue**

Daffodil Woodland and Bandsmen's Memorial Rotunda
The area surrounding the rotunda was planted with 16,000 bulbs in 1933, and in spring is a blaze of yellow.

The Canterbury Museum
Founded in 1868 by geologist Julius von Haast, this museum includes notable permanent collections on early Antarctic exploration and traditional Maori society *(see p230)*.

VISITORS' CHECKLIST

Practical Information
Rolleston Ave (main entrance).
ⓦ **ccc.govt.nz** ⓘ (03) 941 8666. **Open** 7am–1 hour before sunset daily. **Closed** 25 Dec. ♿ ⓒ summer only. 🖊 📷 🎨 Summertimes Festival (Dec–Mar).

Transport
🚍 Worcester Boulevard.

Peacock Fountain
This ornate cast-iron fountain plays amid formal flower beds at the eastern entrance to the gardens.

⑤

| 0 metres | 100 |
| 0 yards | 100 |

⑥   ⑦

ⓘ

Arts Centre
Christchurch's arts and cultural hub was severely damaged during the 2011 earthquake. The centre is re-opening in stages, but restoration is ongoing *(see p230)*.

Sign of the Takahe, on Dyers Pass Road above Christchurch

❷ Port Hills

Road map C6. 🚌

The Port Hills separate Christchurch from Lyttelton Harbour, and were formed as the result of the eruption of the now extinct Lyttelton volcano. Their tussock-covered slopes and volcanic outcrops flank the southern part of the city. Because of their proximity to the city they are extremely popular with walkers, runners, rock climbers and mountain bikers.

The Port Hills are also easily accessed by car, thanks to the work of early 20th-century conservationist and politician Harry Ell, who strove for the creation of a road across the hills. The first stretch of the Summit Road was opened in 1938.

Ell's vision included the construction of a series of rest houses along the Port Hills, the most impressive of which is the Sign of the Takahe, completed in 1949 and now home to a restaurant. Nestled in the hill suburb of Cashmere, this imposing Gothic building was also the most cherished of his projects. Another Ell legacy, the Sign of the Kiwi, is a popular resting place for people travelling along the Summit Road who stop off here for ice creams and other refreshments.

The many tracks on the Port Hills provide striking views of Lyttelton Harbour, the Canterbury Plains and the Southern Alps. The rim of the crater can also be accessed via the Christchurch Gondola (see p231), which runs from Heathcote Valley.

❸ Lyttelton

Road map C6. 🚹 4,000. 🚌
🛈 20 Oxford St, (03) 328 9093.

Lyttelton was the landing place of the Canterbury Pilgrims in 1850, and was named after Lord Lyttelton, the chairman of the Canterbury Association. In 1867, a rail tunnel was drilled through the volcanic rock of the Port Hills to provide a link between Lyttelton's port and Christchurch, and a road tunnel was completed in 1964.

The **Lyttelton Museum** has interesting displays of local maritime history and relics from the colonial past, and a small section on Antarctic exploration. The museum was closed after suffering extensive damage from the 2011 earthquake, with some collections moved to storage. The Thornycroft Torpedo Boat Museum at Magazine Bay exhibits the remains of the torpedo boat purchased by New Zealand in 1883.

The historic Lyttelton Timeball Station stood sentry over the town from its construction in 1875 until 2011, when it was dismantled following irreparable damage during the earthquakes

of 2010 and 2011. The large black ball hanging from its tower once signalled Greenwich Mean Time to the ships in the harbour. It is hoped that the timeball mechanism can be salvaged and reused in a possible reconstruction of the building, which had been one of only five working timeball stations in the world.

A ferry service across the harbour to Quail and Ripapa islands and the small township of Diamond Harbour operates from the Lyttelton docks.

🏛 **Lyttelton Museum**
Gladstone Quay. **Tel** (03) 328 8972. **Closed** for repairs to earthquake damage. 🎟 donation. ♿ ground floor.

❹ Banks Peninsula

Road map C6.

Formed by numerous eruptions of the Lyttelton and Akaroa volcanoes, Banks Peninsula was, until some 25,000 years ago, an island. Reminders of this dramatic geological past are everywhere, including rocky volcanic outcrops, craggy headlands, deep valleys and precipitous bluffs. The Summit Road allows excellent views of this striking scenery.

The peninsula has been settled by Māori for 1,000 years, and until the 1820s was a place of prosperity and security for the Ngai Tahu tribe. That changed as a result of internecine and inter-tribal fighting, conflict which contributed indirectly to the decision taken by the British government to install a governor and sign the Treaty of Waitangi (see pp52–3).

Māori and Colonial Museum and meeting house at Okains Bay

Laverick's Bay, Banks Peninsula

Among the peninsula's many attractions are its beautiful bays and picturesque villages, including Pigeon Bay, Okains Bay, Laverick's Bay and Le Bons Bay. There are many walking tracks, including a 20-minute stroll through the Hay Scenic Reserve, which has one of the peninsula's best remaining stands of lowland podocarp forest; the 5-hour Pigeon Bay Walkway; and the two- to four-day Banks Peninsula Track, which traverses private farmland and the coastline of many of the remote eastern bays. These remote areas can also be visited on the **Eastern Bays Scenic Mail Run**, a mail delivery service that invites up to eight passengers to join its 4-hour mail run.

At Okains Bay is the **Māori and Colonial Museum** which houses an extensive collection of Māori artifacts, including an 1867 Māori *waka* (canoe) used during the Waitangi Day celebrations in February *(see p45)*. Also worth a visit is the boutique **Barry's Bay Cheese Factory**, which continues the peninsula's long tradition of cheese making.

🏛 **Māori and Colonial Museum**
1146 Main Rd, Okains Bay.
Tel (03) 304 8611. **Open** daily.
Closed 25 Dec.

🧀 **Barry's Bay Cheese Factory**
State Hwy 75. **Tel** (03) 304 5809.
Open daily. **Closed** 25 Dec.

🚐 **Eastern Bays Scenic Mail Run**
19 Rue Renard. **Tel** (03) 304 7873.
Open Mon–Sat. **Closed** public hols.

❺ Akaroa

Road map C6. 🚌 580.
ℹ️ 80 Rue Lavaud, (03) 304 8600.
🌐 akaroa.com

This attractive small town, nestled at the head of Akaroa Harbour, is the oldest town in Canterbury, and was founded by a small band of French settlers in 1840. The town boasts many French-influenced historic buildings, narrow streets and a beautiful harbourfront location. Among the many reminders of Akaroa's French heritage is **Langlois-Eteveneaux House**, believed to have been prefabricated in France and

erected in Akaroa in 1841. It is part of the **Akaroa Museum** complex, which also includes the town's old courthouse, opened in 1880. The museum exhibits cover natural and regional history and architecture. A self-guided walk through the town takes in 43 historic sites, including the 1880 **Akaroa Lighthouse**.

A good swimming beach lies at the centre of the town. Harbour cruises operate from the main wharf, and visitors may see Hector's dolphins, penguins and seal colonies. A number of walking tracks lead up to the surrounding volcanic saddles and peaks, affording panoramic views of the harbour. Akaroa also boasts an active art and crafts community, and many shops and galleries. Akaroa has become popular with cruise ships as the nearby Port Lyttelton was heavily damaged during the 2011 earthquake.

🏛 **Langlois-Eteveneaux House and Akaroa Museum**
71 Rue Lavaud. **Tel** (03) 304 1013.
Open daily. **Closed** 25 Dec.

🏛 **Akaroa Lighthouse**
Tel (03) 304 7325. **Open** weekends, public hols & by arrangement.
♿ ground floor.

Jean François Langlois

The man primarily responsible for Akaroa's French heritage was whaler Jean François Langlois. In August 1838, he conceived the idea of a French colony and attempted to buy most of the peninsula from the local Ngai Tahu people. The following year he returned to France to gain support for his plan, and formed the Nanto-Bordelaise Company as the vehicle for his colonizing ambitions.

French navy captain Charles Lavaud was dispatched to provide protection for the 57 colonists who landed at Akaroa in August 1840. However, French ambitions were thwarted by the British who, in the interim, had signed the Treaty of Waitangi and, upon hearing of the settlers' impending arrival, rushed to appoint two magistrates to Akaroa. Despite the assertion of British sovereignty, the settlers stayed, although by 1842 Langlois was back in France. The Nanto-Bordelaise Company was bought out by the New Zealand Company in 1849, opening the way for large-scale British migration to the settlement.

Langlois-Eteveneaux House

❻ Waipara Vineyard Tour

The Waipara district's first vineyards were planted only in the 1980s. However, this wine-growing region has emerged quickly as a promising area, and many of its vineyards have won awards for their wines. Canterbury has more than 30 vineyards, but Waipara, about 65 km (40 miles) north of Christchurch, is the area of most rapid development. Wine-tasting tours can be arranged through the Christchurch i-SITE visitor information centre *(see p227)*.

① Pegasus Bay
This winery crushed its first grapes in 1991 and has since won many awards. Its wine-tasting venue has a charming garden setting overlooking the surrounding countryside.

⑨ Black Estate
Planted in 1993, Black Estate handcrafts artisan Pinot Noir, Chardonnay and Riesling. There is a tasting room and an eatery.

⑧ Mountford Vineyard
Mountford produces top-of-the-range Chardonnay and Pinot Noir. A beautiful homestead overlooks the small vineyard.

⑦ Waipara Springs
With its first vines planted in 1982, Waipara Springs is one of the oldest vineyards in the district, and has won many awards. Its popular wine-tasting venue is set in pleasant gardens.

Hanmer Springs

SH7

Mackenzies Road

Glenmark Drive

Church Road

Waipara

Waipara River

Mt Cass Road

Georges Road

Stockgrove Road

Waipara River

Glasnevin Road

0 kilometres   3

0 miles   3

↓ Christchurch

④ Terrace Edge
Set in a dramatic landscape, this family-owned vineyard and olive grove produces organically grown, award-winning wines and olive oil. Vineyard tours are given on request.

⑤ Torlesse Wines
Torlesse uses both Waipara and Marlborough grapes to produce a wide range of wines, including Gewürztraminer, Cabernet Sauvignon, Sauvignon Blanc and Chardonnay.

⑥ Waipara River Estate
Formerly named Glenmark Wines, the district's first winery, Waipara River Estate's wines have won many awards, and can be tasted in a pleasant, rustic setting.

Tips for Drivers

Tour length: 170 km (105 miles) return from Christchurch. Most of the wineries are located on side roads or driveways off State Hwy 1, so it is important to be careful of fast-moving traffic when travelling between vineyards.

Stopping-off points: Pegasus Bay, Waipara Winds Vineyard & Bistro, Black Estate and Waipara Springs all have restaurants. Booking is advisable.

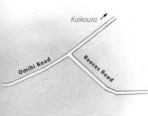

Kaikoura

Omihi Road

Reeces Road

② Waipara Winds Vineyard & Bistro

Opened in 1994, Waipara Winds Vineyard & Bistro specializes in aromatics and is distinguished by a huge stone winery building.

③ Fiddlers Green

Fiddlers Green produced its first vintage in 1998. Its Riesling and Sauvignon Blanc wines have won awards.

Key

■ Tour route

— Other roads

≈ River

Hot pool complex at Hanmer Springs

❼ Hanmer Springs

Road map C5. 🏠 800. 🚌
ℹ 42 Amuri Ave, (03) 315 0020.
ⓦ hanmersprings.co.nz

This small alpine village, 385 m (1,260 ft) above sea level, is best known for the vast **Hanmer Springs Thermal Pools & Spa**. Although hot springs were first discovered in the area in 1859, they were officially opened only in 1883. Today, the complex has 15 thermal and freshwater pools of varying temperatures, as well as private pools and a children's waterslide and activity area.

Surrounding the hot pools is a 168 sq km (65 sq mile) forest park, which offers activities such as mountain biking and walks, ranging from the short Conical Hill walk (one hour return) to the longer Mount Isobel walk (five to six hours return). At the Waiau Ferry Bridge, 5 km (3 miles) from the village, tourist operators offer bungy jumping, jet-boating and rafting down the Waiau River.

🏠 Hanmer Springs Thermal Pools & Spa
42 Amuri Ave. **Tel** (03) 315 0000.
Open daily. **Closed** 25 Dec. 🅿 ♿
🖥 ⓦ hanmersprings.co.nz

❽ Lewis Pass

Road map C5.

Lewis Pass marks the crossing point on State Highway 7 over the South Island's Main Divide. The surrounding 183 sq km (70 sq mile) Lewis Pass National Reserve offers a range of unguided outdoor activities, including hiking, fishing and hunting. Just over the pass, **Maruia Springs Thermal Resort** has a small complex of outdoor hot pools in a natural setting, with views of the surrounding bush and mountain peaks.

🏠 Maruia Springs Thermal Resort
State Hwy 7. **Tel** (03) 523 8840.
Open daily. **Closed** 25 Dec. 🅿 ♿ 🚫

❾ Reefton

Road map C5. 🏠 1,000. 🚌
ℹ 67-69 Broadway, (03) 732 8391.

Founded in 1872, Reefton takes its name from the gold-bearing quartz reefs in the area. The town's gold-mining heritage is evident in the many historic remains of the 1870s boom dotted around the region, especially in the beech forest-clad Victoria Forest Park. A network of tracks provides opportunity for exploration on foot or on mountain bike.

A heritage walk around Reefton takes in many historic buildings, including the **School of Mines**, which operated from 1887 to 1970 as part of a network of similar schools around New Zealand. Two km (1.2 miles) from Reefton, the **Black's Point Museum** exhibits relics from the gold-mining era.

🏫 School of Mines
Shiel St. **Tel** (03) 732 8391.
Open by arrangement. 🅿 🚫

🏛 Black's Point Museum
State Hwy 7. **Tel** (03) 732 8391.
Open Wed–Sun. **Closed** 25 Dec.
🅿 ♿

⑩ Karamea

Road map C4. 🚗 700. 🚌
ℹ️ Market Cross, (03) 782 6652
🎣 Whitebaiters Ball (Oct).
🌐 **karameainfo.co.nz**

Settled by Europeans in 1874, Karamea is an isolated farming community that lies at the northern end of the West Coast's State Highway 67. Nestled in a basin dominated by dairy farming and fringed by the Kahurangi National Park, Karamea is best known as the exit point for the Heaphy Track, which after following the coast from the Heaphy River ends 15 km (9 miles) to the north. Several short walking tracks are based around the Heaphy exit point, including the 40-minute Nikau Loop and the 90-minute Scotts Beach walk.

About 26 km (16 miles) to the northeast of Karamea is the **Oparara Basin**, featuring impressive limestone formations and a 15 km (9 mile) system of caves enveloped by dense forest. Much of the gravel road to the basin is narrow and winding, but can be undertaken in a 2WD vehicle. The highly fragile Honeycomb Caves system, first explored in 1980, is accessible only with a guide, and contains the remains of about 50 species, including the extinct moa and New Zealand eagle. Areas that can be explored without a guide are the Oparara Arch, 43 m (141 ft) high and 219 m (719 ft) long,

Cows, cabbage trees and beach near Karamea

which is reached after a 20-minute walk on a good track through the forest, and the Box Canyon and Crazy Paving caves. It is essential to carry a good torch. For the highly adventurous visitor, local tourist operators run grades four and five white-water rafting trips down the Karamea River.

Karamea is also a base for walkers using the popular three- to five-day Wangapeka Track. The Fenian Track is an historic gold-miners' route, and the four-hour return walk leads to the former mining settlement of Adams Flat.

🌿 **Oparara Basin**
State Hwy 67. **Tel** (03) 782 6652.
🕳️ Honeycomb Caves. 🎫 obligatory at Honeycomb Caves. 🌐 **oparara. co.nz**

⑪ Westport

Road map C5. 🚗 5,000. ✈️ 5 km (3 miles) N of town. 🚌 ℹ️ 123 Palmerston St. (03) 789 6658.
🌐 **buller.co.nz**

Although Westport's origins lie in the gold rush of the 1860s, coal has been its lifeline for much of its history. Until 1954, coal from mines in the surrounding mountains was shipped out through the town's once-busy port at the head of the Buller River, but today the bulk is taken by train to Lyttelton on the east coast *(see p234)*. The **Coal Town Museum** at Westport has extensive exhibits reconstructing aspects of the region's coal-mining heritage. Westport is a base

for a number of outdoor activities, including jet-boating and jet-skiing on the river. Among the most popular activities is underground rafting in the Nile River Canyon area. This can be done only with a guide and involves floating in inner tubes through glowworm grottos and caverns before emerging into the open to float down the Waitakere River rapids and Nile River Canyon. The Metro Cave, which has dramatic limestone stalactite and stalagmite formations, can be explored on foot. Westport's North Beach and Carter's Beach are both popular swimming and surfing spots, as is the scenic Tauranga Bay. On the Cape Foulwind Walkway at the edge of Tauranga Bay is a breeding colony of fur seals *(see p197)*. The walkway, which takes three hours there and back, crosses rocky granite bluffs, grassy downs, swampy streams and sandy beaches.

🏛️ **Coal Town Museum**
123 Palmerston St. **Tel** (03) 789 6658.
Open daily. **Closed** 25 Dec. ♿ 🚻
🌐 **coaltown.co.nz**

Seals at Tauranga Bay, near Westport

Nikau Loop at the exit to the Heaphy Track

Coal-Mining Heritage

Coal was first discovered on the West Coast by explorer Thomas Brunner in 1848. The largest of the early mines were on the Denniston and Stockton plateaus, north-east of Westport, where large-scale exploitation began in 1878. The task of extracting coal from the rugged, mountainous terrain was hazardous, and necessitated some striking feats of engineering. The most famous was the Denniston Incline, a gravity-powered rail system under which laden coal trucks were lowered 520 m (1,700 ft) down the mountainside on a steel cable. Empty wagons were pulled back up by the weight of full wagons. The incline closed in 1967, but during its 87 years of operation it carried 13 million tonnes of coal off the Denniston Plateau. The coal industry continues to be important to the West Coast economy, with over 2 million tonnes exported from the coalfields each year.

Coal wagon on steel tracks for transporting coal in and out of the mine.

The entrance, carefully reinforced to prevent collapse.

Early Mining Towns

Several mining settlements sprang up in the 19th century to support the coal industry, but they are little more than ghost towns today. The 120 km (75 mile) self-guided Buller Coalfields Heritage Trail leads through many mining relics, including the once thriving towns of Denniston, Stockton and Millerton. Information on the trail is available at the i-SITE Visitor Centre in Westport.

Coal miners at the entrance to the Rewanui coal mine

Coal wagons like this one in the Coal Town Museum were used to bring coal down from the mountainous coalfields.

This aerial ropeway is used to lower coal from the opencast Stockton mine down to the coastal settlement of Ngakawau, where it is loaded onto trains bound for the port of Lyttelton on the east coast.

Among the many relics that remain at Denniston, the marshalling point for coal from all over the plateau, are retaining rock walls where coal would be screened before being lowered down the incline, and parts of machinery.

⑫ Paparoa National Park

Road map C5. 🚌 ℹ️ State Hwy 6, Punakaiki, (03) 731 1895.

Established in 1987, this 300 sq km (115 sq mile) park contains varied and dramatic scenery, most famously the Pancake Rocks and blowholes near the small coastal settlement of Punakaiki. Bands of limestone, separated by thin bands of softer mudstone, which has been worn away by thousands of years of rain, wind and sea spray, have created the layered formations of the Pancake Rocks. Over hundreds of thousands of years, caverns have also been formed as carbon dioxide-bearing rain-water has gradually eaten into cracks in the limestone. During high seas, these subterranean caverns become blowholes as the waves surge in under huge pressure and explode in a plume of spray. The Pancake Rocks and blowholes are easily accessible from the main highway via the short Dolomite Point walk. Wheelchair access, if assisted, is also possible.

Other short walks as well as longer hikes are available in the park, including the 15- minute Truman Track through sub-tropical forest to a wild coastline featuring caverns, a blowhole and waterfall, and the two-hour walk to a huge limestone structure known as "the ballroom overhang". A two- to three-day hike through the heart of the park follows a pack track, built in 1867 to avoid dangerous travel along the isolated and rugged coastline.

Left Bank Art Gallery

⑬ Greymouth

Road map C5. 🏔️ 14,000. 🚉 🚌
ℹ️ Historic Railway Station, 164 Mackay St, (03) 768 7080.
🌐 **westcoasttravel.co.nz**

The largest town on the West Coast, Greymouth occupies the site of what was once Mawhera Pa. Although colonial government agents purchased the majority of the West Coast in 1860 for £300, the land under modern Greymouth remained a Māori reserve. Greymouth was laid out in 1865. Around this time, gold was being found in large quantities in the area, and coal had been discovered 17 years earlier. When the gold boom ended, coal mining ensured the district's continued survival. However, the Grey River mouth, which has served the town as a port, has also delivered misfortune. Repeatedly throughout its history, Greymouth has been submerged by flood waters, including twice in 1988. Since then a flood wall has been erected, popularly called "the great wall of Greymouth".

Greymouth's **History House Museum** has a large collection of historical photographs giving insight into the town's heritage. The **Left Bank Art Gallery** features an important greenstone collection, crafted in both contemporary and traditional designs, and hosts a major exhibition every few years. It also displays local art works.

Like other West Coast towns, Greymouth offers a range of adventure tourism activities, including floating through the Taniwha Caves on inflated tubes, and dolphin watching. The Grey River system is known for good fishing.

🏛️ **History House Museum**
Gresson St. **Tel** (03) 768 4028.
Open summer: daily; winter: Mon–Fri.
Closed 25 Dec. 🚫 ♿

🏛️ **Left Bank Art Gallery**
1 Tainui St. **Tel** (03) 768 0038.
Open summer: daily; winter: Tue–Sat.
Closed 1 Jan, 25 Dec. 🚫 ♿
📷 by arrangement. 🏠

Pancake Rocks at Dolomite Point, Punakaiki

Street in Shantytown, a replica gold-mining town

Environs

One of Greymouth's most popular attractions is **Shantytown**, 11 km (7 miles) south. This elaborate replica gold-mining town includes a 1913 steam train, which travels through native bush to a working sawmill and gold claim where visitors can try gold panning and perhaps find a few specks of gold.

Lake Brunner, a restful, scenic spot surrounded by bush-clad mountains 42 km (26 miles) from Greymouth, is excellent for fishing, boating and watersports. The lake area is serviced by the small town of Moana, located at the northern end of Lake Brunner. There is a daily bus between Moana and Greymouth and the TranzAlpine scenic train, which leaves daily from Christchurch, is rated amongst the world's best scenic routes.

Shantytown
Rutherglen Rd, Paroa, Greymouth. **Tel** 0800 742 689, (03) 762 6634. **Open** daily. **Closed** 25 Dec. 🅿️
♿ 🖥️ 📷 **W** shantytown.co.nz

⓮ Hokitika

Road map C5. 🅰️ 3,600. ✈️ 2 km (1.2 miles) N of town. 🚌 ℹ️ 36 Weld St, (03) 755 6166. 🎨 Wildfoods Festival (Mar). **W** hokitika.org and **W** wildfoods.co.nz

With its wide streets, notable historic buildings and excellent local craft studios, Hokitika is perhaps the West Coast's most attractive town. Little more than a shanty town in 1864, by 1866 Hokitika had become a thriving commercial centre thanks to gold. Its river port bustled with ships bearing miners flocking

from the goldfields of Australia, but it was a treacherous harbour where a ship went down every 10 weeks in the years 1865 and 1866. The wreck of one such ship is on the self-guided Hokitika Heritage Trail, which includes 22 historic buildings and sights. The most impressive of these is the 1908 Carnegie Library, now the home of the town's information centre and the **Hokitika Museum**. The museum has displays on gold-mining and an audio-visual display of the town's history. It also houses a collection of rare books about the West Coast.

The **National Kiwi Centre** is a small wildlife centre specializing in kiwi, tuatara, giant long-finned eels and the tiny whitebait for which the West Coast's rivers are renowned. The remarkable Glowworm Dell, on the northern edge of the town, is worth a visit after dark. The

best time to view the lights exuded by these carnivorous larvae is on a wet night.

🏛️ **Hokitika Museum**
Carnegie Centre, Cnr Tancred & Hamilton sts. **Tel** (03) 755 6898. **Open** daily. **Closed** 25 Dec. 🅿️ ♿

⚡ **National Kiwi Centre**
64 Tancred St. **Tel** (03) 755 5251. **Open** daily. **Closed** 1 Jan, 25 Dec. 🅿️ ♿ 📷
W thenationalkiwicentre.co.nz

Environs

There are a number of scenic areas around Hokitika. **Lake Mahinapua**, 10 km (6 miles) south, and **Lake Kaniere**, 20 km (12 miles) east of the town, are peaceful retreats, popular for boating, fishing, swimming and bush walking. The Lake Kaniere Walkway is 13 km (8 miles) and takes about four hours. The West Coast cycle trail stretches from Greymouth to Ross, passing rugged shorelines, rivers, lakes, tidal lagoons and forests (www.westcoastwildernesstrail.co.nz). **Ross** township, 28 km (17 m) south of Hokitika, has a small local museum devoted to its gold-mining history. Walks take visitors past old mine workings. New Zealand's biggest gold nugget was discovered here in 1909, and the area – said still to contain millions of dollars worth of gold – is again being mined.

Hokitika clock tower

Greenstone

Nephrite jade (pounamu), locally known as greenstone, is a hard, opaque, emerald stone. Formed in alpine fault lines under intense heat and pressure, greenstone boulders are eventually flushed from the eroding mountains into West Coast rivers. Greenstone holds great spiritual significance for Māori. Long before European colonization, tribes sent missions to search for the precious stone, later bartering it for food and other items. It was the hardest material known to Māori and was used for making tools, weapons and items of personal adornment. In 1997, ownership of the greenstone resource on the West Coast was handed back to the South Island Ngai Tahu tribe as part of a major Treaty of Waitangi settlement (see p57).

Artisan at the Mountain Jade Greenstone Factory

⑮ Westland/Tai Poutini National Park

Stretching from the top of the Southern Alps in the east, where it shares a common boundary with Aoraki/Mount Cook National Park, to the Tasman Sea in the west, this 1,270 sq km (490 sq mile) national park is renowned for its mountain peaks (which reach a height of 3,500 m or 11,500 ft), dramatic glaciers, dense rainforest, coastal lagoons and beautiful lakes. Despite the intrusions of the West Coast gold rush of the 1860s and pastoral farming on the river flats, the area has remained largely unspoiled.

Guided Glacier Tours
This is one of the best ways to experience the glaciers in the park. Ski-plane and helicopter tours also allow stunning views.

★ Lake Matheson
On clear, still mornings, Aoraki/Mount Cook and Mount Tasman are reflected in the lake, which is enveloped by forest.

0 kilometres 6
0 yards 6

KEY

① **The Copland Valley Track**, accessible from State Highway 6, is popular with hikers. For experienced climbers, the track continues over the challenging Copland Pass and ends at Mount Cook village.

② **Gillespies Beach**, once a historic gold-mining settlement 20 km (12 miles) from Fox Glacier, offers walks along an early miners' track and to a fur seal colony along the beach.

③ **Okarito Lagoon**, one of New Zealand's largest wetland areas, is home to abundant birdlife, including the rare white heron (see p196).

④ **Lake Mapourika**, at the northern end of the park, is a favourite spot for picnickers.

⑤ **Aoraki/Mount Cook and Mount Tasman**, New Zealand's two highest peaks, stand behind Fox Glacier.

Key

▬▬▬ State highway
═══ Minor road
▭▭▭ River
– – Walking track
—·— Park boundary

TASMAN SEA

Gillespies Point

Gillespies Cook River Road

Lake Gault

Cook River

Cook Flat R

KARANGARUA FOREST

Karangarua River

COPLAND RANGE

Copland Track

Copland River

ROCKY RANGE

HOOKER RAN

Lowland rainforest
The park's extremely high rainfall (5,000 mm or 200 inches a year at Franz Josef village) supports lush, densely ferned lowland podocarp forest, featuring local species.

★ Franz Josef Glacier
A 2-hour or so walk up the Waiho
River from the Franz Josef Glacier
village leads to the terminal face.

★ Fox Glacier
Because of the risk of rock and ice falls, it is safe for
visitors to walk only with a guide on the Fox Glacier,
the largest glacier in the park.

Movement of a Glacier

A glacier is a large body of ice that forms on land
and moves slowly downhill at a rate of about
1.5 m (5 ft) a day. Glaciers are fed by snow
accumulating in high-altitude basins (névés)
where it condenses to form bluish ice. This ice
field flows downhill under its own weight,
cracking into a jumble of deep crevasses and
collecting moraine (debris) which scours the
mountain sides to form U-shaped valleys. The
glacier ends at a terminal where the ice melts.
The Franz Josef Glacier 11 km (7 miles) long and
Fox Glacier 13 km (8 miles) long, are unique in
that they descend from regions of perpetual
snow to rainforest close to the coast.

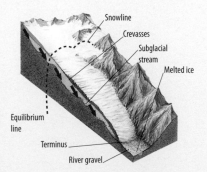

⑯ Arthur's Pass Driving Tour

Arthur's Pass road is the highest and most spectacular highway across the Southern Alps. From Springfield, the road climbs steeply to the 945 m (3,100 ft) Porters Pass before travelling through wide, tussock-covered basins hemmed by mountains and past dramatic limestone outcrops. Entering the eastern flank of Arthur's Pass National Park, the road is enveloped by mountain beech forest. It then climbs to the 920 m (3,017 ft) Arthur's Pass summit, before descending steeply on the western side of the Southern Alps.

① Porters Pass and Lake Lyndon

This area is characterized by distinctive dryland native fauna. Lake Lyndon is a good bird-watching spot in summer and a natural skating rink during the winter months.

② Porters Ski Field

This is the closest ski area to Christchurch and one of six ski fields along State Highway 73. Other than Porters, all are small fields run by local ski clubs where visitors are welcome.

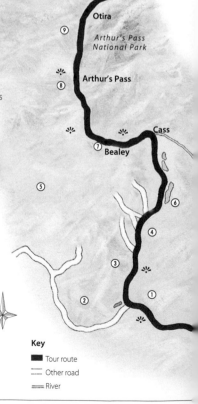

Kumara Junction

Hokitika

Lake Brunner

Taramakau River

Otira

Arthur's Pass National Park

Arthur's Pass

Cass

Bealey

⑩ Jacksons Pub

This is all that remains of what was once a busy railhead and staging post.

⑨ Otira Viaduct

Completed in 1999, this section of State Highway 73 spans the rugged Otira River.

⑧ Beech Forests

The forests on the eastern side of the park are dominated by a canopy of mountain beech, and thus are dramatically different from the dense and varied forests on the western side.

Key

▬ Tour route

╍ Other road

〜 River

③ Castle Hill

The large limestone rock formations of Castle Hill are eerily impressive, and very popular with rock climbers. The area has historical significance to Māori as a seasonal food-gathering spot and as part of the route used by Māori to reach the West Coast.

⑤ Craigieburn Forest Park

The beech-covered hills in the park are popular spots for walking, picnicking and mountain biking.

⑥ Lake Pearson

Lake Pearson and nearby Lake Grasmere are both good trout fishing spots. Lake Pearson is also known for its beautiful mountain reflections.

⑦ Bealey Spur

A rustic cluster of holiday homes marks Bealey Spur, at the fringe of Arthur's Pass National Park.

Springfield

73

0 kilometres 20

0 miles 20

Tips For Drivers

Tour length from Springfield to Kumara Junction: 160 km (100 miles). This is an alpine route that is sometimes closed after snow, and drivers should check conditions.

Stopping-off points: There are many scenic viewpoints and lay-bys along the route. Arthur's Pass is the only township offering services between Kumara and Springfield, although there are hotels at Jacksons and Bealey.

④ Cave Stream

This 360-m (1,180-ft) limestone cave, with waist deep water, takes about 2 hours to navigate, and requires sturdy footwear, warm clothing and a good torch.

The road to Arthur's Pass

⑰ Arthur's Pass

Road map C5. ⛰ 50. 🚌 🚐 ℹ️
Dept of Conservation, State Hwy 73, Arthur's Pass, (03) 318 9211.

The tiny village of Arthur's Pass is nestled in a valley about 5 km (3 miles) east of the summit of Arthur's Pass. It was originally the camping site of contractors engaged to push the road through from Christchurch to the West Coast in 1865–6. In 1908, workers at Arthur's Pass village and at Otira, on the western side of the Main Divide, began construction of the 8 km (5 mile) Otira rail tunnel. In 1912, the population of Arthur's Pass had swelled to about 300, comprised mainly of tunnel workers. It took 10 years for the two ends of the tunnel to meet, and another 5 years before the first train travelled through it. A number of tunnellers' cottages remain in the village, now used as private holiday homes.

Since the 1920s, the village has been a base for day-trippers from Christchurch and Greymouth, walkers, hikers, and mountaineers, as well as skiers who enjoy the splendid views and low-key atmosphere of the nearby Temple Basin ski field. It is also the headquarters of Arthur's Pass National Park (see pp248–9).

An original tunneller's cottage at Arthur's Pass village

⑱ Arthur's Pass National Park

Straddling the Southern Alps 153 km (95 miles) from Christchurch and 98 km (60 miles) from Greymouth, the 1,147 sq km (443 sq mile) Arthur's Pass National Park, the seventh largest in the country, is a place of huge geological and climatic contrasts. On the western side of the alps, where the rainfall is high, the park is clad in dense and varied rainforest through which steep, boulder-strewn rivers rush; on the drier eastern side, mountain beech forests and tussock-covered river flats predominate. Sixteen mountain peaks in the park exceed 2,000 m (6,560 ft). The park offers the well-equipped outdoor enthusiast superb mountain climbing and hiking opportunities, as well as many shorter walks suitable for people of all ages and fitness levels.

★ Dobson Nature Walk
This 30-minute walk on the Arthur's Pass summit gives an excellent introduction to the area's alpine and subalpine plants, which bloom from November to February.

Bealey Valley
A walking track leads from State Highway 73 through mountain beech forest to the beautiful Bealey Valley. It takes about three to four hours' in all to complete the walk.

★ Devil's Punchbowl Waterfall
Although the top of this 131 m (430 ft) waterfall can be seen from the main road, a one-hour walk from Arthur's Pass village takes visitors to the base of the falls.

Kea
These cheeky, inquisitive alpine parrots are sometimes seen in Arthur's Pass village, pecking the rubber from around car windscreens.

Otira Track

Otira River

ARTHUR'S PASS
920 m (3,017 ft)

Upper Twin Ck

MOUNT ROLLESTON
2,275 m (7,462 ft)

Bealey River

Bridal Veil Walk

Cons Track

MOUNT LANCELOT
2,112 m (6,927 ft)

Punc hbowl C

Scotts Track

Mt Aiken Trac

AVALANCHE PEAK
1,833 m (6,012 ft)

Avalanche Peak Track

Arthur's Pass

Crow River

MOUNT BEALEY
1,836 m (6,022 ft)

Bealey

Waimakariri River

For keys to symbols *see back flap*

VISITORS' CHECKLIST

Practical Information
Road map C5. **w** doc.govt.nz
🛈 Arthur's Pass village, (03) 318
9211. **Open** daily. **Closed** 25 Dec.
♿ in village only; not on tracks.
🚻🏪💻

Transport
🚉🚌

Temple Basin
Hikers can enjoy great views
of Temple Basin's mountains and
valleys. In winter, the ski field is
accessible only on foot.

▲ MOUNT TEMPLE
1,913 m (6,274 ft)

Flora and Fauna in Arthur's Pass National Park

As well as the impressive mountain beech forests in the east and
mixed rainforest in the west, the park contains a wide variety of
alpine and subalpine plant species,
including tussock, snow grass,
alpine daisies and herbs, sedge
and ourisia. The park is also rich in
birdlife, and species such as the
paradise shelduck, bellbird, silver-
eye, fantail, kea and rifleman are
often seen or heard. The area is
home to a number of rare species,
including the alpine rock wren,
blue duck and great spotted kiwi.

Blue ducks

▲ MOUNT OATES
2,041 m (6,694 ft)

▲ MOUNT AIKEN
1,859 m (6,097 ft)

0 kilometres   5

0 miles   5

Key

▬▬ State highway

═══ Minor road

── River

■ ■ Walking track

── Tranz Alpine Express route

─ ─ Tunnel

▲ MOUNT WILLIAMS
1,718 m (5,635 ft)

Mingha River

Edwards River

Waimakariri River
The sinuous strands
of this mighty river
transport rock and
shingle from the
Southern Alps
(see p195).

Klondyke Corner

Waimakariri River

Tips for Walkers

The valleys, alpine passes and
scree- and tussock-covered
mountainsides of the park offer
a range of graded walks, from
short, easy strolls to demanding
climbs. However, the climate in
the park is highly changeable and
many routes rudimentary, so it
is important for hiking and
climbing parties to register their
intentions with the visitor centre
at Arthur's Pass village.

BEALEY SPUR ▲
920 m (3,017 ft)   Bealey Spur

Bealey Spur Village
Tussock-covered valleys give
way to tall, craggy hills as the
road approaches Bealey Spur.

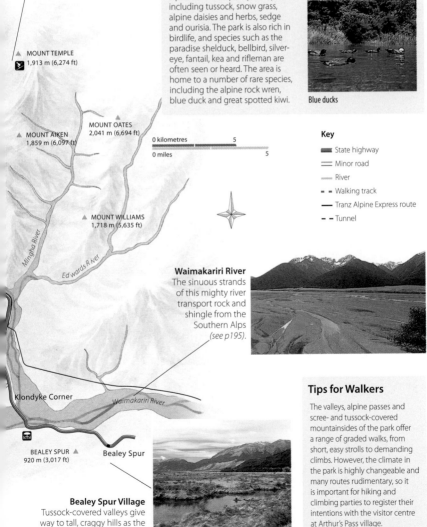

For hotels and restaurants in this region see pp306–7 and pp322–4

Mount Hutt ski field with Lake Coleridge in the distance

⑲ Mount Hutt

Road map C6. 🚌 ℹ️ 121 Main St, Methven, (03) 302 8955. 🎿 New Zealand Walking Festival (Apr).

Mount Hutt, in the foot hills of the Southern Alps, is Canterbury's largest ski field, and claims to have the longest ski season in Australasia (early June to mid-October). The ski field is served by nine lifts and tows, as well as artificial snow-making facilities. From the 2,075 m (6,808 ft) mountain, there are excellent views over the Canterbury Plains.

Environs

The town of **Methven** serves as Mount Hutt's après-ski centre in winter, and reverts in summer to a typical New Zealand farming town. The 42 sq km (16 sq mile) Mount Hutt Conservation Area, 14 km (9 miles) west of the town, has a number of short walking tracks through native forest dominated by mountain beech. The Rakaia Gorge, about 16 km (10 miles) north of Methven, is popular for jet-boating. A 5 km (3 mile) walkway traverses its edge.

⑳ Rakaia

Road map C6. 🏔️ 800. 🚌 🎣 Rakaia Salmon Fishing Competition (end Feb).

Located on the southern bank of the Rakaia River, the small farming settlement of Rakaia claims to be "the salmon capital of New Zealand". A large

fibreglass fish in the middle of the township celebrates the excellent salmon and trout fishing to be had at various spots along the river.

Bridge over the Rakaia Gorge, a popular place for jet-boating

㉑ Ashburton

Road map C6. 🏔️ 16,000. ✈️ 🚌 ℹ️ The Green, East St, (03) 308 1050. 🎡 Wheels Week (May).

Ashburton straddles the Ashburton River and is the principal town in the farming district of mid-Canterbury. The town was named after Lord Ashburton, a member of the Canterbury Association, which settled the province in the 1850s. Although originally dry and tussock covered, irrigation has allowed agriculture to flourish. The well-laid out town has historic brick buildings and many mature trees, including some in the Ashburton Domain. **Ashford Village** produces and

sells a variety of high quality craft work and has a museum housing spinning wheels.

🏛️ Ashford Village
427 West St. **Tel** (03) 308 9085. **Open** daily. **Closed** 1 & 2 Jan, Good Fri, Easter Mon, 25 & 26 Dec. 📷 in factory. ♿ 📷 required in factory. 🏪 🏛️

㉒ Geraldine

Road map C6. 🏔️ 2,000. 🚌 ℹ️ Kiwi Country, 38 Waihi Tce, (03) 693 1101. 🎡 Geraldine Arts and Plants Festival (Nov). 🌐 **aoraki.tourism.co.nz**

This attractive small farming town is a popular stopover for travellers heading south to the Mackenzie Country. First known as Talbot Forest, then Fitzgerald, and finally Geraldine, in 1866, it began as a sheep run and base for sawmillers. Talbot Forest now refers to the lowland podocarp forest that provides a backdrop to Geraldine. The town still has many historic buildings, such as the 1908 Post Office, which can be seen on a self-guided walking trail.

Locally produced juices and condiments can be sampled at **Four Peaks Plaza**. The **Vintage Car and Machinery Museum** has cars dating from 1907 to 1953 and tractors from 1874 as well as a large amount of early agricultural machinery.

🏭 Four Peaks Plaza
76 Talbot St. **Tel** (03) 693 9727. **Open** daily. **Closed** 25 Dec. ♿ 🏛️

🏛️ Vintage Car and Machinery Museum
178 Talbot St. **Tel** (03) 693 8756. **Open** daily in summer; weekends only in winter. **Closed** 1 Jan, 25 & 26 Dec. 📷 ♿ 📷 by arrangement.

Environs

The town is a good base for exploring the forests and rivers of Canterbury, including Peel Forest, 22 km (13 miles) north of Geraldine, as well as the Mount Somers Conservation Area, 47 km (29 miles) north, and the Orari, Waihi and Te Moana gorges, 15 km (9 miles) north, which are good spots for rafting, swimming and picnicking.

High Country Farming

When the "Canterbury Pilgrims" arrived in 1850 to establish their new settlement, they quickly saw the potential of pastoral farming, and the runholders – the farmers who grazed Canterbury's extensive plains, downs, interior and high country – soon became a powerful economic and political force. Although land reform in the late 19th century saw the great estates broken up, large high country stations, where much of the land is leased, have remained a feature of farming in New Zealand, particularly in Canterbury. Good roads and modern communications have reduced the isolation and harshness of station life, but it remains a unique existence defined by the climate and the topography of the high country and the annual cycle of farming.

The Annual Cycle

Stock graze the tussock-covered mountainsides over the summer, and are mustered down to lower ground before winter. This task takes several days and is carried out on horseback or on foot with the aid of teams of highly trained sheepdogs. As shearing, lambing and weaning are completed, stock are released back to the high country for the summer.

Mustering sheep

Selling and buying sheep is a serious business at local livestock auctions as sheep farmers seek to buy stock that will improve the quantity and quality of their wool and meat production.

Shearing is done by skilled teams of contractors, often using manual blade shears which leave a protective layer of wool on the sheep's back. The dominant breed farmed on high county farms is the fine-woolled and hardy merino.

Fodder crops, such as hay and silage, are grown on the farms as supplementary feed for sheep during the cold winter months.

Roast lamb served with vegetables such as baked potatoes, carrots and peas is a favourite traditional meal.

Merino wool from the high country farms of the South Island is very fine, and is used to make luxury knitwear and fine suit fabrics.

㉓ Timaru

About halfway between Christchurch to the north and Dunedin to the south is Timaru. It is built on rolling hills marking the edge of the Canterbury Plains and is the largest town in South Canterbury. Its name derives from Te Maru, meaning "a place of shelter", denoting its historical importance as a safe haven for Maori canoes travelling the coast. It was a whaling station from 1838. The town centre is built on 0.5 sq km (0.2 sq mile) of land acquired by early settlers George and Robert Rhodes, although settlement did not begin in earnest until 1859. Today, Timaru has the appearance of a sturdy and well-appointed regional capital, with many notable buildings gracing its commercial heart.

Aigantighe gallery with new extension and grounds

🌴 Caroline Bay

From 1877, when Timaru's artificial port was first created, the white sand of Caroline Bay accumulated beside it to form a safe and popular swimming beach. The port flanks the southern end of the beach. Behind the beach is an extensive grassed area with a children's playground, an aviary, tennis courts and a mini-golf course. Large-scale redevelopment has added a seaside boardwalk, viewing platforms, volleyball courts and other recreational facilities. The Piazza, a series of staircases and platforms and a lift, links the bay with the central city on the hill above. To the north of the bay are the Benvenue Cliffs and the 1877 Timaru Lighthouse.

🏛 Aigantighe

49 Wa-iti Rd. **Tel** (03) 688 4424. **Open** Tue–Sun. **Closed** 25 Dec. 📷 ♿ 📷 by arrangement.

This charming art museum, pronounced "egg and tie" ("at home" in Scottish Gaelic) is housed in a 1908 building bequeathed to the city by Alexander and Helen Grant, Scottish immigrants who had farmed in the Mackenzie Country. It opened as an art museum in 1956, with much of its fascinating collection donated by the Grant family. Its permanent collection includes works by New Zealand and British painters, as well as English and continental china. The well laid out gallery sits amid a restful garden, which features a permanent exhibition of stone sculptures.

⛪ St Mary's Anglican Church

Church St. **Tel** (03) 688 8377. **Open** Sun, Tue & Thu (for services only).

The foundation stone for St Mary's Anglican Church was laid in 1880, and its nave was consecrated in 1886. The interior of the church features high ribbed ceilings, many fine stained-glass windows, intricate wooden carvings and sturdy columns.

Many of the art pieces and plaques in the church bear the names of influential colonial families in South Canterbury. Steps in the tower can be climbed for an excellent view of the city.

🏛 South Canterbury Museum

Perth St. **Tel** (03) 684 2212. **Open** Tue– Sun. **Closed** 25 Dec. 📷 ♿

This octagonal-shaped museum, opened in 1966, is the main regional museum. Its collections cover the natural history of the area, local Maori history, the early whaling industry and European settlement. The development of the city is shown in a series of photographs. A highlight is a replica of the airplane built by Temuka farmer Richard Pearse, who is believed to have successfully flown in 1903, possibly before the Wright

---

Richard Pearse

Inventor, aviator and farmer, Richard Pearse (1877–1953) has for decades been at the centre of debate about who was the first to achieve powered flight. Pearse was born near Temuka, north of Timaru, and although ridiculed in his lifetime, has been posthumously recognized as an inventive genius. In his farm workshop he constructed a monoplane of bamboo, aluminium, wire and canvas. His first flight in the aircraft is said to have covered 46–91 m (150–300 ft), ending with a crash into a hedge. No records were kept of the flight, but there is some eyewitness evidence that it occurred on 31 March 1903 – about nine months before the 13 December 1903 flight of Orville and Wilbur Wright, officially regarded as the first in the world. Some people even put the date at 1902.

Replica of Pearse's monoplane

Roses in the Timaru Botanic Gardens

brothers in the US. The plane is suspended from the ceiling at about the height at which Pearse is thought to have flown.

🏛 Basilica of the Sacred Heart

7 Craigie Ave. **Tel** (03) 684 4263. **Open** daily. 🏛 daily. ♿
Arguably the most impressive of the many distinguished buildings in Timaru, the Basilica of the Sacred Heart was designed by Francis William Petre and built in 1910–11. Its twin towers and large dome overlook the main route south through the city, and house an equally majestic interior featuring stencilled ceilings, large white pillars and stained-glass windows. Petre also designed the Catholic cathedrals in Christchurch and Dunedin.

🌳 Timaru Botanic Gardens

Queen St. **Tel** (03) 687 7200. **Open** daily. ♿
Opened in 1864, the gardens comprise 19 ha (50 acres) of undulating landforms and water features. Notable highlights include a 1913 statue of Scottish poet Robert Burns, a cabbage tree believed to date from pre-European times and a 1911 band rotunda. The gardens also boast a fine rose collection as well as many rare and threatened plants. The conservatory complex houses desert, tropical and subtropical collections.

Environs

Temuka, about 18 km (11 miles) north of Timaru, is the service centre for a rich farming hinterland, and is also the home of the well-known Temuka Homeware, which makes a wide range of high-quality household ceramics. Although the factory is not open to the public, there is a separate factory shop on the State Highway 1 bypass in Temuka.

State Highway 8 to Tekapo passes through the small

VISITORS' CHECKLIST

Practical Information
Road map C6. 🗺 27,500.
w **aoraki.tourism.co.nz** 🛈
2 George St, (03) 688 4452. 📷
Caroline Bay Carnival (Dec–Jan).

Transport
✈ 12 km (7 miles) N of city.
🚌🚆🚌

township of Pleasant Point, where the **Pleasant Point Museum & Railway** retains a 2-km (1.2-mile) section of the old Timaru to Fairlie line, built in 1875 and closed in 1968. Two steam locomotives ply the track on school and public holidays. The road winds through rolling green farmland and passes through the small towns of Cave, Fairlie and Kimbell, and the turn-off to Mount Dobson Ski Field, before reaching Burkes Pass, which is the entrance to the Mackenzie Country.

🚂 Pleasant Point Museum & Railway

Main Rd. **Tel** (03) 614 8323. **Open** variable. 🚂 ♿ 📷

Timaru City Centre

① Caroline Bay
② Aigantighe
③ St Mary's Anglican Church
④ South Canterbury Museum
⑤ Basilica of the Sacred Heart
⑥ Timaru Botanic Gardens

0 metres   500
0 yards   500

For keys to symbols *see back flap*

Lupins on the shores of Lake Tekapo

❷ Lake Tekapo

Road map B6. 🏔 300. 🚌
ℹ Pukaki, State Hwy 8, (03)
680 6686. 🅦 mtcooknz.com

Lake Tekapo is a place of exceptional beauty and clarity. The remarkable blue of the lake is caused by "rock flour" – finely ground particles of rock brought down by the glaciers at the head of the lake and held in suspension in the melt water. The lake is a very popular venue for fishing, boating, kayaking, swimming and hang-gliding.

On the lake front stands the Church of the Good Shepherd. The foundation stone of this stone-and-oak church was laid in 1935 by the Duke of Gloucester. The front window of the church creates a perfect frame for a view of the lake. Next to the church is a bronze statue of a sheep dog, erected in 1968 as a tribute to the important role played by these animals in the development of high country farming.

Because of the purity of the atmosphere above Lake Tekapo, the University of Canterbury has an observatory atop Mount John to the west of the township. There is a popular walkway to the top of the mountain (about three hours there and back). Cowan's Hill Track (about two hours) also provides good views of the lake and mountains.

Lake Tekapo Village is a good base for skiing at Mount Dobson, Roundhill and Ohau, about 30 km (18 miles) away, while the town's small tourist airport is also a base for scenic flights over Mount Cook. Lake Alexandrina, 10 km (6 miles) from Tekapo, is renowned for its trout fishing.

🏛 Church of the Good Shepherd
Pioneer Drive. **Tel** (03) 680 6516.
Open daily. **Closed** 25 Dec, weddings.
🛕 variable. 🏛 donation. ♿ 📷

❷ Lake Pukaki

Road map B6. ℹ State Hwy 8, (03)
435 3280. 🅦 mountcooknz.com

Like Lake Tekapo, Lake Pukaki is a place of majestic scenery. State Highway 8 hugs the southern tip of the lake, and a large and popular lay-by and picnic area allows stunning views of Mount Cook as well as the Southern Alps. The lake is fed by the waters of the Tasman River, which flows off the Tasman Glacier. It has been artificially raised as part of the Upper Waitaki hydroelectricity network and is also linked by canals to Lake Tekapo and Lake Ohau. On a clear day, Mount Cook is reflected in the waters of the lake.

Glentanner Park Centre, located about 20 km (12 miles) south of Mount Cook village, on the shores of Lake Pukaki, is a major base for helicopter tours over Mount Cook. Other outdoor activites run from

Glentanner Park Centre, backed by the Southern Alps

the centre include horse trekking, mountain biking, boat trips, hunting and fishing. The centre is set amid Glentanner Station, a 182 sq km (70 sq mile) high country farm. Occasional short tours of the farm allow visitors to see sheep shearing and sheepdog demonstrations.

Glentanner Park Centre
State Hwy 80. **Tel** (03) 435 1855. **Open** daily. for activities. some activities. **glentanner.co.nz**

Twizel

Road map B6. 1,500.
Twizel Events Centre, Market Place, (03) 435 3124. **twizel.com**

Twizel was built in 1969 as a construction town for the Upper Waitaki hydro-electric development scheme. Once the hydro scheme was completed, the local people successfully fought to retain the town, and began to exploit its proximity to excellent fishing and boating lakes, and to Mount Cook 61 km (37 miles away. Lake Ruataniwha, a man-made lake just south of Twizel, is popular for watersports. It has an international standard rowing course and is the site of national rowing events every year. From Lake Ruataniwha, a sealed back road leads to Lake Benmore, a 75-sq-km (29-sq-mile) hydroelectric dam that has also become a favourite boating destination.

One of Twizel's most important attractions is the **Kakī Visitor Hide**. The kakī, or black stilt, is one of the rarest wading birds in the world, and the species has been subject to intensive conservation management since 1981 *(see p196)*. Visitors can take tours to view captive breeding birds from specially designed hides.

Kakī Visitor Hide
Twizel Events Centre, Market Place. **Tel** (03) 435 3124. daily (except 25 Dec).

Clay cliffs at Omarama

Environs
South of Twizel, on State Highway 8, lies the small town of **Omarama**. The town has a worldwide reputation for gliding because of its strong northwest thermal updraughts. Various gliding records have been set from Omarama.

About 10 km (6 miles) west of the town are the **Clay Cliffs**, a set of steep, high pinnacles separated by deep, narrow ravines. The cliffs are believed to have been frequented by early Māori travelling into the Mackenzie Country to hunt. Although privately owned, the cliffs are protected by covenant, and are accessible to the public.

Kakī/Black stilt

Clay Cliffs
Henburn Rd. **Tel** (03) 438 9780. **Open** daily.

Lake Ohau
Road map B6.

About 30 km (18 miles) to the west of Twizel, Lake Ohau is a popular swimming, fishing, skiing and boating spot. The six native forests that surround the lake – the Ohau, Temple, Dobson, Huxley, Hopkins and Ahuriri – also provide excellent hiking and walking opportunities. Many huts are scattered in the forests for the use of more experienced hikers.

The Ohau ski field, overlooking the western side of the lake, is a commercial ski field serviced by basic facilities, such as a T-bar and platter lift.

Upper Waitaki Hydro Development Scheme

The power stations of the Upper Waitaki and Mackenzie Country provide about one-third of New Zealand's hydro-electricity. The idea of harnessing the water resources of the region was first mooted in 1904, and today the vast scheme includes the Tekapo A and B power stations, Ohau A, B and C stations, and Benmore, Aviemore and Waitaki stations. An important feature of the scheme is 58 km (36 miles) of man-made canals, which pool the resources of Lakes Tekapo, Pukaki and Ohau, along which there is an attractive scenic drive. The lakes created by the hydro scheme have become popular venues for watersports.

Lake Benmore from the adjacent hills

❷❽ Aoraki/Mount Cook National Park

Aoraki/Mount Cook National Park takes its name from Aoraki/Mount Cook, which at 3,724 m (12,218 ft) is New Zealand's highest mountain. It is sacred to the Ngai Tahu tribe of the South Island, and Māori legend has it that the mountain and its companion peaks were formed when a boy named Aoraki and his three brothers came down from the heavens to visit Papatuanuku (Earth Mother) in a canoe. The canoe overturned, and as the brothers moved to the back of the boat they turned to stone. The 700 sq km (270 sq mile) area was designated a national park in 1953 and includes 19 peaks over 3,000 m (9,842 ft). Glaciers cover 40 per cent of the park.

Flightseeing and Boat Trips
Scenic flights and boat trips operate from Glentanner Park Centre and Mount Cook Airport and cover a range of routes.

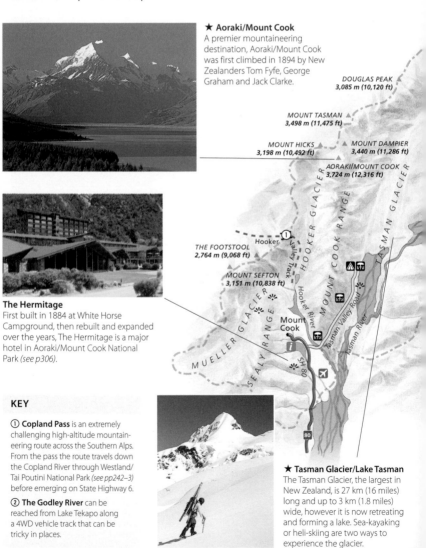

★ Aoraki/Mount Cook
A premier mountaineering destination, Aoraki/Mount Cook was first climbed in 1894 by New Zealanders Tom Fyfe, George Graham and Jack Clarke.

DOUGLAS PEAK
3,085 m (10,120 ft)

MOUNT TASMAN
3,498 m (11,475 ft)

MOUNT HICKS
3,198 m (10,492 ft)

MOUNT DAMPIER
3,440 m (11,286 ft)

AORAKI/MOUNT COOK
3,724 m (12,316 ft)

HOOKER GLACIER
TASMAN GLACIER
MOUNT COOK RANGE

Hooker
Valley Track

THE FOOTSTOOL
2,764 m (9,068 ft)

MOUNT SEFTON
3,151 m (10,838 ft)

Hooker River
Tasman River
Tasman Valley Road

Mount
Cook

MUELLER GLACIER
SEALY RANGE

SH 80

80

The Hermitage
First built in 1884 at White Horse Campground, then rebuilt and expanded over the years, The Hermitage is a major hotel in Aoraki/Mount Cook National Park *(see p306)*.

KEY

① **Copland Pass** is an extremely challenging high-altitude mountaineering route across the Southern Alps. From the pass the route travels down the Copland River through Westland/Tai Poutini National Park *(see pp242–3)* before emerging on State Highway 6.

② **The Godley River** can be reached from Lake Tekapo along a 4WD vehicle track that can be tricky in places.

★ Tasman Glacier/Lake Tasman
The Tasman Glacier, the largest in New Zealand, is 27 km (16 miles) long and up to 3 km (1.8 miles) wide, however it is now retreating and forming a lake. Sea-kayaking or heli-skiing are two ways to experience the glacier.

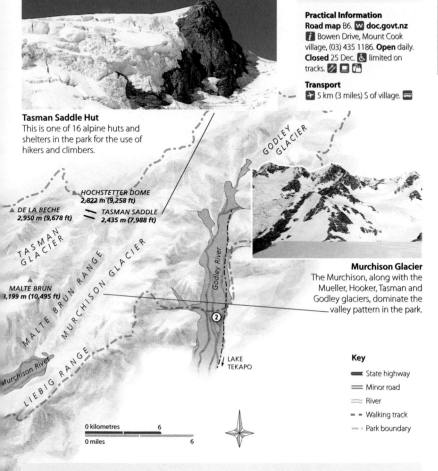

Tasman Saddle Hut
This is one of 16 alpine huts and shelters in the park for the use of hikers and climbers.

VISITORS' CHECKLIST

Practical Information
Road map B6. 🌐 doc.govt.nz
ℹ️ Bowen Drive, Mount Cook village, (03) 435 1186. **Open** daily. **Closed** 25 Dec. ♿ limited on tracks. 🚻 🏪 🏧

Transport
✈️ 5 km (3 miles) S of village. 🚌

Murchison Glacier
The Murchison, along with the Mueller, Hooker, Tasman and Godley glaciers, dominate the valley pattern in the park.

HOCHSTETTER DOME
2,822 m (9,258 ft)

DE LA BECHE
2,950 m (9,678 ft)

TASMAN SADDLE
2,435 m (7,988 ft)

GODLEY GLACIER

TASMAN GLACIER

MALTE BRUN
3,199 m (10,495 ft)

MURCHISON GLACIER

MALTE BRUN RANGE

Godley River

LIEBIG RANGE

Murchison River

LAKE TEKAPO

Key

━━ State highway

══ Minor road

〜 River

▪ ▪ Walking track

▪ ▪ Park boundary

0 kilometres 6

0 miles 6

Walks From Aoraki/Mount Cook Village

There are several walking tracks in the vicinity of Aoraki/Mount Cook village which are well formed and signposted. They are suitable for people who do not have any climbing experience.

Kea Point and Governors Bush are short walking trips that focus on the park's vegetation and birdlife. Longer walks from the village include the Sealy Tarns, Hooker Valley and Red Tarns tracks. Although these tracks are well marked, the ground is rough in places and it is advisable to wear stout shoes or boots and to carry a walking stick. A warm sweater or jacket is needed for places exposed to the wind, even during summer.

Brochures on the walks, giving descriptions and walking times, are available at the visitor centre in the village.

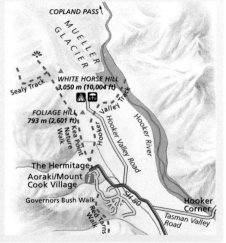

COPLAND PASS

MUELLER GLACIER

Sealy Track

WHITE HORSE HILL
3,050 m (10,004 ft)

FOLIAGE HILL
793 m (2,601 ft)

Kea Point Walk

Hooker Valley Track

Hooker Valley Road

Hooker River

The Hermitage Aoraki/Mount Cook Village

Governors Bush Walk

Red Tarns Walk

SH 80

Hooker Corner

Tasman Valley Road

OTAGO AND SOUTHLAND

With its high, snow-capped mountains, lush rainforests, dry tussocklands, deep glacial lakes, spectacular beaches and rugged coastlines, the Otago and Southland region is one of extreme natural beauty. Set among the area's untamed wilderness and historic settlements is Queenstown, a world centre for adventure sports and one of New Zealand's foremost tourist destinations.

Before the arrival of the first Europeans, Māori settled in coastal areas where seafood was plentiful, although they also hunted, and collected greenstone *(pounamu)*, in the rugged interior. The first Europeans also looked to coastal areas for an environment that would be easy to tame. Members of the Free Church of Scotland were the first to settle the area in an organized way, making Dunedin the centre of their new land. Hopes of an idyllic enclave were dashed in the early 1860s with the discovery of gold.

Gold miners poured into the inhospitable lands of what is now known as Central Otago, in search of an elusive fortune. The money gold brought to the region saw it prosper, and for a time Dunedin became New Zealand's commercial capital. The legacy of the gold mining era lives on in the humblest of stone cottages on remote and rugged landscapes as well as in the splendid buildings that adorn the streets of Dunedin. The region's natural legacy also lives on in many areas, such as the Mount Aspiring and Fiordland national parks, which remain relatively untapped. They are beautifully complemented by other natural attractions, such as Stewart Island and the Catlins area on the southeast coast, while the farmlands that have been tamed provide an attractive contrast. Such is the variety on offer, that each corner of the region provides its own attractions, making exploration very rewarding.

The Octagon in the heart of Dunedin

◄ Mountain view from Glenorchy Lagoon Walkway

Exploring Otago and Southland

The geography, climate and scenery of the Otago and Southland region vary greatly over relatively short distances. To the west, the land rises steeply from the coast through thick rainforest to 3,000 m- (9,900 ft-) high mountain peaks in the space of only 40 km (25 miles) – features that make the Fiordland and Mount Aspiring national parks so spectacular. To the east of these peaks, the ranges and valleys of Central Otago provide a stark contrast. The interior is dry and rugged. Vivid blue lakes nestle among tussock-covered hills and snow-capped mountains to create the scenery and adventure playground that has made resorts such as Queenstown so popular. From the lakes, the land drops down to the eastern and southern coasts and hinterland where extra rainfall has produced fertile farmland to feed the cities of Dunedin and Invercargill.

White-water rafting, Shotover River, Queenstown

Sights at a Glance

Top Outdoor Activities

The places shown here have been selected for their recreational activities. Conditions vary depending on the weather and the time of year, so exercise caution and, if in doubt, seek local advice.

	Aerial Sightseeing	Bungy Jumping	Jet-boating	Paragliding	Skiing	Hiking/Walking	White-water Rafting	Wildlife Watching
Catlins						●		●
Dunedin	●					●		●
Fiordland National Park						●		●
Haast						●		●
Invercargill	●					●		●
Milford Sound	●					●		●
Mount Aspiring National Park	●					●		●
Oamaru						●		●
Otago Peninsula						●		●
Queenstown	●	●	●	●	●	●	●	
Stewart Island	●					●		●
Te Anau	●		●			●		●
Wanaka	●		●	●	●	●	●	

TASMAN SEA

George Sound
Sutherl...
Secretary Island
DOUBTFUL SOUND 16
Breaksea Sound
Resolution Island
Dusky Sound
West Cape
Chalky Inlet
Puysegur Point
Manap...
Manapouri Power Station
Mono...
Lake Monowai
Lake Hauroko
Lake Poteriteri

Key

— Motorway
— Major road
⋯⋯ Minor road
— Scenic route
⋯⋯ Minor railway
— Regional border
△ Summit

The bright blue Lake Hawea, one of the largest southern lakes

Lake Moeraki
Greymouth

HAAST **9**
Jackson Bay
Jackson Bay
Cascade Point
Mount Brewsterz 2515m
Haast Pass 563m
Makaroa
8
Mount Aspiring 3033m
Lake Wanaka
6 LAKE HAWEA
Hawea
Twizel
Omarama
5 LINDIS PASS
Tarras
Mitre Peak 1692m
Milford Sound
Cleddau Valley
Mount Earnslaw 2820m
WANAKA **7**
89
Cardrona
Bendigo
Otematata
Kurow
83
Lake Aviemore
Duntroon
Timaru

GLENORCHY **11**
ARROWTOWN **12**
Moffat Peak 2085m
10
QUEENSTOWN
13 CROMWELL
Clyde
Alexandra
Naseby
Ranfurly
85
OAMARU **4**
Maheno
Herbert
Hampden
MOERAKI BOULDERS SCENIC RESERVE **3**
Shag Point
Palmerston
Waikouaiti

14 KINGSTON
Athol
Roxburgh
Millers Flat
Beaumont
Middlemarch
Hyde
87
Port Chalmers
OTAGO PENINSULA **2**
DUNEDIN **1**
Mosgiel

Lumsden
Waikaka
Tapanui
90
Lawrence
Milton
OTAGO

Mossburn
Dipton
Mandeville
94
18 GORE
Mataura
1
Balclutha

Ohai
Orawia
96
6
Winton
Edendale
Kaitangata
92
PACIFIC OCEAN

Tuatapere
Otautau
Orepuki
Makarewa
Mokoreta
Owaka
Nugget Point
Jack's Blowhole

99
Riverton
Otatara
17 INVERCARGILL
1
CATLINS TOUR
92
Fortrose
Papatowai
21
Cathedral Caves

BLUFF **19**
Toetoes Bay
Waipapa Point
Porpoise Bay

0 kilometres 25
0 miles 25

Mt Anglem 980m
STEWART ISLAND
Oban
20
Mount Allen 750m
Shelter Point
Port Pegasus

Getting Around

Road travel is the main means of getting around the region. There is a range of bus services along the main routes, and for those who choose to drive the state highways are good and generally not too busy, apart from peak holiday periods. Some roads, such as State Hwy 94 to Milford, require care because of the mountainous terrain. There are international airports at Dunedin and Queenstown, while the airport at Invercargill handles domestic flights.

For keys to symbols *see back flap*

❶ Dunedin

One of the joys of exploring Dunedin is that there is a great deal to see in a relatively small area. Its buildings are among the most interesting and architecturally diverse in the country. Many that have survived from Dunedin's heyday following the 1860s gold rush, when the city was the country's commercial centre, are within walking distance of the centre. Others are to the north of the city (see pp268–9) in proximity to Dunedin's many beautiful parks and gardens. The relatively flat central city, which remains the retail hub, is surrounded by hills, which afford a splendid view of the city and harbour below. Dunedin is a designated UNESCO City of Literature.

The striking façade of St Paul's Cathedral, built in a Neo-Gothic style

🏛 The Octagon

When the site of the settlement of "New Edinburgh" was first surveyed in 1846 by its Edinburgh-based surveyors, The Octagon was planned as the focal point. More than 150 years later, The Octagon continues to fulfil that role. It has watched over a passing parade of festivals, protests, parties and royal visits, as well as seeing sporting heroes waved off and welcomed.

This small oasis in the heart of the city – a lunchtime spot – is surrounded by a number of fine buildings. A large bronze statue of Scottish poet Robert Burns, erected in 1887, has a prominent place in front of St Paul's Cathedral. Burns' nephew, the Reverend Thomas Burns, was the spiritual leader for the first group of Scottish settlers to arrive in Dunedin in 1848.

🏛 Municipal Chambers

48 The Octagon. **Tel** (03) 474 3300.
Open Mon–Fri. **Closed** public hols.
📷 inside. 🚻 public areas.

Completed in 1880, the Municipal Chambers is an excellent example of the use of Oamaru stone (see pp272–3). It has undergone considerable restoration and refurbishment both inside and out. It is home to the Council Chambers, where city councillors meet, and features a number of reception and meeting rooms. The size of the chambers is massive, as it is able to incorporate both the 450-seat Glenroy Auditorium and the 2,100-seat Town Hall.

🏛 St Paul's Cathedral

The Octagon. **Tel** (03) 477 2336.
Open daily. 🏛 daily except Sat.
🚻 📷 Summer.

Consecrated in 1919, the Anglican St Paul's stands high above The Octagon on an elevated site, with a broad staircase leading to its doors. It owes its prominent position in a predominantly Presbyterian settlement to the generosity of Johnny Jones, an early whaler and trader. The cathedral, which replaced a smaller church built on the site in 1863, has many fine architectural details, including a vaulted stone ceiling.

🖼 Dunedin Public Art Gallery

30 The Octagon. **Tel** (03) 474 3240.
Open daily. **Closed** 25 Dec. 📷
(special exhibitions only). 🚻 📷 📷
🌐 dunedin.art.museum

This modern gallery, designed to harmonize with The Octagon's historic buildings, has one of the best collections of European art in the country. It features exhibitions on traditional and contemporary art, and a special gallery dedicated to the works of renowned Dunedin artist Frances Hodgkins. (see p36).

Entrance foyer of the Dunedin Public Art Gallery

Key

🟦 Street-by-Street: Central Dunedin pp264–5

For keys to symbols see back flap

🏛 First Church

415 Moray Place. **Tel** (03) 477 7118.
Open daily. 🏛 Sunday only. ♿ 📷

The flagship of the Presbyterian Church in Otago, First Church, consecrated in 1873, is considered to be architect Robert Lawson's greatest contribution to Dunedin's rich architectural heritage. Of note are its beautiful rose window, wooden ceiling and 56 m-(184 ft-) high spire. The church

The Law Courts in Central Dunedin

has undergone considerable restoration work to repair its exterior. Its history is told at the church's heritage centre. Bell Hill, on which First Church stands, was lowered by about 12 m (40 ft) to improve the city's traffic.

🏛 Toitū Otago Settlers Museum

31 Queens Gardens. **Tel** (03) 477 5052.
Open daily. **Closed** Good Fri, 25 Dec.
🅿 ♿ 📷 📷 W **toituosm.com**

New Zealand's oldest social history museum focuses on the lives of the province's settlers from Southern Māori to Scottish pioneers and Chinese gold miners. The displays range from early photographs and household goods to implements and vehicles, including two large steam locomotives, one of which dates back to the 1870s. The Smith Portrait Gallery showcases old photographs

and paintings of the early settlers and the ICT section displays the region's first digital technology. A public archive and an exhibition space are also accessible.

🏛 Law Courts

41 Stuart St.

These were completed in 1902 to a design by government architect John Campbell. The building is distinguished by its combination of local Port Chalmers bluestone and lighter Oamaru stone. Standing just around the corner in complete contrast is the former red brick Dunedin Prison, built to another Campbell design which mimics many aspects of London's New Scotland Yard, although on a smaller scale. Completed in 1895, it also served as the Dunedin Police Station until a new building was built in the mid-1990s.

Dunedin City Centre

Robert Lawson

Many of Dunedin's finest Victorian and Scottish Edwardian-style buildings are attributed to architect Robert Lawson (1833–1902). The Scottish-born Lawson had trained as an architect in his home country before migrating to Melbourne, where he found little work, and instead made a living from gold-mining and journalism. He took up his profession again in 1861 and the following year won a competition for the design of First Church in Dunedin. Lawson moved to Dunedin and so began a successful association with the city. His list of credits includes the Municipal Chambers, Otago Boys High School (a handsome bluestone building completed in 1884) and Knox Church in George Street, which was consecrated in 1876. However, it was his initial Dunedin design, First Church, which many consider to be his masterpiece.

First Church

Street-by-Street: Central Dunedin

Dunedin has close historical links with the Scottish city of Edinburgh. Not only is Dunedin the old Gaelic name for Edinburgh, but many of its street names are Scottish and several Scottish traditions have been preserved since the first Presbyterian settlers arrived in 1848. The Octagon, so-called because of its eight sides, gives the city a central focus. Surrounding it, and within a few blocks, are a number of Victorian and Edwardian public buildings, which are among the finest in the country. Visitors can also enjoy the many cafés and restaurants dotted around the area.

St Paul's Cathedral
St Paul's has the only vaulted stone ceiling in New Zealand (see p262).

Stuart Street Terrace Houses
Built around 1900 as town residences for country folk, these terrace houses are now popular locations for restaurants, boutiques and professional offices.

Dunedin Public Art Gallery (see p262)

Key

— Suggested route

0 metres   300
0 yards   300

First Church (see p263)

Queens Gardens

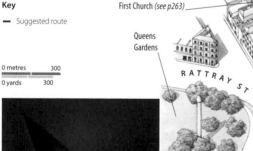

RATTRAY ST

MORAY PLACE

BURLINGTON STREET

CUMBERLAN

Toitū Otago Settlers Museum
New Zealand's oldest history museum tells the story of Otago and its settlers. One wing is dedicated to old forms of transport (see p263).

The Dunedin Chinese Garden
is an authentic example of a late Ming/early Ching Dynasty Scholar's garden and celebrates Otago's Chinese heritage.

The Municipal Chambers
Built in 1880 at a time when Dunedin was revelling in the fortune brought by the gold rush, the building is topped by a 47 m- (155 ft-) high tower *(see p262)*.

VISITORS' CHECKLIST

Practical Information
Road map B7. ⚏ 120,000.
🖳 dunedinnz.com 🛈 i-SITE,
50 The Octagon, (03) 474 3300.
⛷ Chinese New Year (Feb);
Dunedin Fringe Festival (Mar);
Midwinter Carnival (Jun). 📷

Transport
✈ 25 km (16 miles) S of city
centre. Limited international flights
to and from Australia. 🚇 Anzac
Ave. 🚌 Intercity, 7 Halsey St./
Dunedin Railway Station.

★ The Octagon
The Octagon is a popular gathering place for small groups who lunch under the trees, and for bigger crowds during festivals and exhibitions *(see p262)*.

The Otago Daily Times Building, an interesting piece of 1930s Art Deco architecture, is the home of New Zealand's oldest newspaper.

Law Courts *(see p263)*

★ Dunedin Railway Station
Perhaps the finest stone structure in the country, the station has a 37-m- (120-ft-) high square tower, three huge clock faces and a covered carriageway *(see pp266–7)*.

Dunedin Railway Station

Dunedin's Railway Station is one of New Zealand's finest historic buildings and one of the best examples of railway architecture in the southern hemisphere. Although not large by international standards, the station's delightful proportions lend it an air of grandeur. Opened in 1906, the Flemish Renaissance-style building was designed by New Zealand Railways architect George Troup, whose detailing on the outside of the building earned him the nickname "Gingerbread George".

★ Exterior Stonework
Beige Oamaru limestone (see pp272–3) detailing provides a striking contrast to the darker Central Otago bluestone on the walls and the finely polished Aberdeen granite of the columns.

New Zealand Sports Hall of Fame
This features imaginative displays recounting the exploits and achievements of famous New Zealanders.

KEY

① **A frieze** of cherubs and foliage from the Royal Doulton factory in England encircles the ticket hall below the wrought-iron bordered balcony.

② **Dormer windows** projecting from the sloping gable roof are typical Flemish architectural features.

③ **The turret** provides a visual counterbalance to the main clock tower.

④ **The roof** is covered with clay Marseille tiles from France.

⑤ **Finely carved sandstone lions** on each corner of the clock tower guard the cupola behind them.

⑥ **The clock tower** rises 37 m (120 ft) above street level.

⑦ **The platform** is the arrival and departure point for visitors taking the Dunedin Railways (see p268).

Main entrance

Ticket Windows
The ticket windows are ornately deco-rated with white tiles and a crest featuring the old New Zealand Railways logo.

★ Stained-glass Windows
Two imposing stained-glass windows on the mezzanine balcony depict approaching steam engines, lights blazing, facing each other across the ticket hall.

VISITORS' CHECKLIST

Practical Information
Anzac Ave. **Tel** (03) 477 4449.
Open 8am–5pm Mon–Fri,
8:30am–3pm Sat, Sun & public
hols. **Closed** 25 Dec. 🚫 📷

Transport
5-minute walk from the Octagon.

Staircase
Complete with wrought-iron balustrades and Royal Doulton mosaic tiled steps, a staircase sweeps up from the ticket hall to the balcony above.

★ Mosaic Floor
More than 725,000 Royal Doulton porcelain squares form images of steam engines, rolling stock and the New Zealand Railways logo.

North Dunedin and Environs

Dunedin's city centre is enclosed by hills to the north and west, and by water – the Otago Harbour and Pacific Ocean – to the east and south. In the north of the city are several green areas, most notably the Botanic Gardens at the foot of Signal Hill, and several historic buildings. A road along the narrow, scenic harbour leads to lookout points providing panoramic views of the city, harbour and peninsula.

University of Otago clock tower

🌿 Signal Hill

Signal Hill Rd via Opoho Rd.
Open daily. ♿

To the north of the city, the road up Signal Hill leads to a monument built in 1940 to mark 100 years of British sovereignty in New Zealand. From here visitors can get excellent views of the central city, upper harbour and parts of the Otago Peninsula.

🌸 Dunedin Botanic Gardens

Opoho Rd. **Tel** (03) 477 4000.
Open daily. ♿ 🚻 💻 📷

Dunedin's extensive Botanic Gardens were the first to be established in New Zealand, in 1868. The area's varied topography and microclimates are used to grow a diverse range of plants. The flat lower gardens are home to the more formal displays – lawns interspersed with trees and native bush and formal flower gardens – and to the Edwardian Winter Garden, first opened in 1908. On the hill, the upper gardens include more than 3,000 rhododendron varieties in the world-renowned Rhododendron Dell. These provide a springtime feast for the eyes. The gardens are the first in New Zealand to be rated as Garden of International Significance.

🏛 Otago Museum

419 Great King St. **Tel** (03) 474 7474.
Open 10am–5pm daily. **Closed** 25 Dec. 🅿️ donation. ♿ 📷 2pm daily.
💻 📷 🌐 otagomuseum.nz

The displays in the large, Classical-style Otago Museum, opened in 1877, introduce visitors to the region's human, cultural and natural history. There are halls dealing with pre-European Māori life, Pacific culture, marine life, and archaeology of the ancient world. The museum also houses one of New Zealand's leading maritime exhibitions, treasures of Māori life, a Victorian-inspired Animal Attic and a 3D Planetarium. The interactive Discovery World science centre includes a tropical forest with exotic butterflies.

🌿 Tunnel Beach Walkway

Blackhead Rd. **Open** daily.
Closed Aug–Oct.

Located 7 km (4 miles) south of the city, Tunnel Beach is named after the tunnel cut through sandstone cliffs in the 1870s by Edward Cargill so that his family could get down to the pretty beach below. The short but steep walkway to the beach gives breathtaking views of the sandstone cliffs, which have been spectacularly sculpted by wind and sea.

🏛 University of Otago

Leith St. **Tel** (03) 479 1100. **Open** Mon–Fri. **Closed** public hols. ♿ grounds & public areas. 🌐 otago.ac.nz

Founded in 1869, the University of Otago – New Zealand's oldest university – plays a crucial role in the life of the city. The bluestone clock tower registry building dates from 1878 *(see p32)*, while the semi-detached houses close to its northern end were built in 1879. The grounds are a pleasant place to wander.

🌿 The Organ Pipes

Mount Cargill Rd.

Strange multi-sided basalt columns, known as "the organ pipes", are a reminder of Dunedin's volcanic past. Reaching them requires a walk of at least an hour from a signpost on Mount Cargill Road, north of the city. The panoramic views are a bonus.

🚂 Dunedin Railways

Anzac Square. **Tel** (03) 477 4449.
Open departs daily; additional departures during summer. 🅿️ ♿
💻 📷 🌐 dunedinrailways.co.nz

Departing from Dunedin Railway Station, Dunedin Railways offer scenic train journeys. One of the most popular is the Taieri Gorge line, which takes passengers on a 77-km (48-mile) 4-hour return trip west of the city for one of the world's great train journeys. Opened in 1879, the train passes through the greenery of Dunedin's coast, then climbs through a steep-sided river gorge to the arid grasslands and rocky outcrops of the Strath Taieri. It cuts through ten tunnels, crossing bridges and viaducts up to 47 m (155 ft) above the Taieri River.

Rhododendrons in bloom in the Dunedin Botanic Gardens

For hotels and restaurants in this region see p307 and pp324–5

Olveston Historic Home

Olveston, a 35-room Jacobean-style mansion, was completed in 1906 for David and Marie Theomin and their children, Edward and Dorothy. Dorothy left the house and its contents to the city and it remains as it was when the family lived in it. Olveston's grand drawing room, dining room, library, billiard room and great hall contain fine furniture and many treasures collected by the Theomins, who were keen travellers.

VISITORS' CHECKLIST

42 Royal Terrace. **Tel** (03) 477 33 20. W **olveston.co.nz** **Open** daily. **Closed** 25 Dec. (grounds free). ground floor. obligatory; check website for timings.

The kitchen is dominated by a kauri dresser filled with blue and white Delft ware and a kauri table.

Exterior Stonework
The double-brick house gets its warm exterior colour from a cladding of Moeraki pebbles with Oamaru stone highlights *(see pp272–3)*.

★ Dining Room
Attractive features are the oak panelling, semicircular stained-glass windows and richly embossed wallpaper.

Library

The Billard Room
has a full-size table and adjustable overhead lights.

Card Room

Main entrance

Dutch gables and projecting windows add architectural interest to the exterior of Olveston.

★ Great Hall
A centre for receptions, the hall has oak joinery, printed hessian wall covering featuring acanthus leaves, and a collection of porcelain.

The Drawing Room, used for entertaining and music, has the only decorated ceiling in the house.

❷ Otago Peninsula

The 24-km- (15-mile-) long Otago Peninsula offers a wide variety of attractions, including rare and unusual wildlife, historic buildings, woodland gardens and spectacular harbour and coastal scenery. The 64 km (40 mile) round trip, taking the "high" Highcliff Road, which runs over the top of the peninsula, on the outward journey, and returning via the "low" Portobello Road along the coast, can take a full day. The Highcliff Road offers the best views of the surrounding countryside and coastline.

🏰 Larnach Castle
145 Camp Rd. **Tel** (03) 476 1616
Open daily. 🅿️ 🅿️ inside. ♿ ground floor. ☕ by arrangement. ▣ 📷
🌐 **larnachcastle.co.nz**

Located 14 km (9 miles) from central Dunedin along the "high" road, Lanarch Castle is New Zealand's only castle and has been designated a Garden of International Significance. Built between 1871 and 1885 by financier, businessman and politician, William J M Larnach for his wife Eliza, the grand stone mansion, set in 2 sq km (0.8 sq mile) of bush and gardens, is built along Scottish baronial lines. It has many fine features, including elaborately carved and decorated ceilings and a large, hanging staircase. Its magnificent interior was created by English and Italian artisans brought to Dunedin to work on the building. A ballroom was added as a complete wing for Larnach's daughter, Kate. Visitors can climb up the narrow stone steps for a view from the top of the tower. Accommodation is available next to the castle (see p307).

In 1967 the Barker family bought the castle which was by then derelict and spent many years restoring it to its former glory. Margaret Barker has worked particularly hard to restore the gardens and grounds, and they now contain a fine collection of native and exotic plants.

🕊️ Royal Albatross Centre
Taiaroa Head. **Tel** (03) 478 0499.
Open daily. **Closed** 25 Dec. 🅿️
♿ visitor centre, Albatross Tour, Blue penguin Tour. ☕ obligatory; booking essential. ▣ 📷 🌐 **albatross.org.nz**

The prominent Taiaroa headland at the mouth of Otago Harbour is home to the world's only mainland royal albatross colony. Opened in 1989, the centre contains excellent displays about these large birds. With guided tours, visitors can

Black and white royal albatrosses at Taiaroa Head

utilise an observatory where albatrosses can be seen. A colony of Stewart Island shags is also visible from the observatory. Blue penguin viewing tours are also available each evening where they can be watched scurrying up the beach to their burrows after a day out foraging at sea. Taiaroa Head's other main attraction is the Armstrong disappearing gun, a 15-cm (6-inch) diameter naval defence gun installed in 1886 during the "Russian scare". Designed to pop out of the ground, fire and then recoil back into its pit, it is the only one of its kind in the world still in working order in its original position.

Larnach Castle viewed from the gardens

For hotels and restaurants in this region see p307 and pp324–5

Homestead in the Glenfalloch Woodland Gardens

🏠 Glenfalloch Woodland Gardens

430 Portobello Rd. **Tel** (03) 476 1775. **Open** daily. 🏷 donation. ♿ lower gardens. 📷 📠 summer only. 🌐 **glenfalloch.co.nz**

On the "low road", 10 km (6 miles) from Dunedin, the Glenfalloch Woodland Gardens – in Gaelic, glenfalloch means "hidden glen" – have been attracting visitors since the 1870s. An elegant homestead, built in 1871, tearooms (open in summer), and a pottery, where pieces that are made on the spot are sold, are sheltered in grounds containing mature trees, shrubs, and a stream. The gardens are ablaze with rhododendrons and azaleas in spring, and during the summer months they are noted for their colourful displays of fuchsias and roses.

Visitors to Glenfalloch can enjoy several short walking tracks through the trees and woodland gardens.

🐧 Sandfly Bay Recreation Reserve

Seal Point Rd. **Tel** (03) 477 0677. **Open** daily. **Closed** 25 Dec. 🌐 **doc.govt.nz/parks-and-recreation**

Known for its native fauna and flora, this reserve offers brilliant views of the Otago Peninsula coastline and cliff tops. Among the many outstanding attractions, the most striking are the yellow-eyed penguins. To view the penguins, a marked track leads up to a public hide near the southern end of the beach. The best time for viewing is late afternoon or early evening.

🏛 Otakou

Tamatea Rd, Off Harrington Point Rd. **Open** daily, by appointment. 📷 inside. 🌐 **otakourunaka.co.nz**

Otakou is the site of one of the earliest Māori settlements in the area, and it was this word that was anglicized to "Otago" to give the surrounding province its name. The local church and meeting house were built in 1840 to commemorate the centenary of the signing of the Treaty of Waitangi (see pp52–3). What appear to be carvings are actually moulded concrete.

Māori church and meeting house at Otakau

🐧 Penguin Place

45 Pakihau Rd. **Tel** (03) 478 0286. **Open** daily. 🏷 📷 obligatory, bookings essential. 📷 🌐 **penguinplace.co.nz**

The road to Taiaroa Head passes Penguin Place, an award-winning venture to save the yellow-eyed penguin, the world's rarest species of penguin. Yellow-eyed penguins are found only on the Otago Peninsula and other isolated east coast areas of Otago and Southland. An ingenious system of camouflaged trenches at Penguin Place allows visitors to view nesting yellow-eyed penguins at close range without disturbing them. The penguins can be viewed any time of the day during the breeding season.

⑤ Moeraki Boulders Scenic Reserve

Road map B7.

The Moeraki Boulders, 78 km (49 miles) north of Dunedin on State Highway 1, have long been the subject of legend and curiosity. Almost perfectly spherical, with a circumference of up to 4 m (13 ft), the grey boulders lie scattered along a 50-m (164- ft) stretch of the beach. They were formed on the sea bed about 60 million years ago as lime salts gradually accumulated around a hard core.

Māori legend claims that the boulders were the food baskets or Te Kaihinaki of the Araiteuru canoe, one of the great ancestral canoes that brought Māori to New Zealand from Hawaiki. The canoe was wrecked while on a greenstone gathering trip. It is said that the kumara on board became rough rocks, the food baskets became smooth boulders, and the wreck turned into a reef.

It is not unusual to see small black and white Hector's dolphins playing in the surf near the boulders. A nearby café and restaurant service the flow of visitors.

The tiny, picturesque fishing village of Moeraki, a former whaling station established in 1836, is on the opposite side of the bay from the reserve.

Spherical boulders on the beach at Moeraki

❹ Street-by-Street: Oamaru

The main town of North Otago and service centre for a rich agricultural hinterland, Oamaru is a pretty town with wide, tree-lined streets, well-kept gardens, galleries, beaches, colonies of rare penguins, and the best preserved collection of historic public and commercial buildings in the country. The buildings were fashioned in the 1880s from Oamaru stone, a local cream-coloured limestone which is easily cut, carved and moulded. Oamaru was the childhood home of the internationally reputed novelist Janet Frame. A walking tour takes visitors past sites featured in her writing. Steampunk is a genre of science fiction that features steam-powered technology and Oamaru has been reinvented as the 'Steampunk capital' of New Zealand.

★ **Forrester Gallery**
Ornately carved Corinthian columns distinguish this 1882 building, which formerly housed the Bank of New South Wales.

Courthouse
Built in 1883, the Court-house features a Neo-Classical portico with Corinthian columns. It is no longer in use.

Steampunk Headquarters

National Bank (1871)

HUMBER ST

THAMES ST

ITCHIN STREET

★ **North Otago Museum**
Exhibits in the museum, built in 1882, include displays on the quarrying and use of Oamaru stone.

Oamaru's first Post Office, a small Italianate building with a squat clock tower, was built in 1864.

Colonial Bank (1878), now housing the Visitor Centre

St Luke's Anglican Church (1865–1913) contains fine interior woodcarving.

Waitaki District Council
Originally Oamaru's second post office (1883), the building's 28 m (92 ft) clock tower was added in 1903.

Criterion Hotel
Built in 1877, this hotel went "dry" in 1906 during prohibition. Now restored, it serves patrons in a Victorian pub atmosphere.

Harbour Street
At the heart of the port area, this street is lined with 19th-century warehouses, commercial buildings and grain stores.

Harbour Board Office (1876)

HARBOUR STREET

TYNE STREET

Union Bank (1878–9)

Customs House (1884)

Tyne Street, together with Harbour Street, contains over 20 buildings classified for preservation.

| 0 metres | 100 |
| 0 yards | 100 |

Key

— Suggested route

★ **New Zealand Loan and Mercantile Warehouse**
This three-storey Victorian warehouse, built in 1882 for New Zealand's largest stock and station agency, was designed to hold up to 100,000 sacks of grain.

VISITORS' CHECKLIST

Practical Information
Road map B7. ⚑ 12,500.
🇼 visitoamaru.co.nz
ℹ 1 Thames St, (03) 434 1656.
🎭 Victorian Heritage Celebrations (Nov). Forrester Gallery: **Tel** (03) 433 0853. **Open** daily. **Closed** Good Fri, 25 Dec. ♿
North Otago Museum: **Tel** (03) 433 0852. **Open** daily. **Closed** 1 Jan, Good Fri, 25 Apr, 25 Dec. ♿

Transport
🚉 Humber St. 🚌 Cnr Eden & Thames sts.

Oamaru and the harbour as seen from Lookout Reserve

Exploring Oamaru
Apart from its historic harbour precinct which features a number of boutique businesses and cafés, and the Steampunk playground. Oamaru has several scenic and natural attractions. The 1 km (0.6 mile) South Hill Walkway above the harbour leads to Lookout Reserve. Further on is Bushy Beach where a viewing hide allows visitors to see yellow-eyed penguins.

🐧 Oamaru Blue Penguin Colony
Waterfront Rd. **Tel** (03) 433 1195. **Open** daily. **Closed** 25 Apr, 25 & 26 Dec. 🎫 📷 no flash. ♿ 🏪
🇼 penguins.co.nz
At Friendly Bay, in an old quarry at the end of Oamaru's harbour, visitors can see penguins leave to feed at sea, and return at dusk past a special viewing area. From another viewing area, the penguins can be observed in their nesting boxes.

🌿 Oamaru Public Gardens
Chelmer St. **Open** daily, until sunset. Established in 1876, these contain traditional features such as rose gardens, ponds, an azalea lawn and rhododendron dell. A band rotunda, summerhouse, aviary, peacock house and marble fountain are other attractions.

🏛 Totara Estate
State Hwy 1. ℹ (03) 434 7169. **Open** daily. **Closed** end May–end Aug. 🎫 ♿ 🏪
About 8 km (5 miles) south of Oamaru, this is where New Zealand's first shipment of frozen mutton to England in 1882 was processed, heralding the beginning of New Zealand's most important industry. Limestone buildings house displays on the industry's history.

The Lindis Pass winding through tussock-covered hills

❺ Lindis Pass

Road map B6.

The main inland link between Otago and the Waitaki Basin, the Lindis Pass climbs through rocky gorges before reaching the tussock-covered hills of a Department of Conservation reserve near the summit. Early Māori, like today's holiday-makers, used the route in summer to get to Lakes Wanaka and Hawea.

In 1858, John McLean, the first European to settle in the area, established the 2,000 sq km (772 sq mile) Morven Hills Station. Many of the original buildings can still be seen about 15 km (9 miles) south of the summit. These include McLean's original homestead and a massive stone woolshed, built about 1880, which was capable of holding up to 1,500 sheep.

❻ Lake Hawea

Road map B6. 🏔 1,100. 🎿 Hawea Picnic Day & Races (Dec).

Tucked among hills and mountains, the bright blue waters of Lake Hawea make it one of the most beautiful of the southern lakes. The lake, which is 410 m (1,345 ft) deep in

places, is separated from the equally beautiful Lake Wanaka by a narrow, 35 km (22 mile) isthmus, known as "the neck".

Lake Hawea is a popular holiday haven. There are many free camping spots around its shores. It is also well known for its excellent trout and land-locked salmon fishing and for various boating activities. The small town of Hawea on the lake's southern shores is the main base for outdoor activities.

❼ Wanaka

Road map B6. 🏔 7,500.
ℹ 100 Ardmore St, (03) 443 1233.
🎿 Wanakafest (Sep); Warbirds Over Wanaka (Easter, even-numbered years). 🔽 **lakewanaka.co.nz**

Located at the southern end of the lake, Wanaka is one of the country's favourite holiday spots. The willow-lined shores and bays of Lake Wanaka are popular in summer for boating, fishing and water-skiing, while in winter skiers and snow-boarders flock to the local ski areas. Snow-capped peaks provide a beautiful lake setting, and these natural attractions also bring hikers and walkers to the many breathtaking tracks in the nearby Mount Aspiring National Park *(see pp276–7)*.

Aside from the area's natural features, there is plenty to visit and see around the town. One of the chief attractions is **Warbirds and Wheels**, located at Wanaka Airport, which combines classic cars with a variety of World War II fighter aircraft, such as a Hawker Hurricane, Tiger Moth, Vampire, Chipmunk,

a replica of a SE5A and several rare Russian Polikarpovs. Illustrated displays explain the role of New Zealand fighter pilots and crews in several theatres of war. Visitors can also see aircraft being restored in the maintenance hangar. "Warbirds Over Wanaka", a major biennial airshow involving military aircraft, is held every second Easter in even-numbered years. It features aircraft from New Zealand as well as overseas in acrobatic displays and mock battles. Wanaka's open skies and dramatic alpine scenery provide a spectacular backdrop.

Next to Wanaka Airport is the **Wanaka Transport Museum**. Its large private collection of more than 13,000 items includes memorabilia, such as toys and models, as well as military vehicles and aircraft. A special exhibit is a huge Russian Antonov AN-2, the world's largest single engine biplane.

Tumbling Towers at Stuart Landsborough's Puzzling World

Stuart Landsborough's Puzzling World is based around "The Great Maze", 1.5 km (1 mile) of three-dimensional wooden passages and under- and over-bridges. Other attractions include the incredible Illusion Rooms, a Hologram Hall, the bizarre Tumbling Towers/Tilted House, and the Puzzle Centre and Café where you can take a break and try to solve one of the many challenging puzzles on display.

Like many other parts of Central Otago, Wanaka's climate is proving ideal for grape growing. **Rippon Vineyard**, established in 1974 just 4 km (2.5 miles) from the centre of town, is one of the pioneering growers and

Fishing on the shores of Lake Hawea

Rippon Vineyard on the shores of Lake Wanaka

winemakers of the region. The vineyard produces wines from a number of grape varieties.

🏛 Warbirds and Wheels
Wanaka Airport. **Tel** (03) 443 7010. **Open** daily. **Closed** 25 Dec. 🖼 🔁 🖼 **w** warbirdsandwheels.com

🏛 Wanaka Transport and Toy Museum
State Hwy 6. **Tel** (03) 443 8765. **Open** daily. **Closed** 25 Dec. 🖼 🔁 🖼 🖼 **w** nttmuseumwanaka.co.nz

🏔 Stuart Landsborough's Puzzling World
State Hwy 6. **Tel** (03) 443 7489. **Open** daily. 🖼 🔁 🖼 🖼 🖼 **w** puzzlingworld.com

🏔 Rippon Vineyard
Mt Aspiring Rd. **Tel** (03) 443 8084. **Open** daily. **Closed** May–June, 25 Dec. 🖼 wine tasting. 🔁 🖼 🖼 Rippon Music Festival (biennial, even-numbered years in Feb). **w** rippon.co.nz

Environs
Twenty-five km (16 miles) south of Wanaka is the tiny township of Cardrona, consisting of a few cottages and a hotel dating back to 1863.

The surrounding Cardrona Valley, a popular route for gold miners in the 1860s, is now better known for the Cardrona Ski Field on the southeastern slopes of Mount Cardrona, and for cross-country skiing at the nearby Waiorau Snow Farm *(see pp198–9, 335)*.

The **Treble Cone Ski Area**, 20 km (12 miles) southwest of Wanaka, off Mount Aspiring Road, has uncrowded slopes which are great for skiers of all abilities *(see pp198–9, 335)*. Guided back country heli-skiing over the Harris, Richardson and Buchanan moun-tains is another option, flying you to some of the best out-of-the-way ski spots in the area.

Wanaka's Outdoor Attractions

Wanaka is a recreational centre with a wide variety of outdoor pursuits in both summer and winter. Fishing is a popular activity on the lake shore, along rivers and from charter vessels. Waterborne adventures include kayaking, jet-boat and cruise boat trips, white-water sledging on small purpose-designed boards, and canyoning. There are several good walks which leave from or near the township, as well as longer hikes in the nearby Mount Aspiring National Park *(see pp276–7)* for more serious, well-equipped hikers. Horse riding, mountain biking and quad bike motorcycle tours are other ways of exploring Wanaka's back country areas.

Within easy distance of Wanaka lie two commercial downhill ski areas, Treble Cone and Cardrona, as well as the Waiorau Snow Farm cross-country ski area and heli-skiing in the surrounding mountains. From Wanaka Airport, flightseeing tours are available. or, for the more adventurous, acrobatic flights in Tiger Moths or World War II Mustangs.

Skiers on a chairlift at Treble Cone Ski Area, southwest of Wanaka

❽ Mount Aspiring National Park

New Zealand's third largest National Park after Fiordland and Kahurangi, Mount Aspiring National Park enjoys World Heritage status as part of the Te Wāhipounamu/Southwest New Zealand World Heritage Area, which stretches from Aoraki/Mount Cook to the southern tip of Fiordland. Within the park's 3,555 sq km (1,373 sq mile) area, the scenery ranges from snow- and glacier-clad mountains to rugged rock faces, spectacular forested valleys and picturesque river flats. The park, close to the tourist centres of Queenstown and Wanaka, is a popular walking, hiking and climbing destination.

Exploring the park
Opportunities to explore the park on foot are varied, and range from short walks from the road to back country circuits for fit hikers.

★ **Mount Aspiring/Tititea**
Because of its pyramid shape, Mount Aspiring/Tititea is often described as New Zealand's "Matterhorn of the South".

KEY

① **The Rees-Dart Track**, a challenging four- to five-day loop track reached from the head of Lake Wakatipu, offers outstanding scenery but requires a high level of fitness and the proper equipment.

② **The Olivine Wilderness Area**, which constitutes the core of the park, is maintained in an undeveloped state for wilderness recreation and has no tracks or huts.

Okuru

Jackson Bay • Waiatoto

Arawhata River

HAAST RANGE

Waiatoto River

MAIN DIVIDE OF TH

② MOUNT ASPIRING
3,033 m (9,948 ft)

Lake Wilmot

OLIVINE RANGE

ROB ROY GLACIER

Aspiring Hut

Rob Roy Valley Track

Matukituki Ri

Matukituki Valley Track

Rees-Dart Track

① MOUNT EARNSLAW
2,820 m (9,249 ft)

Birdlife in Mount Aspiring National Park

Rock wren

This park is known for its abundant birdlife. Some 59 species, 38 of them native, inhabit the valley floors, riverbeds, forests, subalpine scrub and high alpine regions. Especially symbolic of the park are the kea, rock wren and blue duck. The kea, whose call may be heard echoing through the valleys, is an inquisitive bird well known for its interest in hikers' equipment and food. The hardy little rock wren lives high in the hills in one of the harshest environments in the park, while pairs of blue ducks can be seen feeding on vegetation and insects in the park's swift mountain streams, especially in the hanging valleys.

Matukituki Valley
A track up the west branch of the river from the end of the road takes hikers to the head of the valley and to some challenging climbing in the Mount Aspiring area.

★ **Gates of Haast**
At the Gates of Haast bridge, the Haast River roars down a steep-sided gorge strewn with boulders.

VISITORS' CHECKLIST

Practical Information
Road map A6. Wanaka:
ℹ️ Department of Conservation, Ardmore St, (03) 443 7660.
Open summer: daily, winter: Mon–Sat. **Closed** 25 Dec.
🏕️ Makarora: ℹ️ State Hwy 6, (03) 443 8365. **Open** summer: daily. **Closed** winter, 25 Dec. 🏕️
🌐 doc.govt.nz

Transport
🚌 Ardmore St.

● Haast

Road map B6. 🏔️ 300. ℹ️ Dept of Conservation, cnr State Hwy 6 & Haast–Jackson Bay Rd, (03) 750 0809.

A tiny community on the coast where the broad Haast River meets the sea, Haast is little more than a stopover and supply point for people travelling between the West Coast and the southern lakes, although it does offer good surf and river fishing. The visitor centre provides information on walks and tracks in the area, as well as maps, souvenirs and visitor publications. The staff can also advise on track and weather conditions in this high rainfall area. Fill up with fuel here before driving over the pass to Wanaka.

Environs
The road south to the fishing village of **Jackson Bay** provides a number of walking and sightseeing opportunities, such as the Hapuka Estuary Walk, the Cascade Viewpoint and the Smoothwater Bay track at Jackson Bay itself. The Wharekai Te Kau Walk leads to the Okahu Wildlife Refuge.

There are several places of interest north of Haast, such as the Dune Lake Walk through dense coastal forest stunted by wind at Ship Creek, and the stunning Knights Point viewpoint.

Further on, past **Lake Moeraki**, the Monro Beach Walk passes through luxuriant coastal forest to a remote beach where (from July to December) Fiordland crested penguins are sometimes seen. The road carries on to trout-filled **Lake Paringa** where a 15-minute walk passes through native trees such as silver beech, rimu and kahikatea.

★ **Mount Brewster**
Accessible from State Highway 6, Mount Brewster is a popular climbing and camping spot.

★ **Thunder Creek Falls**
A short forest track from State Highway 6 leads to the 30 m (98 ft) falls which drop from a notch in a rock.

Key

━━━ State highway
═══ Minor road
〰️ River
- - Walking track
-- ▸ Park boundary

0 kilometres 10
0 miles 10

Jackson Bay, surrounded by swamp, bush and mountains

⑩ Queenstown

Situated on the northeast shore of Lake Wakatipu, backed by The Remarkables mountain range, Queenstown enjoys one of the most scenic settings in the world. Since the 1970s, it has developed from a sleepy lakeside town into a leading international resort and a world centre for adventure sports, including bungy jumping *(see pp198–9)*. Like most towns in the area, Queenstown was established during the 1860s gold rushes. Although the pace of development in Queenstown has been dictated by the demands of tourism, it still has the feel of a small town and proudly maintains its links with the days of the gold boom.

TSS *Earnslaw* on Lake Wakatipu

🖼 Lake Wakatipu

There is no mistaking Lake Wakatipu's glacial origins, although Māori legend has it that the lake was formed by the imprint of a sleeping demon burnt to death by the lover of a beautiful Māori girl captured by the demon.

Because his heart did not perish and still beats, the level of the lake rises and falls as much as 7 cm (3 inches) every five minutes. Lake Wakatipu, which is the second largest of the southern glacial lakes, after Te Anau, is up to 380 m (1,246 ft) deep in places.

Adventure Capital of New Zealand

Queenstown offers a range of adventures, from outdoor experiences to total adventure packages *(see pp198–9, 334–9)*. Many activities are centred around the lake and on the several rivers nearby, in particular the Dart, Shotover and Kawarau,

White-water rafting on the Shotover River

where jet-boat trips and white-water rafting offer exciting rides through narrow, rocky canyons. In winter, two ranges within 30 km (19 miles) of Queenstown – the Remarkables and Coronet Peak – provide great skiing. The town's reputation as New Zealand's adventure capital, however, rests on its many airborne activities: bungy jumping, ranging from the 43-m- (141-ft-) high Kawarau Bridge to the 134-m- (440-ft-) high Nevis highwire bungy; hang-gliding from the area's mountainous terrain; tandem parapenting from Bob's Peak; and tandem skydiving.

The steep, rugged slopes of the Remarkables drop down to the lake's edge, leaving downtown Queenstown snuggled on one of the few pieces of relatively flat land in the area. Most private residences and many hotels found on the surrounding hills. During the mining boom, the lake was the principal means of communication, but today it is a focus for recreational activities.

🌳 Queenstown Gardens

Park St. **Open** daily. ♿

Set on a glacial moraine peninsula, the 150-year-old Queenstown Gardens are within walking distance of the town centre. They are surrounded by stands of large fir trees and contain broad lawns and rose beds. The gardens provide a quiet oasis in an otherwise busy tourist town, and are particularly attractive in autumn. An ice skating rink, sporting greens, frisbee golf course, skate park, tennis courts and a walkway around the point are other attractions.

🚢 TSS Earnslaw

Steamer Wharf. **Tel** 0800 656 503. **Open** daily. 🅿 ♿ main deck. 🔲 📷

The TSS (Twin Screw Steamer) *Earnslaw* is a wonderful relic of the mining boom when paddle steamers and other craft plied Lake Wakatipu as the principal means of transport. Launched in 1912, the 51 m (168 ft) vessel, affectionately known as "the lady of the lake", is still powered by its original twin 500-hp coal-fired steam engines. Its interior is finished with wood and brass.

A number of cruises depart daily from Queenstown all year round, from 90-minute cruises to 4-hour dinner cruises in the warmer months. Visitors can also take daytime or evening excursions across the lake to the **Walter Peak High Country Farm**. Enjoy refreshments at the Colonel's Homestead Restaurant, go horse trekking or mountain biking, or see displays of high country activities, such as sheep shearing and sheep dogs in action. Electric bike tours can be booked on www.realjourneys.co.nz.

Underwater Observatory

Main Town Pier. **Tel** (03) 442 6142; 0800 529 272. **Open** daily.

Built beneath the Main Town Pier, Underwater Observatory provides a unique opportunity to see life below the surface of the lake. From a viewing lounge 5 m (16 ft) under the water, visitors can observe brown and rainbow trout peacefully swimming alongside enormous New Zealand long-finned eels, which are often joined by diving black teal ducks.

The Mall

The best way to enjoy and get to know Queenstown is on foot and probably the best place to start is at The Mall, which is a popular meeting place with a food court for visitors and a pedestrian-only street dominated by a variety of restaurants, cafés and pubs, as well as numerous souvenir shops. The Mall leads directly down to the Maintown Pier from which boats and jet boats regularly depart for cruises on the lake.

A number of interesting old colonial buildings, such as the former bank, remain in The Mall.

Skyline Gondola

Brecon St. **Tel** (03) 441 0101. **Open** daily. **skyline.co.nz**

The gondola up to Bob's Peak is synonymous with Queenstown. It rises 450 m (1,476 ft) in just 730 m (2,400 ft) and provides breathtaking panoramic views of The Remarkables, Lake Wakatipu and Queenstown from the observation deck at the top. Visitors can eat at the restaurant or café, take walks in the area, watch parapenters float down from the peak or take an exhilarating ride downhill on the luge – a short, raised toboggan. Many mountainbike trails can be accessed using the Gondola.

Skyline Gondola travelling up to Bob's Peak, with Queenstown below

VISITORS' CHECKLIST

Practical Information
Road map A6. 12,500.
queenstownnz.co.nz
i-SITE, Cnr Camp & Shotover sts, (03) 442 4100; 0800 668 888. Winter Festival (Jul).

Transport
6 km (4 miles) E of town. Steamer Wharf.

Kiwi Birdlife Park

Brecon St. Tel (03) 442 8059. **Open** daily. **Closed** 25 Dec. Kiwi House. one house. kiwibird.co.nz

Queenstown's Kiwi Birdlife Park, below the gondola terminal, is home to several kiwis and other endangered native birds as well as Tuatara. The birds are either part of national breeding programmes for release into the wild, or are being rehabilitated after injury.

A major attraction is the nocturnal Kiwi House where visitors can see kiwis and other species including native owls, large alpine parrots known as kea, parakeets, and the black stilt – a rare wader *(see p255)*. in natural, parklike surroundings.

Queenstown Town Centre

① Lake Wakatipu
② Queenstown Gardens
③ TSS *Earnslaw*
④ Underwater Observatory
⑤ The Mall
⑥ Skyline Gondola
⑦ Kiwi Birdlife Park

0 metres 400
0 yards 400

For keys to symbols *see back flap*

⑪ Glenorchy

Road map A6. 🏔 360. 🛈 Glenorgy Information Centre, Cnr Mull & Oban sts, (03) 409 2049.

Glenorchy is a small township at the head of Lake Wakatipu, 44 km (27 miles) or 45 minutes' drive from Queenstown. The town stands in the shadow of snow-capped peaks with names such as Mount Chaos and Mount Head which rise steeply above the Rees and Dart river valleys.

The town is the transit point for hikers entering the valleys, which are part of the Mount Aspiring National Park *(see pp276–7)*, and which are among New Zealand's Great Walks. For the serious hiker, there is a 77 km (48 mile) loop track which connects both valleys via the 1,447 m (4,747 ft) Rees Saddle. Although it takes four to five days and requires proper equipment, it is also possible to enjoy a few hours' return walk up either valley. A variety of outdoor activities are available at Glenorchy.

⑫ Arrowtown

Road map B6. 🏔 2,700. 🛈 49 Buckingham St (in museum), (03) 442 1824. 🍂 Autumn Festival (Apr).

Nestled at the foot of rugged hills 21 km (13 miles) from Queenstown, Arrowtown is the most picturesque and best preserved gold-mining town in the area. In 1862, a small band of miners, including William Fox and John O'Callaghan, discovered gold in the Fox River and within weeks they had recovered 113 kg (250 lb) of the precious metal. Arrowtown's population peaked at more than 7,000 and is one of the

Lake Hayes near Arrowtown

few boom towns not to have either become a ghost town or been overrun by more modern development. The main street, partly lined with deciduous trees, has many old colonial shops and buildings at one end and, at the other, tiny miners' stone cottages dating back to the 1860s and 1870s.

Chinese miners played a big part in Arrowtown's history after 1865, when they were invited to fill the vacuum created by European miners who had left for the West Coast gold rush. Their legacy is Arrowtown's **Chinese Village** with its pre-served and restored stone buildings, including tiny cottages, an outhouse and a store.

The **Lakes District Museum and Art Gallery** chronicles both Arrowtown and Queenstown's past, focusing on gold-miners and their innovations. It includes a display on New Zealand's first hydroelectric plant, built in 1886 in what is now the ghost town of Bullendale. Other

Stone cottage at the Chinese Village

displays cover local geology, agriculture, sawmilling and domestic life of the gold rush period. The museum doubles as Arrowtown's visitor centre.

🏯 **Chinese Village**
Buckingham St. **Tel** (03) 442 1824. **Open** daily. 🔗 assisted.

🏛 **Lakes District Museum and Art Gallery**
49 Buckingham St. **Tel** (03) 442 1824. **Open** daily. **Closed** 25 Dec. 📷 🔗 📷 📷

Environs
Near to Arrowtown is the much-photographed **Lake Hayes**, at its best in autumn. The back road from Arrowtown to Queenstown passes the access road to Coronet Peak which heads 7 km (4 miles) up to great views from the ski area. **Macetown** is a historic goldfield settlement, and a popular desti-nation for 4WD vehicles. A 26 km (16 mile) return journey from Arrowtown takes visitors up a steep, gold-bearing gorge. Ghost town relics include the remains of old stone buildings and a gold stamping battery.

Gibbston Valley Winery is a good example of vineyards in the area *(see pp40–41)*. Euro-pean varieties thrive in the hot summer days and cool evenings. Gibbston's wine is stored in a cool underground cave, and tours and wine tastings are available.

🍷 **Gibbston Valley Winery**
State Hwy 6. **Tel** (03) 442 6910. **Open** daily. **Closed** most public hols. 🔗 📷 📷 cave. 📷 📷 🌐 gibbstonvalley.com

The main street of Arrowtown

⑬ Cromwell

Road map B7. 5,000.
ℹ️ i-SITE, 2 The Mall (03) 262 7999.

Cromwell survived the gold era to become a service town in one of New Zealand's leading fruit-growing areas. In the 1980s, an electricity generating dam built down river created nearby Lake Dunstan, flooding much of Cromwell's quaint and historic main street, although several of the more notable buildings were relocated stone by stone to a new site. Cromwell now makes its living from farming, horticulture, viticulture and tourism.

Environs
Gold-mining relics in the area include **Bendigo**, a ghost town 4 km (2 miles) off State Highway 8, the main road between Cromwell and Lindis Pass. By 1866 Bendigo was all but deserted until a rich gold-bearing quartz reef was found, and mined for more than 50 years.
    A loop track above Bendigo leads to **Logantown** and **Welshtown**, two associated settlements deserted in the 1880s. It is wise to keep to the tracks because there are many old unmarked mine shafts throughout the area.
    The **Goldfields Mining Centre** in the Kawarau Gorge, 5 km (3 miles) from Cromwell, offers visitors working exhibitions of gold-mining techniques.

The Gold Rush

The Otago gold rush began with the discovery of gold in Gabriel's Gully in 1861, near the present-day town of Lawrence, 92 km (57 miles) west of Dunedin. A tent town sprang up and prospectors soon began pushing further inland. Finds in the Dunstan area around Cromwell and Alexandra followed in 1862, with discoveries in the Wakatipu region soon after. Tens of thousands braved hot, dry summers, cold, harsh winters and starvation in search of a quick fortune. New discoveries were made in other corners of the province, but by the late 1860s the focus had shifted to the West Coast. With the main fields well picked over, more sophisticated methods, such as sluicing, dredging and quartz reef mining, were needed to extract gold. Gold-mining continued well into the 1900s and the development of modern methods has led to large-scale mining operations in the area.

Arrowtown miners at their claim in the 1860s

🏛 **Goldfields Mining Centre**
Kawarau Gorge, State Hwy 6. **Tel** (03) 445 1038. **Open** daily. **Closed** 25 Dec.

⑭ Kingston

Road map A7. 65. Kingston to Queenstown Yacht Race (Jan).

For a long time the little settlement of Kingston served as a railhead and steamer terminal for travellers heading towards Lake Wakatipu from the south. Now a small town, Kingston continues to serve as a lovely stop for visitors, with its beautiful lakeside scenery, picnic spots and cafés.

Environs
To the south of Kingston, on State Highway 6, is **Lumsden**, well known for the trout-filled rivers that crisscross the countryside surrounding the town. Just before Lumsden, State Highway 94 branches west to Te Anau, Manapouri and Fiordland National Park, and east to the farming area of Gore.

Milky blue waters of Lake Wakatipu on the South Island

⓯ Fiordland National Park

Fiordland National Park's 12,500 sq km (4,826 sq miles) make it the largest of New Zealand's National Parks, while its special geology, landscape, flora and fauna have earned it a place in the Te Wāhipounamu – Southwest New Zealand World Heritage Area. It is a region dominated by forest and water. Its 14 fiords and 5 major lakes – the work of Ice Age glaciers – flanked by steep mountains clad with thick, temperate rainforest, make the interior virtually impenetrable except along its 500 km (310 miles) of walking tracks. The park is also known for its wildlife, especially its marine mammals and native birds, including the Fiordland crested penguin.

★ **Doubtful Sound**
This fiord extends 40 km (25 miles) from the foot of the main mountain divide to the open waters of the Tasman Sea *(see pp288–9).*

How the Fiords were Formed

Although named otherwise, Milford Sound/Piopiotahi, Doubtful Sound and the other sounds are, in fact, fiords. Sounds are flooded river valleys whereas fiords are valleys carved by the tremendous pressure and power of glaciers during successive Ice Ages, then later flooded by the sea as the ice melts and sea levels rise.

Rounded peak / V-shaped valley / Horn

10 million years ago, intense pressure in the earth's crust caused the most recent uplift in the area, forming peaks and V-shaped valleys.

Glacier

2 million years ago, the mountains were covered by glaciers. Ridges and peaks became sharper and valleys became U-shaped.

Hanging valley / U-shaped valley

20,000 – 12,000 years ago, the ice melted as the Ice Age receded, leaving the tributaries of rivers as hanging valleys above the main valley.

Flooded valley

6,000 years ago, at the end of the last Ice Age, the sea reached its present levels, flooding the valleys and leaving the peaks exposed.

DOUBTFUL SOUND

DUSKY SOUND

Dusky Sound
This sound can be reached by chartered cruise boat from Lake Manapouri via Doubtful Sound, or, for experienced climbers, via the 10-day Dusky Track.

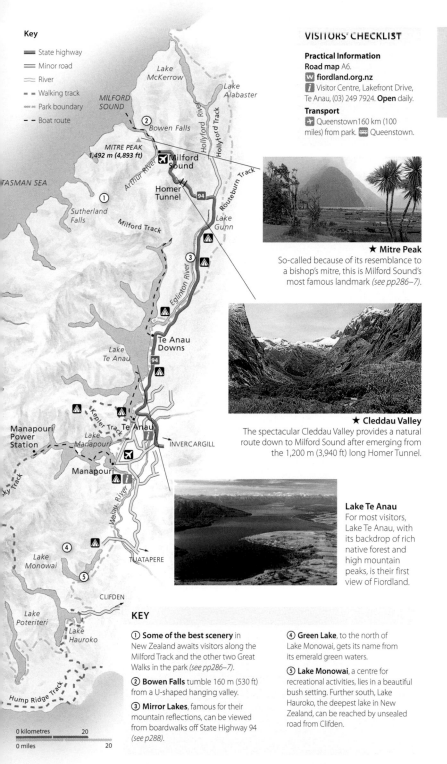

Key

━━ State highway
═══ Minor road
〜 River
- - Walking track
--- Park boundary
- - Boat route

TASMAN SEA

Lake McKerrow

Lake Alabaster

MILFORD SOUND

Bowen Falls ②

MITRE PEAK
1,492 m (4,893 ft)

Milford Sound

Hollyford River

Hollyford Track

Routeburn Track

Arthur River

Homer Tunnel

94

Lake Gunn

Sutherland Falls

①

Milford Track

Eglinton river

③

Te Anau Downs

94

Lake Te Anau

Manapouri Power Station

Kepler Track

Lake Te Anau

Te Anau

INVERCARGILL

Manapouri

Lake Manapouri

Waiau River

④ Lake Monowai

⑤

TUATAPERE

CLIFDEN

Lake Poteriteri

Lake Haurko

Hump Ridge Track

0 kilometres   20
0 miles   20

VISITORS' CHECKLIST

Practical Information
Road map A6.
🌐 fiordland.org.nz
ℹ Visitor Centre, Lakefront Drive,
Te Anau, (03) 249 7924. **Open** daily.

Transport
✈ Queenstown 160 km (100
miles) from park. 🚌 Queenstown.

★ **Mitre Peak**
So-called because of its resemblance to
a bishop's mitre, this is Milford Sound's
most famous landmark *(see pp286–7)*.

★ **Cleddau Valley**
The spectacular Cleddau Valley provides a natural
route down to Milford Sound after emerging from
the 1,200 m (3,940 ft) long Homer Tunnel.

Lake Te Anau
For most visitors,
Lake Te Anau, with
its backdrop of rich
native forest and
high mountain
peaks, is their first
view of Fiordland.

KEY

① **Some of the best scenery** in
New Zealand awaits visitors along the
Milford Track and the other two Great
Walks in the park *(see pp286–7)*.

② **Bowen Falls** tumble 160 m (530 ft)
from a U-shaped hanging valley.

③ **Mirror Lakes**, famous for their
mountain reflections, can be viewed
from boardwalks off State Highway 94
(see p288).

④ **Green Lake**, to the north of
Lake Monowai, gets its name from
its emerald green waters.

⑤ **Lake Monowai**, a centre for
recreational activities, lies in a beautiful
bush setting. Further south, Lake
Haurko, the deepest lake in New
Zealand, can be reached by unsealed
road from Clifden.

For keys to symbols *see back flap*

Exploring Fiordland National Park

With mountains rising 2,750 m (9,020 ft), sheer rock walls climbing 1,200 m (3,940 ft) from deep fiords, and waterfalls tumbling 160 m (530 ft), Fiordland's spectacular landscape attracts visitors from around the world. The Māori were the first to exploit the area's natural resources, then came sealers who from 1792 to the 1820s slaughtered hundreds of thousands of fur seals. Until 1953, when State Highway 94 (the Milford Road) was completed, the only way to Milford Sound was by boat or via the Milford Track. Today, visitors arrive by the busload, and those with the time, fitness and equipment can walk the famous tracks. Others visit the sound by boat or scenic flight.

Milford road along the picturesque Cleddau Valley in summer

Te Anau

Road map A7. 🗺 1,800. 🚌 Miro St. ℹ️ Lakefront Drive, (03) 249 2924.

The picturesque town of Te Anau, on the southeastern shore of Lake Te Anau, is the largest town in Fiordland and a good base for exploring Fiordland National Park. The lake, the largest in the South Island, is 61 km (38 miles) long and 417 m (1,370 ft) deep, the result of glacial action. It is a popular venue for boating and fishing.

🎭 Te Ana-au Caves

ℹ️ Real Journeys Visitor Centre, Lakefront Drive, Te Anau. **Tel** (03) 249 7416. **Open** daily. 🚤 📷

At the Te Ana-au Caves, reached by a boat trip across Lake Te Anau, a combination of carefully formed walkways and small boats allow visitors to explore a series of magical limestone grottos. The caves are home to thousands of tiny New Zealand glowworms, which use their tiny light – the result of a chemical reaction – to attract insects for food. Return trips, which depart several times a day, take two and a half hours.

🎭 The Milford Road

The 121 km (75 mile) road to Milford Sound from Te Anau has earned World Heritage Highway status for its beauty and scenic variety. This includes lush lakeside forest, rugged mountains, cascading alpine rivers and picturesque walks. Although Milford Sound can be reached by road in 2 hours, there are many side trips possible along the way to make the drive more memorable.

Te Anau Downs, 30 km (19 miles) from Te Anau, is the departure point for the boat to the Milford Track. From here there is a 45-minute forest walk to Lake Mistletoe. Further on, the Mirror Lakes are a short five-minute walk from the road across a boardwalk *(see p258)*. On a calm day, beautiful reflections of the surrounding scenery are visible in the lakes. At Lake Gunn, about 46 km (29 miles) from Te Anau Downs, an easy 45-minute loop through beech forest is suitable for all ages and for people in wheelchairs. The Divide, a short distance away, marks the start of the Routeburn Track, which leads overland to the stunning Lake Wakatipu (note that the track does not actually reach the lake, but ends at the road that then leads to the lake 10–15 km (6–9 miles) away). A 3-hour return walk to Key Summit gives rewarding views. The nearby Hollyford Valley also makes a scenic trip.

Nineteen kilometres (12 miles) east of Milford Sound is the 1,200-m- (3,940-ft-) long Homer Tunnel, started in 1935 but not completed until 1954. Leaving the tunnel, the road slopes very steeply downhill to the Milford side where there are spectacular views along the Cleddau Valley. The Chasm, a few kilometres from the tunnel, can be reached by a 20-minute walk to where the Cleddau River drops 22 m (72 ft) through a series of unusual rock formations.

NEXT **35 km**

Sheep warning sign, Milford Road

The impressive, rocky coastline of Te Anau

Milford Sound

Road map A6. 170.

Milford Sound, a 16 km (10 mile) long fiord, is Fiordland's best-known attraction. Its most famous landmark is Mitre Peak, a pyramid-shaped mountain rising 1,692 m (5,550 ft) straight from the deep fiord. Although scenic flights are available, the grandeur of Milford Sound can be best appreciated by boat. Trips pass unusual geological features, such as Lion Mountain, the Elephant and Copper Point, as well as waterfalls: the Bowen Falls drop 160 m (530 ft) into the water, and the Stirling Falls 146 m (480 ft). Fur seals, dolphins, and the occasional Fiordland crested penguin can be seen along the way.

An Underwater Observatory at Milford Sound allows visitors to see the unusual black coral, red coral, anemones, starfish and fish that live in the fiord. High rainfall means there is a 3–4 m (10–13 ft) layer of fresh water above the underlying salt water.

Apart from day trips in the Milford Sound, full-day and overnight cruises take visitors out of the sound to the open Tasman Sea, with stops at other sounds, such as Dusky Sound. Cruises often combine fishing, kayaking and diving.

Great Walks in Fiordland National Park

Hikers on the Milford Track

Fiordland National Park is considered by many to be the best place in New Zealand for hikers. Its three major walking tracks – the Milford, Routeburn and Kepler *(see pp284–5)* – can be walked independently, or on the Milford in a guided group, all year round. Advance booking is essential for the Milford and Routeburn tracks *(see pp334–5)* during the peak hiking season, while all tracks require advance purchase of hut or campsite passes. All three walks are suitable only for experienced, well-equipped parties.

The spectacular 55 km (34 mile) **Milford Track**, which takes four days, climbs through the Clinton Valley to the Mackinnon Pass. It passes the Sutherland Falls before dropping down to Milford Sound. The 39 km (24 mile) **Routeburn Track** usually takes three days. It climbs through forest to spectacular subalpine terrain before crossing the Harris Saddle and descending the Routeburn Valley towards Lake Wakatipu. The **Kepler Track**, a three- to four-day 60 km (37 mile) loop, skirts Lake Te Anau, then climbs to panoramic views from Mount Luxmore before descending to Lake Manapouri.

Typical alpine plant

Milford Sound, Fjordland's most famous attraction

⓰ A Trip to Doubtful Sound

Doubtful Sound was named by Captain James Cook in 1770, on his voyage to New Zealand when, looking at the narrow entrance to the sound, he was doubtful that he could safely get his vessel in and out. The 40-km-(25-mile-) long fiord is Fiordland's second largest and, at 421 m (1,380 ft), the deepest. It is a remote, unspoilt wilderness of mountain peaks, fiords and rainforest that supports a rich array of bird and marine life, including crested penguins, fur seals and bottlenose dolphins. Getting there is an adventure in itself, involving two boat trips and a coach ride over a mountain pass, with a side trip deep underground to the huge Manapouri Power Station generator hall.

① Lake Manapouri
The trip to Doubtful Sound begins at the Pearl Harbour marina on the Waiau River, which feeds into Lake Manapouri. The lake, which is forested to the shoreline, covers 142 sq km (55 sq miles) and is dotted with 34 islands.

⑩ New Zealand Fur Seals
Colonies of New Zealand's most common seal can be seen on the islands dotting the entrance to Doubtful Sound.

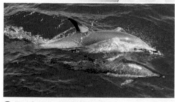

⑨ Bottlenose Dolphins
A resident pod of bottlenose dolphins may be seen playing in the waters at Malaspina Reach. They grow up to 4.5 m (15 ft).

Tasman Sea

Thompson Sound

Secretary Island

⑩

Bauza Island

Bradshaw Sound

⑨

Crooked Arm

Malaspina Reach

⑧

Hall Arm

⑦

Tailrace

⑥

④

⑤

⑧ Commander Peak
To the left at the head of Hall Arm, Commander Peak is one of many awe-inspiring bush-clad peaks that visitors see during a cruise of Doubtful Sound's flooded glacial valleys *(see p284).*

⑦ Deep Cove
The peaceful waters of Deep Cove hide the 10 km (6 mile) tunnel under the mountains from the Manapouri Power Station.

Manapouri Power Station

The Manapouri Power Station is a man-made wonder that takes advantage of the difference in height of the mountains between Lake Manapouri and Doubtful Sound to act as a natural dam. Water is chanelled through vertical penstocks into seven

generators housed in a huge underground room. The water then flows out of a 10 km (6 mile) tunnel to Deep Cove. The electricity generated is used to power the Comalco Aluminium Smelter 171 km (106 miles) to the south, at Bluff.

Underground machine hall

② Manapouri Power Station
Coaches take visitors down a 2 km (1.2 mile) spiral access tunnel to the machine hall, which is carved out of solid granite 213 m (700 ft) under the mountains at West Arm.

④ Moss Gardens
Dozens of species of moss growing on a rock face show how plant life can get a foothold in all sorts of terrain in this high rainfall environment.

③ Wilmot Pass Road
The 22 km (13 mile) Wilmot Pass Road, completed in May 1965 to facilitate the building of the Manapouri Power Station tailrace at Deep Cove, cost more than $2 per cm ($5 per inch) to build.

Tips for Visitors

This trip takes eight hours and can only be undertaken with a commercial tour operator. Winter is the best time of year for clear views and little rain, but the busiest time for tours is spring and summer. Visitors can order a picnic lunch or snack-pack when booking but are advised to take additional food. Insect repellent, warm clothing and a waterproof jacket are also essential.
Boat trips: Real Journeys (03) 249 7416. **Overnight cruises:** Doubtful Sound Cruise (03) 249 6616; Fiordland Expeditions (03) 249 9005; Fiordland Cruises (03) 249 7777; Deep Cove Charters (03) 249 6828. The Sound may also be explored by sea kayak.

⑤ Cleve Garth Falls
The 365 m (1,200ft) high Cleve Garth Falls make a breathtaking entrance from a mountain ridge high above the Wilmott Pass Road.

Lake Te Anau

Te Anau

94

Gore

Kepler Mountains

Waiau River

West Arm

Lake Manapouri

South Arm

Hope Arm

Hunter Mountains

Waiau River

Manapouri

1

0 kilometres 5

0 miles 5

⑥ Wilmot Pass Summit
The 670 m (2,200 ft) summit is reached after a winding drive through cool temperate rainforest. The road then descends a one-in-five slope to Deep Cove.

Key
- - Boat tour route
■ Coach tour route
═ Other roads
▨ River

⑰ Invercargill

New Zealand's southernmost city, and the commercial hub of Southland, Invercargill is a well-planned city with wide, tree-lined streets and many parks and reserves. Settled in the 1850s and 1860s by Scottish immigrants, the city's cultural links with Scotland are reflected in the streets named after Scottish rivers and in its many historic buildings. To the west of the city are several sheltered beaches and walking tracks.

🌳 Queen's Park
Gala St. **Open** daily.
The best-known reserve in the city centre is the 0.8 sq km (0.3 sq mile) Queen's Park, a botanical reserve featuring formal gardens, including rose gardens and the extensive Steans Memorial Winter Garden. There is also a small wildlife park containing deer and wallabies, an aviary, and a challenging 18-hole golf course.

🏛 Southland Museum and Art Gallery
108 Gala St. **Tel** (03) 219 9069.
Open daily. **Closed** 25 Dec. ♿ 🎥 by arrangement. 💻 📷 🎁 donation.
🌐 **southlandmuseum.co.nz**
Apart from its three art exhibition galleries, the Southland Museum and Art Gallery, housed in a pyramid-shaped building near the entrance to Queen's Park, contains displays outlining the area's human and natural

Tuatara at the Southland Museum and Art Gallery

history. It also features a tuatarium *(see p28)* where visitors can see several of New Zealand's "living fossils" at close range. The "Roaring Forties Experience" at the Subantarctic Islands Interpretive Centre provides an introduction to New Zealand's five remote island reserves, which lie hundreds of kilometres to the south of Invercargill.

🏢 Water Tower
Leet St.
A distinctive landmark in the city, the 42-m- (138-ft-) high red

brick water tower, completed in 1889, is a fine example of Neo-Romanesque industrial design of the time.

🏢 Dee and Tay Streets
Invercargill's early prosperity resulted in the construction of many fine commercial buildings and churches. At the northern end of Dee Street lies the former Dee Street Hospital, the oldest public hospital buildings in New Zealand, and the quaint former Porter's Lodge, built around 1866 and reputed to be the oldest house in Invercargill. Nearby is St Paul's Presbyterian Church, whose square tower houses bells manufactured in Italy from captured guns. Further down, the 1901 red-brick Alexander Building is noted for its eclectic style, while the Grand Hotel opposite has fine iron balconies.

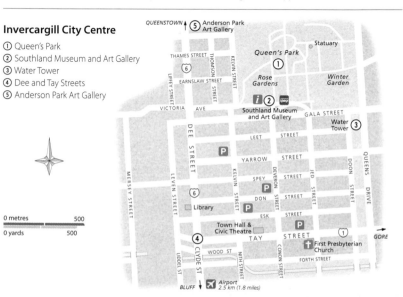

Invercargill City Centre

① Queen's Park
② Southland Museum and Art Gallery
③ Water Tower
④ Dee and Tay Streets
⑤ Anderson Park Art Gallery

0 metres 500
0 yards 500

QUEENSTOWN ⑤ Anderson Park Art Gallery
THAMES STREET
THOMSON STREET
KELVIN STREET
Statuary
Queen's Park ①
⑥
LIFFEY STREET
EARNSLAW STREET
Rose Gardens
Winter Garden
VICTORIA AVE
🛈 ②
Southland Museum and Art Gallery
GALA STREET
Water Tower ③
DEE STREET
LEET STREET
MERSEY STREET
LEVEN STREET
🅿
YARROW STREET
KELVIN STREET
SPEY STREET
DEVERON STREET
DOON STREET
QUEENS DRIVE
⑥
🅿
DON STREET
JED STREET
Library
🅿
ESK STREET
Town Hall & Civic Theatre
TAY STREET
CONON STREET
GORE
④
⑦ First Presbyterian Church
CLYDE ST
WOOD ST
NITH STREET
FORTH STREET
LIDDEL ST
BLUFF ↓ ✈ Airport 2.5 km (1.8 miles)

Anderson Park Art Gallery and gardens

At the intersection of Dee Street and Tay Street (Invercargill's main street) stands the impressive Troopers' Memorial flanked by three elegant bank buildings, erected between 1876 and 1926. In Tay Street is the imposing Renaissance-style Civic Theatre, completed in 1906, and St John's Anglican Church, noted for its stained-glass windows and timber barrel-vaulted ceiling. The Lombardy-style Romanesque First Presbyterian Church, also in Tay Street, features an unusual square 32 m (105 ft) tower.

🏛 Anderson Park and Art Gallery

91 McIvor Rd. **Tel** (03) 215 7432. **Open** 10:30am–5pm daily. **Closed** Good Fri, 25 Dec. 🖼 donation. 📷 inside. 🚻 ground floor. 📷 by arrangement.

Five kilometres (3 miles) north of the city centre, this beautiful Georgian-style house built in 1925 and set in 0.2 sq km (0.08 sq mile) of lovely gardens and native bush, houses a fine collection of New Zealand art.

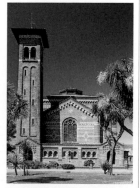

First Presbyterian Church in Tay Street

⑱ Gore

Road map B7. 🔼 8,500. 🚌 🛈 Cnr Hokonui Drive & Norfolk St, (03) 203 9288. 🎸 New Zealand Gold Guitar Awards (May–Jun). 🖥 **gorenz.com**

Lying 66 km (41 miles) north of Invercargill, Gore has varied claims to fame: brown trout in the Mataura River and its tributaries (symbolized by a large trout statue in the middle of the town), sheep (the town is surrounded by fertile farmlands and thrives as an agricultural service town), and a reputation as the country music capital of New Zealand (fans come each May for the New Zealand Gold Guitar Awards).

The Gore Visitor Centre, in the Hokonui Heritage Centre, incorporates the **Gore Historical Museum** and the **Hokonui Moonshine Museum**. The latter covers the period when whisky was made illegally in Hokonui.

The **East Gore Art Gallery** (nicknamed the "Goreggenheim") features major works by New Zealand artists.

Fifteen km (9 miles) west, on State Highway 94, is the **Croydon Aviation Heritage Centre**, which restores vintage aircraft and offers flights to visitors.

🏛 Gore Historical Museum and Hokonui Moonshine Museum

Hokonui Heritage Centre, Cnr Hokonui Drive & Norfolk St. **Tel** (03) 203 9288. **Open** daily. **Closed** 1 Jan, Good Fri, 25 Dec. 🚻 📷

🏛 East Gore Art Gallery

Cnr Hokonui Drive & Norfolk St. **Tel** (03) 208 9907. **Open** daily. **Closed** 1 Jan, Good Fri, 25 & 26 Dec. 🚻 📷

✈ Croydon Aviation Heritage Centre

Tel (03) 208 9755. **Open** daily. **Closed** 25 Dec. 🚻 📷 by arrangement.

⑲ Bluff

Road map A7. 🔼 2,000. 🚌 Gore St. 🚢 Stewart Island Wharf. 🎣 Bluff Oyster & Food Festival (May). 🖥 **bluff.co.nz**

Bluff is New Zealand's southernmost export port and the departure point for ferries to Stewart Island. It is also the base for fishing fleets that cruise the south and west coasts for fish, crayfish and rock lobsters as well as the famous "Bluff oysters". Unique to New Zealand, the oysters are harvested during a limited season from March to the end of August.

Bluff has a long history of human occupation, with Māori settlement dating back to the 13th century. The town is named after the 265 m- (870 ft-) high Bluff Hill which overlooks Foveaux Strait towards Stewart Island, which lies 32 km (20 miles) away. Beneath the hill is Stirling Point – the end of State Highway 1 – where there is a much photographed international signpost. Several walks, including the Foveaux Walkway and the Glory Track, pass through native forest. A 45-minute climb up the hill gives panoramic views of the Foveaux Strait and inland areas.

The **Bluff Maritime Museum** traces the history of whaling, muttonbirding and oyster harvesting, as well as development of the port and the Stewart Island ferry.

🏛 Bluff Maritime Museum

241 Foreshore Rd. **Tel** (03) 212 7534. **Open** daily. **Closed** Good Fri, Easter Sun, 25 Dec. 🖼 🚻 📷 by arrangement. 📷

International signpost at Stirling Point, Bluff

For hotels and restaurants in this region see p307 and pp324–5

⑳ Stewart Island

According to Māori legend, Stewart Island, New Zealand's third largest island, was the anchor of Maui's canoe (the South Island) when he pulled the great fish (the North Island) from the sea. Separated from the South Island by the 32-km (20-mile) Foveaux Strait, 85 per cent of Stewart Island became the Rakiura National Park in 2002. Its unspoilt inlets and beaches, bush-clad hills, rugged coastline and native birdlife combine to make the 1,746 sq km (674 sq mile) island a naturalist's paradise. First settled by Māori in the 13th century, Europeans arrived in the 1820s. Today's small population makes a living from fishing and tourism.

Paterson Inlet from Observation Rock

Oban

Oban, Stewart Island's only settlement, sits snugly around the picturesque, protected shores of Halfmoon Bay. It is easy to explore the town on foot but a 90-minute bus tour along Oban's 28 km (17 miles) of road takes visitors past the main points of interest.

From Oban many short tracks lead through beautiful bush to places of scenic or historic interest, and to lookouts with stunning views, including Observation Rock, which provides splendid views over Paterson Inlet towards Ulva Island. On a clear, summer evening it is easy to see why Māori named Stewart Island "the land of the glowing skies". Several beautiful beaches also lie within walking distance to the north and east of the town.

The island offers a range of accommodation options, such as backpacker inns, beach houses, motels, bed and breakfasts, and the century-old South Sea Hotel. The Rakiura Museum in Ayr Street, which is open daily, provides a fascinating insight into Stewart Island's past, such as Māori settlement, its seafaring history and relics of whaling, sealing, tin mining and timber milling.

Boat charters are also available from Oban, catering for a whole range of interests, including fishing, sightseeing and wildlife spotting. For the more active visitor, diving, kayak hire and guided sea kayak excursions are among the many exciting activities that are on offer.

South Sea Hotel on the shores of Halfmoon Bay

🦞 Paterson Inlet

Over the hill from Halfmoon Bay is the 16 km- (10 mile-) long Paterson Inlet, which extends deep into the hinterland. Charter boats and a water taxi can be hired in Oban and Golden Bay for sightseers, divers and those wanting to catch their own fish. These trips are also a great opportunity to view various seabirds, including yellow-eyed and little blue penguins and molly-mawks, as well as seals and dolphins. The remains of an old sawmill and whaling station are also accessible from the inlet.

⬛ Ulva Island

Located in the centre of Paterson Inlet, Ulva Island is a 10-minute trip by water taxi from the wharf at Golden Bay. The island is predator-free, creating a sanctuary where visitors can get a close look at native New Zealand birds. Walks on the island range from 15 minutes to 3 hours.

⑦

Cod:
Islar

Doughb
Bay

PEA

Muttonbird
Islands

Stewart Island

① Oban
② Paterson Inlet
③ Ulva Island
④ Ocean Beach
⑤ Big Glory Bay
⑥ Titī Islands
⑦ Codfish Island

⚄ Ocean Beach

"Kiwi spotting" (viewing kiwis at night in their natural habitat) is an experience unique to Stewart Island. Licensed tour operators take small groups by boat to the Neck in Little Glory Bay, then on foot through the bush to Ocean Beach where the Stewart Island brown kiwi can be seen feeding as darkness falls.

⚄ Big Glory Bay

Salmon and mussel farming have become important industries in Paterson Inlet. A boat trip takes visitors to a salmon farm at Big Glory Bay, past seal colonies and shag rookeries, with a stopover at Ulva Island on the way.

⚄ Titī Islands

Muttonbirds, or sooty shearwaters, breed on Stewart Island's many offshore islands after a round-the-world migration. Long a source of food, young birds are harvested each April by descendants of the Rakiura Māori. By day, Ackers Point lighthouse gives panoramic views of the islands, and at night during the breeding season (October to April), visitors can hear the muttonbirds returning to land. Some tour operators are licenced to take visitors to the islands to view the birds from the boat.

Muttonbird (sooty shearwater) leaving its burrow

⚄ Codfish Island/Whenua Hou

Codfish Island, about 3 km (2 miles) off the northwest coast of Stewart Island, has been cleared of introduced fauna and is now a protected sanctuary for some 60 species of birds, including the rare and endangered kakapo, a large, flightless, nocturnal parrot. Visitors are not allowed to visit the island.

Walking the Island

Stewart Island has a number of tracks that take visitors into some of New Zealand's most beautiful bush. From Oban, a three-hour return walk through coastal forest to Ackers Point Lighthouse goes past one of New Zealand's oldest buildings, Ackers Cottage, built in 1835. The Ryan's Creek Track is a three- to four-hour loop through coastal forest above Paterson Inlet. For the fitter visitor, there is the Rakiura Track, which is a popular three-day circuit that climbs a high, forested ridge and traverses the sheltered Paterson Inlet.
There are also 10- to 14-day North-West and Southern Circuits, for which hut and camp passes must be obtained from the visitor centre in Oban. For further information on any of the walks call (03) 219 0002.

Hiker on the Rakiura Track, north of Oban

Map labels

North-West Circuit
MOUNT ANGLEM
980 m (3,215 ft) ▲
RUGGEDY MOUNTAINS
Foveaux Strait
Freshwater River
THOMSON RIDGE
Rakiura Track
Port William
BLUFF
⑥
⑦
ⓧ ⓘ
Horseshoe Point
Ackers Point
①
Southern Circuit
Duck Creek
MOUNT RAKEAHUA
681 m (2,234 ft) ▲
②
③
Carter Passage
ADAMS HILL
401 m (1,316 ft) ▲
⑤
④
DOUGHBOY HILL
446 m (1,463 ft) ▲
Rakeahua River
TIN RANGE
Heron River
Gorge Creek
Lords River
Kopeko River
Port Pegasus

0 kilometres 10
0 miles 10

Key

═══ River
– – Ferry route
▪ ▪ Walking track

㉑ Tour of the Catlins

Natural curiosities and beauty combine to make this southeastern corner of the South Island a scenic treasure. Fossilized trees, beautiful waterfalls, golden beaches, high cliffs and secret caves are all part of a unique mix of attractions in this area, commonly referred to as the Catlins after one of the early landowners of the 1840s. A varied coastline of cliffs and golden sand surf beaches provides a home to a wide range of wildlife, from rare Hector's dolphins to penguins, seals and sea lions. The area is made all the more spectacular by the ancient forests of rimu, matai, totara, beech and miro, which reach almost to the sea, and which are filled with the sounds of native birds.

② **Curio Bay**
The fossilized remains of a 160 million-year-old forest from the Jurassic period can be seen on a rock platform at low tide.

① **Waipapa Point**
A picturesque spot but the site of New Zealand's worst shipping disaster when the SS *Tararua* ran aground on a hidden reef in 1881, with the loss of 131 lives.

⑨ **Nugget Point**
A lighthouse, built in 1869, stands sentry on a headland overlooking a series of wave-like pinnacles. The area is home to seals, sea lions, gannets, shags, penguins and shearwaters.

Fortrose

Niagara

Haldane Waikawa

Otara

0 km 5
0 miles 5

Tips for Drivers

Tour length: 172 km (107 miles) from Invercargill to where the tour rejoins State Hwy 1 at Balclutha. It is well worth allowing at least a day to complete the journey because of the number of side tracks and walks taking visitors to the many sights.
Stopping-off points: Most accommodation on this route is on a small scale. There are motels at Papatowai and Owaka, and camping grounds, backpackers hostels and homestays dotted around the area. If an overnight stay is planned, it is wise to book ahead. Food and refreshments are available at several places along the route.

⑧ **Jack's Blowhole**
Sea water surges through a subterranean tunnel before spraying out of this 60 m- (197 ft-) deep blowhole, located in the middle of cliff top pastures.

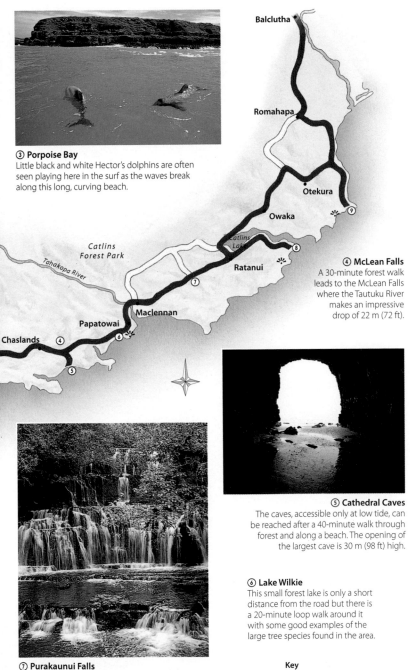

③ Porpoise Bay
Little black and white Hector's dolphins are often seen playing here in the surf as the waves break along this long, curving beach.

④ McLean Falls
A 30-minute forest walk leads to the McLean Falls where the Tautuku River makes an impressive drop of 22 m (72 ft).

⑤ Cathedral Caves
The caves, accessible only at low tide, can be reached after a 40-minute walk through forest and along a beach. The opening of the largest cave is 30 m (98 ft) high.

⑥ Lake Wilkie
This small forest lake is only a short distance from the road but there is a 20-minute loop walk around it with some good examples of the large tree species found in the area.

⑦ Purakaunui Falls
A ten-minute walk through beech and podocarp forest leads to a viewing platform overlooking these attractive waterfalls where the river drops 20 m (65 ft) over a series of wide terraces.

Key

▬ Tour route
═ Other road
〰 River

TRAVELLERS' NEEDS

WHERE TO STAY

A variety of accommodation to suit all budgets is available in New Zealand. At the top end of the range, five-star hotels and wilderness lodges provide luxury accommodation. Mid-range hotels, motels and motor lodges, self-catering apartments, country pubs, farmstays, and bed and breakfasts (B&Bs) cater for travellers on a more modest budget. For those on a very tight budget, camping grounds and backpacker hostels offer good value. Away from the larger cities and resorts, the choice of accommodation can be limited, although there are motels and backpacker hostels in virtually all locations. The listings on pages 302–307 give descriptions of the different types of accommodation throughout New Zealand to suit all budgets.

The beautiful setting of Eagles Nest villas in Russell *(see p303)*

Gradings and Facilities

The country's accommodation grading system, Qualmark, was established in 1994 and now serves as New Zealand tourism's official quality mark. All businesses carrying the Qualmark name have been independently assessed against a set of national quality standards. Accommodation is graded on a star system. One star indicates that the place meets the basic standards of comfort, cleanliness and hospitality; five stars denotes that the facility is superior in every way. The Qualmark system is voluntary, however, and many establishments choose not to participate in it.

Many of the large chain hotels are air-conditioned, but the New Zealand climate does not generally warrant air-conditioning. Hot showers and heating are provided in all types of accommodation. Linen is also provided in hotels and motels. In backpacker hostels and camping grounds, linen is not always provided but can usually be hired for a reasonable fee.

Prices

Luxury lodges start at about NZ$650 a night, while a room in a backpacker hostel can be as low as NZ$20 a night. Most motels are in the range of NZ$100 to NZ$180 per unit, while B&Bs cost between NZ$50 and NZ$100 per person. Many B&Bs, however, offer rooms for a set price, rather than charging per person. Off-season discounts are often available, and it is a good idea to ask about these when making bookings.

Bookings

It is advisable to book accommodation in advance, especially at peak holiday times (December to February). During winter (June to August), hotels and motels in ski resort towns are often fully booked during school holidays (two weeks in early July and late September to early October). Bookings can be made directly, through travel agents or at one of New Zealand's 100 visitor information centres.

In most cases, a credit card number will be requested when a booking is arranged. It is wise to ask about cancellation policies when making bookings as some premises will debit the credit card for one night's accommodation if a cancellation is made

Edwardian façade of the Scenic Hotel, Dunedin *(see p307)*

◀ The Tannery shopping and restaurant centre, Christchurch

Huka Lodge on the banks of the Waikato River *(see p304)*

at short notice. For additional services, such as children's cots, inform the hotel when making a booking.

Children

Travelling with children in New Zealand is easy, with cots and baby-sitting services generally available on request. However, children are not welcome at some exclusive lodges and guesthouses. The definition of a "child" among hotels varies, ranging from under 12 to 17 years. Children enjoy special rates only if they are the third or subsequent occupant of a room and do not request an extra bed. A useful website to look at is www.kidsnewzealand. com, which lists events as well as child-friendly places to visit, to eat at and to stay in.

Disabled Travellers

New Zealand law requires all new buildings as well as old buildings undergoing major renovation to provide "reasonable and adequate" access for the disabled. Many facilities have wheelchair access, but it is best to check in advance.

Luxury Lodges

Often located near a lake, river or beach, luxury lodges provide breathtaking scenery, elegant surroundings and high-quality

service for a limited number of guests at any one time. Many lodges specialise in fishing, hunting and other outdoor activi-ties, and their hosts often have extensive knowledge of the local area. Tariffs at the most exclusive lodges range from NZ$1,500 to NZ$10,000 a night, including meals and alcohol.

Chain Hotels

Several international luxury hotel chains, including the **Hyatt**, **Millennium**, **Novotel**, **Sofitel** and **Sheraton**, are represented in New Zealand. Other chains include the **Copthorne**, **Scenic Hotel Group**, **Heritage** and **Best Western NZ**, which offer a reliable standard of accom-modation in the main cities and resorts of New Zealand. Chain hotels offer a full range of services, including a tele-vision, minibar, telephone and en suite bathroom in all rooms, as well as room service and restaurants. Some hotels also

have sports, business and conference facilities. For hotel listings, see pages 302–307.

Motels and Motor Lodges

Motels are the most common form of visitor accommodation in New Zealand, and even small towns have at least one. They are particularly suitable for large families or groups because they are spacious and have their own cooking facilities. They usually contain one or two bedrooms, a lounge, kitchen and bath-room, and have a television set, radio, telephone and off-street parking. Smaller units, where guests sleep in the lounge or on a small mezzanine, are called studios. Larger motels and motor lodges are similar to hotels, with swimming pools, laundry facilities, restaurants and room service.

Travellers can save money by purchasing a motel accommo-dation pass for one of the local chains such as **Best Western NZ** or **Golden Chain NZ**.

Kauri Cliffs lodge, surrounded by lush forests *(see p302)*

Alpacas grazing in the sprawling grounds of Pete's Farm Stay, Rangiora *(see p306)*

Farmstays, Homestays and B&Bs

Farmstays offer visitors the chance to gain an insight into everyday farming life. Guests stay either in the farmhouse or in separate quarters, and may share meals with their hosts. Bathroom facilities may be either shared with the family or be separate in some cases. In many places, guests can participate in some farming activities if they choose to.

Homestays are located in both urban and rural areas, and, like farmstays, guests stay in the family home or in adjacent quarters and often share meals with their hosts. Tariffs for homestays and farmstays can range from NZ$100 to NZ$400 for a double room per night.

B&B's are also more pocket-friendly options and can be easily found throughout New Zealand. **The New Zealand Bed and Breakfast Book** has details about B&Bs across the country.

Backpacker Hostels and Youth Hostels

New Zealand has more than 250 backpacker hostels in scenic locations. **Budget Backpacker Hostels New Zealand** and **VIP Backpacker Resorts New Zealand** have a comprehensive list of hostels. Hostels are also clearly sign-posted along the main roads. They offer clean and inexpensive accommodation, and are excellent places to meet other travellers and exchange up-to-date information. However, they usually tend to attract younger clientele, so noise-averse travellers should be wary. Prices can be as low as NZ$20 per person for a shared room and NZ$30 for a single room.

Another option for low-budget travellers is the **Youth Hostel Association** (YHA), which has a chain of 56 hostels in strategic locations. Despite the name, youth hostels cater for travellers of all ages. They usually offer separate male and female dormitories, as well as twin, double and family rooms for those wanting more privacy. Linen and blankets are also provided. Youth hostels have well-equipped communal kitchens and comfortable lounges for relaxation. Bathroom facilities in most hostels are shared.

It is not necessary to be a member of the Youth Hostel

Accommodation sign in Marlborough

Association to stay at a hostel. However, non-members incur a surcharge of NZ$3–4 a night in addition to the regular fee.

Camping Grounds

Camping grounds (also called holiday parks and motor camps) offer a cheap way to travel. **Top 10 Holiday Parks** has a list of these. Some contain sites for tents and caravans only, while others have basic cabins fitted with bunk beds, or tourist flats with full cooking and bathroom facilities. Many have kids' playgrounds and games rooms, and are located beside beaches, lakes or rivers in scenic locations. Camping grounds have shared washing and laundry facilities, and fully equipped communal kitchens. Some have shops that sell basic foodstuffs and supplies. Advance booking is advisable during the holiday period, from Christmas to the end of January. Most camping grounds charge about NZ$7 a night per person for a campsite and from about NZ$30 for a double cabin.

Campervans

A popular way to see the country is in a self-drive campervan. Two-, four- and six-berth vans are available, complete with amenities *(see p359)*. Rental charges vary according to the season. Generally, campervan travellers stop for the night at camping

Campervan travellers taking a break by the sea

The Boatshed, a small luxury hotel on Waiheke Island, Auckland *(see p302)*

grounds where they can hire a site with electric power. In remote locations, travellers can park in a rest area near the roadside. Many camping grounds have "dump stations" for the disposal of sewage effluent.

Recommended Hotels

New Zealand is a beautiful island destination where the dramatic coastline is never far

Typical motor camp sign

away, and the plethora of accommodation options makes great use of sea and mountain views and stunning, awe-inspiring locations, right from luxurious top-dollar luxury residences down to more modest camping grounds and cabins.

The establishments that have been listed on pages 302–307 stand out from the crowd in their respective categories:

budget, bed and breakfast, chain, apartment, motel, luxury and boutique. They are listed by price within each area.

These lodgings have been featured for their excellent value, exceptional comfort, wide-ranging facilities, superb service, stunning location or unique character, or a combination of these.

Throughout the listings certain establishments have been highlighted as DK Choice. These offer a particularly special and memorable experience.

DIRECTORY

Luxury Lodges

Luxury Lodges of New Zealand
W lodgesofnz.co.nz

Southern Crossings
17 Falcon St,
Parnell, Auckland.
Tel (09) 309 5912.
W southern-crossings.com

Chain Hotels

Best Western NZ
W bestwestern.co.nz

Copthorne
W mckhotels.co.nz

Heritage
W heritagehotels.co.nz

Hyatt
W hyatt.com

Millennium
W mckhotels.co.nz

Novotel
W novotel.com

Scenic Hotel Group
W scenichotelgroup.co.nz

Sheraton
W sheraton.com

Sofitel
W sofitel.com

Motels and Motor Lodges

Best Western NZ
Tel 0800 700 499.
W bestwestern.co.nz

Golden Chain NZ
Tel (03) 358 0821,
0800 804 653.
W goldenchain.co.nz

Farmstays, Homestays and B&Bs

The New Zealand Bed & Breakfast Book
PO Box 6843, Wellington,
6141. Tel (04) 385 2615.
W bnb.co.nz

Rural Holidays
PO Box 2155,
Christchurch, 8140
Tel (03) 355 6218.
W nzaccom.co.nz

Backpacker and Youth Hostels

Budget Backpacker Hostels New Zealand
208 Kilmore St,
Christchurch.
Tel (03) 379 3014.
W bbh.co.nz

VIP Backpacker Resorts New Zealand
PO Box 60177,
Titirangi, Auckland.
Tel (09) 816 8903.
W vipbackpackers.com/nz, or hostelworld.com/nz

Youth Hostel Association of New Zealand
PO Box 436,
Christchurch.
Tel 0800 278 299.
W yha.co.nz

Camping Grounds

Top 10 Holiday Parks
PO Box 9088, Tower
Junction, Christchurch.
Tel 0800 580 348.
W top10.co.nz

Where to Stay

Auckland

Best Western President Hotel $
Budget **Map** E2
27–35 Victoria St West, 1010
Tel *(09) 303 1333*
W presidenthotel.co.nz
A hotel with comfortable rooms,
from studios and apartments to
suites, all featuring kitchenettes.

YWCA $
Budget **Map** E2
103 Vincent St, 1010
Tel *(09) 377 8763*
W akywca.org.nz
A friendly hostel, with three
women-only floors and three
mixed, a shared kitchen and café.

Heritage Hotel Auckland $$
Boutique **Map** E2
35 Hobson St, 1010
Tel *(09) 379 8553*
W heritagehotels.co.nz
This comfortable hotel has several
pools, a gym, a tennis court and a
sauna. The restaurant is located in
a dramatic palm-lined atrium.

The Langham $$
Chain **Map** E2
83 Symonds St, 1140
Tel *(09) 379 5132*
W langhamhotels.com/auckland
Old-world charm and elegance
with a five-star rating. Centrally
located, with a great spa.

The Old Church Cottage $$
Bed and Breakfast **Map** E2
1 Hastings Parade, Devonport, 0624
Tel *(09) 445 9826*
W oldchurchcottage.co.nz
Colonial charm brimming at this
B&B set in a former 1909 Salvation
Army Citadel. Modern amenities.

SKYCITY Hotel $$
Chain **Map** E2
Cnr Federal and Victoria sts, 1010
Tel *(09) 363 6000*
W skycityauckland.co.nz
On the doorstep of Auckland's Sky
Tower, this hotel offers spacious and
well-appointed rooms and sophis-
ticated in-house restaurants.

The Boatshed $$$
Bed and Breakfast **Map** E2
*Cnr Tawa and Huia sts, Little Oneroa,
Waiheke Island, 1840*
Tel *(09) 372 3242*
W boatshed.co.nz
Chic, luxury accommodation
in a sun-drenched bay just 35
minutes by ferry from Auckland.
Private setting with panoramic
ocean views.

**The Great Ponsonby
Arthotel** $$$
Bed and Breakfast **Map** E2
30 Ponsonby Terrace, Ponsonby, 1011
Tel *(09) 376 5989*
W greatpons.co.nz
A historic villa crammed with New
Zealand and Pacific art. Friendly
staff and trendy, urban atmosphere.

DK Choice

Hilton $$$
Chain **Map** E2
Princes Wharf, 147 Quay St, 1010
Tel *(09) 978 2000*
W auckland.hilton.com
Perched 300 m (985 ft) out on
Princes Wharf with panoramic
views of the marine playground,
the Hilton boasts suites shaped
like the bow of a ship. It has an
aptly named FISH restaurant
featuring a spectacular menu by
acclaimed chef Gareth Stewart.
It also has an outdoor pool.

Latitude 37 $$$
Apartment **Map** E2
20 Pakenham St E, 1010
Tel *(09) 377 5649*
W www.latitude37.co.nz
Boutique-style serviced apartments
with a backdrop of a sheltered
harbour and sleek yachts. Access
is provided to a swimming pool
and gym nearby.

Penthouse 3 $$$
Apartment **Map** E2
3P/148 Quay St, Central Auckland, 1010
Tel *(09) 377 5301*
W 148quay.com
Spacious, two-bedroom luxury
apartment. The enormous decks
at the front and rear are perfect for
admiring the breathtaking views of
Auckland waterfront.

Wainui Country Retreat $$$
Bed and Breakfast **Map** E2
*990 Wainui Rd, Wainui, North
Auckland 0933*
Tel *(09) 420 4567*
W wainuicountryretreat.co.nz
This secluded, self-catering
boutique farm stay has a private
waterfall and bush bath.

Northland

**KERIKERI: Aroha Island Kiwi
Lodge** $
Budget **Map** E1
*177 Rangitane Rd, Kerikeri, Bay of
Islands, 0294*
Tel *(09) 407 5243*
W arohaisland.co.nz
Comfortable eco-lodge set in a
native forest on an island. Stroll
along the private beach, kayak
or do some bird-watching.

KERIKERI: Pagoda Lodge $
Budget **Map** E1
81 Pa Rd, Bay of Islands, 0230
Tel *(09) 407 8617*
W pagoda.co.nz
Chinese-themed 1930s lodge
set in beautiful riverfront gardens
brimming with birdlife. Gypsy
caravans, safari tents and campsites are available.

KOHUKOHU: The Treehouse $
Budget **Map** D1
*168 West Coast Rd, RD1,
Hokianga, 0491*
Tel *(09) 405 5855*
W treehouse.co.nz
Cabins in subtropical gardens and
a forest overlooking Hokianga
Harbour. Shared kitchen/bathroom.

DK Choice

MATAURI BAY: Kauri Cliffs $$$
Luxury **Map** E1
*139 Tepene Tablelands Rd,
Matauri Bay, 0478*
Tel *(09) 407 0010*
W kauricliffs.com
This complex of a Colonial-style
lodge and cottages has access
to beaches, waterfalls and forest
with 2,000-year-old kauri trees.
Stunning vistas out over the
Cavalli Islands and Pacific Ocean.

Elegant lobby at the Colonial-style Kauri
Cliffs, Matauri Bay

OPUA: Crows Nest Holiday Villas $$$
Luxury   Map E1
20 Sir George Back St, Bay of Islands, 0200
Tel *(09) 402 6776*
W crowsnest.co.nz
Two exclusive, nautical-style villas with enormous balconies overlooking Opua harbour. Private and secluded.

PAIHIA: Scenic Hotel $$
Boutique   Map E1
Cnr MacMurray and Seaview rds, Bay of Islands, 0200
Tel *(09) 402 7826*
W scenichotels.co.nz
Set amid subtropical gardens, this refurbished, resort-style, hotel has spacious rooms and island-influenced architecture.

RUSSELL: Eagles Nest $$$
Luxury   Map E1
60 Tapeka Rd, Russell, Bay of Islands, 0202
Tel *(09) 403 8333*
W eaglesnest.co.nz
Five luxury villas with Jacuzzis, balconies and sublime sea views. Fabulous resident chefs, personal trainers and therapists.

WHANGAREI: Little Earth Lodge $
Budget   Map E1
85 Abbey Caves Rd, 0175
Tel *(09) 430 6562*
W littleearthlodge.co.nz
Cosy hostel with Balinese-inspired decor in a serene country setting near to the Glowworm Caves. Daily dive and snorkel tours to the Poor Knights Islands can be arranged.

The Central North Island

COROMANDEL: Beachside Resort $
Boutique   Map E2
20 Eyre St, Whitianga, 3510
Tel *(07) 867 1356*
W beachsideresort.co.nz
This resort offers self-contained one-bed apartments with a private patio, tennis court and pool. One-minute stroll to Buffalo Beach.

COROMANDEL: Seaview Motels Style Bed & Breakfast $
Bed and Breakfast   Map E2
150 Huihana Lane, Long Bay RD1
Tel *(07) 866 8221*
W coromandelseaview.co.nz
This hospitable B&B offers large rooms with panoramic sea views and a spa.

A deluxe villa at Eagles Nest, Russell, with stunning sea views

COROMANDEL: Waihi Waterlily Gardens $$
Luxury   Map E2
441 Pukekauri Rd, Waihi, 3682
Tel *(07) 863 8267*
W waterlily.co.nz
Two pretty self-contained cottages offer a romantic atmosphere in waterlily gardens.

COROMANDEL: Brenton Lodge $$$
Luxury   Map E2
2 Brenton Place, Whangamata, 3691
Tel *(07) 865 8400*
W brentonlodge.co.nz
Tastefully appointed suites with sea views and a pool. Award-winning in-house chocolate maker.

COROMANDEL: Grand Mercure Puka Park $$$
Boutique   Map E2
Pauanui Beach, 3546
Tel *(07) 864 8088*
W pukapark.co.nz
Romantic private chalets set along the native forest slopes of Mt Pauanui. Outdoor dining available.

GISBORNE: Portside Hotel $
Boutique   Map F3
2 Reads Rd, 4010
Tel *(06) 869 1000*
W portsidegisborne.co.nz
This contemporary riverside hotel has a lap pool, hi-tech cardio room and a gym. Spacious rooms.

HAMILTON: Shailers $
Bed and Breakfast   Map E2
1447 Kakaramea Rd, RD 10, 3290
Tel *(07) 825 2729*
W shailers.co.nz
Family-run dairy farm a 12-minute drive from Hamilton city offering hearty food, farm tours and good old-fashioned hospitality.

HAVELOCK NORTH: Mangapapa Petit Hotel $$$
Luxury   Map F4
466 Napier Rd, Hawkes Bay, 4180
Tel *(06) 878 3234*
W mangapapa.co.nz
Twelve magnificent suites make up this boutique hotel and spa

retreat set amongst landscaped gardens and orchards. The restaurant offers a five course set menu by chef Paul Condron.

NAPIER: Albatross Motel $
Budget   Map F4
56 Meeanee Quay, Westshore, 4110
Tel *(06) 835 5991*
W albatrossmotel.co.nz
Renovated studio and two-bed units a short stroll away from the swimming beach, with views over Ahuriri Wildlife Reserve.

OHOPE: Beachpoint Resort $
Apartments   Map F3
5 West End Rd, Ohope Beach
Tel *(07) 312 6100*
W beachpoint.co.nz
Fully equipped, self-service beachfront apartments offering a gym, heated swimming pool and covered parking.

OTOROHANGA: Kamahi Cottage $$$
Bed and Breakfast   Map E3
229 Barber Rd, Rewarewa, RD5
Tel *(07) 873 0849*
W kamahi.co.nz
Try the farm-fresh breakfasts and dinners at this romantic cottage set in a country garden. Billed as New Zealand's only five-star B&B. Sleeps four.

ROTORUA: Alpin Motel $
Budget   Map E3
16 Sala St, 3010
Tel *(07) 348 4182*
W alpin.co.nz
Airy four-star apartments set in a private garden. Rooms have plunge hot tubs with spring water.

ROTORUA: Cleveland Thermal Motel $
Budget   Map E3
113 Lake Rd, 3010
Tel *(07) 348 2041*
W clevelandmotel.co.nz
A family-friendly motel set in large gardens. Outdoor pool, family playground and barbecue area. Outdoor pool.

For more information on types of hotels *see pages 298–301*

The comfortable lounge at Huka Lodge, Taupo

ROTORUA: Rydges Rotorua $
Chain   Map E3
272 Fenton St, 3010
Tel (07) 349 0099
W rydges.com
Well-appointed rooms with
private balconies. There is free
Wi-Fi and a superb breakfast.

ROTORUA: YHA Rotorua $
Budget   Map E3
1278 Haupapa St, 3010
Tel (07) 349 4088
W yha.co.nz
Modern hostel with clean, airy
rooms and free parking. Centrally
located beside Kuirau Park.

ROTORUA: Blossom Cottage $$
Bed and Breakfast   Map E3
62A Sunnex Rd, RD6, 3096
Tel (07) 332 2720
W blossom-cottage.com
Enjoy the old-world charm of
this romantic self-catering B&B.
There are farm animals galore
and a hot tub. Horse riding is
available next door.

**ROTORUA: Paradise Valley
Lodge** $$
Boutique   Map E3
1099 Paradise Valley Rd, RD2
Tel 021 538 311
W paradisevalleylodge.co.nz
A charming lodge set in a large
expanse of gardens. Trout stream
on the boundary and a natural
swimming hole. Family-friendly.

**ROTORUA: Utuhina
Hot Springs Lodge** $$
Bed and Breakfast   Map E3
99 Lake Rd, 3010
Tel (07) 348 5785
Thirteen units make up this historic
lodge set in tranquil gardens. There
are four geothermal mineral pools
and a popular bird aviary.

**ROTORUA: Peppers On The
Point** $$$
Luxury   Map E3
214 Kawaha Point Rd, 3010
Tel (07) 348 4868
W peppers.co.nz/onthepoint
This 1930's lakeside property offers
individually designed rooms, gour-
met dining and a private beach.

ROTORUA: Country Villa $$$
Bed and Breakfast   Map E3
351 Dalbeth Rd, RD2, 3072
Tel (07) 357 5893
W countryvilla.co.nz
A Victorian villa with magnificent
gardens and lake views, friendly
service and superb cooked
breakfasts. Cosy log fire.

DK Choice

TAUPO: Huka Lodge $$$
Luxury   Map E3
271 Huka Falls Rd, 3377
Tel (07) 3785791
W hukalodge.co.nz
Set within 6 ha (17 acres) of
pristine forest and nature reserve,
this tranquil lodge sits just 300 m
(985 ft) upriver from Huka Falls.
The place has its own signature
cuisine and is close to fishing
spots and thermal attractions.

TAURANGA: Casa del Mare $$
Luxury   Map E2
35 Monticello Key, Palm Springs
Estate, Papamoa, 3118
Tel (07) 542 2581
W casadelmare.co.nz
Elegant, Mediterranean-style
accommodation and a private
landscaped courtyard and garden.

TAURANGA: Trinity Wharf $$
Luxury   Map E2
51 Dive Crescent, 3110
Tel (07) 577 8700
W trinitywharf.co.nz
This modern hotel has a private
pontoon, pool, gym and free Wi-
Fi. Dining options on the balcony.

Wellington and
the South

**FEATHERSTON: Wharekauhau
Country Estate** $$$
Luxury   Map E4
Western Lake Rd, Palliser Bay, RD3,
Wairarapa, 5710
Tel (06) 307 7581
W wharekauhau.co.nz
This pretty Edwardian lodge
offers country hospitality,

farm tours, horse trekking,
mountain-biking, archery
and clay-pigeon shooting.

KAPITI COAST: Vista del Sol $$$
Luxury   Map E4
20 Derham Rd, 5581
Tel (06) 364 2173
W vistadelsol.co.nz
Luxury lodge in a serene setting
with views of sand dunes and
rolling farmland. Enjoy lovely
sunsets and birdlife.

WELLINGTON: Comfort Hotel $
Budget   Map D5
213–223 Cuba St, Te Aro, 6141
Tel (04) 385 2156
W hotelwellington.co.nz
Situated on vibrant Cuba Street,
this Edwardian hotel exudes style.
Large rooms are equipped with
kichenettes and chic bathrooms.

WELLINGTON: Hotel St George $
Budget   Map D5
124 Willis St, Te Aro, 6011
Tel (04) 470 7777
W hotelstgeorge.co.nz
This iconic Art Deco hotel offers
affordable, inner city accommoda-
tion along with a great atmosphere.
Communal kitchen and TV area.

WELLINGTON: Nomads Capital $
Budget   Map D5
118–120 Wakefield St, 6011
Tel (04) 978 7800
W nomadsworld.com
This hotel has a wide range of
rooms. Breakfast and dinner
is complimentary.

**WELLINGTON: Aspect
Apartments** $$
Apartment   Map D5
22 Brandon St, Wellington Central, 6011
Tel (04) 384 1070
W villagegroup.co.nz
Large luxury apartments with fully
equipped kitchens, laundry.and
all home comforts. Close to CBD.

**WELLINGTON: Rydges
Wellington** $$
Chain   Map D5
75 Featherston St, Pipitea, 6011
Tel (04) 499 8686
W rydges.com
Apartment-style suites offering
a combination of harbour or city
views and kitchenettes. iPads
available for guests and there
is an on-site pool.

**WELLINGTON: The Wellesley
Boutique Hotel** $$
Boutique   Map D5
2–8 Maginnity St, 6011
Tel (04) 474 1308
W wellesleyboutiquehotel.co.nz
An oasis of calm in the bustling
Lambton quarter, this heritage

hotel boasts spacious, elegant rooms. A short walk for fine dining and great shopping.

WELLINGTON: Bolton Hotel **$$$**
Boutique Map D5
12 Bolton St, Lambton Quay, 6011
Tel *(04) 472 9966*
w boltonhotel.co.nz
This hotel offers luxurious, stylish rooms along with a lap pool, gym, spa and sauna.

WELLINGTON: Boulcott Suites **$$$**
Apartment Map D5
5 O'Reily Ave, Te Aro, 6011
Tel *(04) 384 1070*
w villagegroup.co.nz
Spacious townhouses and luxury suites furnished with real design flair. Fully equipped kitchens.

DK Choice

WELLINGTON: Museum Art Hotel **$$$**
Boutique Map D5
90 Cable St, Te Aro, 6011
Tel *(04) 802 8900*
w museumhotel.co.nz
Close to the shops, waterfront, great nightlife and the Te Papa Museum, this hotel is brimming with original works of art. The rooms are luxurious and its acclaimed Hippopotamus restaurant serves the finest French-inspired cuisine around.

WELLINGTON: Ohtel **$$$**
Boutique Map D5
66 Oriental Parade, Oriental Bay, 6011
Tel *(04) 803 0600*
w ohtel.com
Designer chic with stunning decor, furnishings and large bathrooms situated close to the Yacht Marina. Cable TV and free Wi-Fi provided.

Marlborough and Nelson

DK Choice

BLENHEIM: The Marlborough Lodge **$$$**
Luxury Map D5
776 Rapaura Rd, 7273
Tel *(03) 570 5700*
w themarlboroughlodge.co.nz
Once the Victorian-era home of the Sisters of Mercy, Old Saint Mary's Convent is now a beautifully restored refuge in 25 ha (60 acres) of gardens with vineyards, olive groves, a lake and abundant birdlife.

BLENHEIM: Vintners Retreat **$$$**
Luxury Map D5
55 Rapaura Rd, 7273
Tel *(03) 572 7420*
w vintnersretreat.co.nz
Set along the "golden mile" of vineyards, these spacious and peaceful villas have fully equipped kitchens and great views over the Richmond Range.

KAIKOURA: Austin Heights **$$**
Bed and Breakfast Map D5
19 Austin St, 7300
Tel *(03) 3195836*
w austinheights.co.nz
Enjoy breathtaking mountain and sea views from these self-contained apartments atop Kaikoura Peninsula. Expect to spot dolphins, seals and even whales during your stay.

KAIKOURA: Seaview Motel **$$**
Boutique Map D5
164 Esplanade, 7300
Tel *0800 456 000*
w seaviewmotel.co.nz
Comfortable and private beach-front motel units with kitchenettes. Secured parking.

KAIKOURA: Waves On The Esplanade **$$$**
Apartment Map D5
78 Esplanade, 7300
Tel *(03) 319 5890*
w kaikouraapartment.co.nz
Two-bedroom beachfront apartments offering sea views from the private balconies, outdoor spa, barbecue area and free Wi-Fi.

MURCHISON: RiverSong Cottages **$**
Boutique Map C5
30 Fairfax St, 7007
Tel *(03) 523 9011*
w riversong.co.nz
Tranquil cottages with private decks. Enjoy fresh fruit and vegetables from the gardens.

The historic McCormick House, Picton, surrounded by lush greenery

MURCHISON: Lake Rotoroa Lodge **$$$**
Luxury Map C5
Gowan Valley Rd, RD3, 7077
Tel *(03) 523 9121*
w lakerotoroalodge.com
A historic brown Trout fishing lodge set in a country house in a breathtaking forest location.

MURCHISON: Owen River Lodge **$$$**
Luxury Map C5
173 Owen Valley East Rd, Owen River, 7073
Tel *(03) 523 9075*
w owenriverlodge.co.nz
A five-star fishing lodge next to Kahurangi National Park. 25 fishing rivers within a 90-minute drive make this an anglers' dream.

NELSON: Trailways Hotel **$**
Boutique Map D4
66 Trafalgar St, The Wood, 7010
Tel *(03) 548 7049*
w trailwayshotel.co.nz
This riverside hotel offers modern, stylish rooms, a pool and an award-winning restaurant.

NELSON: DeLorenzo's Studio Apartments **$$**
Apartment Map D4
43–55 Trafalgar St, The Wood, 7010
Tel *(03) 548 9774*
w delorenzos.co.nz
Chic, well appointed studio apartments, some interconnected, as well as comfortable rooms. Located close to markets, shops and restaurants.

NELSON: Stonefly Lodge **$$$**
Luxury Map D4
3256 Motueka Valley Hwy, Stanley Brook, 7096
Tel *(03) 522 4479*
w stoneflylodge.co.nz
Deluxe fishing lodge on the banks of the Motueka River amid a private forest. The four rooms boast magnificent views. Breakfast and dinner are included in the price.

PICTON: Cnoc na Lear **$$**
Boutique Map D4
Queen Charlotte Track, Endeavour Inlet
Tel *(03) 579 8444*
w cnocnalear.co.nz
Peaceful lodge set in a forest landscape offering comfortable suites and home-cooked meals. Close to the beach.

PICTON: McCormick House **$$$**
Bed and Breakfast Map D4
21 Leicester St, 7220
Tel *(03) 573 5253*
w mccormickhouse.co.nz
Beautifully furnished, eco friendly, historic house with tranquil native gardens. Gourmet breakfasts.

For more information on types of hotels *see pages 298–301*

Conservatory at Kapitea Ridge Hotel, Hokitika

PORTAGE: Peppers Portage $$$
Boutique   **Map** D4
2923 Kenepuru Rd, 7282
Tel *(03) 573 4309*
W portage.co.nz
A wilderness retreat on the water-front offering spa baths, decks with views and handsome interiors. The restaurant specialises in seafood.

Canterbury and the West Coast

**AORAKI/MT COOK:
The Hermitage** $$$
Boutique   **Map** B6
Aoraki/Mt Cook Alpine Village, 7946
Tel *(03) 435 1809*
W hermitage.co.nz
Set in a National Park, surrounded by mountains and glaciers, this iconic hotel offers world-class activities and sumptuous food.

**ARTHUR'S PASS: Wilderness
Lodge Arthur's Pass** $$$
Luxury   **Map** C5
Arthur's Pass
Tel *(03) 318 9246*
W wildernesslodge.co.nz
Set in a beech forest, this eco-lodge has well-appointed rooms. Guided nature tours and adventure activities are also offered.

**CHRISTCHURCH: Camelot
Motor Lodge** $
Budget   **Map** C6
28 Papanui Rd, Merivale, 8014
Tel *(03) 355 9124*
W camelot.co.nz
Affordable, central location, this complex offers a wide choice of rooms, a spa, pools, a playground for kids and a garden.

CHRISTCHURCH: Dorset House $
Budget   **Map** C6
1 Dorset St, 8144
Tel *(03) 366 8268*
W dorset.co.nz
Fully refurbished in 2012, this Victorian house offers heritage charm at an affordable price.

Shared bathrooms and kitchen. Located a short walk from the city centre and Hagley Park.

**CHRISTCHURCH: The Old
Country House** $
Budget   **Map** C6
437 Gloucester St, Linwood, 8011
Tel *(03) 381 5504*
W oldcountryhousenz.com
Budget lodgings with colonial villas, spacious rooms, organic herb garden, sauna and spa pool.

**CHRISTCHURCH: Country
Glen Lodge** $$
Motel   **Map** C6
107 Bealey Ave, 8013
Tel *(03) 365 9980*
W glenlodge.co.nz
Located in the heart of the city, close to Hagley Park. Well equipped apartment-style rooms, with kitchens and stylish furnishings.

**CHRISTCHURCH: Heartland
Hotel Cotswold** $$
Boutique   **Map** C6
88/96 Papanui Rd, Merivale, 8540
Tel *(03) 355 3535*
W heartlandhotels.co.nz
Classic, understated charm in this Tudor-style hotel with award-winning gardens. In-house bar and restaurant. Friendly staff.

**CHRISTCHURCH: Orari Bed
and Breakfast** $$
Boutique   **Map** C6
42 Gloucester St, 8013
Tel *(03) 365 6569*
W orari.co.nz
Ten beautifully appointed, spacious suites in a listed Victorian building. Modernised but with plenty of old-world charm. Centrally located.

**CHRISTCHURCH: Clearview
Lodge** $$$
Bed and Breakfast   **Map** C6
8 Clearwater Ave, Northwood, 8051
Tel *(03) 359 5797*
W clearviewlodge.com
Vineyard lodge offering suites with balconies overlooking lovely gardens. Swimming pool.

**FOX GLACIER: Heartland Hotel
Glacier Country** $
Boutique   **Map** B6
39 Main Rd, 7859
Tel *(03) 751 0847*
W heartlandhotels.co.nz
Hospitable hotel on the edge of the Westland World Heritage Park. Unmistakable centre of the Fox Glacier township.

**FRANZ JOSEF GLACIER:
Te Waonui Forest Retreat** $$$
Luxury   **Map** B6
3 Wallace St, 7856
Tel *(03) 752 0555*
W scenichotelgroup.co.nz
Tucked away in the wilderness, this hotel has large rooms and offers a five-course degustation menu, served amongst the trees of the Canopy Restuarant.

DK Choice

**HANMER SPRINGS: Heritage
Hanmer Springs** $$
Boutique   **Map** C5
1 Conical Hill Rd, 7334
Tel *(03) 315 0060*
W heritagehotels.co.nz
Just across the road from Hanmer Springs Thermal Reserve with its healing waters, this well-appointed hotel in a historic building offers a range of accommodation options from three-bedroom villas to garden rooms. It has a restaurant, outdoor pool and tennis courts.

**HOKITIKA: Shining Star
Beachfront Accommodation** $
Budget   **Map** C5
16 Richards Drive, 7810
Tel *(03) 755 8921*
W www.shiningstar.co.nz
Awe-inspiring ocean views from this complex of chalets and log-style cabins. Campsites available.

**HOKITIKA: Kapitea Ridge
Lodge** $$$
Luxury   **Map** C5
Chesterfield Rd, State Hwy 6
Tel *(03) 755 6805*
W kapitea.co.nz
The stylish and private suites here enjoy panoramic views out over wild beaches and rainforest, Enjoy breathtaking ocean sunsets from the garden Jacuzzi.

RANGIORA: Pete's Farm Stay $$
Bed and Breakfast   **Map** C6
45 Mairaki Rd, 7471
Tel *(03) 313 5180*
W petesfarm.co.nz
Help feed the alpaca and sheep at this family-friendly farm stay. Garden-fresh food and complimentary breakfast.

For key to prices *see page 302*

TIMARU: The Grosvenor $
Budget Map C6
26 Cains Terrace, 7910
Tel *(03) 688 3129*
W thegrosvenor.co.nz
Historic hotel with a distinctly
Bohemian atmosphere. Themed
rooms, great bar and pet-friendly.

**WAIAU: The Gates Country
Lodge** $$$
Boutique Map D5
61 Gates Rd, North Canterbury, 7395
Tel *(03) 315 6162*
W thegateslodge.co.nz
Historic lodge in an idyllic 9 ha
(22 acre) farm setting with antique
decor. Pool, croquet lawn, tennis
court, trout fishing and jet boating.

Otago and Southland

ARROWTOWN: Viking Lodge $
Budget Map B6
21 Inverness Crescent, 9302
Tel *(03) 442 1765*
W vikinglodge.co.nz
Self-contained, spacious chalets
with kitchens, washing machines,
cable TV and a pool. Barbecue
area in the garden.

**DUNEDIN: Brothers Boutique
Hotel** $$
Boutique Map B7
295 Rattray St, 9016
Tel *(03) 477 0043*
W brothershotel.co.nz
Charming heritage building with
superb harbour views. Centrally
heated, en suite rooms with Wi-Fi.

DUNEDIN: Scenic Hotel $$
Chain Map B7
123 Princes St, 9016
Tel *(03) 470 1470*
W scenichotelgroup.co.nz
This inner-city hotel offers large,
airy rooms, award-winning
design, modern facilities and
displays attractive local artworks.

A plush room at Scenic Hotel
Dunedin City

**DUNEDIN: Scenic Hotel Southern
Cross, Dunedin City** $$
Chain Map B7
118 High St, 9054
Tel *(03) 477 0752*
W scenichotelsgroup.co.nz
Dunedin's largest hotel offers
elegant rooms and superb service.
Central location, on site parking.

DK Choice

**DUNEDIN: Camp Estate,
Larnach Castle** $$$
Luxury Map B7
100 Camp Rd, Larnach Castle, 9077
Tel *(03) 476 1616*
W larnachcastle.co.nz
A beautiful country house in
the grounds of New Zealand's
only genuine castle, along with
Camp Estate, which has five
spacious rooms decorated in
Neo-Classical style. Rooms offer
fireplaces and views of the
surrounding countryside.
Additional accommodation is
available in 19th-century stables.

**DUNEDIN: Glendinning
House** $$$
Bed and Breakfast Map B7
222 Highgate, Roslyn, 9010
Tel *(03) 477 8262*
W glendinninghouse.co.nz
A heritage house in Dunedin's
premier hilltop suburb, less than 3
minutes' drive to the city centre.
Modern facilities and great service.

FIORDLAND: Possum Lodge $
Budget Map A6
13 Murrell Ave, Manapouri, 9679
Tel *(03) 249 6623*
W possumlodge.co.nz
Cosy holiday park with motel
units, self-contained cottages,
cabins and tent sites on the
edge of Lake Manapouri.

**HAAST: Heartland World
Heritage Hotel, Haast** $
Budget Map B6
7844 State Hwy 6, 7886
Tel *(03) 3775767*
W heartlandhotels.co.nz
Tranquil hotel nestled in a world
heritage park. Great base to
explore the surrounding ancient
forests, mighty glaciers, rare
wildlife and dramatic coastlines.

**MILFORD SOUND: Milford
Sound Lodge** $
Budget Map A6
State Hwy 94
Tel *(03) 249 8071*
W milfordlodge.com
Basic but comfortable dorm-style
rooms, cabins, tent sites, riverside
and mountain-view chalets.
There is also an in-house café.

**QUEENSTOWN: Nomads
Queenstown** $
Budget Map A6
5/11 Church St, 9300
Tel *(03) 441 3922*
W nomadsworld.com
Hostel with dorms and some
private rooms with en suite
bathrooms. There is a pool table
in the lounge, a sauna, ski storage
and even a cinema.

**QUEENSTOWN: YHA
Queenstown Central** $
Budget Map A6
48 Shotover St, 9300
Tel *(03) 442 7400*
W yha.co.nz
Busy backpacker hostel with a
selection of private rooms with
en suite baths. Close to many
cafés, bars and restaurants.

QUEENSTOWN: The Ferry $$
Bed and Breakfast Map A6
92 Spence Rd, 9371
Tel *(03) 442 2194*
W ferry.co.nz
Historic homestead in an English
cottage garden overlooking the
Shotover River. Home-cooking
and great service, perfect base
for fishing and skiing enthusiasts.

**QUEENSTOWN: Azur
Luxury Lodge** $$$
Luxury Map A6
*23 Mackinnon Terrace,
Sunshine Bay, 9300*
Tel *(03) 409 0588*
W azur.co.nz
Nine stunning open-plan villas
offer peace and tranquillity.
Complimentary breakfast, after-
noon tea and evening canapes.

QUEENSTOWN: Forty Two $$$
Luxury Map A6
42 Man St, 9300
Tel *(03) 450 0855*
W touchofspice.co.nz
Immaculate three-bed apartment
by the lake and mountains with
barbecue area and pool.

**QUEENSTOWN: Queenstown
Country Lodge** $$$
Luxury Map A6
497 Frankton–Ladies Mile Hwy, 9371
Tel *(03) 441 8548*
W queenstowncountrylodge.co.nz
Lavishly appointed lodge set in
secluded gardens and farmland,
and surrounded by mountains.

QUEENSTOWN: Scenic Suites $$$
Apartment Map A6
27 Stanley St, 9348
Tel *(03) 442 4718*
W scenichotels.co.nz
Spectacular mountain and lake
views can be enjoyed from the
hotel's elevated position.

For more information on types of hotels *see pages 298–301*

WHERE TO EAT AND DRINK

Both New Zealand's restaurants and cuisine have undergone a revolution in the past few decades. Eating in restaurants was once reserved for special occasions and usually included a traditional British meal, such as roast lamb and vegetables, New Zealand now has a wide variety of eating places to suit all tastes and all budgets. Although plainer fare is still available, the country's multicultural population has meant that restaurants serving traditional food sit alongside those offering cuisine from almost every corner of the world. Influences from Asia and the Pacific have been particularly significant. New Zealand restaurants make good use of home-grown produce, such as fresh fish (including whitebait), oysters, mussels, crayfish (rock lobsters), beef, lamb and venison, as well as vegetables and fruit. These can be enjoyed with a glass of New Zealand wine (see pp312–13). A popular experience is a Māori hangi, where food is wrapped and cooked on heated rocks under the ground.

The lounge bar at Herzog Winery and Restaurant in Blenheim (see p321)

Types of Restaurants

New Zealand's major cities have a vibrant restaurant scene ranging from formal dining to a multitude of casual cafés. Diners can experience haute cuisine or eat in a café offering cheaper, simpler food. Some eateries feature courtyard, garden or pavement seating. There is every type of ethnic restaurant imaginable, offering the cuisines of every continent, such as Chinese, Cambodian, Malaysian, Turkish and Greek. Some high-quality restaurants can be found in provincial and rural areas. Many vineyard restaurants serve ploughman's lunches with seating among the vines as well as more formal meals in picturesque restaurant settings. Pubs also offer food that can range from cheap and basic fare to more sophisticated, restaurant-quality dishes. A typical and very popular pub meal is a roast.

A meal in a café or ethnic restaurant can cost as little as NZ$15 for a one-course meal. Restaurant prices range from NZ$25 to more than NZ$100 per person for a three-course meal. A range of fast-food chains, such as McDonalds, KFC and Burger King, have franchises in New Zealand, and there are the traditional, local fish and chip shops as well as gourmet burger and pizza outlets.

Eating Hours and Reservations

Many restaurants serve lunch from noon to 2pm and dinner from 6 to 10pm. Some establishments open earlier and serve increasingly popular "all day breakfasts". Late-night and 24-hour cafés are gaining in popularity.

Bookings are often necessary at more formal restaurants. Cafés and bars vary in their booking policies, with some taking reservations and others operating on a casual basis. It pays to ring and check to avoid disappointment.

Paying and Tipping

The majority of restaurants and cafés accept credit cards, though it is a good idea to check when booking. Most restaurants will not accept personal cheques or traveller's cheques. Government taxes are included in the menu prices and there are no service charges. Tipping is not standard

Exquisite views from the restaurant at Cable Bay Vineyard (see p315)

Tables outside a café at Mount Maunganui

Dress

Dress in New Zealand is informal compared to many other parts of the world, especially when dining out for lunch. It is unlikely that a jacket or tie will be needed, although visitors may feel more comfortable if they are formally dressed at the more upmarket restaurants. Informal but tidy dress is appreciated at less formal restaurants. Street fashion is acceptable at inner-city cafés.

Smoking

Along with most other indoor workplaces and on all public transport, restaurants, cafés and bars became smoke-free zones by law at the end of 2004. At present, the ban does not apply to outdoor dining areas, and where possible, restaurateurs make every effort to satisfy a customer's requirements. It is common for most restaurants in New Zealand to have dedicated gardens or gazebos for smokers to retreat to, away from other diners.

Recommended Restaurants

The restaurants on pages 314–25 have been carefully selected to give a cross-section of the best options from across the country: from the smartest and most upmarket establishments to the best budget food vendors.

Many eateries boast spectacular rural locations and views of New Zealand's dramatic coastline, but some of the tastiest (and cheapest) meals are to be enjoyed in urban environments, especially in Auckland and Wellington, where there is a good selection of fantastic Asian restaurants.

The DK Choice category draws attention to the truly exceptional establishments: those that boast superb cuisine, beverages, presentation, service, atmosphere or location, or provide an outstanding overall experience.

procedure, although a tip will be appreciated for very good service. Patrons can leave tips in cash on the table or a tip jar on the counter, or include them in credit card payments.

Children

Most restaurants cater for children. If travelling with very young children, it is best to check with the restaurant to ensure that children are welcome. An option in busy cafés is to book early before large numbers of adult diners arrive. Chinese, Greek and other ethnic restaurants tend to have more relaxed attitudes towards children. Fast-food chains can be found in most cities and towns, and children usually enjoy a take-away meal at the park or beach. Families staying in motels with kitchens may find that putting together a meal from a local supermarket provides a break from having to take small children to restaurants.

Wheelchair Access

Government regulations require building owners to ensure that new and redeveloped buildings are accessible by wheelchair. Most restaurants provide toilet facilities for the disabled.

Vegetarians

Many restaurants offer some vegetarian meals and will usually be happy to adapt menus, especially in areas where there is an abundance of home-grown produce. Many restaurants also have dairy-free and gluten-free options. Most Asian restaurants in New Zealand also offer vegetarian food on their menus. There are more than 50 vegetarian and vegan restaurants in Auckland alone. The Happy Cow website (www.happycow.net) has a full lists of vegetarian establishments.

BYO Restaurants

BYO means "bring your own" alcohol. Instead of a full liquor licence, restaurants may have a BYO licence that allows diners to bring their own alcohol. This is cheaper than buying alcohol on the premises, although a fee may be charged for corkage. Some fully licensed restaurants allow diners to bring their own wine, but corkage charges can add NZ$5–10 to the bill.

Alcohol and Other Drinks

Licensed restaurants and bars serve a range of alcohol, including wine, beer and spirits. Many cafés are also fully licensed, but offer a more limited range of alcohol. Many restaurants and cafés highlight New Zealand wines and boutique beers. Restaurants in wine-growing areas usually specialize in wine from that region. Tap water is safe in all urban and town supply areas, and bottled still and sparkling water is available in all dining establishments.

The Flavours of New Zealand

Cuisine in New Zealand is most likely to be characterized by its freshness and diversity and, as a relatively youthful nation, there is a willingness to experiment with food and flavours. Surrounded by clean ocean and with extremely fertile land, New Zealand offers food of the very highest standards, and many of its producers are certified organic, reinforcing its clean, green image. New Zealand's cuisine has been described as Pacific Rim, drawing inspiration from Europe, Asia, Polynesia and its indigenous people, the Māori. Chefs hailing from New Zealand are among the most sought-after in the world, due to their contemporary approach and passion for good ingredients.

Avocado oil

Visitors at a fruit stall at the Rotorua Night market

Meat

There are over 25 million sheep in New Zealand, all bred on natural, free-range pastureland. New Zealand lamb is world-famous and features on menus in a wide variety of dishes. Offerings range from a traditional rack of lamb to a Moroccan-style lamb tagine – and you can always expect to see a few chops on a barbecue. For a change from lamb, there are plenty of other meats available, such as beef, pork, chicken and cervena, which is a lighter, leaner style of farmed venison.

Fish and Seafood

New Zealand has a plentiful supply of *kaimoana* (seafood), with many local varieties – in particular blue cod from the South Island and the Chatham Islands, oysters from Bluff, Southland, and the amazing green lip mussels of Havelock, Marlborough Sounds. Snapper, blue cod, *tarakihi* and *hapuku* (the Māori name for grouper) are the most common saltwater fish. There is also wonderful farmed salmon

Mussels · Lobster · Samphire · Red snapper · Salmon · Cockles (clams) · Whitebait
Selection of seafood found in the waters of New Zealand

New Zealand's Varied Cuisine

Cuisine in New Zealand is very diverse. Fine dining often has a French influence with a modern edge, and you will find great bistros serving classics such as *boeuf bourguignon* and *tarte au citron*. Cafés in New Zealand tend to have a more relaxed, Mediterranean approach. Most pubs serve a wide range of dishes, such as fish, salads, steaks and, of course, roast meats. There are increasing numbers of pubs serving restaurant-quality food. New Zealand is part of the Asia-Pacific region, and there is a vibrant Asian flavour to be found in many dishes. Look out for whitebait fritters on the West Coast from August to September, when the season is at its peak. The Blue Cod in Southland is not be missed. Eating at one of the many wonderful vineyard restaurants is highly recommended, as is the chance to sample a genuine Māori *hangi*.

Manuka honey

Kumara soup Made with the native sweet potato, this soup is especially delicious topped with goat's cheese croutons.

Basket of *kumara* in a local farmers' market

(wild salmon cannot be sold commercially). Other popular fish include, John Dory, monkfish and blue warehau. As for shellfish, New Zealand has a native clam called *tuangi*, as well as bivalves called *tuatua* and *pipi*. Oysters, mussels and crayfish are also popular.

Upmarket fish and chips, best enjoyed outdoors by the sea

Fruit and Vegetables

The almost perfect farming conditions in New Zealand mean that the enormous variety of produce cultivated is of a consistently high quality. All common vegetables are farmed here, alongside some native varieties. Kumara is a local sweet potato, and a traditional Māori food. They are often baked in their jackets, and also boiled, roasted, fried, mashed or scalloped (sliced, seasoned, and slowly cooked in milk). Other common root vegetables are parsnips and yams. The tamarillo (tree tomato), kiwifruit and feijoa are all local fruits. During harvest time, look out for roadside stalls near farms, selling fresh vegetables and fruit cheaply. Honey from the native Manuka plant is popular worldwide for its woody, earthy

aromas and supposed medicinal properties. Also gaining fame around the globe is the delicious and decadent avocado oil from the North Island.

Dairy Produce

The conditions in New Zealand are perfect for dairy farming. Wonderful cheeses, yoghurt and ice cream, made by small producers can be found all over the country. Hokey-pokey ice cream is a New Zealand speciality – delicious vanilla ice cream loaded with caramel chunks.

Māori Food *(Kai)*

New Zealand's abundant supply of food is explained in Māori legend as a gift from the gods. From Tane, god of the forest, come the game birds, from Tangaroa seafood, from Haumia wild plants, and from Rongo cultivated vegetables.

The main traditional method for feasting is the *hangi* (pronounced hung-ee). Men heat stones in a fire and dig an earth pit, while women prepare the meat and vegetables. The stones are placed in the pit with the food (placed in hangi baskets and covered in cloth), and earth is piled back into the pit. The food cooks slowly for up to 4 hours. The results are worth the wait – succulent, tender meat and smoky, delicious vegetables.

Pan fried hapuka Roasted shallots, pancetta and rocket give this popular fish a Mediterranean flavour.

Grilled lamb Simple, fresh flavours, such as polenta and red pepper sauce, complement this superb meat.

Pavlova Aussies and Kiwis disagree over who invented this delicious meringue, cream and fruit dessert.

What to Drink in New Zealand

New Zealanders were, until the 1960s, a nation of beer drinkers and wine consumption was not that common. However, the meteoric rise of New Zealand's wine industry, which has scooped many international awards, means wine has enjoyed a dramatic rise in popularity since the early 1960s. New Zealand's temperate maritime climate is ideal for maximizing grape ripeness and the production of premium, intensely flavoured wines. There are almost 700 wineries throughout the country, many near the coast *(see pp40–41)*. Guides on wines, vineyards and vineyard restaurants are available at larger book shops or can be found at www.nzwine.com.

Wine tasting at C J Pask Winery, Hastings *(see pp154–5)*

White Wine

Sauvignon Blanc is regarded as New Zealand's most outstanding white wine, with critics naming New Zealand Sauvignon Blanc as the world's finest. New Zealand's white wines, produced by both modern and traditional methods, are known for their fruit flavours. There is also a fascinating range of Chardonnays to choose from, ranging from cheaper Chardonnays fermented in stainless steel tanks and bottled young to more expensive Chardonnays fermented and aged in oak barrels. Riesling is growing in popularity, with New Zealand Riesling often described as similar to the light and elegant German style. Pinot Gris is also increasingly popular.

Huia Sauvignon Blanc   Palliser Sauvignon Blanc

Sweet White Wine

New Zealand sweet wines are also winning international recognition and awards. The most interesting of these sweet wines are made from botrytis-affected grapes, with the Marlborough region emerging as a leading producer of the finest wines *(see pp210–11)*. However, the weather conditions needed to produce botrytis-type wines occur irregularly in New Zealand, and therefore prices for these luscious dessert wines tend to be somewhat higher than other wine varieties.

Cave cellar at Gibbston Valley winery *(see p282)*

Wine Type	Regions	Recommended Producers
Chardonnay	All key wine regions	Allan Scott, Church Road, Clearview, Cloudy Bay, Corbans, Hunters, Morton Estate Wines, Vavasour
Chenin Blanc	Central Otago, Gisborne, Hawke's Bay	Collard Brothers, Lazy Dog, The Millton Vineyard, Queensbury
Gewürztraminer	Central Otago, Gisborne, Hawke's Bay, Marlborough	Brookfields, Chifney Wines, Dry River, Eskdale, Gatehouse, Lawson's Dry Hills, Stonecroft
Muller-Thurgau	Gisborne, Hawke's Bay, Marlborough	Corbans Gisborne Winery, Pleasant Valley Wines, Vidal of Hawke's Bay, Villa Maria
Pinot Gris	Canterbury, Hawke's Bay, Marlborough	Ash Ridge Wines, Brookfields, Bushmere Estate, Cape Campbell Wines, Dry River, Margrain, Martinborough Vineyard
Riesling	Canterbury, Central Otago, Hawke's Bay, Marlborough, Nelson, Wairarapa	Allan Scott Wines and Estates, Collards, Cooper's Creek, Corbans, Framingham Wine Company, Grove Mill, Martinborough Vineyard, Neudorf, Stoneleigh
Sauvignon Blanc	Canterbury, Gisborne, Hawke's Bay, Marlborough	Cloudy Bay, Grove Mill, Hunters, Jackson Estate, Nautilus, Palliser, Selaks, Villa Maria
Sémillon	Gisborne, Hawke's Bay, Marlborough	Collards, Huntaway, Kim Crawford, Pleasant Valley, Vidal of Hawke's Bay
Sweet wines	Central Otago, Gisborne, Hawke's Bay, Marlborough	Church Road, Cooper's Creek, Cottage Block, Dry River, Framingham Wine Company, Villa Maria

Sparkling Wine

New Zealand sparkling wines are world class and have won a number of awards. Deutz Marlborough Cuvée was voted "Sparkling Wine of the Year" in the Great Wine Challenge held in Britain in 1998 and has been awarded numerous medals since. Visitors should be aware that there are two types of sparkling wine. At the bottom end of the market, "bubblies" are carbonated wines and tend to be rather sweet. However, the middle and top ends of the market feature *méthode traditionnelle* labels made by bottle fermentation methods. Marlborough is regarded as the country's top region for bottle-fermented *méthode traditionnelle*, although other regions in the country are now also gaining a reputation for producing high quality products.

Huia
Marlborough
Brut

Wine Regions of New Zealand	
Auckland	Cabernet Sauvignon, Cabernet blends, Chardonnay, Merlot, Pinot Noir
Northland	Cabernet Sauvignon, Chardonnay, Merlot, Pinot Gris, Pinotages Chambourcin, Syrahs, Viogniers.
Waikato and Bay of Plenty	Pinot Gris, Pinot Noir Sauvignon Blanc
Gisborne	Chardonnay, Muller-Thurgau, Muscat, Pinot Gris, Sémillon
Hawke's Bay	Aromatic white wines, Cabernet & Merlot blends, Chardonnay, Syrah
Wairarapa	Chardonnay, dessert wines, Pinot Noir, Riesling, Sauvignon Blanc, Syrah
Nelson	Chardonnay, Pinot Noir, Riesling, Sauvignon Blanc
Marlborough	Chardonnay, Pinot Noir, Riesling, Sauvignon Blanc
Canterbury	Chardonnay, Pinot Gris, Pinot Noir, Riesling
Otago	Chardonnay, Pinot Noir, Riesling, Sauvignon Blanc

Alana Estate
Pinot Noir

Red Wine

Although New Zealand is still primarily known for its white wines, its red wines are gaining in importance as wine makers discover better sites, perfect their viticulture methods and as vines mature, making them more stable. Pinot Noir is the most widely planted red variety, but Cabernet Sauvignon, Merlot and Cabernet Franc are also well suited to New Zealand's soil and climatic conditions. Wine makers frequently blend red wines from different areas and provinces.

Clearview Estate's popular seaside restaurant, Hawke's Bay
(see pp154–5)

Wine Type	Regions	Recommended Producers
Cabernet Sauvignon	Auckland, Hawke's Bay, Northland, Waikato	Benfield, Brookfields, Church Road, Delamere Esk Valley, Goldwater, Morton Estate, Villa Maria
Merlot	Auckland, Gisborne, Hawke's Bay, Marlborough	Arahura, Babich, Church Road, C J Pask, Clearview Estate, Corbans, Delegates, Esk Valley, Villa Maria
Pinotage	Auckland, Gisborne, Hawke's Bay, Marlborough	Cottle Hill Winery, Kerr Farm Vineyard, Landmark Estate Wines, Ohinemuri Estate Wine, Pleasant Valley
Pinot Noir	Canterbury, Central Otago, Hawke's Bay, Marlborough, Nelson, Wairarapa	Ata Rangi, Black Ridge, Cloudy Bay, Cooper's Creek, Dry River, Martinborough Vineyard, Palliser, Rippon Vineyard

Beer

Beer remains a popular drink in New Zealand and beers such as Steinlager and Kiwi Lager have won international recognition. There has been an explosion of craft breweries since 2012 and there are now more than 85 in the country producing styles that range from light lagers to draft beers and malt ales. Beer is usually served chilled and is available on tap in bars and hotels. Low-alcohol beers as well as overseas bottled and canned beers are available in supermarkets, bars and restaurants.

Steinlager

Other Drinks

New Zealand's climate, which ranges from subtropical to alpine, allows the cultivation of a large variety of fresh fruit for juicing, including its famous kiwifruit *(see p133)*. Its apples are made into cider. Other bottled drinks and mineral waters are also widely available. A speciality is Lemon and Paeroa, a lemon-flavoured carbonated mineral water originally from Paeroa on the Hauraki Plains. Coffee and tea are other popular drinks with New Zealanders.

Kiwifruit

Where to Eat and Drink

Auckland

Art Gallery Café
Café **Map** E2
Kitchener St, CBD, 1010
Tel (09) 369 1149
This daytime café has art-themed dishes, an "aspiring artists" menu for children and plenty of gluten-free, dairy-free and vegetarian options.

Barilla Dumpling $
Chinese **Map** E2
571 Dominion Rd, Balmoral, 1446
Tel (09) 638 8032
Come here for all sorts of dumplings – boiled, steamed or fried. They are fragrant, flavourful and inexpensive. Cash only.

Bikanervala $
Indian **Map** E2
2 White Swan Rd, Mt Roskill, 1041
Tel (09) 625 2807
Indulge in Bikanervala's extensive range of mouth-watering, spicy vegetarian meals, including an exquisite selection of *dosas* (rice batter and black lentil pancakes). There is also a sweet shop on site.

Bird On A Wire $
Rotisserie **Map** E2
136/146 Ponsonby Rd, Ponsonby, 1011
Tel (09) 361 3407
Succulent free-range rotisserie chicken that comes every which way – breaded, basted or in a burger bun.

Eden Noodles $
Chinese **Map** E2
105 Dominion Rd, Mt Eden, 1024
Tel (09) 630 1899 **Closed** Mon
Tiny, bustling restaurant with loyal patrons enjoying spicy Sichuan soup, noodles and dumplings. Extensive menu; no credit cards.

Happy Japanese $
Japanese **Map** E2
4038 Great North Rd, Kelston, 0602
Tel (09) 813 1078
This big, bustling establishment offers a wide range of à la carte dishes, set menus, sushi and even Japanese-flavoured burgers. Wash it down with some sake.

Jai Jalaram Khaman $
Indian **Map** E2
39 Boundary Rd, Blockhouse Bay, 0600
Tel (09) 627 6200 **Closed** Mon
Sit down and savour vegetarian Gujarati and South Indian street food. Try the amazing *pau bhaji* (bread with a thick, tangy curry) and the spicy veggie burgers. Takeaway is available.

Jolin Shanghai $
Chinese **Map** E2
248 Dominion Rd, Mt Eden, 1024
Tel (09) 631 5575
Head here for Chinese food on a budget. The marinated pork ribs and soupy dumplings are fantastic.

Kati Grill $
East Indian **Map** E2
146 Karangahape Rd, CBD,1010
Tel (09) 302 5284
Delicious Kati rolls, made with paratha (Indian flat bread), are stuffed with various fillings such as tandoor cooked chicken, lamb or spicy vegetables.

Kokako $
Café **Map** E2
537 Great North Rd, Grey Lynn, 1021
Tel (09) 376 6086
Daytime café where everything is fresh, organic and vegetarian. The salads are meals in themselves, and the coffee is divine.

Contemporary interior of Kokako, Auckland, known for its organic fare

Price Guide
Prices are based on a three-course meal per person, without drinks, and inclusive of taxes and service charges.

$	up to NZ$50
$$	NZ$50–NZ$150
$$$	over NZ$150

Mamak Malaysian $
Malaysian **Map** E2
Chancery Square, Chancery, 1010
Tel (09) 887 8361 **Closed** Mon
Expect friendly, helpful service at one of Auckland's best Malaysian eateries. Don't miss the crispy, soft-shelled crab or the incredible *laksa* – spicy noodles with curry.

Original California Burrito Company $
Tex Mex **Map** E2
350 Queen St, CBD, 1010
Tel (09) 302 3345
This is a franchise with multiple branches, but the food is hearty and reliable. Extensive menu.

Sanchun Bamboo House $
Korean **Map** E2
9 Commerce St, CBD, 1010
Tel (09) 377 8377 **Closed** Sun
The food at this small, charming restaurant is the next best thing to home-cooked Korean cuisine.

Seafood Central $
Seafood **Map** E2
22 Jellicoe St, Westhaven, 1011
Tel (09) 303 0262
A treat for seafood lovers, located on Auckland's wharf. Fish straight off the boats is cooked any way you want.

Takapuna Beach Café $
Café **Map** E2
22 The Promenade, Takapuna, 0622
Tel (09) 484 0002
This excellent beachside venue offers delicious casual dining. Try the hand-made ice creams.

Basque Kitchen and Bar $$
Spanish **Map** E2
61 Davis Crescent (entrance on Short St), Newmarket, 1023
Tel (09) 523 1057 **Closed** Sun
This restaurant serves excellent Spanish tapas and wines.

Café Hanoi $$
Vietnamese **Map** E2
Cnr Galway and Commerce St, Britomart, 1010
Tel (09) 302 3478
Authentic Vietnamese dining with shared plates. Deft seasonings and free-range meat ensure a gastronomic treat.

Casita Miro $$
Mediterranean Map E2
3 Brown Rd, Onetangi, Waiheke Island, 1081
Tel *(09) 372 7854*
Specializing in Spanish and Mediterranean cuisine, the menu here features delicious tapas as well as larger plates to share.

Coco's Cantina $$
Italian Map E2
376 Karangahape Rd, Newton, 1010
Tel *(09) 300 7582* **Closed** *Sun*
Coco's is an Italian-style bistro: casual dining, no bookings and a great place to hang out. Try the juicy steaks.

DK Choice

**Depot Eatery and
Oyster Bar** $$
Seafood Map E2
86 Federal St, CBD, 1010
Tel *(09) 363 7048*
Fine dining in an informal atmosphere features at this award-winning restaurant. Simple dishes using seasonal produce are prepared over charcoal or hard wood. Try a selection of small plates. Swift service. No reservations.

The Engine Room $$
Bistro Map E2
115 Queen St, Northcote Point, 0627
Tel *(09) 480 9502* **Closed** *Sun & Mon*
A fine dining restaurant, the Engine Room has won a number of awards for its classic bistro dishes made with local produce.

Moochowchow $$
Thai Map E2
23 Ponsonby Rd, Ponsonby, 1010
Tel *(09) 360 6262* **Closed** *Sun & Mon*
This Thai restaurant offers delectable, fragrant dishes that delight the palate. The jasmine-smoked salmon is a good choice.

Antoine's $$$
Fine dining Map E2
333 Parnell Rd, Parnell, 1052
Tel *(09) 379 8756* **Closed** *Sun*
Antoine's has been serving delicious French-European cuisine since 1973. Try the timeless favourites such as roast duck with Grand Marnier sauce.

Botswana Butchery $$$
Fine dining Map E2
99 Quay St, CBD, 1010
Tel *(09) 307 6966*
Slow-roasted lamb shoulder and rib-eye steak count among the specialities here in the sumptuous historic Ferry Building overlooking the harbour.

Cable Bay restaurant, Auckland, set amid sprawling grounds

Cable Bay $$$
Vineyard Map E2
12 Nick Johnstone Drive, Oneroa, Waiheke Island, 1971
Tel *(09) 372 5889* **Closed** *Mon*
Enjoy amazing views of the Hauraki Gulf at this restaurant, and a delicious à la carte menu featuring fresh local produce; alternatively, the adjoining wine bar offers small plates.

Cibo $$$
Fine dining Map E2
91 St Georges Bay Rd, Parnell, 1149
Tel *(09) 303 9660* **Closed** *Sun*
Housed in an old chocolate factory, the award-winning Cibo offers seasonal dishes prepared with flair. There is a courtyard for alfresco summer dining.

Clooney $$$
Fine dining Map E2
33 Sale St, Freemans Bay, 1010
Tel *(09) 358 1702*
Winner of several awards, including Metro magazine's coveted Best Restaurant 2012 in the greater Auckland area, Clooney serves classic dishes with a contemporary twist.

Cocoro $$$
Japanese Map E2
56A Brown St, Ponsonby, 1021
Tel *(09) 887 8592* **Closed** *Sun & Mon*
Japanese cuisine with a difference. The exquisite dishes are a world away from takeaway sushi. The octopus sashimi is a popular choice.

Euro $$$
Fine dining Map E2
Shed 22, Princes Wharf, Viaduct
Tel *(09) 309 9866*
Euro boasts an exceptional, diverse menu created under the leadership of chef Simon Gault. Try the pizzas or the Bluff oysters. Lovely waterfront views.

The French Café $$$
French Map E2
210 Symonds St, Eden Tce, 1010
Tel *(09) 377 1911* **Closed** *Sun & Mon*
Winner of the prestigious Cuisine Restaurant of the Year 2016 award, this place offers delectable food and premium wines served by knowledgeable staff.

Sugar Club $$$
Fusion Map E2
Level 53, Sky Tower, 90 Federal St, CBD, 1010
Tel *(09) 363 6365*
In this fourth incarnation of the iconic Sugar Club, chef Peter Gordon expertly combines Asian and European cuisine 57 floors above Auckland in the Sky Tower.

Northland

DARGAVILLE: Funky Fish Café $
Café Map E1
34 Seaview Rd, Baylys Beach, 0377
Tel *(09) 439 8883*
A classic New Zealand fish 'n' chips experience with a difference: this is a restaurant, café and bar in one with live music, and nature on its doorstep.

KAITAIA: Bushman's Hut $$
Steakhouse Map D1
5 Bank St, 0410
Tel *(09) 408 4320* **Closed** *Sun & Mon*
Casual dining in a rustic atmosphere, often with live music. The steak is legendary and portions are generous.

KAWAKAWA: Railway Station Café $
Café Map E1
102 Gillies St, 0210
Tel *(09) 404 1110*
Located right on the railway, this café has a great vibe and offers superb coffee and large portions of food in a cosy setting.

For more information on types of restaurants *see pages 308–309*

Alfresco dining in the subtropical gardens at Food At Wharepuke

KERIKERI: Ake Ake Vineyard and Restaurant $$
Vineyard   Map E1
165 Waimate North Rd, 0293
Tel *(09) 407 8230*
This bistro-style restaurant uses fresh local produce to create fulsome flavours that complement the organic wines.

KERIKERI: The Black Olive Restaurant $$
Mediterranean   Map E1
380 Kerikeri Rd
Tel *(09) 407 9693*   **Closed** *Mar–Dec: Mon*
Mediterranean-inspired cuisine with classic pizzas, fish dishes, salads and special kids' meals.

DK Choice

KERIKERI: Food At Wharepuke $$
Fusion   Map E1
190 Kerikeri Rd, 0230
Tel *(09) 407 8936*   **Closed** *Sun & Mon*
Serving European and Thai-inspired dishes, Food At Wharepuke wins awards and critics' accolades year after year for its tasty concoctions made largely from the restaurant's own organic produce. Its accent on Thai flavours complements the airy garden setting.

KERIKERI: Marsden Estate $$
Café   Map E1
56 Wiroa Rd, 0293
Tel *(09) 407 9398*
Come here to enjoy exquisitely prepared fresh food with excellent wines on a terrace overlooking the vineyard and lake. A great experience.

For key to prices *see page 314*

KOHUKOHU: Koke Pub and Café $
Café   Map D1
1372 Kohukohu Rd, 0491
Tel *(09) 405 5808*
Hearty dishes, such as creamy mushroom pies, fish 'n' chips, and great coffee, are served at this delightful open-air café in a remote village. The portions are generous and the prices reasonable.

MANGAWHAI: The Cow Shed Restaurant $
Pub   Map E1
53 Pebblebrooke Road, 0573
Tel *(09) 431 2354*   **Closed** *Sun–Wed*
Housed in a converted cow shed and operated by a local family, this BYOB eatery serves generous servings of home-style food. Book ahead for the 3-course set menu.

MANGAWHAI: Frog and Kiwi $$
French   Map E1
6 Molesworth Drive, 0505
Tel *(09) 431 4439*
An intimate, charming restaurant serving genuine Gallic dishes, the Frog and Kiwi invites patrons to linger. Good service.

MANGAWHAI: Harvest Blue Café and Bistro $$
Café   Map E1
198 Molesworth Drive, 0505
Tel *(09) 431 4111*   **Closed** *dinner*
A reliably great daytime café, Harvest has an extensive menu of flavourful dishes made using fresh, local produce. The eggs Benedict is a must.

MANGAWHAI: Sandbar Eatery $$
European   Map E1
7 Wood St, Mangawhai Heads, 0505
Tel *(09) 431 5587*   **Closed** *Sun–Tue dinner*
The food at Sandbar and Grill is prepared with locally sourced produce, perfectly paired with local wines. The ambience is relaxed – a good place to enjoy a full meal or just linger over coffee.

MANGONUI: Waterfront Café and Bar $$
Café   Map D1
1A Waterfront Drive, 0420
Tel *(09) 406 0850*
Excellent brunches featuring simple, fresh-cooked produce with a wine list to match, feature here. There is also a kids' menu.

MATAKANA: Ascension Osteria Restaurant $$
Italian   Map E2
480 Matakana Rd, 0982
Tel *(09) 422 9601*   **Closed** *Tue in summer; Mon–Thu in winter*
The famous Ascension vineyards offer an extensive and authentic Italian menu along with fine wines.

MATAKANA: Plume $$
Fine dining   Map E2
49A Sharp Rd, 0982 (near Warkworth)
Tel *(09) 422 7915*   **Closed** *Mon*
Fusion food made with local produce is served at this restaurant with panoramic vineyard views.

OMAPERE: Bryers Room Restaurant $$
New Zealand   Map D1
State Hwy. 12, 0473
Tel *(09) 405 8737*
Housed in a hotel, this restaurant specializes in seafood and offers a great selection of Northland wines.

OPUA: Marina Café $
Seafood   Map E1
Opua Marina Bldg, Baffin St, 0200
Tel *(09) 402 6991*
This family-run daytime venue serves an award-winning seafood chowder and has great views of the Marina and Kawakawa river. There is live music in summer.

PAIHIA: Alfresco's Restaurant and Bar $$
New Zealand   Map E1
6 Marsden Rd, 0200
Tel *(09) 402 6797*
Enjoy inspired food, made with fresh produce, and waterfront views. A great place to relax.

Lunching on the terrace at Marsden Estate, Kerikeri

**PAIHIA: Jimmy Jack's
Rib Shack** $$
American **Map** E1
9 Williams Rd, 0200
Tel *(09) 402 5002*
An unpretentious eatery whose
speciality is prime rib platters.
Big portions, cooked just right,
for a reasonable price.

RUSSELL: The Gables $$
Fine dining **Map** E1
19 The Strand, 0202
Tel *(09) 403 7670* **Closed** *Tue*
Housed in a heritage building, The
Gables serves perfectly cooked,
fresh local cuts of beef and lamb
as well as a range of seafood.
Stunning waterfront views.

WHANGAREI: Killer Prawn $$
Seafood **Map** E1
26–28 Bank St, 0110
Tel *(09) 430 3333* **Closed** *Sun*
A seafood-oriented delight,
Killer Prawn's menu includes
large seafood plates to share
and pizzas. It also has a busy bar.

The Central
North Island

**GISBORNE: Muirs Bookshop
and Café** $
Café **Map** F3
62 Gladstone Rd, 4010
Tel *(06) 867 9742*
Located above one of New
Zealand's finest independent
bookstores, this lovely daytime
café offers delicious coffee,
cakes, salads and savouries.

GISBORNE: Cantina Caliente $$
Tex-Mex **Map** F3
7 Oneroa Rd, 4010
Tel *(06) 868 6828* **Closed** *Mon*
A lively beachside Mexican
restaurant with famously large
portions and a selection of
rare tequilas.

**GISBORNE: Colosseum Banquet
and Bistro** $$
Mediterranean **Map** F3
10 Riverpoint Rd, Matawhero, 4071
Tel *(06) 867 4733* **Closed** *Sun–Tue*
A large restaurant, Colosseum
offers Mediterranean-style cuisine
with New Zealand touches. All
ingredients are sourced from
the garden and local farms.

**GISBORNE: Marina
Restaurant** $$
French **Map** F3
Vogel St, Whataupoko, 4010
Tel *(06) 868 5919* **Closed** *Sun
& Mon*
Fine French cuisine, cooked
by Michelin-trained chefs, is

Well-stocked bar at The Gables restaurant in Russell

served in an elegant setting –
a beautiful former ballroom
by the river.

**GISBORNE: Ussco Bar
and Bistro** $$
Bistro **Map** F3
16 Childers Rd, 4010
Tel *(06) 868 3246* **Closed** *Sun*
Set in a historic shipping company
building by the inner harbour,
Ussco's award-winning cuisine
features seasonal, local produce.

GISBORNE: Works Café $$
Café **Map** F3
41 Esplanade, Kaiti, 4010
Tel *(06) 868 9699* **Closed** *Sun dinner*
Lovely pub food is offered in a
beautiful old brick building with
indoor as well as outdoor dining.
Extensive beer and wine selection.

**GISBORNE: Bushmere
Arms** $$$
Fine dining **Map** F3
*Main Rd, Waerenga-a-Hika,
Gisborne, 4071*
Tel *(06) 862 5820* **Closed** *Mon*
In an exquisite, country garden
setting, Bushmere Arms has been
awarded the New Zealand Beef
and Lamb Hallmark of Excellence
Award every year since 1999.

HAMILTON: The River Kitchen $
Café **Map** E2
237 Victoria St, 3204
Tel *(07) 839 2906*
This daytime café keeps winning
Best Café awards for its delicious,
fresh, organic food.

HAMILTON: Vegan Buffet $
Chinese **Map** E2
148 Ward St, Hamilton Central, 3204
Tel *(07) 838 0805* **Closed** *Sat
& Sun*
Hamilton's Vegan Buffet is not
just popular with vegans and
vegetarians – many meat eaters
enjoy the tasty Chinese dishes
offered here.

**HAMILTON: Gothenburg
Restaurant** $$
Tapas **Map** E2
21 Grantham St, 3204
Tel *(07) 834 3562* **Closed** *Sun*
Specializing in tapas, this restaurant
also serves vegetarian, vegan and
gluten-free options. It has a huge
selection of mostly Belgian beers
and a stunning cheese board.

**HAMILTON: Jaipur Indian
Restaurant** $$
Indian **Map** E2
793 Victoria St, 3204
Tel *(07) 839 3400*
A traditional restaurant with
a wide-ranging menu offering
an authentic taste of India. Try
the butter chicken and *biryani*
(flavoured rice mixed with
meat, fish or vegetables).

**HASTINGS: Taste Cornucopia
Organic Café** $
Café **Map** F4
219 Heretaunga St East, 4122
Tel *(06) 878 8730* **Closed** *Sun*
Winner of numerous awards,
this café aims to use locally
grown organic food. It has a
kids' menu and a play area.

**HASTINGS: Te Awa Restaurant
and Winery** $$
Vineyard **Map** F4
2375 State Hwy 50, Hawkes Bay
Tel *(06) 879 7602* **Closed** *Sun; dinner*
Try the seven-spice pork belly at
this long-established restaurant
in the heart of wine country.

**HAVELOCK NORTH: Namaskar
India** $
Indian **Map** F4
10 Joll Rd, Hawkes Bay, 4130
Tel *(06) 877 7208*
World-class Indian chefs mix
spices by hand and use only
the freshest ingredients to
create a range of traditional
dishes here, all gluten-free.
All meat is free range.

For more information on types of restaurants *see pages 308–309*

Scenic outdoor terrace at the Terrôir Restaurant at Craggy Range, Havelock North

HAVELOCK NORTH: Deliciosa Tapas and Wine Bar $$
Spanish   Map F4
21 Napier Rd, Hawkes Bay, 4130
Tel *(06) 877 6031*   **Closed** *Sun*
Customers are encouraged to linger over and enjoy their food at this tapas restaurant with indoor and outdoor seating.

HAVELOCK NORTH: Terrôir Restaurant at Craggy Range $$
Vineyard   Map F4
253 Waimarama Rd, 4292
Tel *(06) 873 0143*   **Closed** *Mon & Tue in winter*
Enjoy delicious, French-style treats in an amazing setting at one of Hawkes Bay's most legendary wineries. The menu features seasonal offerings.

NAPIER: Crab Farm Restaurant $
Vineyard   Map F4
511 Main Rd, Bay View, 4104
Tel *(06) 836 6678*   **Closed** *Mon–Wed*
The small but delightful lunch menu at this winery includes fabulous seafood platters and seasonal specials made with fresh local produce are also on offer. Open for dinner on Friday.

NAPIER: Groove Kitchen Espresso $
Café   Map F4
112 Tennyson St, Hawkes Bay, 4110
Tel *(06) 835 8530*
The divine coffee alone makes this daytime café worth a visit, but the Groove Kitchen whips up great brunches as well, and, as the name implies, it plays the grooviest tunes.

NAPIER: Indigo $
Indian   Map F4
24A Hastings St, Hawkes Bay, 4110
Tel *(06) 834 4083*
This restaurant boasts chefs trained at five-star hotels, an extensive wine list that includes local wines and authentic Indian food prepared in a traditional charcoal oven.

NAPIER: Restaurant Indonesia $
Indonesian   Map F4
409 Marine Parade, Hawkes Bay, 4110
Tel *(06) 835 8303*   **Closed** *Mon*
Since1983 Restaurant Indonesia has been providing an inviting atmosphere and attentive service to accompany its authentic *Rijsttafel* (small plate) dishes.

NAPIER: SOURCE Café $
Café   Map F4
2 Puketapu Rd, Taradale, 4112
Tel *(06) 650 6930*
Homemade healthy food is served at this daytime eatery. Vegetarian and gluten-free options are available.

NAPIER: Caution Dining Lounge and Shed 2 $$
Contemporary   Map F4
56 West Quay, Ahuriri, 4110
Tel *(06) 835 2202*
Housed in a historic building that was once a wool shed, this eatery offers harbour views, intimate dining booths, craft beer and the best wood-fired pizzas in Napier.

DK Choice

NAPIER: Mission Estate Restaurant $$
Vineyard   Map F4
198 Church Rd, Taradale
Tel *(06) 845 9350*
Inside a seminary building, this award-winning restaurant serves contemporary cuisine with a European influ-ence. Diners can enjoy distinguished wines with delicious cuts of beef and lamb while gazing out over vineyards to the horizon.

NAPIER: Trattoria alla Toscana $$
Italian   Map F4
180 Emerson St, Hawkes Bay, 4110
Tel *(06) 834 1988*   **Closed** *Mon*
This beautiful family-owned restaurant serves fine traditional dishes. The homemade pasta and salsa are the house specialities.

NAPIER: Wine Street Restaurant $$
Fine dining   Map F4
12 Browning St. 4110
Tel *(06) 835 7800*
This sophisticated restaurant in the County Hotel offers a relaxed atmosphere, an oyster bar and an extensive cocktail menu.

ROTORUA: The Pizza Library Co $
Italian   Map E3
54 Springfield Rd, 3015
Tel *(07) 349 2328*
A family-run, rustic pizza eatery that takes you all the way to Italy. The amazing creations use a wide variety of toppings.

ROTORUA: Aorangi Peak Restaurant $$
European   Map E3
353C Mountain Rd, Ngongotaha, 3015
Tel *(07) 347 0036*
Photo opportunities abound at this amazingly scenic location that also boasts reasonably priced, award-winning food. Visit during the day for the stunning views.

ROTORUA: Mokoia Restaurant $$
Fine dining   Map E3
77 Robinson Ave, 3010
Tel *(07) 343 5100*
Award-winning beef and lamb dishes made with indiginous ingredients, herbs and spices, are the highlights at this restaurant with lovely views of Lake Rotorua.

TAURANGA: Mount Bistro Restaurant $$$
Bistro   Map E2
6 Adams Ave, Mt Maunganui, 3010
Tel *(07) 575 3872*   **Closed** *Mon*
The award-winning fusion food at Mount Bistro is made from fresh local produce.

Eating outside at the Mission Estate Restaurant, Napier

Chic, modern interior of Satori Lounge, Tauranga

TAURANGA: Satori Lounge $$
Sushi   **Map** E2
309 Maunganui Rd,
Mt Maunganui, 3116
Tel *(07) 575 0979*   **Closed** *Mon*
Satori Lounge is a unique
combination of sushi and cocktail
bar with resident DJs. The sushi
is rolled fresh when you order.

TURANGI: Lakeland House
Restaurant $$
New Zealand/European   **Map** E3
88 Wihi Rd, 3381
Tel *(07) 386 6442*
Stunning views of Lake Taupo
and the mountains compliment
the à la carte menu at this eatery.
Try the superb seafood chowder.

Wellington and
the South

MARTINBOROUGH: Tirohana
Restaurant $
Fine dining   **Map** E4
42 Purutanga Road, 5711
Tel *(06) 306 9933*
Located on the Tirohana Estate
Vineyard, this restaurant offers a
Mediterranean menu of superb
dishes. Wine tastings and platters
are also available.

NEW PLYMOUTH: Flame $
Indian   **Map** D3
151 Devon St East, Taranaki, 4310
Tel *(06) 758 0030*
Friendly staff, generous portions
of north Indian favourites and a
great selection of New Zealand
wines characterize this restaurant.

NEW PLYMOUTH: Sushi Ninja $
Japanese   **Map** D3
89 Devon St East, Taranaki, 4310
Tel *(06) 759 1392*   **Closed** *Sun*
This authentic sushi restaurant
is a casual dining experience by
day and a sake bar at night.

NEW PLYMOUTH: Gusto
Restaurant $$
New Zealand/European   **Map** D3
Ocean View Parade, 4310
Tel *(06) 759 8133*
Perched on the port, Gusto
offers sophisticated cuisine
and lovely sea views.

PALMERSTON NORTH:
The Bean Café $
Asian   **Map** E4
92 Broadway Ave, 4410
Tel *(06) 353 6556*   **Closed** *Sun & Mon*
Good-value, cheerful eatery
in a charming old building. This
is the place for stone bowl garlic
pepper chicken and bubble tea.

PALMERSTON NORTH:
Moxies Café $
Café   **Map** E4
67 George St, 4410
Tel *(06) 355 4238*
A daytime café, Moxies has a
broad all-day breakfast menu,
and separate menus for those
with gluten or dairy allergies.

PALMERSTON NORTH:
Aberdeen on Broadway $$
Steakhouse   **Map** E4
161 Broadway Avenue, 4410
Tel *(06) 962 5570*
This steakhouse has delectable
meat dishes on offer plus the
sauces and sides to match.
Vegetarians are also catered for.

PALMERSTON NORTH: Yatai
Japanese Izakaya $$
Japanese   **Map** E4
316 Featherston St, 4410
Tel *(06) 356 1316*   **Closed** *Sun*
Enjoy authentic dishes to share
and Japanese beers, cocktails
or sake at this restaurant in a
lovely old building.

TARANAKI: Volcanoview Grand
Café and Restaurant $
Family   **Map** D3
1917 Egmont Rd, Inglewood, 4386
Tel *(06) 756 6112*   **Closed** *Mon–Wed*
This alpine restaurant with endless
menu options is attached to a kids'
playground and campsite.

WELLINGTON: Cinta Malaysian
Kitchen $
Malaysian   **Map** D5
119 Manners St, Wellington
Central, 6011
Tel *(04) 385 8622*
A local favourite, Cinta Malaysian
Kitchen has basic decor but offers
great food in huge portions.

WELLINGTON: Memphis Belle
Coffee House $
Café   **Map** D5
38 Dixon St, Wellington Central, 6011
Tel *(021) 244 8852*
The food is fresh and healthy,
but Memphis Belle is really
about the coffee. Regular
winner of "Best Café" plaudits.

WELLINGTON: Rasa Malaysian $
Malaysian/South Indian   **Map** D5
200 Cuba St, Te Aro, 6011
Tel *(04) 384 7088*
This family-run restaurant serves
authentic, well prepared food.
The *Dosai* (South Indian pancake)
are a speciality and worth visiting
this restaurant for.

WELLINGTON: Saigon Taste $
Vietnamese   **Map** D5
17 Majoribanks St, Mt Victoria, 6011
Tel *(04) 801 6866*
Come here for reasonably
priced authentic Vietnamese
fare. Unpretentious venue
and warm service.

WELLINGTON: Ti Kouka Café $
Café   **Map** D5
76 Willis St, Wellington Central, 6011
Tel *(04) 472 7682*   **Closed** *Sun*
Expect fresh, organic dishes
made with local ingredients,
as well as great service, at the
daytime Ti Kouka Café.

WELLINGTON: Viva Mexico $
Mexican   **Map** D5
210C Left Bank, Wellington
Central, 6011
Tel *(04) 382 9913*   **Closed** *Mon*
This is a great restaurant for
hearty, authentic Mexican food
with both meat and vegetarian
options, in a rustic dining room.

Gusto Restaurant in New Plymouth, with a backdrop of Mt Taranaki

For more information on types of restaurants *see pages 308–309*

Guests at Havana Bar and Restaurant, an eatery popular for tapas in Wellington

WELLINGTON: Boulcott St Bistro and Winebar $$
Bistro   **Map** D5
99 Boulcott St, Wellington Central, 6011
Tel *(04) 499 4199*
This delightful bistro serves classic dishes with an innovative twist in a fabulous old villa. Specials include the Sunday roast and dessert with wine, and the $20 lunch which changes monthly.

WELLINGTON: Café Polo $$
Bistro   **Map** D5
82 Rotherham Terrace, Miramar, 6022
Tel *(04) 380 7273*   **Closed** *Mon*
The accent here is on Slow Food cooking using local organic produce and free-range meat and eggs. The coffee is organic and fair trade.

WELLINGTON: Capitol $$
Italian   **Map** D5
10 Kent Terrace, Wellington Central, 6011
Tel *(04) 384 2855*
Classic Italian dishes are served with a New Zealand twist.

WELLINGTON: Field and Green $$
European   **Map** D5
262 Wakefield St, Te Aro, 6011
Tel *(04) 384 4992*   **Closed** *Mon & Tue; Sun dinner*
The menu at this eatery changes weekly with the seasons and is rustic, understated and delicately cooked. You can dine at a bar in the kitchen and watch all the action.

WELLINGTON: The General Practitioner $$
Pub   **Map** D5
100 Willis St, Wellington Central, 6011
Tel *(04) 499 6001*   **Closed** *Sun*
A gastro-pub in a former doctor's residence, famous for "wild food". The dinner menu changes daily.

WELLINGTON: The Green Man $$
Pub   **Map** D5
25 Victoria St, Wellington Central, 6011
Tel *(04) 499 5440*   **Closed** *Sun*
This big gastro-pub is always busy. The super-spicy chicken wings are a speciality.

WELLINGTON: Havana Bar and Restaurant $$
Cuban/Spanish   **Map** D5
32a–34 Wigan St, Wellington Central, 6011
Tel *(04) 384 7039*   **Closed** *Sun*
A Cuban-themed eatery serving tasty tapas. There is live music most evenings.

WELLINGTON: Hummingbird Eatery and Bar $$
Bar   **Map** D5
22 Courtenay Place, Wellington Central, 6011
Tel *(04) 801 6336*
Unpretentious, tasty food, good cocktails and an extensive wine list make this a popular venue.

WELLINGTON: The Larder $$
New Zealand   **Map** D5
133 Darlington Rd, Miramar, 6022
Tel *(04) 891 0354*   **Closed** *Mon*
Flavourful, fresh and locally grown seasonal produce is used at this great café situated close to the town centre.

WELLINGTON: Muse Eatery and Bar $$
New Zealand/European   **Map** D5
56 Victoria St, Wellington Central, 6011
Tel *(04) 499 7548*   **Closed** *Sun*
Local organic produce is used to prepare the New Zealand–European fusion dishes here.

WELLINGTON: Olive Café $$
Mediterranean   **Map** D5
170/172 Cuba St, Te Aro, 6011
Tel *(04) 802 5266*   **Closed** *Sun & Mon dinner*
A restaurant, café and bar, this secluded haven has an inner city garden courtyard furnished with palm trees and wooden décor. Menu changes with the seasons.

WELLINGTON: Ortega Fish Shack and Bar $$
Seafood   **Map** D5
16 Majoribanks St, Wellington Central, 6011
Tel *(04) 382 9559*   **Closed** *Sun & Mon*
A popular restaurant for seafood lovers, with a relaxed, casual environment. Serves quality dishes.

WELLINGTON: Shed 5 Restaurant and Bar $$
Seafood   **Map** D5
3 Queens Wharf, Wellington Central, 6011
Tel *(04) 499 9069*
Super-fresh seafood picked by the restaurant's own fishmonger and top New Zealand wines make this one of Wellington's leading seafood restaurants. Also serves quality lamb, beef and wild meats.

WELLINGTON: Shepherd Restaurant $$
New Zealand   **Map** D5
1/5 Eva St, Te Aro, 6011
Tel *(04) 385 7274*   **Closed** *Mon & Tue*
This popular restaurant is perfect for a relaxed evening out in a cosy atmosphere. The menu features dishes made with locally sourced ingredients. Excellent staff.

WELLINGTON: Two Souls Bistro $$
Bistro   **Map** D5
290 Wakefield St, Wellington Central, 6011
Tel *(04) 803 3137*
This restarant offers great-value and perfectly cooked dishes. The service is excellent.

WELLINGTON: Charley Noble Eatery and Bar $$$
New Zealand   **Map** D5
Huddart Parker Building, 1 Post Office Sq, Wellington Central, 6011
Tel *(04) 282 0205*
Locally sourced grass-fed steaks are cooked over a manuka-fired open-pit grill at this rustic restaurant. For those craving something fresh, there is a raw bar.

The cosy Hummingbird Eatery and Bar, Wellington

Lavish interior of the award-winning Logan Brown restaurant, Wellington

WELLINGTON:
Hippopotamus $$$
European **Map** D5
Museum Art Hotel 90 Cable St,
Wellington Central, 6011
Tel *(04) 802 8935*
Enjoy breathtaking harbour
views and superb dishes in
this quirky French-influenced
restaurant inside the Museum
Art Hotel *(see p305)*. Booking
is essential.

DK Choice

WELLINGTON:
Logan Brown $$$
New Zealand **Map** D5
Cnr Cuba and Vivian sts,
Wellington, 6011
Tel *(04) 801 5114* **Closed** *Mon*
Since it opened in 1996
Logan Brown has won many
awards. Contemporary dishes
containing fresh local produce
are prepared using classic
cooking methods. The elegant
but relaxed atmosphere,
extensive wine list and
excellent service make for an
exceptional dining experience.

WELLINGTON: MariLuca
Ristoro $$$
Italian **Map** D5
55 Mulgrave St, Thorndon, 6011
Tel *(04) 499 5590* **Closed** *Sun*
Dishes that emphasize freshness
and simplicity, including hand-
made pasta, are served here.

WELLINGTON: Portlander Bar
and Grill $$$
Steakhouse **Map** D5
75 Featherston St, Wellington
Central, 6011
Tel *(04) 498 3762*
It is hard to argue with the
Portlander Bar and Grill's claim
to being the best steakhouse

in Wellington. The excellent
food is served in a relaxed
environment.

WELLINGTON: Whitebait $$$
New Zealand **Map** D5
Clyde Quay Wharf, Te Aro, 6001
Tel *(04) 385 8555*
Come to this restaurant for tasty
food made with local ingredients
such as fish from the harbour,
foraged wild edibles, *kaimoana*
(shellfish) and wild game.

Marlborough and Nelson

BLENHEIM: The Burleigh $$
Deli **Map** D5
72 New Renwick Rd, 7201
Tel *(03) 579 2531* **Closed** *Sun; dinner*
Renowned for its delicious
gourmet pies with both classic
as well as unusual fillings such
as pork belly and jerk chicken.
Baguettes, French cheeses and
good coffee are also available.

BLENHEIM: Twelve Trees $
Vineyard **Map** D5
229 Jacksons Rd, 7273
Tel *(03) 572 7123*
Located at the famous Allan
Scott vineyard, Twelve Trees is
a popular lunchtime destination
with a great seasonal menu.
The name refers to the original
walnut trees that lined the
winery's entrance.

BLENHEIM: Raupo Riverside
Café and Restaurant $$
French **Map** D5
6 Symons St, 7201
Tel *(03) 577 8822*
In an eco-friendly building
overlooking the river, this eatery
offers fresh innovative cuisine as
well as an in-house patisserie.

BLENHEIM: St Clair
Vineyard Kitchen $$
New Zealand **Map** D5
Corner of Raupara and Selmes Rd, 7273
Tel *(03) 570 5280*
A lunchtime restaurant that
overlooks the stunning Richmond
Ranges. Try the vine-wrapped
Merino lamb loin paired with
an award winning wine.

Blenheim: Wither Hills $$
Vineyard **Map** D5
211 New Renwick Rd, Burleigh, 7272
Tel *(03) 520 8284*
This beautiful restaurant, in
one of New Zealand's most
celebrated wineries, is named for
the Wither Hills range that forms
its backdrop. Everything on the
menu is handmade on site.

DK Choice

BLENHEIM: Herzog Winery
and Restaurant $$$
Vineyard **Map** D5
81 Jeffries Rd, RD3 Marlborough,
7273
Tel *(03) 572 8770* **Closed** *Mon &*
Tue; May–Nov
A famous Marlborough vineyard
restaurant, Herzog specializes
in a tasting menu that is a
multi-course offering of flavours
to complement perfectly the
accompanying wines (there
are over 500 wines to choose
from). There is a charming
Mediterranean-style garden
with views of the vineyard
for outdoor dining.

HAVELOCK: Mussel Pot $
Seafood **Map** D4
73 Main Rd, 7100
Tel *(03) 574 2824* **Closed** *late Jun–*
Aug
This iconic restaurant specializes
in green-lipped mussels. There
are different menus for breakfast,
lunch and dinner. Vegetarian and
gluten-free options, too.

NELSON: Akbabas $
Turkish **Map** D4
130 Bridge St, 7010
Tel *(03) 548 8825*
A family-run restaurant that
offers authentic Turkish kebabs
(Iskenders) and *mezze*. A special
kids menu is available.

NELSON: East St Vegetarian
Café Bar $
Café **Map** D4
8 Church St, 7010
Tel *(03) 970 0575* **Closed** *Mon*
All the tasty dishes are freshly
prepared at this vegetarian
café and include vegan and
gluten-free options.

For more information on types of restaurants *see pages 308–309*

NELSON: La Gourmandise $
French   Map D4
276 Hardy St, 7010
Tel *(03) 546 6348*   **Closed** *Sun & Mon*
Only organic, local produce is used and half the menu is gluten-free at this friendly, unpretentious creperie. As well as sweet and savoury crepes there are also salads and sandwiches.

NELSON: Morrison Street Café $
Café   Map D4
244 Hardy St, 7010
Tel *(03) 548 8110*
Winner of many café awards, the Morrison Street Café serves a variety of platters, burgers, salads and excellent coffee. There are also two art galleries on site, with frequently changing exhibitions.

NELSON: Urban Oyster Bar and Eatery
Street Food $ Map D4
278 Hardy St, 7010
Tel *(03) 546 7861*   **Closed** *Sun*
Run by the award winning Michelin trained chef Matt Bouterey, this casual eatery serves top quality local innovative food in a relaxed setting right on the street.

NELSON: Ford's Restaurant & Bar $$
New Zealand/European   Map D4
276 Trafalgar St, 7010
Tel *(03) 546 9400*
Housed in a historic villa and boasting a diverse tapas menu and European-style dishes with New Zealand influences, this family-run restaurant is a Nelson secret worth discovering. Open for breakfast, lunch and dinner.

NELSON: Hopgoods $$
Bistro   Map D4
284 Trafalgar St, 7010
Tel *(03) 545 7191*   **Closed** *Sun*
An award winning fine-dining restaurant, Hopgoods mixes great service with a relaxed

The bright, arty interior of Morrison Street Café, Nelson

atmosphere. The seasonal menu consists of simple dishes made from local ingredients. Nelson wines feature strongly on the drinks list.

NELSON: Tides Restaurant & Bar $$
Seafood   Map D4
66 Trafalgar St, 7010
Tel *(03) 548 7049*
With an accent on seafood, this restaurant's diverse menu also includes game, beef and lamb. There is also a kids menu. The balcony offers lovely river views.

PICTON: Cortado Restaurant, Bar & Café $$
European   Map D4
Cnr High Street & London Quay, 7220
Tel *(03) 573 5630*   **Closed** *Mon & Tue in winter*
Located on the waterfront promenade, Cortado offers a relaxed atmosphere in which to enjoy European-inspired dishes, including tapas, seafood and Italian-style pizzas made with local produce There is also good coffee and craft beers

PICTON: Le Café $$
European   Map D4
12 London Quay, 7220
Tel *(03) 573 5588*
Divided into formal and casual dining areas, Le Café combines

great sea views with European-inspired dishes cooked with care and pride. There is regular live music in the evenings. Open for breakfast, lunch and dinner.

Canterbury and the West Coast

AORAKI/MT COOK: Alpine Restaurant $$$
International   Map B6
The Hermitage, Terrace Road Aoraki Mt Cook Village
Tel *(03) 435 1809*
Sumptuous buffets for breakfast, lunch and dinner combined with breathtaking views of Aoraki Mt Cook from every table. A range of fare to suit different taste buds including soups, salads, seafood, meats and desserts.

CHRISTCHURCH: Bamboozle Oriental Fusion $
Asian   Map C6
151 Cambridge Terrace, Christchurch Central, 8013
Tel *(03) 366 9991*
Chef Phillip Kraal's Asian restaurant offers traditional oriental dishes as well as some with fusion leanings, such as steamed buns filled with Caesar salad ingredients.

CHRISTCHURCH: Beat Street Café $
Café   Map C6
324 Barbadoes St, Christchurch Central, 8011
Tel *(03) 366 6324*
This café offers the best egg-laced breakfasts in Christchurch. All ingredients are sourced locally and the food is cooked in an open-plan kitchen.

CHRISTCHURCH: Dimitri's Greek Food $
Greek   Map C6
84A Riccarton Road, 8011
Tel *(03) 377 7110*   **Closed** *Sun & Mon*
A bustling daytime restaurant that never skimps on meat or flavour. The decor is basic, but the food is great. The *souvlaki* is a highlight.

CHRISTCHURCH: Mrs Hucks Eatery and Events $
Café   Map C6
12 Show Place, Addington, 8024
Tel *(03) 982 5471*
Refreshing beverages, salads and sandwiches are on offer in the warm ambience of this contemporary daytime café. Quality wines and beer on tap also on the menu.

A rack of New Zealand lamb served with couscous and a pomegranate sauce

For key to prices *see page 314*

Modern, stylish dining room at Christchurch's Pescatore Restaurant

CHRISTCHURCH: Mum's 24 Restaurant $
Asian   Map C6
62 Manchester St, Christchurch Central, 8011
Tel *(03) 365 2211*
This restaurant offers traditional, slow-cooked Korean and Japanese food with fresh spices and ingredients.

DK Choice

CHRISTCHURCH: The Thai Kitchen $
Thai   Map C6
239A Colombo St, 8023
Tel *(03) 332 8280*
Fresh, flavoursome Thai fare, considered by many to be the best in Christchurch, is offered at The Thai Kitchen. The portions are generous, and there are vegetarian and gluten-free options too. Welcoming atmosphere.

CHRISTCHURCH: 50 Bistro $$
Bistro   Map C6
50 Park Terrace, 8013
Tel *(03) 371 0250*
This place, overlooking Hagley Park, has a stylish interior and an extensive outdoor area. The menu features classic bistro dishes with a twist and there is a wine selection to match.

CHRISTCHURCH: Casa Nostra Italian Restaurant $$
Italian   Map C6
2 Waterman Place, Ferrymead, 8023
Tel *(03) 384 3186*
A family-run restaurant and bar serving authentic homemade Italian cuisine from breads and salads to pasta and risotto. The seafood dishes are highly recommended. Takeaways are also available.

CHRISTCHURCH: Cook 'N' With Gas $$
Bistro   Map C6
23 Worcester Boulevard, Christchurch Central, 8013
Tel *(03) 377 9166*   **Closed** *Sun*
Housed inside a 19th-century villa, this celebrated eatery is all about fine dining on a budget. The menu offers modern New Zealand cuisine and over 200 beers and wines.

CHRISTCHURCH: Curator's House Restaurant $$
Spanish   Map C6
7 Rolleston Ave, Botanic Gardens, 8013
Tel *(03) 379 2252*
Enjoy the view of the Botanic Gardens while dining on tasty Spanish-influenced dishes.

CHRISTCHURCH: Dux Dine $$
Seafood/Vegetarian   Map C6
28 Riccarton Road, 8011
Tel *(03) 348 1436*   **Closed** *Sun & Mon*
Housed in a renovated villa, this Christchurch institution has been revamped into a Mediterranean-style restaurant. It serves good platters and caters for children.

CHRISTCHURCH: Misceo Café & Bar $$
Café   Map C6
Cnr Ilam & Clyde Rd, Ilam, 8041
Tel *(03) 351 8011*
Buzzing upmarket pub-style food is served in this popular suburban eatery.

CHRISTCHURCH: The Old Vicarage Café, Restaurant and Bar $$
Fine dining   Map C6
335 Halswell Rd, Halswell, 8025
Tel *(03) 322 1224*
The warm and inviting Old Vicarage offers European and New Zealand dishes. Open for breakfast, lunch and dinner.

CHRISTCHURCH: The Station Restaurant $$
Korean   Map C6
1 Restell St, Papanui, 8053
Tel *(03) 354 9003*
Enjoy spicy, mouth-watering Korean food, and a karaoke "train booth" in the garden.

CHRISTCHURCH: Pescatore Restaurant $$$
Seafood   Map C6
50 Park Terrace, 8011
Tel *(03) 371 0257* **Closed** *Sun & Mon*
This premium restaurant offers contemporary fine dining and lovely views of Hagley Park.

CHRISTCHURCH: Saggio di Vino $$$
Modern Italian   Map C6
179 Victoria St, 8014
Tel *(03) 379 4006*
The Italian-inspired cuisine here is simple and refined, and the wines are exquisite.

HAAST: The Cray Pot $
Seafood   Map B6
The Espalanade, Jacksons Bay, Westland, 7886
Tel *(03) 750 0035*
A simple cabin at the end of the road with a brilliant view. Serves fresh seafood - tender fillets in the lightest batter, fish and chips, crayfish and chowder. Impeccable location and value.

HAAST: The Salmon Farm Café $
Café   Map B6
6156 Haast Hwy, Paringa, Westland, 7886
Tel *(03) 751 0837*
In a beautiful forest setting, this café at the South Westland Salmon Farm offers delectable, fresh fish dishes.

For more information on types of restaurants *see pages 308–309*

Marine-themed booths at Fishbone Bar & Grill, Queenstown

HANMER SPRINGS: Monteiths Brewery Bar $$
Pub   **Map** C5
47 Amuri Avenue, 5133
Tel *(03) 315 0035*
Welcoming, comfortable bar with huge steaks and fresh blue cod. Wash down the superb food with locally made craft beer. Located next to the thermal pools, this is the place to eat after a hot soak.

HOKITIKA: Ocean View Restaurant $$
Seafood/Mediterranean   **Map** C5
111 Revell St, Westland, 7810
Tel *(03) 755 8344*
Enjoy the catch of the day while gazing at the panoramic view of the ocean at this restaurant in the Beachfront Hotel Hokitika.

HURUNUI: The Mud House Winery Café $$
Vineyard   **Map** C5
780 Glasnevin Rd, Waipara, 7447
Tel *(03) 314 6900*
Set among vines and rolling hills, The Mud House specializes in classic New Zealand fare such as game pies and fish 'n' chips.

KARAMEA: Karamea Village Hotel $
Pub   **Map** C4
141 Waverly St, 7893
Tel *(03) 782 6800*
This lovingly restored old country pub serves hearty home cooked food. Try the whitebait fritters.

Otago and Southland

DUNEDIN: Buddha Stix $
Asian   **Map** B7
678 George St, 9016
Tel *(03) 421 6706*
Savour a vibrant fusion of Asian culinary styles in a fine dining setting at this restaurant. On the menu are spicy soups and

salads along with noodles and rice dishes. The sharing menus are value for money.

DUNEDIN: Luna Bar $$
Bar   **Map** B7
314 Highgate, Roslyn, 9010
Tel *(03) 477 2227*
Enjoy spectacular views of Dunedin, an extensive wine list and inspired dishes. Relax in the bar or on the sunny deck.

DUNEDIN: Salt Bar & Restaurant $$
Bistro   **Map** B7
240 Forbury Rd, Saint Clair, 9012
Tel *(03) 455 1077*
A café by day and a bar and restaurant by night, Salt offers a diverse range of culinary options in a beautiful Art Deco venue.

DUNEDIN: Speights Ale House $$
Southern New Zealand   **Map** B7
200 Rattray St, Dunedin, 9016
Tel *(03) 471 9050*
One of New Zealand's oldest breweries, Speights Ale House

Freshly baked bread at Riverstone Kitchen, Oamaru

features classics such as seafood chowder, blue cod, lamb shanks, steak and venison. There are good vegetarian options. Package deals include tours of the brewery.

INVERCARGILL: Level One Restaurant and Bar $$
Southern New Zealand   **Map** A7
20 Kelvin St, 9810
Tel *(03) 218 2829*
Situated on the first floor of the Kelvin hotel, Level One is a sophisticated restaurant with a diverse range of menu options. Try the beer battered southern blue cod.

OAMARU: Riverstone Kitchen $$
Southern New Zealand   **Map** B7
1431 State Hwy 1, 9493
Tel *(03) 431 3505*   **Closed** *Tue & Wed*
Famed chef Bevan Smith's "always seasonal, always local" dishes have won many awards. The daily-changing chef's tasting menu with seasonal ingredients is particularly recommended.

QUEENSTOWN: Eichardt's Bar $
Tapas   **Map** A6
2 Marine Parade, 9348
Tel *(03) 441 0450*
Fresh organic produce is served in an array of tapas-style platters at this bar, also famous for its cocktails. Comfortable sofas and a cosy fireplace give it a homely atmosphere.

QUEENSTOWN: 1876 $$
Tapas   **Map** A6
45 Ballarat St, 9300
Tel *(03) 409 2178*
Located in a former courthouse, this restaurant offers tapas platters to share, as well as salads, burgers, steaks and a children's menu. There is a sunny courtyard for alfresco dining.

QUEENSTOWN: Birches Restaurant $$
Fine dining   **Map** A6
146 Arthurs Point Rd, Queenstown-Lakes, 9371
Tel *(03) 441 0288*
Part of the Distinction Hotel, Birches offers sophisticated dishes made with prime local produce. Stunning alpine views.

QUEENSTOWN: Fishbone Bar & Grill $$
Seafood   **Map** A6
7 Beach St, 9300
Tel *(03) 442 6768*
Choose from the freshest seafood, including dishes such as crumbed blue cod with tartare sauce. Fishbone sources only sustainable fish, and much of the produce is grown on their own farm.

QUEENSTOWN: Lombardi $$
New Zealand **Map** A6
10 Brunswick St, 9300
Tel *(03) 442 4990*
In the Hotel St Mortiz, Lombardi
has three dining spaces: tapas in
the bar; pizzas in the dining room;
and fine dining in The Library, all
with lovely alpine and lake views.

QUEENSTOWN: Public
Kitchen & Bar $$
Regional **Map** A6
*Ground floor, Steamer Wharf,
Beach St, 9300*
Tel *(03) 442 5969*
In a spectacular location, this fine
restaurant has stunning lake
views and an excellent wine list
to match the food. The kitchen
uses local produce.

QUEENSTOWN: The Bunker
Restaurant and Bar $$$
Fine dining **Map** A6
4 Cow Lane, 9300
Tel *03 441 8030*
An intimate, rustic restaurant with
an extensive wine and cocktail list,
The Bunker showcases produce
from New Zealand's regions,
including game and red meat.
There is a superb tasting menu.

QUEENSTOWN: Gantleys
Restaurant $$$
Fine dining **Map** A6
*172 Arthurs Point Rd, Arthurs
Point 9371*
Tel *03 442 8999*
Housed in a historic stone
building that was once a wayside
inn for gold miners, Gantleys offers
superb New Zealand cuisine.

QUEENSTOWN: Rata $$$
Fine dining **Map** A6
43 Ballarat St, 9300
Tel *(03) 442 9393*
Michelin-trained star chef Josh
Emmett is the talent behind Rata,

Cosy interior of Gantleys Restaurant,
Queenstown, in an old stone building

with its emphasis on slow cooked,
full-flavoured dishes. It also has a
courtyard for outdoor dining.

DK Choice

QUEENSTOWN: Roaring
Meg's Restaurant $$$
Fine dining **Map** A6
53 Shotover St, Queenstown, 9300
Tel *(03) 442 9676* **Closed** *Mon*
This restaurant has won many
accolades for its beef and lamb
dishes. Try the award-winning
rack of Canterbury lamb. The
elegant Victorian decor and
candlelit dining room give it a
refined, romantic atmosphere.

QUEENSTOWN: True South
Dining Room $$$
Fine dining **Map** A6
377 Frankton Rd, 9300
Tel *(03) 450 1100*
Located in the Rees Hotel, True
South offers elegant dining with
awe-inspiring views of the lake
and mountains, and a selection
of wines so good that it wins

international awards. A children's
menu and vegetarian options are
available on request.

STEWART ISLAND: Church
Hill Restaurant and
Oyster Bar $$
Seafood **Map** A7
36 Kamahi Rd, Oban, Southland, 9846
Tel *(03) 219 1323* **Closed** *Jun–Sep*
This amazing restaurant has
a menu that focuses on local
seafood, including the famous
Stewart Island oysters.

WANAKA: Amigos Mexican
Grill $
Mexican **Map** B6
71 Ardmore St, 9305
Tel *03 443 7872*
Family-owned Amigos offers
a budget-conscious selection
of traditional favourites. The corn
chips are cooked fresh everyday,
and the margaritas are delicious.
Children are very welcome and
there is a kids' menu, puzzles
and games.

WANAKA: Wanaka Bullock
Bar – The Grill Restaurant $$
Steakhouse **Map** B6
71 Ardmore St, 9305
Tel *(03) 443 7148*
A meat lovers' delight, The Grill
is famous for its 1 kg (2.2 lb) plate
of BBQ ribs, juicy steaks and large
range of local wines. It is very
child-friendly, with high-chairs,
a children's menu and even
crayons and colouring sheets.

WANAKA: Bistro Gentil $$$
Fine dining **Map** B6
76A Golf Course Rd, 9305
Tel *03 443 2299*
Dine on exquisite French cuisine
while enjoying fabulous mountain
views. The kitchen uses seasonal
ingredients from its garden.
Good selection of Gallic wines.

Façade of Public Kitchen, Queenstown

SHOPPING IN NEW ZEALAND

New Zealand has a lot to offer the visiting shopper, including goods not available in most other countries. Such items range from traditional Māori bone and greenstone carvings to sheepskin rugs and handmade wool sweaters. Many small towns in popular tourist areas have galleries where local crafts people sell their goods, and Auckland, Wellington and Christchurch have major markets where artisans sell unique products. Because New Zealand is one of the most open economies in the world, with few tariffs and no import licensing, goods such as cameras and audio equipment are very reasonably priced. New Zealand's wines *(see pp312–13)*, meats, seafoods, dairy products and fruits are also well worth sampling.

Kirkcaldie and Stains, Wellington's leading department store

Shopping Hours

Most shops in New Zealand are open from 9am to 5pm or 5:30pm, Monday to Saturday. Most stores are open on Sundays also for shorter hours. In big cities, late-night shopping is usually available on Thursdays or Fridays, when stores stay open until 9pm.

Supermarkets and shopping malls in urban areas are open seven days a week, and many supermarkets stay open until 8pm or 9pm and some offer a 24-hour service. In towns, suburbs and rural areas, dairies stay open long hours.

How to Pay

Credit and debit cards are accepted by most stores, usually with a minimum purchase limit. If your card is encoded with a PIN number, you can withdraw cash from one of the many automatic teller machines at banks and shopping centres. Identification, such as a passport or driver's licence, is required when presenting traveller's cheques. Personal cheques are accepted less and less now; shops prefer debit or credit cards. New Zealand shopkeepers are not accustomed to bargaining and many also prefer cash transactions.

All goods sold in New Zealand are levied a Goods and Service Tax (GST) of 15 per cent, which is included in the purchase price. GST is not refunded when you leave New Zealand.

Rights and Refunds

The **Consumers' Institute** (04) 384 7963) can provide detailed information about your rights as a buyer. If the goods purchased are defective, you are entitled to a refund. If you decide you do not like an item, many shops will allow you to return or exchange it for something else. If you want to return or exchange an item, you will need to present the receipt.

Department Stores

Each of the four main cities has a major department store selling high quality goods. In Auckland, it is **Smith and Caughey's**; in Wellington, **David Jones**; in Dunedin, **H&J Smith**, and in Christchurch, **Ballantynes**.

Farmers, Kmart and The Warehouse sell a wide range of lower priced goods, and have numerous branches throughout the country.

Shopping Malls

Large indoor shopping malls are a feature of cities and larger towns. Most are located in the suburbs rather then central city areas, and usually include at least one supermarket plus a range of shops selling items such as clothing, sports equipment, household appliances and books. Many also have food halls selling a variety of inexpensive meals.

Shop assistant arranging a display of Zambesi fashion clothes

Dairies

Dairies are small convenience stores that can be found in most towns and suburbs (though they are slowly disappearing). Hours of opening vary, but most are open seven days a week from about 7am until 8pm. They sell basic food supplies, snacks, drinks, newspapers and cigarettes.

Roadside Stalls

Roadside stalls selling fruit and vegetables are common in major horticultural areas such as the Bay of Plenty, Marlborough, Nelson and Central Otago. Many orchards and berry farms encourage people to "pick their own", and may also sell the produce at a reduced price. Strawberries can be found everywhere in late spring and summer; cherries in Marlborough at Christmas; apricots, nectarines and peaches in Otago around January–February, and kiwifruit in the Bay of Plenty and Tasman from April to September. Visitors should also look out for the many cheese factories in Waikato, Taranaki, Marlborough and Canterbury which sell delicious, locally made dairy products.

Markets

Most New Zealand markets specialize in crafts rather than foods, although Otara Market in South Auckland (*see p95*) specializes in Pacific foods. Farmers' markets, such as at Hastings and Dunedin, are also increasingly popular. Auckland, Christchurch and Nelson have craft markets. Opening times vary: in Auckland, the Victoria Park Market (*see p95*) is open daily; while Christchurch's Arts Centre market (*see p230*) and Nelson Market (*see p215*) are open at the weekend.

New Zealand-made crafts and souvenirs for sale in Blenheim

Handicrafts

A wide variety of shops selling locally made crafts and souvenirs can be found in New Zealand's main cities, tourist towns and resorts. In areas where the local craft industry is particularly strong, such as Coromandel (*see p131*) and Nelson (*see p217*), small galleries maintained by individual artists and crafts people are dotted along the roadsides. Museum shops, such as at the **Museum of New Zealand Te Papa Tongarewa**, Wellington (*see 170–71*), and **Auckland War Memorial Museum** (*see pp82–3*), also sell top-of-the-range handcrafted products.

The variety and quality of New Zealand handicrafts is continually improving. Products worth buying are traditional Māori flax baskets, bone and greenstone jewellery and ornaments, *paua* (abalone) shell jewellery, ceramics, hand-blown glassware, wood products made from New Zealand's native timbers, and sheepskin and wool items (*see pp328–9*).

Designer Labels

New Zealand has a number of internationally successful fashion designers, whose clothing can be bought in boutiques in the main cities. Labels to look for are Trelise Cooper, Karen Walker, World, Zambesi and NomD. Top quality casual wool clothing is available under several labels, including Untouched World.

Quality outdoor clothing and equipment is available under the Canterbury, Heritage and Macpac (*see p329*) brands. Arthur Ellis manufactures high quality Fairydown equipment. Icebreaker merino outdoor gear is very popular.

Goods on sale at Creative Queenstown Arts and Crafts Market

What to Buy in New Zealand

New Zealand offers a wide range of unique goods. Some, such as bone and greenstone carvings and jewellery, and *harakeke* (woven flax) items, are reflective of the country's Māori heritage, while others, such as sheepskin rugs and wool garments, reflect its strong agricultural base. Other good buys are wood products made from New Zealand's native timbers, ceramics, outdoor equipment, and food and wine. Hundreds of gift and craft shops, as well as department stores and museum shops, make it easy to find New Zealand-made products to suit every budget.

Sheepskin floor rug with thick, combed wool

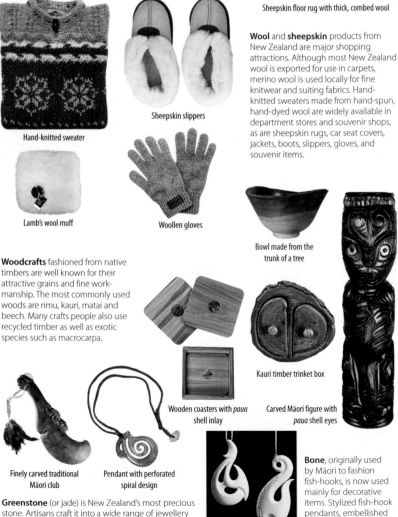

Hand-knitted sweater

Sheepskin slippers

Lamb's wool muff

Woollen gloves

Wool and **sheepskin** products from New Zealand are major shopping attractions. Although most New Zealand wool is exported for use in carpets, merino wool is used locally for fine knitwear and suiting fabrics. Hand-knitted sweaters made from hand-spun, hand-dyed wool are widely available in department stores and souvenir shops, as are sheepskin rugs, car seat covers, jackets, boots, slippers, gloves, and souvenir items.

Bowl made from the trunk of a tree

Woodcrafts fashioned from native timbers are well known for their attractive grains and fine workmanship. The most commonly used woods are rimu, kauri, matai and beech. Many crafts people also use recycled timber as well as exotic species such as macrocarpa.

Kauri timber trinket box

Wooden coasters with *paua* shell inlay

Carved Māori figure with *paua* shell eyes

Finely carved traditional Māori club

Pendant with perforated spiral design

Greenstone (or jade) is New Zealand's most precious stone. Artisans craft it into a wide range of jewellery and ornaments using both traditional Māori and contemporary designs (see p241).

Bone, originally used by Māori to fashion fish-hooks, is now used mainly for decorative items. Stylized fish-hook pendants, embellished with delicate tracery, are popular purchases.

Paua (abalone) is a shellfish mollusc found around the New Zealand coastline, but it is treasured more for its iridescent inner shell than for its meat. It is used to make pendants and earrings, and for inlays in woodcrafts and traditional Māori carvings.

Paua shell and silver pendants and necklace

Box with inset *paua* shell

Hand-painted dish

Wine goblet

Red glass vase

Ceramics and glassware are widely available craft items in New Zealand. Ceramics range from rustic earthenware pieces to delicate ornamental works and top quality tableware. Hand-blown glassware is of high quality, and many artisans are happy to allow visitors to watch them at their work *(see p217)*.

Perfume bottle

Earthenware coffee mug

Cat-shaped coffee pot

Outdoor equipment made in New Zealand is among the best in the world. One of the leading brands is Macpac, which regularly tests its own equipment in the mountains of the South Island. The best places to buy such goods are specialist outdoor equipment shops in the main cities.

Tent in bag

Windcheater

Backpack

Food and drink, products of New Zealand's extensive farmlands, include excellent meats, fruit, dairy produce and wines. As well as lamb and beef, speciality meats such as ostrich and venison are available. Cheeses made by small boutique factories are worth trying, as is New Zealand's delicious ice cream and its honey from native plants. New Zealand wines have also gained a strong international reputation *(see pp40–41, 312–13)*.

Selection of Kapiti cheeses

Kiwifruit flavoured chocolates

Jars of local honey

Sauvignon Blanc from Marlborough

ENTERTAINMENT IN NEW ZEALAND

From professional theatre, opera and ballet to Māori and Pacific Island culture, music and dance and "Down Under" rock music, New Zealand has a diverse entertainment scene. The liveliest places are the main cities, but even small provincial towns boast their own local bands and amateur performance societies.

New Zealand is on the itinerary of many international performers, although some of these venture no further than Auckland and Wellington. Māori culture is an important theme in New Zealand art, and is showcased at festivals and specialist venues, such Te Puia, a Māori arts and crafts centre situated in Rotorua.

Information Sources

Tourism New Zealand posts a yearly calendar of events around the country on its website *(see p331)*. Daily newspapers and magazines such as *North and South*, *The Listener* and *Metro* also provide details about current and upcoming performances.

Auckland Live, Auckland's main entertainment complex

Major Venues

The major entertainment venues for the performing arts are located in New Zealand's four main cities. They include Auckland's **Auckland Live**, which comprises the Aotea Centre, Town Hall and Civic Theatre; Wellington's **Michael Fowler Centre** and **TSB Bank Arena**; Christchurch's **Town Hall** and **Isaac Theatre Royal**, and Dunedin's **Town Hall**.

Booking Tickets

It is wise to book in advance for most live performances. The easiest way is to use the nationwide **Ticketek** and **Ticketmaster** systems, either via the internet or by telephone through their many agencies around the country. In many cases, tickets can also be purchased at the venue.

Theatre

Professional theatre companies are restricted to the main cities, while the smaller provincial towns are served by amateur troupes. Wellington has the most vibrant theatre scene, with two professional theatre companies *(see pp160–61)*: **Circa**, a co-operative established in the 1970s, known for its consistently excellent plays; and **Bats**, best known for experimental theatre performances. New Zealand's only national Māori theatre company, **Taki Rua**, specializes in indigenous ethnic drama and is based in Wellington, but also tours the country regularly with new productions. Other professional theatre groups are the **Auckland Theatre Company**, which performs at the Maidment, Herald and Sky City theatres; the **Court Theatre** in Christchurch's historic Arts Centre; and the **Fortune Theatre**, located in Dunedin in an historic inner-city church.

Classical Music, Opera and Dance

The **New Zealand Symphony Orchestra** is based in Wellington *(see pp160–61)* but tours the country regularly, covering about 50,000 km (31,000 miles) a year, making it one of the most travelled orchestras in the world. It sometimes performs outdoor city concerts in the summer.

New Zealand's regional professional orchestra companies are of a high standard and perform regularly. The principal opera company is the **New Zealand Opera**, which performs mainly at the Aotea Centre in Auckland and in Wellington. Canterbury is home to Southern Opera.

Reece Mastin performing on his Beautiful Nightmare tour at the Michael Fowler Centre

A Royal New Zealand Ballet Company performance

The **Royal New Zealand Ballet** is the oldest professional dance company in Australasia. It tours the country frequently with a wide range of work *(see pp160–61)*.

Footnote Dance, New Zealand's only national contemporary dance troupe, also tours the country regularly, presenting productions created by New Zealand's own choreographers and composers.

Rock, Jazz and Country

Kiwi rock music has a quirky charm that attracts fans worldwide. The Mutton Birds, Dave Dobbyn, Neil Finn and The Datsuns are among New Zealand's most internationally successful rock performers, and they occasionally perform in the country. Many local bands perform in pubs and popular venues such as **Auckland Live**.

Events such as Wellington's International Arts Festival attract both local and international jazz performers *(see pp160–61)*, as do regional festivals such as the Bay of Islands Jazz and Blues Festival each August.

Country and Western has a strong following in New Zealand and there are a number of excellent singers and bands. Lovers of traditional country music should make their way to Gore in Southland during May and June to watch the Gold Guitar Awards.

Māori Music and Dance

Traditional Māori performing arts are showcased at a number of venues, including **Te Puia**, a Māori arts and crafts centre, at Rotorua *(see pp142–3)*, and at the **Auckland War Memorial Museum** *(see pp82–3)*, both staging daily concerts. The biennial three-day Aotearoa Traditional Māori Performing Arts Festival, held at different locations, features Māori culture, music and dance from around New Zealand. Tourist operators specializing in Māori heritage include music and dance in their programmes *(see p339)*.

Māori cultural performance at an arts festival in Wellington

DIRECTORY

Information Sources

Ticketek
Tel 0800 842 538.
w ticketek.co.nz

Ticketmaster
Tel (09) 970 9700.
w ticketmaster.co.nz

Tourism New Zealand
Tel (09) 914 4780.

Major Venues

Isaac Theatre Royal, Christchurch
Tel (03) 366 6326.

Michael Fowler Centre, Wellington
Tel (04) 801 4231.

Auckland Live, Auckland
Tel (09) 309 2677.

Town Hall, Christchurch
Tel (03) 366 8899.

Town Hall, Dunedin
Tel (03) 479 4398.

TSB Bank Arena, Wellington
Tel (04) 801 4231.

Theatre

Auckland Theatre Company
Tel (09) 309 0390.

Bats Theatre, Wellington
Tel (04) 802 4175.

Circa Theatre, Wellington
Tel (04) 801 7992.

Court Theatre, Christchurch
Tel 0800 333 100.

Fortune Theatre, Dunedin
Tel (03) 477 8323.

Taki Rua
Tel (04) 385 3110.

Classical Music, Opera and Dance

Footnote Dance
Tel (04) 384 7285.

New Zealand Opera
Tel 022 071 8850.

New Zealand Symphony Orchestra
Tel (04) 801 2035.

Royal New Zealand Ballet
Tel (04) 381 9000.

Māori Music and Dance

Te Puia, Rotorua
Tel 0800 405 623.

Film and Popular Music

New Zealand arts and entertainment are in the midst of a mini renaissance. Local music has benefited from a music commission that helps to market the industry both at home and overseas, so more New Zealand bands are now heard on the radio. The big theatres and cinema chains are found in the main centres *(see p96)*, but many smaller towns also have vibrant entertainment venues, many of which play host during the international festivals.

Film and Festivals

Although major New Zealand productions such as the *Lord of the Rings* trilogy have been making the headlines since 2001, for every Peter Jackson there are countless other filmmakers working on short films and digital feature films. New Zealanders love going to the cinema and advances in digital projection have prompted the revival of boutique suburban cinemas and an explosion of "small" big screen theatres that seat about 50 moviegoers in comfortable surroundings.

Alongside the growth in screen numbers there is an explosion in the number of specialist film festivals. The biggest of them all is the **International Film Festival**, now in its 40th year. It presents a programme of critically acclaimed films from the international festival circuit alongside classics and director showcases, and includes world premieres of works by new and established New Zealand filmmakers. The festival travels the country starting in the main centres in July and takes in the provinces until the end of the year. The magnificently refurbished **Embassy Theatre** in Wellington is one beneficiary of the festival's popularity. Dunedin's arthouse cinema **Metro** and the **Academy Gold** in Christchurch also host festival showings.

Out Takes is a festival for gay and lesbian film that takes place in May and June in Auckland, Wellington and Christchurch, while The Date Palm Film Festival in September focuses on film from the Middle East. The Documentary Edge Festival takes place in February and March, with showings in both Wellington and Auckland, including at Auckland's independent **Academy Cinema**. "The Italian Film Festival takes place in the main centres and provincial towns during October and November.

Popular Music

There is no definitive New Zealand sound, but artists who are able to instil a local flavour to whatever genre they work in stand out from the crowd. The Wellington-based dub/soul/funksters Fat Freddy's Drop picked up a major New Zealand Music award in 2005 for their album *Based on a True Story*.

New Zealand hip hop is popular, with producer P Money leading the way, and MCs such as Scribe and Ladi 6 topping the charts. Local hip hop often fuses American gangster styles with Pacific Island rhythms and tales. Dub, roots and reggae are also popular, especially at summer festivals; The Black Seeds, Katchafire and Kora are leaders in these genres.

The Datsuns are a three-piece rock band from the provincial town of Cambridge who have exported their AC/DC style power chords to the rest of the world. Led Zeppelin bass player John Paul Jones produced their second album. Bands such as the Sneaks and the Checks are following in their wake. Stereogram, Pluto and Elemeno P are mainstream pop rockers who have benefited from commercial radio's current inclusive approach to local music. Most of the live music action takes place in pubs and clubs, but established artists such as Neil Finn, Dave Dobbyn and Bic Runga now also play seated concerts in larger theatres such as the Opera House in Wellington and Auckland Live *(see p78)*.

Jazz festivals are held in Wellington, Nelson and on Waiheke Island, and the national country music awards are held annually at the bottom of the South Island in Gore.

Pubs, Bars, Cafés and Clubs

The traditional New Zealand pub with at least three bars and accommodation is alive in the provinces, but in the cities it is rapidly being replaced by smaller bars and cafés offering good food and live entertainment as well as drinks. Many bars and cafés turn the lights down and the music up later in the evening, however, with the entertainment starting when the food stops. It is worth checking whether food is still being served when you arrive. Irish-themed bars, with Guinness on tap and Irish music, can be found in most reasonable sized towns.

It is often said that Wellington has more bars, cafés and restaurants per head then New York City. That may or may not be true, but the most vibrant areas are in and around Courtenay Place and on Cuba Street. The bohemian-themed **Fidel's Café** is famous for Cuban brews, while nearby **Goldings Free Drive Bar** is known for its selection of craft beers. Bars cater for most musical tastes with **San Francisco Bathhouse**, **Refuel** and **Bar Bodega** flying the flag for live music while clubs like **Garden Club** and **Red Square** cater for the dance crowd. **The Matterhorn** and **Lagerfield** are some of the many that offer good food and an eclectic selection of DJs.

Auckland's nightlife is more dispersed. Viaduct Basin *(see p76)* was developed in the late 1990s to cater for followers of the Americas Cup yachting regatta. The cup may have gone but bars such as **Soul Bar & Bistro** and **Chic Lounge** remain. The city's dance clubs are mainly found on High Street, Ponsonby Road and Karangahape Road.

Cassete Number Nine and the **Golden Dawn** host live bands and DJs, and among the bars near High Street are **Impala** and **1885**. **Occidental Belgian Beer Café** is an institution and **Federal Delicatessen** is a charming deli. **Danny Doolans**, an Irish pub located in the Viaduct, has live music daily. Two main band venues are the **Kings Arms** and **Dogs Bollix**. Karangahape Road is home to such clubs as **K'Road Ballroom**, **Charlies Bar** and **Rising Sun**.

Christchurch is the home of New Zealand drum 'n' bass music. The premiere venues for live music are **Dux Central**, **Orleans, Churchills, The Physics Room** and **Mashina Lounge** that play host to local and touring bands. **Wunderbar** in nearby Lyttelton also has live music.

Dunedin's rich musical heritage can be experienced by a self-guided walking tour covering major landmarks of the celebrated **Dunedin's Sound of the 1980s**. Starting with Empire Tavern on Princes St, walking past Sammy's all

the way up to Coronation Hall on Māori Hill and further, on Otago Peninsula, to Lovers Leap. Dunedin was the birthplace of some of New Zealand's more influential guitar bands such as The Chills.

Chicks Hotel is a well-known haunt of a number of iconic Dunedin artists. It has a great atmosphere with locals and students converging to watch Dunedin music being performed. **Refuel** has local Dunedin bands playing live music most weekday nights. The **Crown Hotel** and **10 Bar** both host DJs and live music.

DIRECTORY

Film and Festivals

Academy Cinema
City Library Building,
44 Lorne St, Auckland.
Tel (09) 373 2761.

Academy Gold Cinema
The Colombo 22/363
Colombo St, Sydenham.
Tel (03) 377 9911.

Embassy Theatre
10 Kent Tce, Wellington.
Tel (04) 384 7657.

International Film Festival
ⓦ nziff.co.nz

Metro
Town Hall, Moray Place,
Dunedin.
Tel (03) 471 9635.

Pubs and Bars

10 Bar
10 The Octagon, Dunedin.
Tel 027 588 7447.

Bar Bodega
101 Ghuznee St,
Wellington.
Tel (04) 384 8212.

Charlies Bar
368 Karangahape Rd,
Auckland.
Tel (03) 369 1153.

Chicks Hotel
2 Mount St, Port
Chalmers.
Tel (03) 472 8736.

Crown Hotel
179 Rattray St, Dunedin.
Tel (03) 477 0132.

Dogs Bollix
2 Newton Rd
(K Rd End), Auckland.
Tel (09) 378 1845.

Goldings Free Drive Bar
14 Leeds St,
Wellington.
Tel (04) 381 3616.

Kings Arms
59 France St, Auckland.
Tel (09) 373 3240.

Occidental Belgian Beer Café
6–8 Vulcan Lane,
Auckland.
Tel (09) 300 6226.

Refuel
640, Cumberland St,
Dunedin.
Tel (03) 479 5300.

Rising Sun
373 Karangahape Rd,
Auckland.
Tel (09) 358 5643.

San Francisco Bathhouse (San Fran)
171 Cuba St, Wellington.
Tel (04) 801 6797.

Southern Cross
39 Abel Smith St,
Wellington.
Tel (04) 384 9085.

The Twisted Hop
616 Ferry St,
Woolston, Christchurch.
Tel (03) 943 4681.

Wunderbar
19 London St, Lyttelton.
Tel (03) 328 8818.

Cafés

Cassette Number Nine
9 Vulcan Ln, Auckland.
Tel (09) 366 0196.

Dux Central
10 Poplar Lane,
Christchurch.
Tel (03) 943 7830.

Federal Delicatessen
86 Federal St,
Auckland.
Tel (09) 363 7184.

Fidel's Café
234 Cuba St, Wellington
Tel (04) 801 6868.

Lagerfield
21 Blair St, Wellington.
Tel (04) 801 5212.

The Matterhorn
106 Cuba St,
Wellington.
Tel (04) 384 3359.

Soul Bar & Bistro
Viaduct Harbour Ave,
Auckland.
Tel (09) 356 7249.

Clubs

1885
27 Galway St,
Britomart, Auckland.
Tel (09) 551 3100.

Churchills
441 Colombo St,
Sydenham.
Tel (03) 379 0503.

Danny Doolans
204 Quay St,
Auckland Viaduct.
Tel (03) 358 2554.

Golden Dawn
Cnr Richmond and
Ponsonby St, Auckland.
Tel (09) 376 9929.

Garden Club
13 Dixon St,
Wellington.
Tel 027 522 5522.

Impala
7 Shortland St,
Auckland Viaduct.
Tel 09 309 9764.

K'Road Ballroom
214 Karangahape Rd,
Auckland.
Tel (09) 366 0340.

Mashina Lounge
30 Victoria St,
Christchurch.
Tel (03) 365 9999.

Orleans
48 Customs St,
Britomart, Auckland.
Tel (09) 309 5854.

The Physics Room
209 Tuam St,
Christchurch.
Tel (03) 379 5583.

Red Square
28 Blair St, Wellington.
Tel 021 243 2788.

Smash Palace
172 High St,
Christchurch Central.
Tel (03) 366 5369.

SPECIALIST HOLIDAYS AND ACTIVITIES

Lovers of the outdoors will find New Zealand an ideal place to pursue their interests, or to experience something they have never tried before. From quick thrills, such as bungy jumping, jet-boating and helicopter rides to mountain climbing, abseiling, white-water rafting and skiing, New Zealand offers a huge range of activities for outdoor enthusiasts. The best places to find out what is available are at the Department of Conservation (DOC) offices, visitor information centres (i-SITES) and travel agents.

Hiking and Walking

With its 14 national parks, as well as many forest parks and protected natural areas, New Zealand offers immense opportunities for walking and hiking at all levels; "tramping" is the term New Zealanders use for trekking or hiking. A national network of walkways, ranging from short, well-graded paths to rudimentary alpine routes, thread their way throughout New Zealand, and every location boasts tracks and trails that allow visitors to experience the locality's finest aspects.

The best hiking routes are in the national parks, which are serviced by basic but comfortable huts costing between NZ$10 and NZ$45 per night. Nine of these tracks – world famous for their beauty – have been designated "Great Walks". Hiking can be done with a guide or independently. In the latter case, hikers are required to be self-sufficient in food, carry suitable clothing and sleeping gear. Tramping huts vary in size and facilities, and it is wise to check with the DOC before setting off. It is also vital to check track and weather conditions with the DOC. Always sign in at the local DOC office or in intentions books provided at the beginning of major tracks. Although New Zealand has a sophisticated search and rescue system, it cannot operate if trampers do not leave a record of their where-abouts and expected date of return. On popular routes, such as the Abel Tasman Coastal Track and the Routeburn and Milford tracks, advance booking is essential.

Mountaineering and Rock Climbing

With 30 peaks at heights over 3,000 m (9,840 ft), the South Island's Southern Alps provide climbers many opportunities for technically demanding mountain climbing. The principal climbing regions are the Aoraki/Mount Cook, Westland/Tai Poutini, Tititea/Mount Aspiring, Arthur's Pass and Fiordland national parks, while in the North Island the Central Plateau offers the best climbing. The main season is from November to March. Weather in the mountains can change extremely rapidly, and it is important that climbers get an up-to-date weather forecast, are adequately equipped, and post their intentions with the DOC before setting off. Experienced mountain guides, such as Aoraki/Mount Cook's **Alpine Guides (Aoraki) Ltd**, are available in many of the major climbing regions.

There is also plenty of scope for rock climbing. Among the best locations are the volcanic rock outcrops of Christchurch's Port Hills (*p234*) and the limestone formations of Castle Hill in Canterbury (*see p247*).

Caving and Abseiling

New Zealand has extensive cave systems, among the most notable being the Waitomo Caves in the central North Island (*see pp124–5*) and the Takaka region in northwest Nelson (*see p220*). Some caves are easily accessed, while others are more suited to experienced cavers. A popular way of experiencing New Zealand's cave formations

Guided walk on Franz Josef Glacier (*see pp242–3*)

Abseiling in the Mangapu Cave system, Waitomo *(see pp124–5)*

is with the **Legendary Black Water Rafting Co™**. Participants float in rubber tubes through extensive cave systems illuminated by glowworms. Two of the best locations for this activity are Waitomo *(see p124–5)* and Westport *(see p238)*, where rafting operators run tours.

Both the North and South islands offer exhilarating abseiling. In the Waitomo area, tourists can descend down a 100-m (330-ft) hole into the "Lost World" *(see p125)* Mangapu Cave system with **Waitomo Adventures**.

Cycling

Cycle touring on New Zealand's highways and back roads is a popular way of seeing the country. Among the many scenic roads suited to cycling are the Queen Charlotte Drive in the Marlborough Sounds *(see p204)* and State Highway 6 on the West Coast. The **Otago Central Rail Trail** offers three to five days cycling along a 150 km (93 mile) old rail line, upgraded specifically for cyclists. An extensive network of off-road tracks is also available for mountain bikers. Hanmer Springs *(see p237)* and Victoria Forest Park *(see p237)* are among

the best mountain biking destinations. **The New Zealand Cycle Trail (Nga Haerenga)** has many cycle routes dotted around the country, with the long-term aim of developing a nationwide cycle network.

Skiing

New Zealand has numerous ski fields, ranging from highly commercialized fields to small fields owned by local ski clubs. Major fields are **Whakapapa Ski Area** and **Turoa Ski Resort** on the slopes of the North Island's Mount Ruapehu *(see pp146–7)*, the **Mount Hutt Ski Area** in Canterbury *(see p250)*, and **Coronet Peak**, the **Remarkables Ski Area**, **Cardrona Alpine Resort** and **Treble Cone** in Central Otago *(see pp198–9)*.

The ski season runs from mid-June to September. In the South Island, heli-skiing operators take skiers to untouched powder snow. Ski touring and cross-country skiing take place in many locations, including the **Waiorau Snow Farm** near Wanaka *(see pp198–9)*.

DIRECTORY

Hiking

w doc.govt.nz
provides information on "Great Walks" and how to make bookings.

Mountaineering and Rock Climbing

Alpine Guides (Aoraki) Ltd
PO Box 20, Mt Cook Village. **Tel** (03) 435 1834.
w alpineguides.co.nz

Mount Aspiring Guides
58 McDougall St, Wanaka
Tel (03) 443 9422.
w aspiringguides.com

Caving and Abseiling

Legendary Black Water Rafting Co™
39 Waimoto Village Road, Waimoto **Tel** (07) 878 8228, 0800 533 115.
w waitomo.com/
black-water-rafting

Underwater Adventures
182 Queen St, Westport.
Tel (03) 788 8168, 0800 11 6686 **w** caverafting.com

Waitomo Adventures
654 Waimoto Village Road, Waimoto. **Tel** (07) 878 7788, 0800 924 866.
w waitomo.co.nz

Cycling

Mountain Bike Station
27 Goldfinch St, Ohakune Shopping Centre,
Ohakune. **Tel** (06) 385 9018. **w** mountainbike-station.co.nz

The New Zealand Cycle Trail (Nga Haerenga)
w nzcycletrail.com

New Zealand Pedaltours
218e Marua Rd, Mt Wellington, Auckland.
Tel (09) 585 1338.
w pedaltours.co.nz

Otago Central Rail Trail
i-SITE Visitor Centre,
26 Princes St, Dunedin.
Tel (03) 474 3300.
w otagocentralrailtrail.co.nz

Pacific Cycle Tours
Unit 3, 14 Kennaway Rd, Christchurch.
Tel (03) 329 9913.
w bike-nz.com

Skiing

Cardrona Alpine Resort
20 Helwick St, Wanaka
Tel (03) 443 8880.
w cardrona.com

Coronet Peak
Tel (03) 442 4620.
w nzski.com

Harris Mountains Heli-skiing
Tel (03) 442 6722.
w heliski.co.nz

Mount Hutt Ski Area
PO Box 14, Methven.
Tel (03) 308 5074.
w nzski.com

Remarkables Ski Area
PO Box 359, Queenstown.
Tel (03) 442 4615.
w nzski.com

Treble Cone
PO Box 206, Wanaka.
Tel (03) 443 1406.
w treblecone.com

Turoa Ski Resort
Tel (06) 385 8456.
w mtruapehu.com/
winter

Waiorau Snow Farm
Cardrona, Wanaka.
Tel (03) 443 7542.
w snowfarmnz.com

Whakapapa Ski Area
Tel (07) 892 4000.
w mtruapehu.com

Surfing at Whale Bay, Raglan
(see pp120–21)

Watersports

With a coastline 18,200 km (11,300 miles) long and an abundance of lakes and rivers, New Zealand offers plenty of opportunities for visitors to participate in watersports. From Auckland's Hauraki Gulf *(see pp92–3)* northwards is a yachting paradise where experienced sailors can hire boats for "bareboat" cruising. Skippered sailing is more common, however, as the country's gusty winds can test even the most capable "boaties".

Surfing is popular, especially in the North Island at beaches like Piha *(see p90)*, Raglan *(see pp120–21)* and in the Bay of Plenty *(see pp130, 132)*. The calm waters of the country's harbours and lakes are suitable for windsurfing, and boards can be hired at many water-front locations.

The Bay of Islands, Auckland's Hauraki Gulf, Nelson's Abel Tasman National Park, the Marlborough Sounds, Fiordland and Stewart Island are prime venues for sea kayaking. Tours can take as long as a week. Kayaks can also be hired for a few hours' paddling around the harbours of Auckland, Wellington and other coastal cities.

New Zealand's fast-flowing rivers are excellent for white-water rafting and kayaking. Among the most challenging rivers are the Motu *(see p136)*, Rangitikei and Tongariro in the North Island, while the South Island has dozens of rivers, from the Buller on the West Coast to the Clarence in Canterbury. Among the rivers suitable for the inexperienced is the Whanganui River, which winds its way through the historic Whanganui National Park *(see p183)*.

There are many good dive spots, including the network of marine reserves around the New Zealand coastline *(see pp30–31)*. Near Whangarei, the dramatic underwater caves of the Poor Knights Islands *(see p103)* are rated as one of the world's top diving destinations. Further north, the Greenpeace boat, the *Rainbow Warrior*, is a well-known underwater wreck. In Fiordland, a unique marine eco-system, tempered by huge quantities of freshwater run-off, attracts deepwater species nearer to the surface than in other areas.

Hunting

Because many of the animals introduced into New Zealand by Europeans have no natural predators, they have become pests, and therefore hunting of big game is encouraged by the authorities. No licence is required, there is no restriction on the numbers killed and the season is generally open all year round.

Professional guiding companies operate throughout the country, many with access to extensive tracts of private land. Seven species of deer, wild pigs and goats are common in forests, while chamois and thar can be found in mountain areas of the South Island. The duck shooting season starts in May and lasts eight weeks. All native birds are endangered and protected.

Fishing

New Zealand is justly renowned for the quality of its sea and freshwater fishing. Lake Taupo and the rivers surrounding it (especially the famed Tongariro) are internationally regarded as the Mecca of trout fishing *(see p145)*, although there are good rivers throughout the country. The trout fishing season runs from October to May. The main salmon rivers are on the east coast of the South Island. A licence is compulsory in order to fish for trout and salmon, and tackle is readily available.

The Bay of Islands is the centre of deep-sea marlin fishing *(see p107)*. The best

Kayaking over rapids on the Tongariro River

Fishing in the Waikato River near Huka Lodge *(see p299)*

deep-sea angling is found on the North Island's east coast, northwards from the Bay of Plenty. The best fishing months are from January to May and licences are not necessary.

Ecotours

A long tradition of environmental activism in New Zealand has led to numerous ecotourism developments. There are many specialist nature tour operators to choose from, and guides working in the adventure tourism area, such as black-water rafting *(see p124)*, often have a good knowledge of local flora and fauna.

There are numerous opportunities for bird watching *(see pp196–7)*, including at the Royal Albatross colony on Otago Peninsula, ocean birds at Kaikoura *(see p213)*, the white heron colony at Okarito and the immense birdlife of Farewell Spit *(see p221)*.

Kaikoura is synonymous with whale watching *(see p213)*. During winter there is nearly a 100 per cent chance of seeing sperm whales. Dolphin watching tours operate from many areas, including Banks Peninsula, the Bay of Islands and Southland.

Whale Watch® tour at Kaikoura *(see p213)*

DIRECTORY

Rafting

Queenstown Rafting
35 Shotover St,
Queenstown.
Tel (03) 442 9792,
0800 723 8464.
W queenstownrafting.
co.nz

Wet 'n' Wild Rafting Company
58a Fryer Rd, Hamurana,
Rotorua.
Tel (07) 348 3191,
0800 462 7238.
W wetnwildrafting.
co.nz

Kayaking

Abel Tasman Kayaks
Main Rd, Marahau.
Tel (03) 527 8022.
W abeltasmankayaks.
co.nz

Abel Tasman Wilson's Experiences
409 High St, Motueka.
Tel (03) 528 2027.
W abeltasman.co.nz

Go Orange Kayak
74 Shotover St,
Queenstown.
Tel (03) 249 8585,
0800 246 672.
W goorangekayaks.
co.nz

Diving

Dive! Tutukaka
Marina Rd, Tutukaka,
Whangarei.
Tel (09) 434 3867, 0800
288 882. W diving.co.nz

Splash Gordon
432 The Esplanade,
Island Bay, Wellington.
Tel (04) 939 3483.
W divewellington.co.nz

Hunting and Fishing

Chris Jolly Outdoors
PO Box 1020,
Lake Taupo.
Tel (07) 378 0623.
W chrisjolly.co.nz

South Pacific Safaris
Glencree Lodge, Kaikoura.
Tel (03) 319 5189.
W huntingnewzealand.
co.nz

Eco Tours

Albatross Encounter
96 Esplanade, Kaikoura.
Tel (03) 319 6777,
0800 733 365.
W albatrossen
counter.co.nz

Caitlins Scenic Tours
744 Catlins Valley Rd,
Tawanui.
Tel (03) 415 8613.
W catlinsmohuapark.
co.nz

Explore NZ
PO Box 400, Cnr Marsden
& Williams rds, Paihia, Bay
of Islands. **Tel** (09) 359
5987, 0800 397 567.
W exploregroup.co.nz

Heritage Expeditions
53b Montreal St,
Christchurch. **Tel** (03) 365
3500. W heritage-
expeditions.co.nz

Whale Watch® Kaikoura Ltd
Kaikoura.
Tel (03) 319 6767.
W whalewatch.co.nz

Paraglider near Queenstown

Aerial Adventures

Hot-air ballooning, tandem parapenting (paragliding) (see p199) and tandem sky-diving are more adventurous ways of taking to the air than flying. Commercial operators offering all three types of aerial thrill exist in the main cities and major resorts (see p339). A hot-air balloon ride is a spectacular way to view the extensive Southern Alps and Canterbury Plains, while para-penting from Te Mata Peak in Hawke's Bay (see p153) and the Remarkables near Queenstown is a unique experience (see pp198–9). Check with local visitor centres or travel agents for details of available services.

Aerial sightseeing is also popular throughout the country, either in small planes, helicopters or float planes. Highlights in the North Island include flights over the volcanically active White Island (see p134) and volcanic Tongariro National Park (pp146–7). In the South Island, flights over Mount Cook, the Fox and Franz Josef glaciers (see pp256–7) and Fiordland

Flightseeing over Fiordland National Park (pp284–7)

(see pp284–5) are popular and readily available. Many flights touch down in spectacular locations, such as White Island and the glaciers of the Southern Alps.

Bungy jumping from the Kawarau Bridge, Queenstown (see p280)

Bungy Jumping

Ever since A J Hackett used a historic bridge over the Kawarau River in Queenstown (see pp198–9) to launch the bungy jumping phenomenon in 1988, tourism operators have set up bungy jump sites in picturesque locations, usually on bridges above river gorges, in both the North and South islands.

Safety is a key issue in bungy jumping. Jumpers are weighed so that the correct length of bungy cord can be calculated for their jump. The cord is securely attached to their ankles before the jump from a bridge or platform.

Jet-Boating

Bill Hamilton, a local engineer and farmer, perfected the design of the jet-boat so it is no coincidence that these highly manoeuvrable craft are so popular on the nation's waterways. In locations such as Waikato and Queenstown (see pp198–9), jet-boat operators take tourists through narrow canyons, across the shallowest of water and whirl 360 degrees "on a sixpence". Some operators offer jet-boat safaris, taking visitors on longer trips into the scenic back country. Mandatory life jackets are supplied.

Golf

There are more than 400 golf courses in New Zealand, more per head of population than virtually any other country. Green fees can be as low as NZ$5 for a club in rural areas. Even the more exclusive city courses charge no more than NZ$50. Weekends are often reserved for members, although a number of clubs have reci-procal membership with overseas clubs, allowing visitors to play at any time. Major clubs have carts and clubs for hire.

Four-Wheel Drive Touring

In the high country and rural areas of New Zealand are hundreds of rough tracks, many of which were created to provide access to farms, timber mills, gold mines and mining settlements. A four-wheel drive vehicle offers a physically undemanding way to explore these locations. Numerous tour operators exist throughout the country, offering both day trips and longer safaris through varied terrain.

Horse Trekking

The wide open spaces of the country encourage horse riding and there are many operators who offer horse trekking through forests, high country trails or along one of the many beaches. Options range from half-day or all-day treks to multi-day camping safaris. Some

Horse trekking at Hanmer, North Canterbury

operations are conveniently located close to cities. Most operators cater for a range of riding abilities and provide all equipment.

Spectator Sports

New Zealanders are passionate about rugby. It is worth visiting a match during the rugby season from March to October (see pp42–3). The Super 14 and Air New Zealand Cup are the major competitions. Matches generally attract large crowds, as do one-day cricket test matches. Highly entertaining,

the atmosphere is best at the day–night matches which begin in the afternoon and are played through the evening under lights.

Horse racing is a national passion, and a number of big race meetings are held between November and April (see pp42–3). Netball also has a large following, with the most exciting games often involving the national team, the Silver Ferns.

Tickets for sports events can be obtained from Ticketek (see p331).

Māori Heritage Tours

Tour companies offering genuine encounters with Māori heritage operate in a number of locations. Tours may include a visit to a *marae*, where participants share a *hangi* (a traditional feast) and learn about Māori protocol, myths and legends, dance and art. One such operator near Rotorua, **Te Urewera Treks**, offers a range of eco-cultural treks and guided tours through the Urewera country, spiritual home to the Tuhoe people.

Waikato supporters at a provincial rugby match

DIRECTORY

Aerial Adventures

Air Safaris
PO Box 71,
Lake Tekapo.
Tel (03) 680 6740.
W airsafaris.co.nz

Fiordland Helicopters
6 Milford Cres,
Te Anau.
Tel (03) 249 7575.
W fiordland helicopters.co.nz

Sky Trek
45 Camp St,
Queenstown.
Tel 0800 759 873.
W skytrek.co.nz

Sunrise Balloons
121 Main St,
Methven.
Tel (03) 442 0781,
0800 486 247.
W ballooning.nz

Bungy Jumping

A J Hackett Bungy
PO Box 488,
Queenstown.
Tel (03) 450 1300.
W bungy.co.nz/
queenstown

Taupo Bungy
202 Spa Rd, Taupo.
Tel (07) 377 1135,
0800 888 408.
W taupobungy.co.nz

Four-Wheel Driving

Eco Wanaka
Lakeside Road,
Wanaka.
Tel (03) 443 2869.
W ecowanaka.co.nz

Nomad Safaris
37 Shotover St,
Queenstown.
Tel (03) 442 6699.
W nomadsafaris.co.nz

Jet-Boating

Hukafalls Jet
200 Karetoto Rd,
Wairakei.
Tel (07) 374 8572.
W hukajet.co.nz

Shotover Jet
Shotover Jet Beach,
Gorge Rd, Queenstown.
Tel (03) 442 8570.
W shotoverjet.co.nz

Horse Trekking

Alpine Horse Safaris
Waitohi Downs,
Hawarden, Canterbury.
Tel (07) 314 4293.
W alpinehorse.co.nz

Cape Farewell Horse Treks
23 McGowan St,
Puponga, Collingwood.
Tel (03) 524 8031.
W horsetreksnz.co.nz

Dart Stables
58 Coll St, Glenorchy.
Tel (03) 442 5688.
W dartstables.com

Pakiri Beach Horse Rides
317 Rahuikiri Rd, Pakiri,
RD 2, Wellsford.
Tel (09) 422 6275.
W horseride-nz.co.nz

Māori Heritage Tours

Tamaki Tours
Highlands Loop Rd,
Ngakaru, Rotorua.
Tel (07) 349 2999.
W tamakimaorivillage.
co.nz

Te Urewera Treks
3891 Ruatahuna Rd,
Ngaputahi.
Tel (07) 929 9669.
W teureweratreks.co.nz

Waimarama Māori Tours
PO Box 8065, Havelock
North Hawkes Bay.
Tel 021 057 0953.

SURVIVAL GUIDE

PRACTICAL INFORMATION

Tourism is one of New Zealand's most important industries, attracting over 2.5 million overseas visitors a year. As the industry has grown, services and facilities have improved to keep pace with demand. Visitors are well served by a wide range of accommodation and restaurants (*see pp298–307, 308–25*). There is easy and free access to good quality information through the many i-SITE visitor centres, which are co-ordinated by Tourism New Zealand, the national tourism body. Many of the best attractions in New Zealand are free – particularly when enjoying the natural landscape of national parks, beaches, lakes and rivers. New Zealanders are friendly people who are generally willing to offer assistance to tourists, although it is advisable for visitors to have a basic grasp of English as few New Zealanders are fluent in other languages.

Enjoying the sun at Scorching Bay, Wellington *(see p173)*

When to Go

Spring (Sep–Nov), summer (Dec–Feb) and autumn (Mar–May) are the most popular seasons for travellers, although the ski season is a major attraction during the winter months (Jun–Aug). Average summer temperatures range between 20 and 30° C (68 and 86° F), and winter between 10 and 15° C (50 and 60° F), but the weather in New Zealand is changeable: temperatures can drop 10–20° C (50–68° F) in a short space of time when a cold southerly front blows in.

The climate has strong regional variations. The north of the North Island is subtropical, while the remainder of the country is temperate. The country also has a pronounced west–east climate: the west coasts are wet and humid, the east coasts drier and sunnier.

Snow in winter falls mainly in the mountains of the South Island, when temperatures can fall below 0° C (32° F).

Visas and Passports

Visitors to New Zealand must have a passport valid for at least three months longer than the intended period of stay. Visas are not required for Australian or British citizens, who are issued with a six-month visitor permit on arrival, or for visits of up to three months by residents of any of the 50 countries with which New Zealand has a visa-waiver agreement. All visitors should check visa requirements prior to travelling on the New Zealand Immigration Service website: www.immigration.govt.nz.

A reciprocal working holiday scheme exists between New Zealand and a further

Mount Cook
National Park and
Alpine Resort

Turnoff 700m

Resort signboard

34 other countries, entitling 18–30-year-olds to travel and work in the country temporarily for up to a year. It is also possible to obtain a work permit if you have been offered a job or have skills that are in demand; plan to set up a business or invest; or are visiting the country as an artist or athlete participating in a performance or sporting event. For full details visit the New Zealand Immigration Service website.

Travel Safety Advice

Visitors can get up-to-date travel safety information from the **Foreign and Commonwealth Office** in the UK, the **State Department** in the US and the **Department of Foreign Affairs and Trade** in Australia.

Customs Information

New Zealand relies heavily on its agricultural industries and the bio security of its native flora and fauna. Great efforts are made to keep the country free of introduced pests and diseases. All plant and animal materials must be declared on arrival, including fresh food-stuffs. Failure to declare quarantine items can lead to a fine of NZ$100,000 or five years in jail. If in doubt about an item, declare it to the inspectors on arrival. Tents or shoes that have been used recently in the countryside should be declared. For other restrictions and allowances,

◀ Paragliding in Queenstown

visit the New Zealand Customs Service website: www.customs.govt.nz

Class A, B and C drugs are prohibited, as are firearms and weapons unless a permit is obtained from the New Zealand Police on arrival. The country is also party to an international convention designed to prevent trade in all endangered species, and various animal products, which include anything made of ivory, turtle shell, clam shells and whalebone.

Visitors can buy duty-free goods on arrival, departure and at duty-free stores in cities (see p94). For travellers over 17 years old, the customs allowances are: 200 cigarettes, 250 grams of tobacco or 50 cigars, or a mixture of all three weighing no more than 250 grams; 4.5 litres of beer or wine and up to three 1,125 ml (40 oz) bottles of spirits or other beverages.

Tourist Information

The official information service that most visitors have contact with is the **i-SITE** visitor centre network. Independently owned but coordinated by the central tourism body, **Tourism New Zealand**, there are over 80 i-SITE centres scattered throughout New Zealand, sporting a distinctive green and black logo. They provide information on local attractions and activities, sell maps and guidebooks, and book accommodation.

Department of Conservation visitor centres are the best

source of information on national parks. They provide maps and information on conditions for walkers.

Admission Prices

Admission charges to attractions vary. Many galleries and museums request a donation or modest entry charge. Entry into the national parks is free, although access to certain areas is possible only with an approved tour company or guide. There is also a charge for overnight stays in Department of Conservation huts. Private companies run the many adventure tourism ventures, and charges vary.

Opening Hours

Most major tourist attractions are open seven days a week in season, but it is best to check in advance. Business hours are generally from 8:30am to 5pm. Shops open 9am–5:30pm Monday–Friday and Saturday morning, with late-night shopping on Thursday. Shopping malls may stay open all day Saturday and Sunday. Many supermarkets open until 10pm.

Language

English is the main language in New Zealand, but Māori also enjoys official status. Government departments and agencies often have bilingual names. Kia ora is a traditional

Māori greeting and haere mai means "welcome". Wharepaku is the word for "toilet" – wahine for women and tane for men. "Wh" is pronounced "f".

Etiquette and Smoking

New Zealand is a relatively informal society. On the whole, people are friendly and easygoing, and are happy to assist tourists. Dress codes vary, but casual wear is the norm.

Smoking is banned in cafés, bars, restaurants, shops and on public transport. It is not acceptable to smoke in private homes without asking permission. If invited to a New Zealander's home for a meal, take a bottle of wine or an item of food to share.

Public Conveniences

Public conveniences can be found in town centres and shopping malls, at public beaches and at roadside service stations. They are generally free to use, open 24 hours and serviced regularly. Many, though not all, are wheelchair-accessible. Cafés, bars and restaurants have toilets for customers. The New Zealand Automobile Association website (www.aa.co.nz) has a searchable map of public toilet locations.

Taxes and Tipping

A Goods and Services Tax (GST) is charged on most goods and services in New Zealand at a rate of 15 per cent. GST is usually included in the quoted price, but may occasionally be added at the end. There is currently no GST refund scheme for tourists.

Tipping in restaurants and hotels is not obligatory, although it has become more widespread with the increase in overseas tourists. Many New Zealanders do not tip taxi drivers, bartenders and porters, but it is becoming more common to reward good service in a restaurant (about 10 per cent of the bill).

Visitor information centre, Viaduct Basin, Auckland (see p76)

New Zealand has much to offer families on holiday

Travellers with Specific Needs

Disabled travellers are well catered for in New Zealand. Every new or substantially renovated building is required by law to have adequate access for people with disabilities. As a result, most hotels, restaurants and tourist sites have wheelchair facilities, and guide dogs are welcome.

Airports provide staff to assist disabled passengers, but national trains and buses are often inaccessible without assistance. City transport is more accessible, but it is best to check with the operating companies. Avis car rentals, can supply cars with hand controls (see p359). All major towns have taxis that carry wheelchairs.

Accessible Kiwi Tours offer tour packages for disabled and mature travellers. **Enable New Zealand** offers support and information to disabled visitors on how to get around. **CCS Disability Action** can help with parking concessions when supplied with a home mobility card and a medical certificate. **Accomobility** provides information on accommodation suitable for disabled travellers.

Travelling with Children

New Zealand is a safe place to take children for a holiday. Many top attractions, such as beaches and national parks, appeal equally to children and adults. Children are well catered for, especially in motels with family rooms and self-catering facilities. Restaurants often have children's menus and high chairs. Breastfeeding in public is accepted and changing facilities are available in most public toilets. Children under five years must be restrained in an infant car seat.

Senior Travellers

New Zealand is a popular destination for retired people. Most sights and activities are accessible to senior travellers, but participation in extreme sports will depend on individual age, health and fitness.

Some travel insurance policies set age limitations and many exclude pre-existing medical conditions, but it is possible to find policies targeted at older travellers. Ask about discounts on transport, tours and admission charges when booking.

Gay and Lesbian Travellers

New Zealanders are generally accepting of homosexuality, though this is more true in the liberal cities than in the rural hinterland. The Human Rights Act 1993 made it unlawful to discriminate on grounds of sexual orientation, and travellers are highly unlikely to face discrimination. The **Gay Travel New Zealand** website provides useful information about the gay scene in New Zealand.

Travelling on a Budget

Students with a valid ISIC (International Student Identity Card) or young people with an IYTC (International Youth Travel Card) can obtain substantial discounts on flights, coach travel, tours and car hire, and at hotels and hostels. Cardholders are also entitled to reduced charges at art galleries, museums and attractions. The ISIC card can be acquired only by school, college or university students. The IYTC can be purchased by anyone aged 12–26. To find out about special deals, go to www.isiccard.com.

New Zealand is well equipped for budget backpacker travel, with a network of backpacker hostels in all the main towns and resorts around the country. **Backpacker bulletin boards** online and at hostels are a great place to pick up budget travel tips before you go or while on the road.

Several companies offer cost-effective group coach tours. **Stray New Zealand** and **Flying Kiwi Adventure Tours** are well-known operators offering packages that combine travel with activities.

An International Student Identity Card (ISIC)

Time

New Zealand is 12 hours ahead of Greenwich Mean Time and 2 hours ahead of Sydney. Clocks are put forward 1 hour each October and back 1 hour in March.

Electricity

The electrical current is 230/240 volts 50 hertz, although most hotels and motels provide 110 volt AC sockets for electric razors.

For all other equipment, an adaptor is necessary, as power outlets accept only flat, two- or three-pin plugs.

Responsible Tourism

New Zealand is proud of its clean, green image, encapsulated in its "100% Pure NZ" tourism brand. It has 14 national parks, protecting a third of the country's land, and its wildlife sanctuaries preserve the country's unique native flora and fauna.

New Zealand was one of the first countries to pledge a carbon-neutral future, with a number of tourism companies achieving CarboNZero certification. The New Zealand tourism industry recognizes environmentally sustainable tourism with Qualmark Enviro certification, awarded to operators and accommodation providers for high levels of environmental responsibility. Eco-lodges committed to a sustainable accommodation

can be found in the most beautiful and remote locations such as **Hapuku Lodge**, found

Hapuku Lodge & Tree Houses, Kaikoura

in the Kaikoura forests. Organic food and produce is available from farmers' markets and specialist health shops.

Māori Tourism

Māori tourism has moved on from the once limited "cultural shows" involving a *kapa haka* performed by indigenous people in traditional dress. Today Māori-led tours, such as those by **New Zealand Māori Tourism**, combine hiking, kayaking or whitewater-rafting with storytelling and interpretation.

DIRECTORY

Personal Security and Health

New Zealand is one of the safest countries in the world to visit. New Zealanders have a reputation for being friendly and law-abiding, and the political and economic climate is stable. Crimes do occur in New Zealand as in any other society, and visitors need to take sensible precautions to protect themselves and their property. The greatest risks, however, are environmental; many tourists have been caught out on the water, or in the mountains or bush with inadequate food and clothing, having underestimated the dangers of the terrain and the speed with which New Zealand's weather can change.

Travellers should be aware that New Zealand is situated on the Pacific Rim of Fire. Big earthquakes are infrequent but they do happen – Christchurch suffered major earthquakes in 2010 and again in 2011, both causing widespread damage. The Ministry of Civil Defence website (www.getthru.govt.nz) gives details on what to do in the event of an earthquake.

Police

The New Zealand Police force are professional and helpful. They are divided into 12 districts, which between them run more than 400 community-based police stations across New Zealand.

Police officers are identified by their dark blue uniforms with epaulettes indicating rank. Police are highly visible patrolling the cities' streets day and night, in a non-aggressive manner. It is common to see highway police at roadsides in most cities and in rural districts, carrying out breath-tests on suspected drunk drivers.

To report a crime, visit the nearest police station: addresses and contact details can be found at www.police.govt.nz or in the blue pages of the telephone directory under "police".

Police car

What to be Aware of

There are few areas in New Zealand that are not suitable for tourists to visit. However, use common sense to ensure your personal safety. Streets are often deserted after dark and it is not advisable, particularly for women, to walk alone at night. Licensed taxis are readily available and are safe to use. Hitch-hiking is not recommended, especially for women and lone travellers.

Fire engine

Road accidents are a major public health issue and tourists planning to drive should be aware of the rules of the road in New Zealand.

In an Emergency

In an emergency, police, fire and ambulance services can be contacted by dialling **111**.

In the event of a non-emergency road traffic incident, call *555.

Ambulance

Lost and Stolen Property

Travellers need to use common sense to safeguard their property in New Zealand. Theft from cars can occur so lock vehicles and make sure valuable items remain out of view. Passports and credit cards should be kept in a hotel safe deposit box, a money belt or a zipped bag. A comprehensive travel insurance policy is advisable.

Stolen property should be reported to the police, who will issue a report, which can be used to support an insurance claim. Local police stations are easily located in all towns and cities. Most airports, bus and train stations, and the public transport networks in the big cities, have lost property offices and it is worth checking with the service in case any lost items have been handed in.

Hospitals and Pharmacies

Urgent medical treatment, including emergency dental care, can be received at hospital A&E departments or at 24-hour walk-in GP surgeries. New Zealand has an extensive network of pharmacies (known as chemists), which offer over-the-counter remedies and prescription drugs. Qualified chemists can provide free advice but a doctor must write out prescriptions. All major towns have chemists, that open 9am–5:30pm daily and later on Thursday and Friday. Contact details for hospitals, GP and dental surgeries and pharmacies are listed in the front of local telephone directories.

A Golden Bay chemist, Takaka

Environmental Hazards

New Zealand poses few risks to the visitor, as long as sensible precautions are taken. Its changeable climate is probably the greatest threat, but the vast majority of accidents befall people who venture into the wilderness unprepared. The **New Zealand Mountain Safety Council** outdoor safety code advises that you: plan your trip, let someone know where you are going, be aware of the weather, know your limits and take enough supplies – food, warm clothes, first aid kit and a means of communication – even when going for a day's walk in the bush or mountains. Hypothermia can set in quickly and be fatal.

Many hikes involve river crossings, and water levels can rise rapidly after heavy rain. It is often necessary to take shelter and wait until rivers drop to a safe level.

Lifeguards patrol popular beaches, and red and yellow flags indicate areas where it is safe to swim. Patrols are run by individual clubs under the umbrella of **Surf Life Saving New Zealand**. However the New Zealand coastline is extensive and in areas where there are no lifeguards there may be dangerous rip tides.

Sunburn can occur quickly so a good hat and sun block with a rating of at least SPF 30 are essential in summer.

It is best to avoid drinking water from rivers, lakes or ponds without boiling or treating the water first.

The tiny sandfly bites exposed skin, causing an annoying itch. They can usually be kept at bay with insect repellent.

Travel and Health Insurance

New Zealand has excellent medical services. Under its accident compensation scheme, **ACC**, visitors may be covered for the cost of treatment if they are injured. ACC does not cover continuing costs of injury-related rehabilitation or loss of earnings once visitors return home. The no-fault scheme precludes the option of suing for damages, so it should not be regarded as a substitute for medical insurance. Non-accident medical treatment is not free. Reciprocal publicly funded medical care is available for Australian and British citizens, but not for other nationalities. Visitors are strongly advised to take out travel insurance to cover medical care. No vaccinations are needed.

Surf rescue boat at Mount Maunganui *(see p132)*

DIRECTORY

In an Emergency

AA Road Service
Free call **Tel** 0800 500 222
(24 hours, all areas).

Police, Fire and Ambulance
Free call **Tel** 111
(24 hours, all areas).

Search and Rescue
Free call **Tel** 111
(24 hours, all areas).

Lost and Stolen Property

Auckland
Lost Property & Baggage, Auckland Airport.
Tel 0800 247 7678.

Christchurch
Lost & Found, Travel & Tourism Centre, Christchurch Airport.
Tel (03) 353 7749.

Wellington
General Lost Property, Main terminal, Wellington Airport. **Tel** (04) 385 5100.

Hospitals

Auckland
2, Park Road, Grafton.
Tel (09) 367 0000.

Christchurch
2, Riccarton Avenue, Addlington 8011.
Tel (03) 364 0640.

Dunedin
201, Great King Street.
Tel (03) 474 0999.

Wellington
Riddiford Street, Newton.
Tel (04) 385 5999.

Pharmacies

Auckland Newmarket Day and Night Pharmacy
Tel (09) 520 6634.

Christchurch Urgent Pharamacy
Tel (03) 366 4439.

Dunedin Antidote Central
Tel (03) 477 0890.

Wellington Urgent Pharmacy
Tel (04) 385 8810.

Environmental Hazards

New Zealand Mountain Safety Council
W mountainsafety.org.nz

Sunsmart
W sunsmart.org.nz

Surf Life Saving New Zealand
W slsnz.org.nz

Travel and Health Insurance

ACC
W acc.co.nz

Banking and Currency

A large number of banking institutions operate in New Zealand, all of them foreign owned apart from government-owned Kiwibank, which is a subsidiary of New Zealand Post and operates from PostShops around New Zealand. Major banking chains include ANZ, ASB, Bank of New Zealand (BNZ), HSBC and Westpac. Branches can be found in the central business districts of the major cities and in suburban shopping centres. Foreign currency can be readily exchanged at banks and private bureaux de change. There is no restriction on the amount of foreign currency that can be brought in or taken out of New Zealand, although people carrying more than NZ$10,000 in cash must make a declaration to customs.

Banks and Bureaux de Change

The New Zealand banking system is modern and efficient. However, electronic banking has led to a decline in the number of bank branches and some small rural towns no longer have a local banking service. Banks are generally open from 9:30am to 4:30pm Monday to Friday, and some also open on Saturdays.

Bureaux de change can be found at international airports, in city centres and in resort areas. They are generally open from 8am to 8pm on weekdays, and from 10am until early evening on weekends. Commissions and fees are higher than at banks.

ATMs

ATMs are widely available in New Zealand and can be found outside banks in town centres. Travellers should check with their own bank whether there will be a charge for using their debit card to access cash through ATMs in New Zealand. It is possible to withdraw cash from an ATM using a credit or debit card with a PIN number: the "Plus" logo indicates this service is available to VISA card holders, while the symbol for Master-Card holders is "Maestro".

Credit and Debit Cards

All major credit and debit cards are used in New Zealand. **Visa**, and **MasterCard**, **Diners Club**, and **American Express**, are the most widely accepted, and can be used to book and pay for hotels, rental cars and airline tickets, as well as to pay for entry to tourist attractions and purchases from shops. China UnionPay (CUP) cards are also increas-ingly accepted. Check with your bank regarding fees for using your credit or debit card abroad.

Currency Cards

Pre-paid currency cards (also known as Cash Passports) are a safe alternative to travelling with a debit or credit card. Before leaving from home, load the card with money from your bank account. The currency will be fixed at that day's exchange rate. You can then use the card to buy goods, and withdraw cash from ATMs.

An ATM, widely available throughout New Zealand's towns and cities

Currency

The unit of currency in New Zealand is the New Zealand dollar (NZ$), divided into 100 cents (c). In 2006 a set of smaller coins came into circulation and prices for cash purchases were rounded up to the nearest 10 cents. These coins are now legal tender, replacing the 1 cent, 2 cent and 5 cent coins. Small shops, cafés and taxis may not be able to provide change for NZ$50 or NZ$100 notes, so it is advisable to carry cash in NZ$10 and NZ$20 notes. To make it more difficult for counterfeiters to operate and to ensure notes can stay in circulation for longer, plasticized notes have replaced paper ones.

Bank Notes

New Zealand's bank notes are issued in denominations of NZ$5, NZ$10, NZ$20, NZ$50 and NZ$100. Sir Edmund Hillary, the first man to climb Mount Everest features on the NZ$5 note, and 19th-century women's suffrage campaigner Kate Sheppard is on the NZ$10 note. The reverse sides feature native fauna.

NZ$100 note

NZ$50 note

NZ$20 note

NZ$10 note

NZ$5 note

10 cents (10c)

20 cents (20c)

50 cents (50c)

Coins

Coins currently in use in New Zealand are 10c, 20c, 50c, NZ$1 and NZ$2. The 10c piece features a traditional Māori carving, while the NZ$1 coin showing the national icon, the flightless kiwi, brings reality to the colloquial term the "kiwi dollar".

1 dollar (NZ$1)

2 dollars (NZ$2)

Communication and Media

Despite serving a small, widely dispersed population, New Zealand's telecommunications industry has kept pace with the rest of the developed world. Mobile phones are ubiquitous, broadband internet access has reached most areas and Wi-Fi is increasingly available in the cities, small town centres and popular tourist areas. Visitors can make cheap phone calls within and outside New Zealand by subscribing to one of the mobile networks or taking advantage of cheap calling card schemes. New Zealand's traditional media – newspapers, magazines, television and radio – are high quality, but the widespread use of the internet has brought easy access to international media too.

International and Local Telephone Calls

To make telephone calls within New Zealand, visitors may consider purchasing a pay-as-you-go mobile phone. Alternatively, public payphones, available in public spaces, are operated with phonecards, purchased at supermarkets, dairies (convenience stores), visitor information centres or PostShops. Some accept credit cards, but few accept coins. If using a payphone to make an international call, it is cheaper to use one of the discounted Telecom

Phonecard-operated public payphone in New Zealand

prepaid cards, such as the Yabba card, available from the same outlets as local phonecards. There is no charge for making emergency 111 calls.

Each region in New Zealand has a White Pages and a Yellow Pages telephone directory, listing residential and business numbers respectively. Both are available online at www.yellow.co.nz. In many regions the White Pages and Yellow Pages are in one directory but in larger regions, such as Auckland, Wellington and Christchurch, they come in separate volumes.

Reaching the Right Number

- For long distance calls within New Zealand (STD calls), first dial the national access code **0**, then the area code and the number.
- For an international number (IDD call), dial **00** followed by the country code, then the area code and number.
- For local and national directory enquiries, dial **018** (charges vary).
- For international directory enquiries, dial **0172** (charges vary).
- For collect calls (reverse charges) to NZ numbers, dial **010** (charges vary).
- The prefixes **021**, **022**, **027** and **029** are mobile telephone numbers.
- **0800** and **0508** numbers are toll free.
- See also Emergency Numbers, *p347*, or search for national numbers on yellow.co.nz/whitepages.

Mobile Phones

New Zealand has analogue and GSM digital mobile phone networks, and mobile phones can be used throughout most of New Zealand, apart from remote and mountainous areas. International roaming is available with most providers, but it may be cheaper to buy a pay-as-you-go phone or a New Zealand SIM card. New Zealand's main mobile phone providers are **Vodafone** and **Spark**. Another option is **2degrees**, which offers competitive prepaid prices and rates for international texts and calls.

Internet

Broadband internet coverage now extends to most of New Zealand, apart from some of the very remote areas. Cybercafés still exist around the country, providing email and internet services to travellers, but Wi-Fi hotspots can increasingly be found in cafés and public spaces such as libraries, museums and university

Cybercafés with internet access are found all over New Zealand

campuses, especially in Auckland and Wellington. All hotels, motels and campsites offer broadband or Wi-Fi facilities for guests to check emails and access the internet. Major hotel chains offer internet access as a complimentary service *(see p299)*.

Postal Services

New Zealand's very efficient postal service is run by **New Zealand Post**. Letters and parcels can be sent through PostShops, many of which are located in bookshops. Most are open from 9am to 5pm Mon–Sat. Stamps can be bought at supermarkets, dairies (convenience stores) and newsagents as well as at PostShop branches. There are two main classes of domestic mail: FastPost, which arrives the day after posting, and standard post, which takes two to three days to arrive. International airmail takes four to ten days to reach most countries.

The main post office in each town serves as a *Poste Restante*. You will need a passport or some other form of identification to claim *Poste Restante* mail.

New Zealand has several excellent domestic courier companies, offering same- or next-day delivery to anywhere in New Zealand. **Courier Post** is operated by New Zealand Post, and you can mail parcels using this service from their PostShops, found in all towns and cities. Or you can opt for one of the well-known international courier services, that ship parcels overseas such as **DHL**, **Fedex** or **UPS**. For all

Newspapers and magazines for sale

courier companies you will need to phone the 0800 number to arrange a pick-up or find the nearest depot. All companies offer an online tracking service for packages; a tracking number will be provided by the courier office.

Newspapers and Magazines

Each of the main cities has its own morning newspaper. *The New Zealand Herald*, the country's largest, is published in Auckland. The Christchurch *Press* is the South Island's largest newspaper. The *Otago Daily Times* is published in Dunedin, the *Dominion Post* in Wellington and the *Southland Times* in Invercargill. Excellent weekend reading is contained in *The Sunday Star Times*, which is published nationally. The best current affairs magazines are *The Listener* and *North and South*.

Foreign newspapers and magazines are available in bookshops and at newsstands in larger towns, but can also be accessed via the internet.

Televison and Radio

The three main free-to-air television channels are TV1 and TV3, which screen mostly local programmes, and TV2, which relies more heavily on US programmes. Pay channel Sky offers specialist channels, such as CNN and National Geographic. Māori Television broadcasts programmes nationally, often

Standard and FastPost boxes

in *te reo Māori* (the Māori language), and can provide an insight into Māori culture.

The state-owned, non-commercial Radio New Zealand (similar to the BBC) is renowned for the quality of its broadcasting. Other stations provide regional news and traffic reports.

TRAVEL INFORMATION

The vast majority of visitors arrive in New Zealand by air. Auckland is the busiest port of entry, followed by Christchurch. Once in New Zealand, many tourists use the domestic air network to get around, particularly to travel between the North and South islands. The coach network covers most major routes in the country. The rail network is limited, but travels through spectacular scenery. For visitors wanting to explore at their own pace, a car or campervan is the best way to travel. The roads are in good condition, but extra care is needed on alpine routes and back country roads.

Arriving by Air

Despite New Zealand's clean, green image and attempts to make the cities less polluted, it is hard to reach the country in an environmentally responsible way. The country is also reliant on air travel for its domestic travel network *(see pp354–5)*.

Around 15 international airlines fly into New Zealand daily. Others, such as **British Airways**, serve the country on a codeshare basis (sharing routes with a partner airline). The national airline, **Air New Zealand**, has an extensive international network, with links with more than 130 countries worldwide.

Air New Zealand and **Qantas** fly into New Zealand from the west coast of the United States, while **Cathay Pacific**, **Emirates**, **Japan Airlines**, **Korean Air**, **Malaysian Airlines**, **Royal Brunei**, **Singapore Airlines** and **Thai Airways** depart from major Asian airports for New Zealand. **Aerolineas Argentinas** flies direct from Buenos Aires to Auckland and **Lan Chile** direct from Santiago. Pacific Blue, a low-cost subsidiary of Virgin, flies from various Australian cities to Auckland, Hamilton, Wellington, Christchurch, Queenstown and Dunedin, and many other airlines fly via Australia.

New Zealand is a 3-hour flight from eastern Australia, 10 hours from Pacific Rim cities such as Singapore, Hong Kong and Tokyo, and between 13 and 16 hours from the USA and South America. Taking account of delays and transfers, a flight from Europe can be very taxing and it is worth making a stopover in Asia, the USA or on one of the Pacific Islands.

Airports

New Zealand has two main international terminals. Auckland is the major gateway, accommodating international and domestic flights, followed by Christchurch, where flights arrive from Singapore, Bangkok and Dubai. This airport is known as the New Zealand's tourism gateway, due to its location on the south island close to major tourist sights. Wellington Airport, in the country's capital, is used mainly as a domestic hub and can only be reached direct from Australia or via a connecting flight from Auckland or Christchurch. Queenstown offers flights to and from Brisbane, Sydney and Melbourne in Australia as well as domestic inland flights, while Hamilton links with Australia and some Pacific destinations. By international standards, none of the airports is congested and the airports are rarely affected by adverse weather conditions.

International signpost at Christchurch Airport

Tickets and Fares

Air fares to New Zealand can be expensive, particularly during the peak season from December to February when airlines charge premium rates. The cost of flights also goes up during the northern hemisphere summer (July–August). Cheaper air fares are available during the "shoulder" season between the high and low seasons. Shop around and get several prices before making

The "City of Sails" design of Auckland International Airport

a booking. Online booking and internet travel comparison sites make it easier to check ticket prices, but you may still save time and money by going through a travel agent. Air New Zealand may bundle in onward domestic flights with its international flights and sometimes offers cheap seats on www.grabaseat.co.nz. Always check the limitations and penalties before buying a cut-price ticket.

On Arrival

During international flights to New Zealand, visitors are given a Passenger Arrival Card to complete and hand in on arrival, along with their passports. Travellers must declare any restricted items and items subject to agricultural quarantine *(see pp342–3)* and place fresh food in bins before the immigration area, where they will go through passport control, customs and bio security checks.

Auckland and Christchurch airports have a wide range of food and retail outlets, telecommunication services, visitor information and banking facilities *(see p348)*. Bookings can be made for further domestic air travel, if flights have not already been arranged in advance.

Transport to and from the Airport

Transfer to the city centres from the airport is straightforward: taxis and shuttles (shared mini-vans with trailers for luggage) are available for door-to-door service, and buses run regularly. Taxis are an expensive option, with buses being the cheapest. Auckland is the only city to suffer from traffic congestion; it can take up to 1 hour to reach the city centre. Christchurch is a 15-minute drive from the airport.

Departure Tax

An airport user fee is levied on passengers aged 12 and above departing from New Zealand's international airports. It is now included in the ticket price for departures from Auckland and Christchurch. Security checks are as stringent at New

Zealand's airports as anywhere in the world. Make sure you pack restricted items such as liquid cosmetics or nail scissors in your checked baggage.

Package Deals

Although New Zealand mostly attracts independent travellers, a range of package deals are on offer, from basic fly-drive deals to all-inclusive coach tours, backpacker and adventure tours, and ski/snowboard packages. Alternatively, there are plenty of local tour operators who can plan activities on arrival. The Tourism New Zealand website *(see p345)* is an excellent place to start, as is www.destination-nz.com. **Discover New Zealand** offers a good selection of these tours and travel packages, which also includes coach and rail holidays.

Airport bus, a cheap option for reaching the city centre

DIRECTORY

Arriving by Air

Aerolineas Argentinas
Tel 0810 222 86527.
W aerolineas. com.ar

Air New Zealand
Tel (09) 336 2400,
0800 737 000.
W airnz.co.nz

British Airways
Tel (09) 966 9777.
W ba.com

Cathay Pacific
Tel 0800 441 289.
W cathaypacific.co.nz

Emirates
Tel 050 836 4728.
W emirates.com/nz

Japan Airlines
Tel 0800 885 880.
W nz.jal.co.jp/en

Korean Air
Tel (09) 914 2000.
W koreanair.com

Malaysia Airlines
Tel 0800 777 747.
W malaysiaairlines.
com.my

Qantas
Tel 0800 808 767.
W qantas.co.nz

Singapore Airlines
Tel 0800 808 909.
W singaporeair.com

Thai Airways
Tel (09) 377 0268,
0800 100 992.
W thaiair.com

Airports

Auckland
Tel (09) 275 0789.
W aucklandairport.co.nz

Christchurch
Tel (03) 353 7777.
W christchurchairport.
co.nz

Queenstown
Tel (03) 450 9031.
W queenstownairport.
co.nz

Wellington
Tel (04) 385 5100.
W wellingtonairport.
co.nz

Package Deals

Discover New Zealand
Tel 0800 468 624.
W discovernew
zealand.com

Domestic Air Travel

New Zealand has an extensive domestic air transport network, linking all of the major and provincial cities as well as many smaller towns. Although it is a small country, New Zealand's long, thin shape means that land travel between major centres, such as Auckland, Wellington and Christchurch, is time-consuming. As a result, air services play a crucial transport role. The main domestic carrier is Air New Zealand, which also owns airline companies that operate services to provincial centres. A wide range of heavily discounted fares are always available, particularly on the internet or if travellers are flexible and book well in advance.

Air New Zealand domestic flight arriving at Wellington airport

Airports

Some 26 domestic destinations are serviced by scheduled flights that connect the main cities – Auckland, Wellington, Christchurch and Dunedin – with provincial centres. These include Nelson, Gisborne, Napier/Hastings, Taupo, Whangarei, Kaitaia, Hokitika and Timaru and tourist resorts such as Queenstown, Rotorua and the Bay of Islands, Mount Cook and Te Anau/Manapouri. It is also possible to fly from Invercargill to Stewart Island, from Auckland to Great Barrier Island, from Wellington to Blenheim, Picton or Nelson (as an alternative to the ferry) and from Wellington to Takaka in the South Island. Scenic flights over Mount Cook, Fiordland and other areas are also on offer.

Domestic flights within New Zealand save travelling time and the comprehensive network of airports and regular flights make every part of the country accessible.

Domestic Airlines

Air New Zealand operates the main national network, incorporating the Air New Zealand Link carriers – Air Nelson, Mount Cook Line and Eagle Air – which service some provincial centres. All bookings for these services are made through Air New Zealand. **SoundsAir** operate across the Cook Strait, with up to eight return flights a day from Wellington to Picton, up to 20 return flights a week to Nelson and up to 12 return flights a week to Blenheim. **Golden Bay Air** flies the Wellington–Takaka route once a day out of season, two to four times daily in summer. **Steward Island Flights** fly three times a day between Invercargill and Stewart Island. **Great Barrier Airlines** fly from Auckland and North Shore to Great Barrier Island, as well as from Auckland to Kaitaia.

Fly–Drive Deals

A convenient way to travel in New Zealand is to fly to a destination and then continue by car. Rental cars can be picked up and dropped off at different points; for example, it is possible to fly from Auckland to Queenstown, then drive from Queenstown to Christchurch. Air New Zealand and other airlines have links with car hire firms (see p359), which offer discounts to passengers travelling on those airlines.

A wide range of fly–drive packages operate from Auckland to the South Island during the ski season, including deals combining flights, car rental and ski lift passes. Travel agents offer a variety of special promotions, and it is best to shop around.

Fly-drive packages operate to Mount Cook Line ski-planes

DIRECTORY

Domestic Airlines

Air New Zealand
Tel 0800 737 000.
W airnewzealand.co.nz

Golden Bay Air
W goldenbayair.co.nz

Great Barrier Airlines
W barrierair.kiwi

SoundsAir
Tel 0800 505 005.
W soundsair.com

Stewart Island Flights
Tel (03) 218 9129.
W stewartislandflights.co.nz

Domestic Airports

Dunedin
Tel (03) 486 2879.
W dnairport.co.nz

Hamilton
Tel (07) 848 9027.
W hamiltonairport.co.nz

Invercargill
Tel (03) 218 6920.
W invercargillairport.co.nz

Nelson
Tel (03) 547 3199.
W nelsonairport.co.nz

Taupo
Tel (07) 378 7771.
W taupoairport.co.nz

Special Passes

Star Alliance
W staralliance.com

Passengers checking in at Christchurch International Airport

Checking In

On domestic flights, airlines require passengers to check in at least 30 minutes before departure. This may be done at self check-in kiosks. All economy class passengers on domestic flights have a baggage allowance of 20 kg (44 lb) and a one bag limit, which is less than on international flights and is strictly enforced. If you are connecting with an international Air New Zealand flight, you should be able to check your baggage through from your domestic check-in point, and they may be more lenient about weight. The maximum weight for cabin baggage is 7 kg (11 lb). Personal articles, such as a coat, handbag, camera or laptop may also be carried into the aircraft.

Air Fares and Special Passes

Standard domestic fares can be expensive, but airlines allocate a variety of fares to each flight. Even at short notice you can sometimes get a good deal: to find discounted last-minute fares on Air New Zealand flights, go to the website and click on the "grabaseat" option. It is usually cheaper to buy your first onward domestic flight along with your international flight booking. Various air passes allow visitors to make a number of single domestic flights for a set price. Air New Zealand offers a "South Pacific Airpass" to travellers flying in on any **Star Alliance** flight (Air New Zealand, Singapore Airlines and Thai Air). The Star Alliance South Pacific Airpass offers options between three to ten flights within ten countries in the South Pacific, which include New Zealand, Australia, Fiji, Cook Islands and French Polynesia. Customers are provided with various choices to plan a South Pacific flight itinerary, with considerable savings on airfares. The airpass is only available in conjunction with an intercontinental ticket to or from the South Pacific region, on one of the 25 Star Alliance member airlines. It is necessary to have two stopovers in order to qualify for the pass. The fare is calculated by the mileage travelled.

Principal Domestic Air Routes

Domestic flights operating between major cities, complemented by a host of connecting flights between smaller towns and tourist resorts, cover the country quite comprehensively. Flying is ideal for those with limited time to spend in the country.

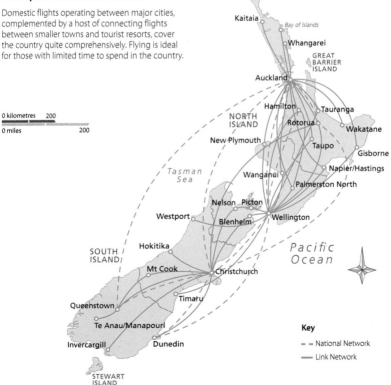

0 kilometres 200
0 miles 200

Kaitaia
Bay of Islands
Whangarei
GREAT BARRIER ISLAND
Auckland
Hamilton
Tauranga
NORTH ISLAND
Rotorua
Wakatane
New Plymouth
Taupo
Gisborne
Tasman Sea
Wanganui
Napier/Hastings
Palmerston North
Nelson Picton
Westport
Blenheim
Wellington
Hokitika
Pacific Ocean
SOUTH ISLAND
Mt Cook
Christchurch
Timaru
Queenstown
Te Anau/Manapouri
Invercargill
Dunedin
STEWART ISLAND

Key
− − National Network
— Link Network

Travelling by Coach, Train and Inter-Island Ferry

New Zealand's coach service is extensive and efficient, connecting most points throughout the country. Coaches cater for independent travellers as well as those who prefer guided tours. Although New Zealand does not have an extensive rail network, trains connect the main cities and passenger journeys are outstanding for their breathtaking scenery, some not visible from any road. The mountainous terrain has forced railway engineers to build spectacular viaducts and long tunnels. The North and South islands are connected by ferry, with several sailings each day.

Magic Bus coach

Coach Travel

Coach travel is a safe, efficient and popular means of transport for tourists in New Zealand. Coach travellers can take regular scheduled services or use one of the travel pass options available to independent travellers. Most New Zealand cities and towns are linked by **InterCity Coachlines**, while **Newmans Coach Lines** offers tours around Queenstown and its environs. Northliner Bus operates between Auckland and all Northland centres, whereas Mana Bus offers a low-cost service between Wellington and Auckland. Discounts are available on scheduled services, subject to cancellation penalties. InterCity sometimes offers NZ$1 tickets.

NakedBus offers a travel pass system, targeted at backpackers. Travellers buy a national coach pass, which is valid on selected routes at any time within 12 months of purchase. **Kiwi Experience** offers travel passes for backpackers and sightseeing tours.

Tickets and Reservations

InterCity and Newmans coach tickets can be booked in advance by phone, online or from agents, based at i-SITE visitor centres (see p345) and independent travel agencies in most towns. InterCity offers a range of Travelpasses, valid for one to 14 days of travel on selected itineraries. They can be used over a 12-month period, and are priced from NZ$43 to NZ$1,249, according to the distance travelled and number of stops. The Flexipass, which is priced in blocks of time from 15 to 60 hours' travel and can be used over a 12-month period, is more flexible and costs NZ$443. Discounted backpacker rates are available.

Magic Bus passes range from NZ$290 to NZ$1,994, purchased at the Magic Bus office in Auckland or online.

Travelling by Train

The New Zealand rail network is operated by a private company, **KiwiRail,** who conduct the Great Journeys of New Zealand with choices of Tranz-Coastal, TranzAlpine and OverLander trains offering scenic rail journeys for tourists. Passenger rail services connect the major cities as well as a number of provincial centres, including Ohakune, Palmerston North, Picton, Kaikoura and Greymouth. In the North Island, the OverLander train connects Auckland to Wellington, and vice versa, and is mainly used by tourists.

The TranzAlpine journey from Christchurch to Greymouth crosses the Canterbury Plains before cutting dramatically through the Southern Alps via the Otira viaduct (see pp246–7), and on through the rainforests of the West Coast. The Tranz-Coastal, which runs between Picton and Christchurch, is popular for viewing the Kaikoura coast scenery.

Otago has a privately run excursion train: Dunedin Railways (see p268).

Tickets and Reservations

Bookings for rail travel can be made through travel agents, by calling Tranz Scenic Reservations seven days a week from 7am to 9pm, or online. There is a multi-tier fare structure for both rail and ferry travel, and discounts of up to 50 per cent on standard fares are often available, during off-peak periods. Always ask for the best possible price when making a booking.

An economical and independent way to travel is to use the Tranz Scenic rail and ferry pass, similar to the passes available in the UK and Europe, where all travel must be completed by a certain date.

Inter-Island Ferry Services

The main inter-island ferry service between Wellington and Picton is provided by the **Interislander** fleet, which carries passengers, cars and freight. The Interislander service operates five return trips a day, taking about 3 hours each way. The trip is one of the most

The TranzAlpine crossing Kowai Bridge near Springfield

A ship from the Interislander ferry service fleet

scenic cruises in the world, offering stunning views, and the three ships in the fleet are all comfortable, with a wide range of facilities on board, including restaurants, bars, cafés, children's rooms, observation decks and also "quiet rooms" for business people, which can booked when on board the ferry.

The **Bluebridge Cook Strait Ferry** runs twice daily and offers similar facilities to the Interislander ferries. A number of ferry companies operate services around Auckland Harbour.

Tickets and Reservations

Bookings for Interislander ferries and Bluebridge Cook Strait Ferry services can be made online, by telephone, at travel agents or at i-SITE visitor information centres *(see p345)*. It is advisable to book in advance particularly during school holidays and if you are taking a car across the strait. However, it is possible to buy tickets at the ferry terminals on the day, if they are not sold out. For joint rail and ferry passes, *see p356*.

DIRECTORY

Rail Companies

KiwiRail
Tel 0800 872 467. W kiwirail.co.nz
W greatjourneysofnz.co.nz

Coach Companies

InterCity Coachlines
Tel (03) 548 1539.
W intercity.co.nz

Kiwi Experience
Tel (09) 336 4286.
W kiwiexperience.com

NakedBus
Tel (09) 979 1616.
W nakedbus.co.nz

Newmans Coach Lines
Tel (03) 442 4922.
W intercity.co.nz

Ferry Companies

Bluebridge Cook Strait Ferry
Tel 0800 844 844.
W bluebridge.co.nz

Interislander
Tel 0800 802 802.
W interislandline.co.nz

Principal Coach, Rail and Ferry Routes

In New Zealand, travel by the national coach network, the scenic rail network and the inter-island ferry services enables visitors to cover much of the country. Local bus companies service smaller towns. Note that the following rail services do not carry passengers: Wellington to Napier, Auckland to Tauranga, Auckland to Rotorua, and Christchurch to Invercargill.

Key

— Principal coach route
— Principal rail route

For keys to symbols *see back flap*

Travelling by Car

Although the public transport system offers plenty of options for travelling between towns and cities, a car allows you to thoroughly explore New Zealand's scenic rural areas, and gives you the flexibility to stop at beaches, lakes, country cafés, wineries and restaurants, and other points of interest along the way, or pause to admire a view. Outside the main cities the roads are relatively uncongested. They are generally in good condition, but even major highways have winding, hilly sections. Multi-lane motorways occur on the approaches to the main cities and the first 80 km (50 miles) between Auckland and Hamilton.

State Highway 1 parallelling the railway line along the Kaikoura coast

especially in the main cities. Auckland's motorways in particular can get close to gridlock. Traffic reports and updates are regularly broadcast on local radio stations *(see p351)*.

Car Insurance

Car and campervan rental rates usually include insurance cover for collision damage and theft from the vehicle. However, policies often carry a very high excess payment. Many companies offer worthwhile "excess waiver" options. Personal accident plans are available, but this risk should be covered by comprehensive travel insurance. Insurance for drivers under the age of 25 is more expensive.

Parking

Outside the main cities, parking in New Zealand poses few problems. In most town centres there is a combination of free and metered parking, and car parks. Parked cars must face the same direction as the flow of traffic. Parking is usually under the control of local councils and patrolled by wardens who can issue fines to vehicles that are parked illegally or that have expired meters.

Most cities have clearway zones and vehicles parked in these areas during certain times may be towed away. If this occurs, call the local traffic authority or police to find out where your car has been impounded.

Driving in New Zealand

Holders of a current driving licence can drive in New Zealand for up to 12 months. Foreign licences must have an authorised English translation if they are not in English. If you do not hold a driving licence, you will need an International Driving Permit. All drivers must carry their licence when driving.

New Zealanders drive on the left-hand side of the road. The speed limit is 100 km/h (60 mph) on the open road and 50 km/h (30 mph) in urban areas. Excessive speed is a major hazard and speeding, erratic drivers will be fined.

A yellow line down the centre of the road means it is illegal to overtake. Main highways have passing lanes at regular intervals. Similar to most left-hand drive countries, traffic crossing or approaching from the right has to give way.

Drink-driving laws are strictly enforced in New Zealand. A driver

may be required to give a breath test at any time. The legal blood alcohol level is 50 milligrams of alcohol per 100 millilitres of blood for drivers 20 and over. There is zero-tolerance for drivers under 20.

It is compulsory for the driver and passengers to wear a seat belt, while children under seven years must use an approved car seat.

It is illegal to use a hand-held mobile phone while driving, but bluetooth head-set and no-hands speaker phones are permitted. You may not make or answer calls, nor send or read text messages.

Traffic accidents involving injury must be reported to the police within 24 hours.

When driving in cities, an up-to-date street map or Sat Nav is essential, especially for spotting one-way streets. Wherever possible, avoid peak traffic between 7:30–9am and 4:30–6pm,

One-lane
bridge ahead

Fuel

The majority of New Zealand cars run on petrol, which is available in regular and premium unleaded. Most four-wheel drive vehicles and campervans use diesel, which is cheaper than petrol. Fuel is sold at service stations which stay open late or even 24 hours in cities, but may be closed in the evenings and at weekends in rural settlements. Larger rural petrol stations often have cafés and convenience stores for handy stop-off points.

Service station selling both petrol and diesel

Breakdown Services

Car hire companies deal with breakdowns involving their own vehicles, and will arrange to provide a replacement if necessary. The **Automobile Association** (AA) is a nationwide motoring organization providing breakdown services. Members of most overseas motoring organizations, except AA UK and RAC UK, receive reciprocal services with the New Zealand AA. To benefit, take your home motoring organization card into any AA office in New Zealand.

New Zealand AA membership entitles you to six free breakdown call-outs a year, and discounted rates at some hotels and for car hire.

Car and Motorcycle Rental

Rental cars are readily available with a range of companies to choose from. Large companies such as **Avis**, **Budget** and **Hertz** have nationwide networks. Smaller local companies may be cheaper, but offer less flexibility. Most rental companies will not hire to anyone under the age of 21. Companies are likely to ask for a credit card imprint as security against loss or damage.

Several companies offer specialized motorbike rental, guided motorbike tours or can help to plan routes, especially in the South Island. Try Christchurch-based **South Pacific Motorcycle Tours** for a fleet of bikes including BMWs, Triumph Thunderbirds and Harley Davidsons. **New Zealand Motorcycle Rentals**, with a fleet of mainly Japanese bikes, has bases in both Christchurch and Auckland, offering the option of picking up at one and dropping off at the other.

Rates start from about NZ$100 a day for a small bike, going up to about NZ$285 a day for a top-of-the-range bike. Rental should include a helmet and any other safety equipment, full insurance, breakdown cover, road maps and GPS hire.

Campervan Rental

A popular form of transport with visitors is a campervan, motorhome or RV. Camping grounds can be found in beautiful locations around the country *(see p301)*. Campervans are available in a range of sizes and come with a refrigerator and gas cooker. Some have their own shower, toilet and microwave. One of the largest campervan rental companies in New Zealand, **Kea Campers** have gained CarboNZero certification for their campervans, which have engines that comply with EU standards, solar panels to heat water and self-contained waste, making them suitable for free camping.

Kea Campers, **Maui Rentals** and **Britz NZ** have depots in Auckland, Christchurch and Queenstown. You may be asked for a large deposit and the insurance excess may also be high. It is usually possible to pay a higher insurance premium to reduce or waive the excess and deposit.

Maui Rentals campervan parked near Auckland waterfront

Road Conditions

The quality of New Zealand's roads is excellent. However, with few motorways, only a painted centre line separates opposing traffic on most roads, and winding stretches are common. Many back roads are unsealed and require extreme care as it is easy to lose control on the uneven surface.

Check road conditions with the Department of Conservation (www.doc.govt.nz) or AA before travelling on roads in the snowbound mountainous and inland areas of the South Island in winter, on any back roads leading to scenic areas. Take care on unsealed roads such as the one leading to the Oparara Basin north of Karamea *(see p238)*. These roads are often narrow and driving can be dangerous on the gravel surface or on verges.

DIRECTORY

Breakdown Services

Automobile Association
Tel 0800 500 222. W aa.co.nz

Car and Motorcycle Rental

Avis
Tel 0800 655 111.
W avis.co.nz

Budget Rent A Car
Tel 0800 283 438.
W budget.co.nz

Hertz
Tel 0800 654 321.
W hertz.com

New Zealand Motorcycle Rentals
W nzbike.com

South Pacific Motorcycle Tours
W motorbiketours.co.nz

Campervan Rentals

Britz NZ
W britz.co.nz

Kea Campers
W keacampers.com

Maui Rentals
W maui-rentals.com/nz

Getting Around Towns and Cities

Although rural New Zealand is very car-dependent, it is possible to get around the main towns and cities on foot and using public transport. Auckland, Wellington and Christchurch have a mix of suburban trains, buses and trams, which can be supplemented by taxis. Auckland is a sprawling city and some means of transport is necessary to travel between its suburbs, although the central business district can be traversed on foot. Central Wellington is compact, but its outlying districts are steep and hilly. Christchurch, by contrast, is flat and is ideally suited to touring by bicycle.

Buses

Auckland has an extensive bus network. The **Britomart Transport Centre**, its downtown hub, has an information kiosk open daily. Alternatively, check Auckland Transport's MAXX website (www.maxx.co.nz) for route maps, timetables, fares and a useful journey planner.

In Wellington, the main bus routes traverse downtown. Buses are operated by several companies and information for all services can be found on the **Metlink** website.

Christchurch's **Central Bus Exchange** is the main bus service provider. Information is available on the Metro website. Leopard Coachlines run a fleet of biodiesel buses that run on animal fat, identified by a "biodiesel" tag.

Queenstown's **Connectabus** service links the resort centre to outlying areas.

Historic hop-on, hop-off tram, Christchurch

Trams

Christchurch has a historic tram service which runs on a 2.5 km (1.5 mile) loop around the city centre. It offers a hop- on, hop-off service, with a two-day ticket costing NZ$17. Buy tickets from the **Christchurch Tramway** website, at the tram station or from the conductor.

Wellington has a system of trolleybuses that run on electric overhead cables.

Tickets

Single bus tickets and day passes can be paid for as you board the bus, or cheaper 10-ride tickets can be bought at dairies (convenience stores) and newsagents. Single tram tickets, day passes or 10-ride tickets can be purchased at train stations or on the trams.

Both Auckland and Wellington offer a "top-up" Snapper Card, which gives a 20 per cent discount on bus travel. Cards can be bought from the **Snapper** website or at dairies. The card can also act a form of payment in some shops.

Christchurch has a prepaid Metrocard, offering users a 30 per cent discount on cash fares and can be purchased on the **Metro** website or at the Central Bus Exchange.

Walking

Walking is an eco-friendly way to get around New Zealand's cities, offering the chance to take in the local architecture at a leisurely pace.

Sprawling Auckland, covering 100 sq km (39 sq miles), is not immediately conducive to walking, but the central business district is easily covered on foot, and suburbs such as Ponsonby, Newmarket and Parnell, as well as the city parks, are pleasant to walk around. The **Short Walks in Auckland** website offers free self-guided circular routes throughout the city.

Wellington's scale is more walker-friendly, but its steep hills may be a deterrent to all but the keenest. To encourage walkers, **Greater Wellington Regional Council** offers a walking journey planner, which not only gives directions from A to B, but shows how hilly the trip will be and how many calories you will burn.

Central Christchurch is easily covered on foot, and has the advantage of being flat. Getting around Queenstown's central business district is likely to be an easy stroll for outdoor enthusiasts using the resort town as a base for arduous mountain hikes.

Bus en route to the railway station, Wellington

Taxis

Taxis are readily available in all the cities, operated by private companies and licensed by the New Zealand Transport Association (NZTA). To find a taxi, look in the Yellow Pages of the telephone directory or ask at your hotel. Taxi ranks are found at airports, in city centres and near shopping malls. **Wellington Combined Taxis** are New Zealand's first CarboNZero certified taxi company.

Cycling

Cycling is a good way to get around Auckland, although cyclists have to contend with the traffic. Bikes can be rented from **BikeCentral** near the Britomart Transport Centre. The MAXX website (www.maxx. co.nz) has a cycle route map, making cyclists aware of crash hotspots and indicating the location of bike lockers and parking, cycle-friendly cafés and cycle repair shops.

Hilly Wellington offers a challenge to cyclists. Greater Wellington Regional Council offers an online cycle journey planner showing the hills. To rent bikes, go to **Mud Cycles** in Karori or **Dirt Merchants** in Brooklyn.

Central Christchurch is flat, compact and ideal for cycling, with on-road cycle lanes and off-road paths for cyclists. **Christchurch City Council** publishes a guide, with route maps and information for cyclists. The Metro website has a map of bus routes that carry bikes. Bikes can be hired from **City Cycle Hire**.

Guided Tours

A host of tourism providers offer guided tours of Auckland and its environs, including the North Shore and West Coast beaches, with transport by car and minivan included. **NZ Tours & Travel** offer a wide range of full- and half-day tours.

Several companies offer guided walking tours of all the main sights in Auckland, Wellington and Christchurch. All can be contacted through the i-SITE Visitor Information Centre *(see p345)*. **Walk Wellington** offers daily tours taking in the main downtown sights in a 2-hour walk. Evening walks are available in summer and personalized walks can be arranged. **Zest Food Tours** follow foodie trails around the city, which boasts that it has more cafés and restaurants per capita than any other in the world.

Christchurch Tours offer daily guided tours of the South Island city, beach and harbour by coach, departing from Cathedral Square.

Cycling on South Island

DIRECTORY

Buses

Britomart Transport Centre
Commerce St, Auckland.
Tel 0800 10 30 80 or (09) 366 6400.
W **at.govt.nz**

Central Bus Exchange
Cnr Colombo and Lichfield sts, Christchurch.
Tel (03) 66 88 55.
W **metroinfo.org.nz**

Connectabus (Queenstown)
Tel (03) 3 441 4471.
W **connectabus.co.nz**

Metlink (Wellington)
Tel 0800 801 700.
W **metlink.org.nz**

Trams

Christchurch Tramway
W **welcomeaboard.co.nz**

Tickets

Metro (Christchurch)
W **metroinfo.co.nz**

Snapper (Wellington)
W **snapper.co.nz**

Walking

Greater Wellington Regional Council
W **journeyplanner. org.nz**

Short Walks in Auckland
W **walksinauckland.com**

Taxis

Auckland Co-op Taxis
Tel (09) 300 3000.

Wellington Combined Taxis
Tel (04) 384 4444.
W **taxis.co.nz**

Cycling

BikeCentral
Tel (09) 365 1768.
W **travelwise.org.nz**

Christchurch City Council
W **ccc.govt.nz/ cycling**

City Cycle Hire (Christchurch)
Tel (03) 377 5952.
W **cyclehire-tours.co.nz**

Dirt Merchants
93 Aro St, Wellington.
Tel (04) 831 1512.

Mud Cycles
Tel (04) 476 4961.
W **mudcycles.co.nz**

Guided Tours

Christchurch Tours
W **hasslefreetours. co.nz**

NZ Tours & Travel
W **newzealandtours. travel**

Walk Wellington
W **wellingtonnz.com**

Zest Food Tours
W **zestfoodtours.co.nz**

General Index

Page numbers in **bold** type refer to main entries

Acknowledgments

Dorling Kindersley would like to thank the many people whose help and assistance contributed to the preparation of this book.

Contributors
Helen Corrigan is a Wellington-based writer, editor, researcher and publicist. She has a background in journalism and radio and since 2002 has been a parliamentary press secretary.

Roef Hopman is a public relations consultant and freelance writer in Auckland. Formerly Chief Editor of *Design Trends*, he organizes public relations projects for Pacific Rim countries and contributes to various publications.

Gerard Hutching is a freelance journalist who specializes in natural history and the environment. He has written several books, including *The Natural World of New Zealand* which won the 1999 Montana Book of the Year (environment).

Rebecca Macfie is an award-winning Christchurch-based journalist. She specializes in business and current affairs feature writing, and contributes to a range of New Zealand newspapers and magazines.

Geoff Mercer lives in Hastings. He has written for daily newspapers in Wellington and Hawke's Bay. He now compiles oral histories, writes and publishes biographies, and contributes articles to various publications.

Simon Noble lives in Nelson and has a long involvement in the region's natural, historic and scenic areas. He is the author of *The Treasured Pathway*, a guide to a heritage highway through northern Nelson and Marlborough.

Peter Smith is an Auckland artist, educator, writer and yachtsman, and former principal of Auckland College of Education.

Michael Ward is a chef who has worked in the food industry for some twenty years. Michael has a keen interest in promoting New Zealand food and wine.

Mark Wright is a Dunedin-based freelance writer whose work ranges from articles on travel, technology and health to classic cars. He has a background in radio and writes scripts for television and video.

Additional Contributors
Georgina Palffy; Simon Vita

For Dorling Kindersley
Picture Research Rachel Barber, Marta Bescos, Sumita Khatwani, Ellen Root
Publishing Manager Kate Poole
Cartographic Editors Casper Morris, David Pugh
Production Michelle Thomas
Publishing Director Gillian Allan
Revisions Editor Neil Lockley
Revisions Designers Mariana Evmolpidou, Supriya Sahai

Indexer
Kay Lyons

Additional Photography
Peter Bush, Louise Goossens, Gerard Hindmarsh, Ian O'Leary, Rough Guides/Paul Whitfield

Revisions Team
Emma Anacootee, Avanika, Lydia Baillie, Stuti Tiwari Bhatia, Sheeba Bhatnagar, Frances Chan, Richard Czapnik, Alice Fewery, Rhiannon Furbear, Jenn Hadley, Christine Heilman, Gerard Hindmarsh, Brendan Hutching, Zafar ul Islam Khan, Bharti Karakoti, Sumita Khatwani, Tanya Mahendru, Hayley Maher, Alison McGill, Sam Merrell, Kate Molan, George Nimmo, Rakesh Kumar Pal, Garima Pandey, Susie Peachey, Scarlett O'Hara, Georgina Palffy, Helen Partington, Helen Peters, Marianne Petrou, Rada Radojicic, Rituraj Singh, Susana Smith, Roseen Teare, Conrad Van Dyk, Deepika Verma.

Special Assistance
Debbie Ameriks and Amelia Manson, Office of Treaty Settlements, Wellington; Tim Amos, Department of Conservation, Wellington; Lane Ayr, Bay of Islands Swordfish Club; Kate Banbury, Waitomo Glow Worm Caves New Zealand, Otorohanga; Jennifer Beatson, Latitude Nelson; Black's Point Museum, Reefton; Hughie Blues and Amanda Turner, Waikokopu Café, Waitangi; Julia Bradshaw, Lakes District Museum and Art Gallery, Arrowtown; Linda Burgess, Wellington; Dennis Buurman, Ocean Wings; Elizabeth Caldwell, Arts Council of New Zealand; Cathedral Church of St Paul, Wellington; Alan Cooper, Geology Department, University of Otago, Dunedin; C.P. Group, Auckland; Croydon Aviation Heritage Centre, Gore; Jo Darby, Tourism Industry Association New Zealand; Carol Davidson, New Zealand Festival 2000; Department of Conservation Visitor Centres; Jenny Dey, Photosource New Zealand Ltd; Richard Doyle and Lisa Hoffman, Christchurch City Council; Far North Regional Museum, Kaitia; Tammy Fromont and Nineke Metz, Destination Northland Limited; Dianne Gallagher, New Zealand Mountain Safety Council Inc.; Jane Gilbert, Film New Zealand; Gillooly family, Farewell Spit Safari, Collingwood; Donna Gray, Abel Tasman National Park Enterprises; Lesley Grey and Sharon Pasco, Stewart Island Promotion Association; Frank Habicht, Paihia; Haoni Waititi Marae, Auckland; Lee Harris, Fiordland Travel Limited, Queenstown; Tania Harris, Waitangi National Trust; Christine Harvey, Whale Watch®, Kaikoura; Cameron Hill, Air New Zealand; Hillary Commission; Barbara Hinkley and Suzanne Knight, Museum of New Zealand Te Papa Tongarewa; InterCity Coachlines; Anne Irving, City Gallery Wellington; Peter Jackson, Blenheim; Jean Johnston, Wellington City Council; Kapiti Cheese; Kelly Tarlton's Sea Life Aquarium, Auckland; Michael Liao, Kiwifruit Country, Te Puke; Fay Looney, New Plymouth; Peter McCleavey Gallery, Wellington; Ruth McGirr, Robert McDougall Art Gallery and Annex, Christchurch; Bill and Joan MacGregor, Lake Hawea; Robert McGregor, Art Deco Trust, Napier; Annabelle MacKenzie and Cathy Muker, New Zealand High Commission, Kuala Lumpur; Cathy Maslin, Key-Light Image Library; Heather Mathie and Betty Moss, Alexander Turnbull Library; Darryl May, Oamaru; Montana Marlborough Winery; Anita Moreira, Air New Zealand, Kuala Lumpur; Morven Hills Station, Oamaru; Museum of Caves, Waitomo; Newmans Coach Lines; Okarito Nature Tours, Westland; Old Mandeville Airport, Gore; Otago Early Settlers Museum, Dunedin; security staff, Parliament House, Wellington;

Libby Passau and Nick Turzynski, Hodder Moa Beckett Publishers Ltd; Jacky Payne; Penguin Place, Otago Peninsula; Meng-Chong Phang, New Zealand Tourism Board, Singapore; Clive Ralph, Napier; Rewa's Village, Kerikeri; Chris and Phil Rose, Wairau River Wines; Royal Albatross Centre, Taiaroa Head; Russell Museum; Mary Sharrock, Ansett Airways, Australia; Jenny Shipley, MP, Wellington; Stone Store, Kerikeri; Annalese Taylor, New Zealand Tourism Board, Auckland; Judith Tizard, MP; Tourism Auckland Office; Tourism Industry Association New Zealand; Tranz Rail Ltd; Tom Van der Kwast, Picton; Andrew and Jeannie Van der Putten; Visitor Information Centres; Warbirds and Wheels, Wanaka; Tim Warren, Visual Impact Pictures Ltd; concert staff, Whakarewarewa Thermal Village, Rotorua; Whangarei Museum of Fishes; Dr Rodney Wilson, Auckland War Memorial Museum; Jane Wynyard, The Royal New Zealand Ballet.

Photography Permissions
The publisher would like to thank the following for their assistance and kind permission to photograph at their establishments.

Graham Abbott, Hanmer Springs Thermal Reserve; Art and Gourd Gallery, Golden Bay; Ashford Craft Village, Ashburton; Auckland International Airport; Auckland Zoological Gardens; Avis, Auckland International Airport; Babich Winery, Auckland; Grant Barron, Olveston Historic Home, Dunedin; Café de Paris, Hokitika; Canterbury House Vineyards, Waipara; Christ Church Cathedral, Christchurch; Dr Fiona Ciaran, Aigantighe Art Gallery, Timaru; Clapham Clock Museum, Whangarei; Coal Town Museum, Westport; Dargaville Maritime Museum; DFS Galleria, Auckland; Driving Creek Railway and Potteries, Coromandel; Dunedin Public Art Gallery; Dunedin Railway Station; The Edwin Fox, Picton; Ana Foreman, Weta Shop, Coromandel; Gibbston Valley Winery, Queenstown; Lindsay Hazley, Southland Museum and Art Gallery, Invercargill; Helen and Ross Ivey, Glentanner Station; Kevin Judd, Cloudy Bay; Steve Jones, Science Centre, Manawatu Museum and Art Gallery, Palmerston North; Kauri Kingdom, Kaitaia; Stuart Landsborough's Puzzling World, Wanaka; Left Bank Art Gallery, Greymouth; Le Brun family, Blenheim; Malcolm McLaughlan and Peter Thornley, Icon Restaurant, Wellington; Maori Arts and Crafts Institute, Rotorua; Royce McGlashen, Nelson; Matakohe Kauri Museum, Dargaville; Mountain Jade Greenstone Factory, Hokitika; Mt Bruce Wildlife Centre, Wairarapa; Mountford Vineyard, Canterbury; Museum of Transport and Technology, Auckland; New Zealand Automobile Association; New Zealand Rugby Museum, Palmerston North; North Otago Museum, Oamaru; Nigel and Teresa Ogle, Tawhiti Museum, Hawera; Outdoor Heritage, Newmarket; Out of New Zealand, Auckland; Parnell Fire Service; Parnell Police Station; Pegasus Bay, Canterbury; Provincial Council Buildings, Christchurch; Queenstown Rafting; Rainbow's End Adventure Park, Auckland; Rippon Vineyards, Wanaka; St John's Ambulance; St Paul's Cathedral, Dunedin; Shantytown, Greymouth; Sheraton Auckland Hotel; Shotover Jet, Queenstown; Southward Car Museum, Paraparaumu; Stockton Mine, Westport; Thames School of Mines and Mineralogical Museum; Tramway Museum, Paekakariki; Waiau Waterworks, Coromandel; Waipara Springs, Canterbury; Whakarewarewa Thermal Village, Rotorua; Whale Watch®, Kaikoura; Wellington Museum; Whanganui Riverboat Centre; Zambesi, Wellington.

Picture Credits
Key: a = above; b = below/bottom; c = centre; f = far; l = left; r = right; t = top.

The publisher would like to thank the following individuals, companies and picture libraries for permission to reproduce their photographs:

111 Emergency: Derek Quinn: 346clb; **123RF.com**: Anastasia Raspopina 65br.

Airbus Express: 353cr; **AGL Aerial Imagery**: 43br; **Alamy Images**: Rafael Ben-Ari 1c; Jon Bower New Zealand 12bl; Greg Balfour Evans 13b, 296–7; Andrew Court 138br; Carpe Diem - New Zealand 156; Cephas Picture Library 200; Paul Grogan 113tl; Paul Thompson Images 311tl; Douglas Fisher 311cl; frans lemmens 20; Vincent Lowe 12tr; Henk Meijer 346cl; MJ Photography 171crb; North Wind Picture Archives 8–9; robertharding 220b; theatrepix 331t; UrbanZone 351cla; David Wall 62–3, 344tl; WENN Ltd 330br; Kim Westerskov 133tr; WinePix 211bc; **Art Deco Trust**: 150bl; **Auckland Museum Tāmaki Paenga Hira**: 83tl.

Bay of Islands Swordfish Club: 107tc, 107cla; **The Boatshed Hotel**: 301t; **Britomart Limited**: 74cla; **Peter Bush**: 37cr, 42bl, 42br, 75tr, 123clb, 161bl, 331cr.

Cable Bay Vineyards: 308br, 315tr; **Christchurch City Council**: 222; **Christchurch and Canterbury**: 229tl, 229tr; **Christchurch International Airport**: 355tl; **ChristchurchNZ**: 229bl; **City Gallery Wellington**: 168tr; **Corbis**: Jami Tarris 180–81; Miz Watanabe 278–9.

Department of Conservation, Wellington: 195tr, 223b; **Destination Northland Limited**: 100cl, 107cra, 112bc; **Destination Wairarapa**: 176t; **Dreamstime.com**: Rafael Ben Ari 80tl, 231br, 310cl; Blagov58 84–5; Dirkr 11cr; Filipe Frazao 283b; Ivan Gorpolski 65tl; Grace5648 327bc; Pablo Hidalgo 129b; Fritz Hiersche 350c; Hugoht 15br; In Sung Choi 286tr; Irina88w 122tr, 286bl; Krug100 82tr; Light & Magic Photography 244–5; Lucidwaters 109crb, 109bl, 346bl; Christopher Meder 270b; Millaus 24t; Christian Mueringer 14bl, 231tr; Dmitry Naumov 4tr; Cloudia Newland 2–3, 116; Mohd Nadly Aizat Mohd Nudri 258; Gaid Phitthayakormsilp 224tr; Dmitry Pichugin 4crb, 58–9, 148–9; Pstedrak 211tl; Uros Ravbar 338tl; Dennis Richardson 288clb; Natalia Sergeeva 170tr; Gina Smith 5tc; Alexey Stiop 222; Jordan Tan 273tr; Maksim Toome 322bl; Tupungato 13tr, 226tr, 230b; Ventura69 202cl; Mark Ward 15tc; Naruedom Yaempongsa 47c; **Drylands Restaurant**: 322t.

Eagles Nest: 298cl, 301t, 303tr.

Fiordland Travel Limited: 284tr, 288–9 all; **Fishbone Bar & Grill**: 324tl; **Food At Wharepuke**: 316tl.

The Gables: 317tr; **Gantleys Restaurant**: 325tc; **Gareth Eyres, Exposure**: 43tl, 45bc, 46cr, 112c, 125r, 243cr, 275br, 287tr, 335tl, 336tl, 336b, 337t; **Getty Images**: Alexandre Cappi 361cr; Mark Daffey 25tr; Paul Kennedy 130tl; Doug Pearson 104–5; Darryl Torckler 103br, 190–91; Matthew Micah Wright 70; **Greater Wellington Regional Council**: 360bl.

Hapuku Lodge & Tree Houses: 345tl; **Havana Bar and Restaurant**: 320tl; **The Hermitage, Mt Cook**: 256tr, 256clb.

Herzog Winery & Luxury Restaurant: 308cl; Gerard Hindmarsh: 274tl, 301c; Hodder Moa Beckett Publishers Ltd: 37bl; The Huka Retreat: 304tl; 2015 Hundertwasser Archive, Vienna: Richard Smart 111ca.

Interislander: 357tl.

Kapitea Ridge: 306tl; Kauri Cliffs: 299br, 302bc; Key-Light Image Library: Andy Belcher 147crb; Nic Bishop 248bl, 277ca; Gary Bowering 41bc; Brian Chudleigh 198tr; Richard Cory-Wright 123br; Brian Enting Photography 27tl, 51bl, 68br, 146clb; Tim Hawkins 256bc; Caroline Hobbs 243cra; Warren Jacobs 26–7, 30tr, 187br, 276cl, 339tl; Peter Laurenson 187crb; Geoff Mason 68tr, 199br, 251cl, 334bl, 354bc; Graham Meadows 38bc; Michael Pole 38tr; Graham Radcliffe 46bl, 177br, 356br; Andy Radka 30cl; Peter Reese 294cl; Nick Servian 34br, 34–35cr, 38br, 169tr; James White 38clb; Kokako: 314bl.

Lakes District Museum and Art Gallery: 283c; Holger Leue: 26br, 30cr, 31bl, 38cla, 38–39c, 53bc, 69cr, 69br, 72cl, 77clb, 78tl, 79bl, 81tr, 82br, 87bc, 93t, 96bl, 117b, 124cl, 126bc, 131br, 134tr, 135crb, 147cra 194tr, 194cla, 198–199c, 236tl, 248br, 256cla, 257tl, 271c, 276br, 281c, 282tr, 284br, 286cr, 287cl, 287b, 292cl, 292bc, 293br. Logan Brown Restaurant & Bar: 321tl; Rob Lucas: 28bl, 28bc, 28br, 29cla, 29bl, 29crb, 276tl, 287cr.

Magic Travellers Network: 356cla; Marsden Estate: 316br; Maui, New Zealand: 300br; Darryl May: 272tl, 272cla, 272clb, 273ca, 273ca; McCormick House: 305bc; Robert McDougall Art Gallery and Annex: 36bl; Mission Estate Winery: 318br; Rod Morris: 28clb, 28cb, 28crb, 29tl, 29tr, 29cl, 29cr, 29tl, 51cr, 93c, 196tr, 196cl, 196bl, 196br, 249cr, 255cl, 270tr, 276bl, 293cr, 295tl; Museum of New Zealand Te Papa Tongarewa: 33bl, 34bl, 35tl, 35cr, 37tl, 50tr, 50bc, 51cra, 55cb, 61bl, 170bl, 171tl; NZTA: 360c.

Napier City Council: 152tr; National Party Office: 57bc; Nelson Tasman Tourism: 14tr, 23b, 201b, 219tl; New Zealand Festival 2000: 160clb, 160–161c; The New Zealand Herald: 22b, 57tr, 121bl, 161tc.

Office of Treaty Settlements: 57cl.

Lloyd Park: 27br, 39bl, 39bc, 194–195c, 195br, 251cra, 251cr; Pescatore Restaurant: 323br; Pete's Farm Stay: 300tl; Peter McLeavey Gallery: Russell Kleyn 160cl; Photosource

New Zealand Ltd: 39cl, 39cr, 39clb, 42ca, 43clb, 43clb 44bl, 46bl, 47b, 66cl, 113cra, 123bl, 125tl, 165cl, 186tr, 186bl, 197tr, 198br, 199tl, 242cl, 249tl, 257cr, 285cr, 339cr.

River Restaurant and Vineyard: 319br; Riverstone Kitchen: 324bc; The Royal New Zealand Ballet: 94cr, 161br.

Satori Lounge: 319tl; SCENIC HOTEL GROUP: 307bl; Sky City Auckland Limited: 78tl; Stewart Island Promotion Association: 292tl.; SuperStock: age fotostock 98, /Charles O. Cecil 184cl, /Ignacio Palacios 340–41; Travel Library Limited 208–9;

Te Manawa Museums Trust: Andrew Blayney 179 all; Terrôir Restaurant at Craggy Range: 318tl; Tourism Auckland: 75cr; 88b; Tourism Dunedin: 264bl, 268bl; Tourism New Zealand: 60bl, 61br, 64cla, 99b, 193tr, 338bl, 359bc; Tourism Northland: 102tl, 107bl, 114cr; Fullers Great Sights Bay of Islands 101tl; Tourism West Coast: 242tr Alexander Turnbull Library: 22c, 34tr, 35tr, 35b, 37br, 40cl, 48, 49bl, 50cl, 50bl, 50cla, 51tc, 51br, 52tl, 52c, 52bl, 52br, 53br, 54tr, 54clb, 54bl, 55c, 55bc, 55br, 56tl, 56clb, 56cb, 66tl, 66bl, 66–67c, 67tl, 67cr, 89bc, 141br, 175br, 230cr, 239cl.

Visual Impact Pictures Ltd: 30bl, 31cr, 31br, 32tr, 39cra, 39crb, 39cla, 43ca, 44cr, 107br, 113crb, 121cla, 127bl, 132bl, 146tr, 194clb, 195tl, 199bl, 218tr, 250tl, 295cr.

Wai Restaurant: 325b; Wairau River Wines: 211cr; Waitangi National Trust: 45cr, 100br, 108cl, 108bl, 109tl; Wellington City Council: 91br, 160br; Dr Kim Westerskov: 107crb, 153br, 197tl, 197cr, 197clb; Westpac Limited: 348cl; Whale Watch®, Kaikoura: 213cla; Women's Golf New Zealand: 43tr.

Front Endpaper:
All special photography except
Alamy Images: Carpe Diem – New Zealand Rtr; Cephas Picture Library Rcr, Dreamstime.com: Cloudia Newland Lcl; Mohd Nadly Aizat Mohd Nudri Rbr; Alexey Stiop Rbc; Getty Images: Matthew Micah Wright Ltl; SuperStock: age fotostock Ltc.

Cover images:
Front and spine: AWL Images: Doug Pearson; Back: Dreamstime.com: Vlnasmartin

Further Reading

Art and Culture

100 New Zealand Craft Artists Schamroth, H., Godwit, Auckland 1998.

100 New Zealand Paintings Brown, W., Godwit, Auckland 1997.

Contemporary Painting in New Zealand Dunn, M., Craftsman House, Auckland 1996.

Dream Collectors: 100 Years of Art in New Zealand Wedde, I., Walsh, J. and Johnson, A., Te Papa Press, Wellington 1998.

A History of New Zealand Architecture Shaw, P., Hodder Moa Beckett, Auckland 1998.

Looking for the Local: Architecture and the New Zealand Modern Clark, J. and Walker, P., Victoria University Press, Wellington 2000.

Mau Moko: The World of Maori Tattoo Te Awekotuku, N. & Nikora, L.W., Penguin, Auckland 2007.

New Zealand Pottery: Commercial and Collectable Henry, G., Reed Publishing, Auckland 2007.

Old New Zealand Houses 1800–1940 Salmond, J., Reed Publishing, Auckland 1998.

Fiction

100 New Zealand Poems Manhire, B. (ed.), Godwit, Auckland 1994.

Believers to the Bright Coast O'Sullivan, V., Penguin, Auckland 1998.

The Best of Katherine Mansfield's Short Stories Mansfield K., Random House, Auckland 1998.

The Best of Owen Marshall Marshall, O., Random House, Auckland 1997.

The Bone People Hulme, K., Picador, Auckland 1986.

Land of the Long White Cloud: Maori Myths, Tales and Legends Kanawa, K.T. and Foreman, M., Penguin Auckland, 1997.

Mister Pip Jones, L., Penguin, Auckland 2006.

The Matriarch Ihimaera, W., Reed Publishing, Auckland 1996.

Once Were Warriors Duff, A., Tandem Press, Auckland 1990.

Plumb Gee, M., Penguin, Auckland 1981.

Potiki Grace, P., Penguin, Auckland 1986.

Reconnaissance Kassabova, K., Penguin, Auckland 1999.

Season of the Jew Shadbolt, M., David Ling Publishing, Auckland 1988.

Skylark Lounge Cox, N., Victoria University Press, Wellington 2000.

Geography and Geology

Aotearoa and New Zealand: A Historical Geography Grey, A., Canterbury University Press, Christchurch 1995.

Awesome Forces: The Natural Hazards That Threaten New Zealand Campbell, H. and Hicks, G., Te Papa Press Wellington 1998.

Contemporary Atlas of New Zealand Kirkpatrick, R., David Bateman, Auckland 1999.

Historical New Zealand Atlas Malcolm McKinnon et al (eds.), David Bateman, Auckland 1997.

History and Politics

A Concise Encyclopaedia of Maori Myth and Legend Orbell, M., Canterbury University Press, Christchurch 1998.

The Discovery of Aotearoa Evans, J., Reed Publishing, Auckland 1998.

Historical Dictionary of New Zealand Jackson, K. and McRobie, A., Addison, Wesley, Longman, Auckland 1996.

Making Peoples: A History of New Zealanders from Polynesian Settlement to the End of the 19th Century Belich, J., Penguin, Auckland 1996.

New Zealand, the Story So Far: A Short History Bohan, E., Harper Collins, Auckland 1997.

The Oxford History of New Zealand Oliver W.H. (ed.), Oxford University Press, Wellington 1981.

Politics in New Zealand Mulgan, R. Auckland University Press, Auckland 1997.

Penguin History of New Zealand, King, M., Penguin, 2003.

The Treaty of Waitangi Orange, C., Bridget Williams Books, Wellington 1991.

Natural History

A Field Guide to the Alpine Plants of New Zealand Salmon, J., Godwit, Auckland 1999.

Field Guide to the Birds of New Zealand Heather, B. and Robertson, H., Viking, Auckland 1996.

Game Animals of New Zealand Roberts, G., Shoal Bay Press, Blenheim 1998.

Ghosts of Gondwana, Gibbs, G., Craig Potton Publishing, Nelson 2006.

Kiwi: New Zealand's Remarkable Bird Peat, N., Godwit, Auckland 1999.

Native Trees of New Zealand Salmon J., Reed Publishing, Auckland 1996.

Natural History of New Zealand Bishop, N., Hodder and Stoughton, Auckland 1992.

The Natural World of New Zealand Hutching, G., Viking, Auckland 1998.

Outdoor Activities

Bird's Eye Guide: Tramping in New Zealand Barnett, S., Craig Potton Publishing, Nelson 2006.

Classic New Zealand Mountain Bike Rides Kennett, P., Kennett, S. and Kennett, J., Reed Publishing, Auckland 1998.

Classic Walks of New Zealand Potton C., Craig Potton Publishing, Nelson 1997.

New Zealand: Pure Adventure McLennan, C., David Bateman, Auckland 1999.

A Tramper's Guide to New Zealand's National Parks Burton, R. and Atkinson, M., Reed Publishing, Auckland 1998.

Glossary

Culture

Aotearoa: Maori name for New Zealand, literally "Land of the Long White Cloud", coined by the explorer Kupe's wife *(see p21)*

haka: war dance and song performed by males *(see p34)*

hangi: style of cooking food in an earth oven where the heat is provided by special stones or embers *(see p141)*

hongi: greeting by pressing noses together. When people *hongi*, their *hau* or life essence intermingles

iwi: tribe, people. A *hapu* is a subtribe and *whanau* an extended family

kai: food. Any word with *kai* in it relates to food, for example, *kai moana* (seafood) *(see p113)*

kete: woven basket made from the fibre of flax, kiekie or pingao plants *(see p35)*

mana: authority, prestige, psychic power

māori: ordinary or usual, used by indigenous New Zealanders from the 19th century to distinguish themselves from *pakeha* (stranger or different)

Maoritanga: Maori culture

marae: gathering place, open courtyard in front of a village meeting house where important meetings, funerals and entertainment take place *(see p120)*

mere: flat greenstone war club, most highly valued of weapons *(see image on p204)*

moko: tattoos incised on the faces, buttocks and thighs of men and the lips and chins of women *(see p34)*

pa: fortified village or stockade *(see p49)*

pakeha: stranger, person of European descent

poi: ball made of leaves attached to a piece of string and used by women in graceful dances *(see p34–35)*

tane: man, male

tangi: funeral

taonga: treasures, cultural items such as carvings or woven cloaks passed down through the generations

tapu: holy, sacred, forbidden; taboo in English

tiki: from *heitiki*; prized greenstone figure worn around the neck. Debate continues over the origins and religious significance of this ornament *(see p34)*

wahine: woman, female

waiata: songs. There are many types, for example *waiata tangi* (laments) and *waiata aroha* (love songs)

waka: canoe. The masterpieces were elaborately carved 30-metre *waka taua* or war canoes *(see p50)*

whare: house. There are a number of different houses: *whare runanga* (meeting house) *(see p32)*; *whare whakairo* (carved house); *whare puni* (family sleeping house)

Geography and Nature

kauri: huge forest tree growing in northern New Zealand *(see p28)*

kea: uncommon but inquisitive alpine parrot whose name is derived from its call *(see p29)*

kiwi: flightless, nocturnal indigenous bird which uses its long beak to probe in the earth for worms *(see p28)*

koru: the spiral, the principal motif used in Maori carving, inspired by the unfurling fern frond or *koru (see p28)*; it signifies "awakening, the process of growth, joy"

kumara: sweet potato, transported from Polynesia to New Zealand where it became a staple food *(see p49)*

manuka: shrubby plant popularly known as the tea tree with proven anti-bacterial qualities, source of honey and oils *(see p28)*

paua: black coloured shellfish known elsewhere as abalone, prized for its beautiful shell which is worked into jewellery *(see p329)*

pohutukawa: large spreading coastal tree covered in scarlet flowers during early summer, hence described as the "Christmas tree" *(see p29)*

ponga: tree fern

pounamu: greenstone or jade, the most precious stone used in jewellery and weapons, found in the South Island and traded with North Island tribes *(see p 241)*

Te Ika a Maui: the fish of Maui, the North Island

Te Wai Pounamu: South Island

Everyday Words and Phrases

Haere mai: Welcome

Haere ra: Goodbye (from the person staying to the one going)

E noho ra: Goodbye (from the person going to the one staying)

Ka pai: Thank you

Kia ora: Thank you, good luck, good health

Tena koe: Hello (to one person)

Tena koutou: Hello (to more than three people)

Kei te pehea koe: How are you?

Kei te pai: Very well, thank you

Words Commonly Forming Place Names

ao: cloud

atua: spirit or gods

awa: river or valley

hau: wind

ika: fish

iti: small

kai: food

kainga: village

kare: rippling

manga: stream, tributary

manu: bird

maunga: mountain

moana: sea or lake

motu: island

nui: big

one: beach, sand or mud

papa: flat, broad slab

po: night

puke: hill

puna: water spring

rangi: sky, heavens

roa: long

roto: lake

rua: two, hole

te: the

wai: water

wero: challenge

whanga: bay or inlet

whenua: land or country

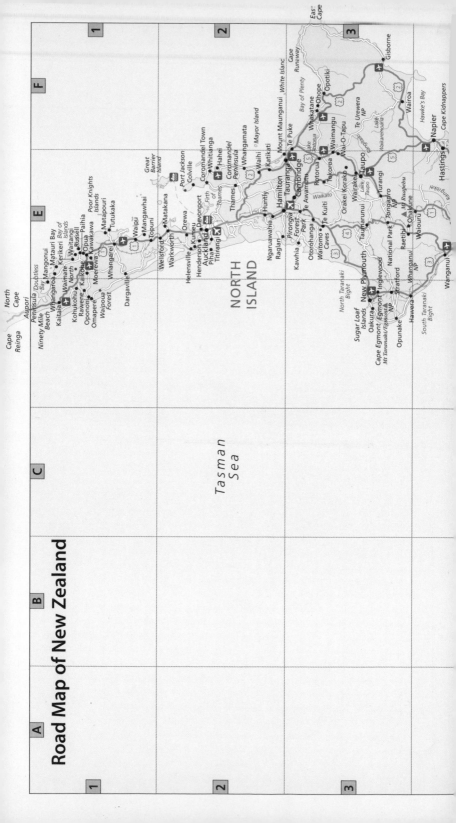